# The Hub *of the* Universe

A Century and More of Sturmey-Archer

Tony Hadland and Alan Clarke

This edition is dedicated to all the people of Sturmey-Archer, past and present, and in particular to Alan Clarke, who has done more than anyone to preserve, collate and make available the history of the company and its products.

This expanded 2nd edition published in 2020 by Pinkerton Press, the publishing wing of the Veteran-Cycle Club

© The authors

ISBN 978-1-9993429-2-0

British Library Cataloguing-in-Publication Data
A catalogue record for this book is available from the British Library

All rights reserved. Except for the purpose of review, no part of this book may be reproduced, stored in a retrieval system, or transmitted, in any form or by any means, electronic, mechanical, photocopying, recording or otherwise, without the prior permission of the publishers.

Cover, presentation box and typesetting by Stephen Morris www.stephen-morris.co.uk
Printed and bound in Slovakia via Akcent Media

# Contents

Foreword  7

Epicyclic fundamentals  9

Chapters

1. The Crypto principle  11
2. William Reilly and the Hub  16
3. Archer's involvement  24
4. Sturmey's contribution  30
5. The 'Sturmey-Archer-Reilly-Mills-Pellant' gear  35
6. Reilly at Nottingham  44
7. A motorcycle excursion  68
8. Competition and conflict  79
9. Conservative consolidation  91
10. Innovative diversification  108
11. War and peace  157
12. From jubilation to rationalisation  181
13. Small wheels and big triggers  215
14. The secret seven  234
15. A wavering relationship  254
16. The rise and fall of Derby  271
17. Sun Race sunrise  297

Postscript  315

Appendices

A  Production date list (1902-2018)  319
B  Glossary  323
C  Manufacture  329
D  Efficiency  313
E  Derailleur converters  332
F  Dating Sturmey-Archer hubs  334
G  Triggers, 1938 to 1960  336
H  Sources  344
I  Repairs and maintenance  352
J  Auctioneer's list of Sturmey-Archer plant, 2000  355
K  Lubrication  359
L  Sturmey-Archer Heritage website  360
   Index  362

Fig. 0.1. The author's plate from the first edition of this book, published in 1987

## Abbreviations and symbols

" = inch (25.4 mm)
mm = millimetre
cm = centimetre (10 mm)
cc = cubic centimetres
km = kilometre (0.62 miles)
£ = British pound
s. = shilling (20th of a British pound, pre-decimalisation)
d. = old penny (240th of a British pound, pre-decimalisation)
p. = new penny (100th of a British pound)
lb = pound weight
oz = ounce (16 to the pound weight)
kg = kilogramme
gm = gram (1,000 to the kilogramme)
hp = horsepower
DDRN = reference prefix for a document held by Nottinghamshire Archives
Fig. = Figure

Weights and measures throughout the book are generally based on manufacturer's figures and should be regarded as approximate.

Present day equivalents of prices are rounded approximations based on figures available at the time of writing.

Where the terms 'left' and 'right' are used, this means as viewed by the rider of the bike.

# Foreword

I was given my first bike when I was about 9 years old: a pre-war Raleigh Speed Sports that my uncle bought in the mid 1930s. It was fitted with a strange-looking Sturmey-Archer 3-speed called a KS that my father told me was 'close-ratio'. This meant nothing to me except that it was harder to climb the hill on which we lived than with an ordinary 3-speed. I was quite relieved when the supposedly irreparable toggle chain broke and my father built me a replacement wheel around a BSA wide-ratio 3-speed.

At the age of 15 I saved up for a Moulton Speed and was thus introduced to the FW 4-speed and the GH6 Dynohub. They served me well for everything from newspaper deliveries to continental touring.

During the following two decades I rode the AW, AG and AM 3-speeds and FWs converted to 5-speeds. I also experimented with hybrid gearing – derailleurs with two or three sprockets used in conjunction with a 5-speed hub gear. And I started a modest collection of Sturmey-Archer hubs but did not regard myself as an expert on the subject.

I was quite surprised when in 1983 Denis Watkins contacted me and asked whether I would be interested in using his research as the basis for a book on Sturmey-Archer. With some trepidation I journeyed to his home in Castle Bromwich and soon found myself thoroughly engrossed in the project.

Fig. 0.2.
The author's first Sturmey-Archer gear, a 1935 KS close-ratio 3-speed.

I was fortunate in having Denis's assistance and encouragement. Another stroke of good luck was the publication in *The Boneshaker* of extracts from letters written by I.C. Cohen, who had worked at Sturmey-Archer in the early days. This material gave vital leads and direction to my research and I was able to read the original Cohen correspondence, for which I am greatly indebted to Derek Foxton.

Some thirty years after publication of the first edition, the Veteran-Cycle Club offered me the opportunity to produce an updated edition. I have been delighted to work on this with

Alan Clarke, Sun Race Sturmey-Archer's own historian, who has brought a huge amount of information and first-hand experience to the project. It has been a pleasure working with him.

Since I started researching this story in 1983, numerous other people (some no longer with us) have helped in one way or other. They include John S. Allen, Ron Beams, Patrick Bramman, Dave Connley, Chris Deegan, John Fairbrother, Vernon Forbes, Jim Gill, Irene Griffin (granddaughter of James Archer), Martin Hanczyc, Brian Hayes, Tony Hillyer, Mark Hunt, Ron Kitching, Jack Lauterwasser, Barry Lawson, Peter Lawson, John Macnaughtan, John Pinkerton, Stephen Ransom, Peter Read, Derek Roberts, Victor Rumak, Peter Shirtcliffe, David Sore, Hilary Stone, Frances Theobald, Ted Tyndall, Dave White and many more. My thanks go to all of them.

What then is the purpose of this book? It is not a service manual: there is no need for that as Sturmey-Archer published comprehensive servicing instructions for their products and, as Appendix I shows, most of this material is readily available. This book is instead a company history, product history and technical history of one of the most important and enduring cycle component makers. It includes not only the products that reached the market but many others that were never mass produced.

Alan Clarke and I hope you enjoy reading this book as much as we did researching and writing it.

Tony Hadland
Oxfordshire, 2019

# Epicyclic fundamentals

### How a typical 3-speed hub works

To enjoy the design history of Sturmey-Archer it is not necessary fully to understand the workings of all the gears. However, if you find the technicalities interesting, the following explanation of simple epicyclic gearing principles may prove helpful.

### In Figure 0.3:

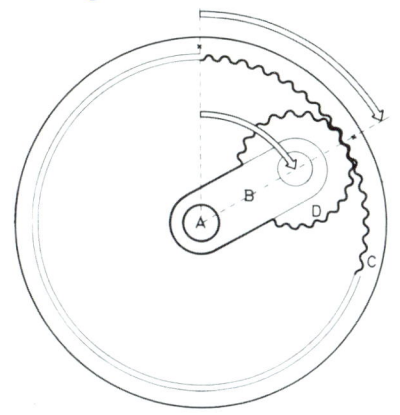

A is a fixed axle
B is an arm, free to rotate about A
C is a gear ring, also free to rotate about the fixed axle A
D is a cog, which meshes with ring C and is locked to arm B (so cog D cannot rotate relative to arm B).

For every revolution of arm B, ring C will also rotate once.

### In Figure 0.4:

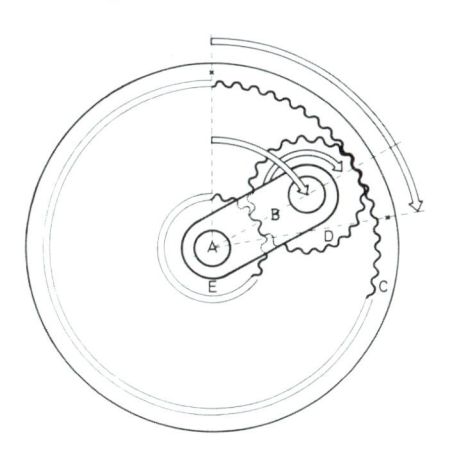

Everything is the same as in Figure 0.3 except:
there is a cog E, rigidly fixed to the axle A and meshing with cog D
cog D can rotate relative to arm B.

For every revolution of arm B, gear ring C revolves more than once. It gets the extra motion from cog D, which is now rotating not only relative to axle A but also relative to arm B. The amount of extra rotation is equivalent to the circumference of the fixed cog E around which cog D rolls.

This arrangement is at the heart of what is known as epicyclic or planetary gearing. Fixed cog E is referred to as a sun pinion; cog D, because of its orbital motion around the sun, is referred to as a planet pinion. (A pinion is a small cog.)

For practical reasons there are usually three or four planet pinions; a 'planet cage' then takes the place of arm B. The number of the planet pinions has no effect on the gearing ratios. Neither, in a simple epicyclic gear, does the number of teeth on the planet pinions.

Engineers sometimes refer to the gear ring as the *annulus* (Latin for ring), although Sturmey-Archer always preferred the more explicit plain English term.

### Practical use
The arrangement in Figure 0.4, when built into the rear hub of a bicycle, forms the basis of the familiar wide-ratio 3-speed gear:

- When the drive from the bicycle chain is fed direct to arm B (in the form of the planet cage), and gear ring C is connected direct to the hub shell, the wheel rotates faster than the chain sprocket: this is high gear.
- When the drive is fed direct to gear ring C, and arm B (the planet cage) is connected direct to the hub shell, the wheel rotates slower than the sprocket: this is low gear.
- When the drive is fed direct to the hub shell, the wheel rotates at the same rate as the sprocket: this is middle or normal gear.

2-speed hub gears merely use two of the available speeds.

### What's the difference?
The difference between the various speeds is easily calculated:

- If cog E has 20 teeth and gear ring C has 60, high gear will cause the wheel to rotate (20 + 60)/60 times normal gear, i.e. 1⅓ times – an increase of 33⅓%.
- Low gear will cause the wheel to rotate 60/(20 + 60) times normal gear, i.e. ¾ times – a decrease of 25%.

Although the steps between normal gear and low gear (-25%) and between normal gear and high gear (33⅓%) are unequal, the two upward steps – low to normal and normal to high – are both 33⅓% per cent; and the two downward steps – high to normal and normal to low – are both 25%.

### Beyond 3-speeds
Reading this book, you will discover many hub gears that are more complicated than the simple 3-speed described above. Some use more than one epicyclic train, either by switching between differently proportioned trains or by one train driving another. At the time of writing, commercially available epicyclic hub gears offer from two to fourteen speeds. The spread of ratios can range from ultra-close to ultra-wide, though current hubs are mostly wide-ratio.

Throughout the twentieth century, Sturmey-Archer produced excellent instructions for servicing and repairing their hubs. What they rarely did was explain how the mechanisms worked: that is one of the aims of this book. But if that aspect does not interest you greatly, you can skip the technical explanations. You will still be able to enjoy the fascinating design history of one of the world's greatest bicycle component makers.

# Chapter 1

# The Crypto principle

### From the earliest cycle gears to the first compact 2-speed hubs, 1868 to 1895

In the second half of the 1860s front-wheel drive semi-recumbent bicycles, known as velocipedes, became popular in France. By 1867 'velocipedomania' had broken out. There were soon about 150 French makers, mostly artisans copying the leading Parisian manufacturer Michaux and its successor, Compagnie Parisienne. It was not long before the first patent for bicycle gearing was filed.

## Villepigue's big idea
On 9 March 1868 Ferdinand Floran Villepigue applied for a British patent concerning 'Improvements in the Construction of Velocipedes' (GB 708 of 1869). The brief specification covered a dozen wide-ranging ideas including rubber tyres, adjustable metal spokes and an adjustable saddle.

Villepigue's tenth idea was this:

> The application of a differential movement to the fore wheel, whereby communicating a difference of velocity, or a difference in the number of revolutions made respectively by the crank and the fore wheel; that is to say, that according to the slope or other conditions of the road you are travelling over, or the speed which you wish to attain in relation to the force expended, you can make the wheel describe more or fewer revolutions than the crank. Thus, for example, if the road be good the wheel may perform two revolutions, while the crank revolves once; or contrariwise the wheel may be made to make only half a turn while the crank is making a whole one if the ground should be bad and the inclination steep.

What Villepigue described was the concept of change-speed gearing for bicycles. But he did not specify how the principle was to be put into practice and his patent never got beyond provisional acceptance, probably because it was too vague and all-encompassing.

Villepigue had formed a partnership with Louis Marie Stoffel, trading as the Veloce Company to make French-style velocipedes in England. They were based off The Strand in London and also in Birmingham. Villepigue may have had good ideas but inventiveness is not enough to ensure commercial success. Stoffel ended up in the London and Middlesex debtors' gaol and in July 1869 *The London Gazette* announced that his partnership with Villepigue had been dissolved by mutual consent.

## Barberon and Meunier's 2-speed velocipedes
Alphonse Barberon and Joseph Meunier were meanwhile manufacturing velocipedes near Bourges in central France. They began to equip their machines with a 2-speed drive system (French patent 86,459 of 1870; GB 2626 of 1869). When the rider pedaled forwards, the pedal shaft connected via a pawl and ratchet system directly to the concentric front wheel hub. But pedaling backwards drove the wheel forwards via a belt drive system, the pulleys being sized

to give a higher gear. An 1870 addendum to the patent described a 3-speed variable drive system in which either a belt or a chain would be shifted from one set of pulleys or sprockets to another by means of a lever but the Franco-Prussian war ended the venture.

### Growing interest in change-speed gearing
Barberon and Meunier's specification was followed by an outburst of interest and activity in cycle gear development. James Starley, 'the father of the cycle industry', and William Hillman patented a gear similar to Barberon and Meunier's (GB 2236 of 1870). Starley also produced a crank, the length of which could be varied while in use. This was not a gearing system as such but had a similar objective: greater leverage for hill climbing and a short throw for faster riding. Something similar was advertised by the French Compagnie Parisienne in 1870.

In his 1908 book *Variable Gears*, Logos summed up the early days of cycle gearing development:

> Telescopic cranks, expanding and contracting chain-wheels, variable pulleys, elliptical chain-wheels, telescopic levers, and other devices almost too numerous to mention, were described, and, in many instances, tried, but nothing really satisfactory was found until someone, more observant than his predecessors, recognized the possibilities of the epicyclic train, a perfectly well known piece of mechanism in common use since the days of James Watt at least.

### Scott and Phillott's hub gears
The earliest British patent for an epicyclic cycle gear appears to be that of Scott and Phillott (GB 860 of 1878). George Dennistoun Scott was an engineer from Derby; George Henry Phillott an architect from Cheltenham. Scott and Phillott's gear was fitted into the hub of a front-driving cycle. It employed a variant of the simple epicyclic principle, whereby two equal-sized co-axial bevel gears took the place of the sun and gear ring. Meshing with both was another pair of bevel gears acting as planet pinions. These were mounted on a cross-head taking the place of a planet cage. Because the sun and gear ring equivalents were of equal size, the gear changes were very widely-spaced: 100% increase or 50% decrease.

Two versions of the gear were described. The first was a 2-speed offering direct drive, a manually selected freewheel and a doubling in wheel speed relative to the crank. Gear change was by sliding the cranks sideways with the feet. The second version was a 3-speed that offered additionally a halving of wheel speed. It was necessary to declutch the first bevel wheel from the driving wheel and instead clutch the cross-head to the driving wheel and clutch the crankshaft to the first bevel wheel. Although Scott and Phillott's gear worked, it was hardly user friendly.

### Epicyclic gears in the tricycle boom
Thereafter came other patents for epicyclic gears, including those of Kirby (GB 5043 of 1879), Peirce (GB 134 of 1880), Harvey and Paddock (GB 2174 of 1882), Shaw and Sydenham (GB 3230 of 1882), Britain (GB 4803 of 1882), Jay (GB 2957 of 1883), Latta (US 294,641 of 1884) and Simpson (GB 4414 of 1884). Most of these were 2-speeds but some were 3-speeds. The tricycle boom of the 1880s was the stimulus for much of this development, which also included other forms of change-speed gearing.

Harvey and Paddock's gear was probably the first really practicable epicyclic. It was closely followed by that of William Thomas Shaw and William Sydenham. Shaw and Sydenham's gear was marketed as the Crypto Dynamic 2-speed and was first applied to tricycles. It was produced by the Crypto Cycle Company Limited of 47 Farringdon Road, London.

## Impact of the safety bicycle

Various attempts were made to produce bicycles that were safer than the high-wheeler, subsequently referred to as the 'ordinary' or 'penny farthing'. ('Penny farthing' because the proportionality of the front and rear wheels was reminiscent of the largest and smallest British coins then in circulation.)

The best known early safety bicycle, the Rover, was invented by James Kemp Starley, nephew of James Starley. To drive the rear wheel it used Hans Renold's new 'floating roller' chain. The first version of the Rover safety bicycle was demonstrated early in 1885 and later that year an improved direct steering version was put on sale.

Also in 1885 the Raleigh bicycle brand was established in Nottingham by local man Richard Woodhead and French immigrant Paul Angois, who took over a small workshop in Raleigh Street. The 'Raleigh Works' had previously been used to build bicycles by Richard Jennison Ball, whose partnership with local industrialist Ernest Jardine terminated in 1879 and who went bankrupt in 1883. Woodhead and Angois were trading from the site by spring 1885.

The firm of Woodhead and Angois (later briefly Woodhead, Angois and Ellis) was noted for the quality and innovative design of its safety bicycles. One of the selling points was the Raleigh patent interchangeable chainwheel. To change gear, the rider had to stop, unbolt the chainwheel, substitute another of different size and then lengthen or shorten the chain; a tedious and messy process that took several minutes. This system was nonetheless considered innovatory and advanced, which highlights how primitive bicycle change-speed gearing was at the time.

## Collier 2-speed chainwheel

1889 saw the introduction of the Collier bracket-mounted 2-speed gear (GB 8893 of 1889). Its chainwheel ran on a hollow axle within which the crank axle was eccentrically mounted. Fixed to the crank axle was an internally toothed ring which, for low gear, engaged with teeth on the outside of the chainwheel axle. For direct drive the crank was locked to the chainwheel axle.

A special bottom bracket was needed to house the oversized chainwheel axle and the gear was heavy, weighing about 4½ lb. (2.05 kg). It gave a reduction of 15–20%, depending on what the customer ordered. It was not an epicyclic gear but it was simple and reliable. The Collier was one of the more successful early gears for the new pneumatic-tyred safety bicycles.

## Geared front drivers

The high-wheeler evolved from the desire to travel further for each turn of the cranks, the smaller wheeled direct-drive velocipede being at a disadvantage when it came to speed. But by the mid 1880s high-wheelers were under threat from the new safety bicycles.

The safeties, with their geared-up chain drive to the rear wheel and their lower riding position, were easier to steer and safer to ride. In a rear-guard action that started in 1890 the Crypto Cycle Company tried to maintain the front-wheel-drive tradition while offering a less daunting riding position than the high-wheeler. They did this by building a single-speed epicyclic gear into the front hub. By using, for example, a gear giving a 36% increase the front wheel size could be reduced from 60" (152 cm) to 44" (112 cm) while the bicycle still travelled the same distance for each rotation of the cranks.

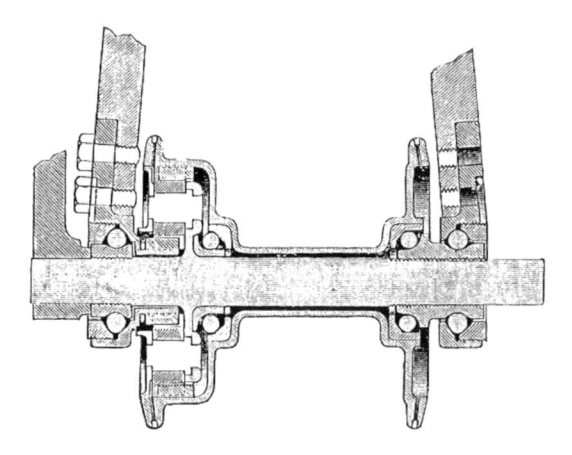

Fig. 1.1. Section through a Crypto single-speed epicyclic front hub (from a catalogue). The gearing is in the drum on the left.

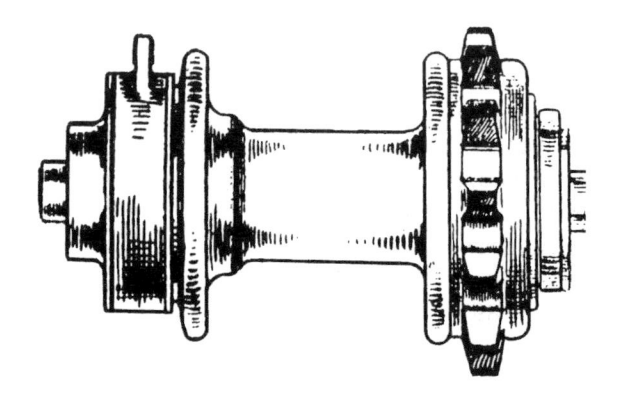

Fig. 1.2. The Crypto Dynamic 2-speed hub.

By 1891 Crypto were offering two ranges of geared front drivers: the Geared Ordinary and the smaller FD (= Front Driver). The Geared Ordinary had driving wheels of 42" to 46" diameter, with other sizes made to order; the FD had driving wheels of 34" to 38" diameter. Frank Shorland, riding a Crypto FD Light Roadster, broke the 12 hour, 50 mile and London to York records, which suggested that the epicyclic mechanism was efficient.

Crypto launched the smaller Bantam in 1894, with driving wheels of 22" to 26" diameter, and the even smaller Bantamette, with a 20" driving wheel. Some other makers, such as Raleigh, offered similar machines but front drivers soon disappeared from the market. However, the practice of describing bicycle gearing in terms of the equivalent direct-drive wheel diameter expressed in inches persists in English speaking countries. In mainland Europe the term 'development' is used: this is the distance in metres covered by the machine for one rotation of the cranks in a particular gear. To convert the English gear to the development, multiply by 0.08. Thus, a 60" gear has a development of approximately 4.8 metres.

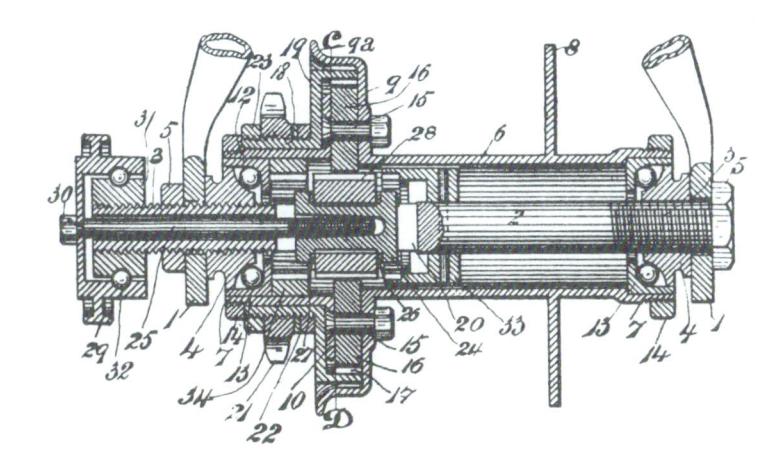

Fig. 1.3. Section through Johnson's 2-speed hub (patent drawing).

### Compact epicyclic rear hubs

So great was Crypto's dominance of the market for epicyclic single-speed front drivers that among cyclists 'the Crypto principle' became the generic term for how epicyclic gears worked. Despite Shaw and Sydenham's preference for front drivers, in 1891 they patented the first compact 2-speed epicyclic hub gear for chain drive safety bicycles (GB 7,940 of 1891). A reviewer in *Cycling* magazine enthused about it, remarking on its neat appearance, its slim shell and the fact that all the moving parts ran on ball bearings.

But this hub appears never to have gone into production. Crypto's catalogue for the 1891 Stanley cycle trade show makes no mention of it, nor is there any reference to the hub in the spring 1892 catalogue or in any later edition. It seems probable that the gear did not stand up to heavy or prolonged use. However, the idea of a compact epicyclic 2-speed hub for chain-drive safety bicycles was an attractive one. It fell to two other inventors to develop the idea.

In 1895 the American machinist Seward Thomas Johnson, dubbed by Logos 'father of the modern speed-gear', patented a compact 2-speed hub gear that went into production. Hot on its heels came the first such gear to achieve widespread popularity. Simply called the Hub, it was the brainchild of William Reilly, the forgotten hero of epicyclic bicycle gearing.

# Chapter 2

# William Reilly and the Hub

### The compact 2-speed hub gear overtakes the opposition, 1895 to 1908

### Boom and bust
The early and mid 1890s were boom years for British cycling. The number of cyclists increased by about 75,000 a year and Britain's rich and fashionable elite took to the bicycle, making cycling socially respectable, albeit briefly. The consequent speculation in bicycle company shares led to over-capitalisation, over-production, a slump and numerous bankruptcies. Although the 'society boom' ended about 1899, cycling continued to increase in popularity well into the twentieth century, as bicycles became ever more affordable.

### Early change-speed systems
The 1890s saw the introduction of a number of marketable change-speed gear systems. The Cycle Gear Company's 2-speed epicyclic bracket gear could be fitted to a standard safety bicycle; different ratios could be supplied and the gear had handlebar control. The Kynoch gear was another epicyclic that could easily be fitted to a safety bicycle; it had unusual elliptical sun and planet pinions and typically gave gears of 72" and 54". The Kynoch was based on A.W. Bevis's patent (GB 379 of 1898). The purpose of the elliptical pinions was to vary 'the speed of the work in each revolution so as to give a quicker, or slower, motion to it during that portion of the revolution when the driving power is applied to greatest advantage'. Locking the elliptical sun with its long axis in line with the crank gave the effect of a large diameter sun with a small diameter planet; whereas locking the sun with its short axis in line with the crank gave the opposite effect. However, these characteristics were only substantially true for the 'quarter of pedal path during which power is applied' and they gave a non-uniform motion, particularly at high speed.

Some other bracket gears did not use the Crypto principle and needed two bottom bracket barrels, one being for a layshaft. Such gears included the Sharp and the Eite & Todd but the need for frame modifications limited their appeal.

The spring of 1895 saw the introduction of the Protean or Whippet gear, patented the previous autumn. It was made by Linley and Biggs of 29 Clerkenwell Road, London, who had introduced the Whippet spring-frame safety bicycle in 1887. The first Protean was a 4-speed expanding chainwheel gear; the overall range was about 16% which could give gears in the order of 63, 66, 69 and 73" – very close ratios, especially for that time.

The Protean was soon followed by the Paradox, another expanding chainwheel gear. It gave 27% change of speed in seven steps, each about 3" apart. It could therefore offer gears in the order of 62, 65, 68, 71, 74 and 77" – again very close.

The first practicable chain-shifting gears were introduced during this period. Before the anglicised French name 'derailleur' became widely used they were known as 'chain gears'. They were inspired no doubt by similar change-speed systems widely used in industry, which usually employed belts rather than chains. The earliest patented derailleur seems to be La Polyceler, meaning The Multispeed, which was invented by Jean Loubeyre of Paris (French patent 245,148 of 1895).

Although two of the most successful early chain-shifter gears, the Gradient and the New Protean, were British, derailleurs made little headway in Britain until they had undergone three decades of further development on the Continent. E.H. Hodgkinson's Gradient was introduced in 1896 and was a 3-speed gear that incorporated a chain tensioner under the bottom bracket. The gear was changed by a sideways movement of the sprockets, thereby maintaining a true chainline for maximum efficiency.

The New Protean derailleur replaced the earlier Protean expanding chainwheel. C.M. Linley's patent (GB 18,240 of 1899) allowed for three or more sprockets but the production version was a 2-speed. It used a special chain in which the links were arched to facilitate shifting from one sprocket to another. The chainwheel was double width to enable the chain to run in line, and the chainwheel and sprockets had flanges to stop the chain falling off.

This period saw considerable interest in shaft drive systems. Wyatt's 3-speed gear of 1897 had three circles of pins on a driving wheel that took the place of the chainwheel. Any of these circles could be made to engage with roller teeth on an adjustable drive shaft.

## Johnson's hub gear

It was compact epicyclic hub gears that were to prove the most significant innovation of this period. In 1895 Seward Thomas Johnson successfully applied for GB patent 12,681 for 'a bicycle wheel hub with driving mechanism'. Johnson was a machinist living in Noblesville, Indiana, USA. Johnson's gear established the format for many subsequent 2-speed hubs. It housed the epicyclic mechanism in a 'drum' adjacent to a drive sprocket that was threaded onto the gear ring.

Within the gear ring were four planet pinions, the drum of the hub shell forming the planet cage. The planet pinions revolved around a sun wheel that could slide on the fixed axle. This enabled the sun to be clutched to the hub shell for direct drive and higher speed, or to the fixed axle for gearing down and increased torque.

Johnson's sliding sun mechanism was considered a major advance in enabling the construction of practicable compact hub gears. The right-hand side of the fixed axle was hollow and slotted for part of its length; the left half of the axle was solid. This arrangement enabled a bush to slide along the right-hand part of the axle within the epicyclic gear drum. The sun pinion was free to rotate on this bush.

Either side of the sun wheel was a clutch sleeve, the inside of which was the shape that would be obtained by pushing the sun pinion axially into a piece of modelling clay. One of these clutch sleeves was fixed to the hub shell, the other to the fixed axle. They were far enough apart to allow the sun to be parked midway between the two clutches to allow freewheeling.

When the sun was inside the hub clutch sleeve, it locked the epicyclic mechanism solid. The sun being disconnected from the fixed axle, the whole mechanism could rotate as one, giving direct drive.

When the sun was inside the axle clutch sleeve, the sun could not rotate. Because the hub shell formed the planet cage, the hub had to rotate slower than the sprocket (fixed to the gear ring), giving a lower gear.

To freewheel the rider selected the 'neutral' position, which left the sun engaged with neither hub nor axle. Engagement of either gear gave a fixed-wheel condition.

The gear change was effected by a sliding rod within the hollow section of the axle. One end was threaded into the sliding bush on which the sun was mounted; the other was fixed to a sleeve fitted over the right-hand axle end. This sleeve had an internal helical groove which ran on ball bearings. A control cable was wrapped around the sleeve and, when pulled, caused the sleeve to rotate. The helical groove made it move sideways along the axle, thus moving the rod and sun, thereby changing gear.

The following year, 1896, saw the publication of Archibald Sharp's classic book *Bicycles and Tricycles: An Elementary Treatise on their Design and Construction*. This described and illustrated the J & R 2-speed hub, based on Johnson's patent. Unlike the version in the patent, the sun was mounted on a sliding sleeve around the axle. The sleeve was moved by a rack and pinion mechanism.

Having established the new compact 2-speed hub gear format, the J & R was rapidly eclipsed by William Reilly's Hub.

## Enter William Reilly

William Reilly was born 11 January 1867 at the family home, a dairy run by his parents at 10 Wood Street, Salford. The city merges almost imperceptibly with Manchester, the two being separated by the River Irwell. Both cities were granted charters in the thirteenth century but it was the Industrial Revolution that led to their rapid growth, providing numerous job opportunities in the rapidly expanding world of engineering.

William's father Peter Reilly was born in Kinglet, Co. Cavan in 1826. He would have been in his late teens and early twenties during the worst years of the potato famine, which was probably why he moved to England. Peter Reilly married a local woman, Rosanna Brown, four years his junior. They set up home five minutes' walk from Salford's Catholic cathedral. William Reilly was one of ten siblings who survived infancy. But William's mother died in 1873 when he was only six years old and his father died six years later.

As a young teenager William Reilly worked as an engine turner, a skilled job entailing mechanised decoration of metalwork. He lived at 1 Lee Grove, Salford, the home of his eldest brother John, a mechanic, and John's wife Jane. Also in the household were William's other brothers: railway worker Joseph and schoolboy Arthur Harry.

William Reilly married Martha Jones from Galway in 1890 when he was 23 years old. When six years later he invented the Hub, he was living in Wellington Street, Salford, near Collier Street where his invention would be manufactured.

Reilly applied for his first hub gear patent in March 1896 and it was accepted in January 1897. It was entitled 'Improvements in Two-Speed Driving Gear for Bicycles' (GB 6062 of 1896) and was also in the name of Charlton Haigh, a draughtsman who lived in Grafton Street, Manchester.

In most respects this gear was similar to Johnson's. The sprocket was shown as integral with the gear ring. The gear could be made with or without a neutral position, this being merely a matter of adjusting the distance between the axle clutch sleeve and the hub shell clutch sleeve.

Unlike Johnson's gear, Reilly's had an axle that was hollow for its full length. In the original design the shifting rod within the axle was operated by a lever that pushed the shifting rod, moving the sun and changing gear. The shifting rod was connected to a gear adjustment indicator rod protruding from the right-hand axle end.

In September 1896 Reilly and Haigh applied for British patent 19,859, which was accepted the following spring. This covered an improved changing mechanism. The left end of the axle now featured a teardrop-shaped cam which was free to rotate about the axle. A control rod

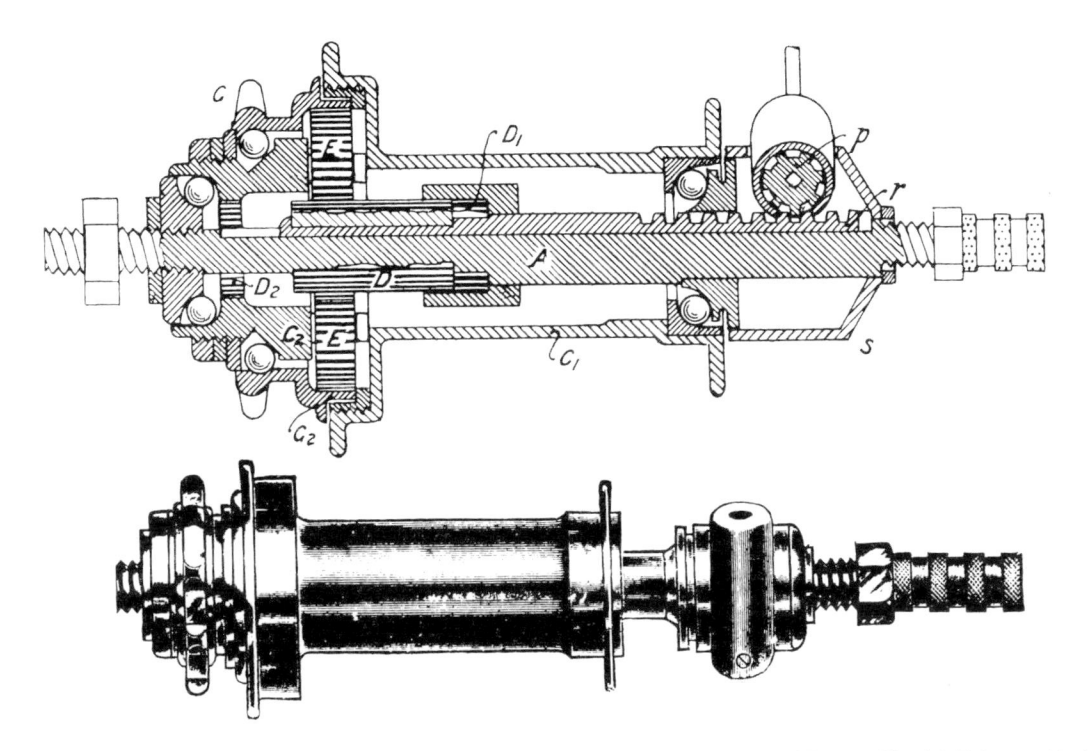

Fig. 2.1. The J & R 2-speed hub.

Fig. 2.2. William Reilly.

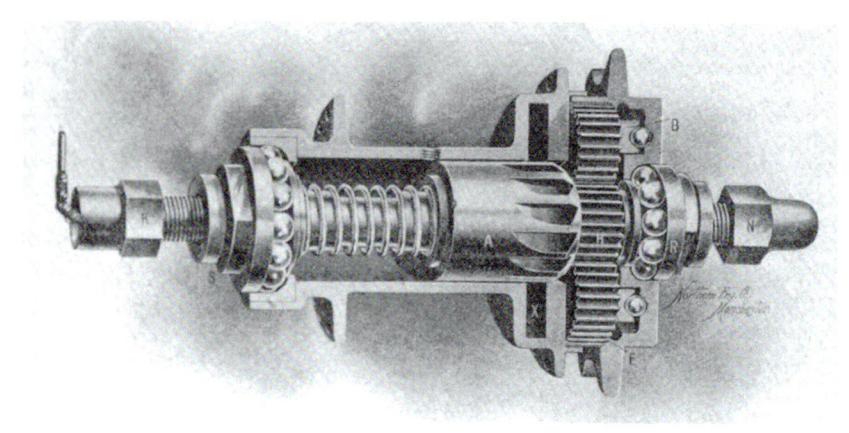

Fig. 2.3. Cutaway illustration of the Hub 2-speed.

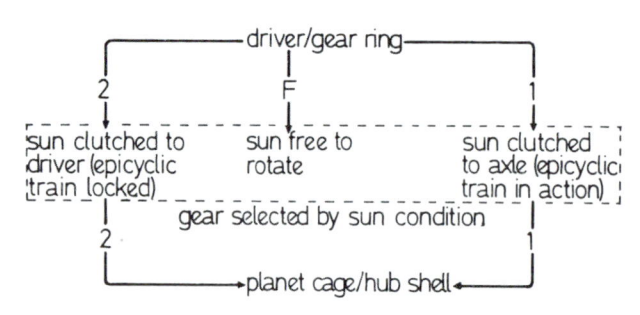

Fig. 2.4. Hub 2-speed flowchart.

or cable was connected to the pointed end of the cam so that movement of the control rotated the cam through an arc. The cam was connected, via the hollow axle, to a quick-pitch screw device that moved a sleeve along the axle inside the hub, sliding the sun along the axle and changing gear.

In 1898 Reilly's gear was put into production by the Hub Two-Speed Gear Company Limited of Collier Street, Greengate, Salford which was backed by The Green Economizer Company. The founder, Edward Green, was responsible for GB patent 10,986 of 1845 for 'Economizing fuel, retaining and applying heat for generating steam and heating water'. Unfortunately, Reilly signed a contract with the Hub Company that gave them the rights to any of his future bicycle gear inventions. He soon fell out with his employers and went to work for the Manchester electrical engineers Royce, a forerunner of Rolls-Royce.

Late in 1899 the Hub Two-Speed Gear Company and W.H. Palmer of Middleton applied for GB patent 22,342. This referred to Reilly's earlier patents and dealt with another modification to the Hub's shifting mechanism: the familiar flared nut and toggle chain seen on vast numbers of subsequent hub gears throughout the twentieth century.

## Cohen's testimony

Israel Cohen, usually known as I.C. Cohen and informally as Ike, had been apprenticed to Hetheringtons of Manchester on machine tools and textile machinery. He became Reilly's assistant at Sturmey-Archer and was chief designer at Raleigh for 12 years. Cohen later worked for Cammel Laird (as tutorial foreman and experimentalist); Wadkin Mills (as technical assistant to the head of the company); the Cubitt Car Company (as assistant works manager); John Jardine Limited (as gearbox designer); The Gramophone Company (as chief tool designer); Plessey (also as chief tool designer); Aircraftings Limited (as technical director); and was later an independent consultant. He was a contributor to *Cycling* magazine as late as the 1950s.

Cohen believed that it was Reilly alone who was responsible for the flared nut and toggle chain combination. Logos, in his 1908 book *Variable Gears*, wrote of the 'clever application of the flared or bell-mouthed nut for pulling through the chain connected to the control rod in the axle'. Logos described it as 'just one of those simple and apparently self-evident devices which have made the speed-gear a practical bit of mechanism' and added that 'nothing so simple, cheap, and effective as the flared nut has ever been devised'. The little chain itself was similar to the fusée chains used for centuries in clock making.

The Hub was a great success. At first it was denigrated for being so small and light: critics described it as 'watch work' and said that it would never stand up to normal use. Yet by 1901 its reputation was firmly established. Early in that year the Hub Company's advertisements claimed hundreds of satisfied users; before the year's end they claimed thousands. In 1902 Henry Sturmey, editor of *The Cyclist*, praised the Hub for its lightness, compactness, ease of fitting and for being the first gear to offer 'reasonably correct proportions' for the ratios. By 1903 Cycling was reporting that the Hub 'has won praise on all hands and we have been struck by the virtual absence of complaint'.

The Hub added about 1 lb (450 gm) to the weight of a bicycle and in 1903 it cost £3 8s. 0d. exclusive of fitting. This may sound cheap today but it was the equivalent of two weeks' wages for many workers.

By 1903 the Hub was available in three standard sizes and could be supplied 'to suit any chainline, any width or pitch of chain and to have any required number of teeth on the chain ring' ('chain ring' in this case meaning the rear sprocket). It was also made to the specification of some large cycle manufacturers. It gave direct drive and a 23.8% reduction and typical ratios thus provided were 116 and 88" or 73 and 56".

The gear was modified in 1901 to give a constant freewheel on the high gear, although low gear was still fixed. All parts of the new Hub were interchangeable with those of the original version. The freewheel modification seems to have been the suggestion of Alfred Pellant, the Hub Company's London representative. He was a notable cycle dealer who broke the Amateur 50 mile road record in 1893. He operated from 74 Shaftesbury Avenue and described himself variously as 'cycle expert' and 'wholesale factor'. Pellant was responsible for a number of patents, some of which related to cycle technology and others to power-driven applications. He had a particular interest in freewheels and clutching arrangements in hub gears. His GB patent 19,064 of 1900 covered an improved screw-on freewheel sprocket. Later that year Pellant applied for GB patent 22,202 which was granted in 1902. This related particularly to the Hub: it introduced a friction roller or spring pawl freewheel mechanism between the direct drive clutch sleeve and the hub shell and required a larger cylindrical hub shell.

The Hub Company applied for its own freewheel patent in August 1901 (GB 15,775 of 1902). This was accepted just three months after Pellant's. It likewise gave a freewheel only in top gear but was a more elegant solution and enabled the gear to retain a relatively compact appearance, complete with the familiar drum on the driving side. It was this version that went into production. The patent was in the names of the Hub Two-Speed Gear Company and its chairman Walter Goodbrand. Most later Hub Company patents were jointly in the names of

2.5. Advertisement for the Hub 2-speed.

the company, its general manager Charles Hilton Reynolds and works manager William Henry Palmer. The Hub Two-Speed Gear Company continued to improve the gear and was responsible for a number of patents during the period 1901–6. The Irish cycle engineer John Fagan patented an external freewheel for the Hub that could be retro-fitted (GB 8,672 of 1902).

By 1907 the pioneering Hub was not as prominent as hitherto and the patent rights were bought by the Birmingham Small Arms Company (BSA). Reilly's gear, renamed the Manchester Hub, continued in production for a short time but was withdrawn about 1908. It had been on sale for a decade and had taken the Crypto principle, as refined by Johnson, and turned it into a reliable marketable product. It had confounded the critics and established the practicability of compact hub gears. And although Reilly had left the Hub Two-Speed Gear Company about 1899, he had not stopped thinking about epicyclic gearing.

# Chapter 3

# Archer's involvement

### Reilly patents a 3-speed hub under a colleague's name

### Jay's 3-speed tricycle gear

The idea of a 3-speed epicyclic gear dates back at least to 1883. In that year Robert Charles Jay applied for a patent entitled 'Improvements in Tricycles and other Velocipedes' (GB 2957 of 1883). Jay was a barrister in the Bayswater district of London. His gear gave direct drive and two higher gears, and also permitted freewheeling.

Jay used bevelled gear rings and pinions similar to those used in many hand drills. In fact, his gear resembled two hand drills grafted together (if you ignore the handles and chucks). There was therefore no inner sun pinion or outer gear ring as we normally know them.

The sprocket on the rear axle of the tricycle housed a pair of compound pinions, thus taking the place of the planet cage. (Compound pinions are 'stepped', with two sets of teeth.) On one side of the sprocket, and concentric with it, was a bevelled gear ring, similar to the drive ring of a hand drill: this meshed with the larger section of the compound pinions. On the other side of the rear sprocket, also concentric with it, was a smaller bevelled gear ring that meshed with the smaller part of the compound pinions.

For low gear, the sprocket drove the axle direct, both bevelled gear rings being disengaged.

For middle gear, the larger bevelled gear ring was locked solid and the smaller gear ring was locked to the tricycle axle for drive. The sprocket was free to rotate independent of the tricycle axle and, as the sprocket rotated, it imparted a faster rotation to the small bevelled

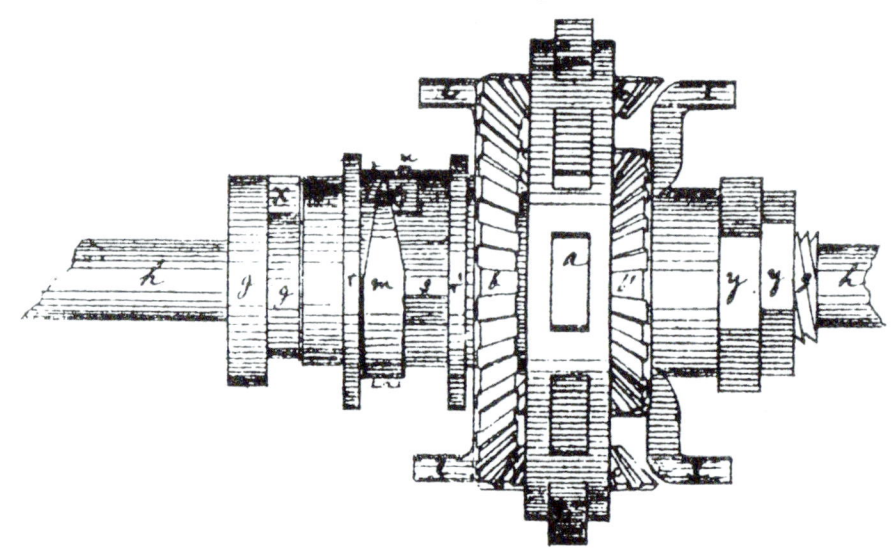

Fig. 3.1. Jay's 3-speed epicyclic tricycle gear used bevelled pinions (patent drawing).

gear ring and hence to the tricycle axle. The fixed larger bevelled gear ring acted like a fixed sun while the smaller gear ring acted like the gear ring in a conventional epicyclic gear.

For high gear, the same principle applied, except that the smaller bevelled gear ring was held static while the larger one was driven by the sprocket containing the bevelled pinions.

Jay's gear raised awareness of the possibilities offered by epicyclic mechanisms but the most successful subsequent epicyclic 3-speeds bore little resemblance to his.

### Reilly designs a 3-speed

In 1898 the Hub 2-speed Gear Company started producing Reilly's 2-speed. Shortly afterwards Reilly left the Hub company to join Frederick Henry Royce's electrical engineering firm, across the River Irwell in Manchester. While working at Royce, Reilly developed his thoughts on epicyclic bicycle gears. On the quiet he got a fellow workman, Tom White, to manufacture the parts for prototypes. But Reilly had a problem patenting any future bicycle gear inventions: he had signed away his rights to his previous employer. He therefore persuaded another colleague, a Londoner called James Samuel Archer, to sign the patent applications. It is for this reason that the name Archer became known to millions of cyclists.

### Archer and his patents

James Samuel Archer was born 7 January 1854. At the age of 21, at St Andrew and St Phillip's Church in Kensington, he married Emma Parsons, who bore him 11 children in less than 20 years. Emma died in 1899 and James married again the following spring at Oldham Register Office. His second wife, Florence Todd, bore him two more offspring.

In 1901 Archer and family were living at 17 Linwood Street, Hulme, Manchester, near the Royce works. His first patent application for a cycle gear on behalf of Reilly was made on 14 June 1901 but was declared 'void or abandoned' (GB 12,135 of 1901). Five days after Archer's patent application *The Cyclist & Bicycling & Tricycling Trades Review* carried an editorial entitled 'Variable Speed Gears'. Assistant editor H. Walter Staner wrote:

> Next year will undoubtedly be a year of gears. Two and 3-speed gears are no novelty in the cycle world; in fact, they were used and practically discarded long before pneumatic tyres had been fitted to a cycle. However, like many another good idea, they were handicapped by the clumsy way in which they were made … it remained for the 2-speed Hub to demonstrate to riders at large what could really be done in this direction by a properly designed and perfectly made 2-speed gear.

Staner went on 'to consider what is really wanted'. His ideal was a gear that could

> be instantly changed at any speed without removing the hand from the handle-bar, and by which any combination can be effected between, say 40 and 120 [inches], and it should provide an automatic freewheel which can be locked solid when desired without dismounting.

He decided that such a combination was not yet practicable and concluded that the aim should be an epicyclic hub gear with direct drive for the most frequently used gear, a lower gear (similar to that offered by the Hub) and a higher gear. A fortnight later in the same magazine, Staner returned to the subject and developed his thoughts on whether the 3-speed should have fixed drive or an automatic freewheel. He concluded that 'the arrangement which, in addition to the three speeds, gives the perpetual freewheel, will be the more successful'.

Many years later Henry Sturmey, editor of *The Cyclist*, wrote that Staner's first editorial on the subject had inspired James Archer (in reality Reilly) to develop a 3-speed hub. But the timing of the article's publication arouses the suspicion that Archer's abortive patent application may have inspired the editorial. Whichever came first, the idea of a 3-speed compact epicyclic hub was in the air at this time.

On 2 August 1901 James Archer, now of 6 Pinder Street, Hulme, made a second application (GB 15,638 of 1901), this time successfully. It described a gear 'by which the rider may have the option of using three different gears or speeds low, high, normal and a free wheel as desired, and so constructed that the rider may change the gears whilst riding'.

This patent was later amended to include the following statement from Archer in accordance with the decision of the Chief Examiner:

Fig. 3.2. James Archer.

> I wish it to be understood that I am aware that it is not new to employ epicyclic gear for varying the speed of cycles or motor vehicles and that it is not new with such variable gear to employ a hollow axle, a sliding sleeve, controlling springs and a cord or its equivalent for bringing about the changes of gear and I therefore make no general claim thereto.

On 8 January 1902 Archer applied successfully for a further patent (GB 519 of 1902), covering improvements to the earlier 3-speed patent 'to provide for the more perfect working of the apparatus and to allow of a better control and variety of gears'. It contained a similar statement to that quoted above and was accepted on 25 June 1902. This new patent dealt principally with the clutching arrangements, pawls and control lever.

## Pellant promotes the new gear

The Hub company's London representative Alfred Pellant, acting independently, became promoter of the 'Archer' 3-speed. F.T. Bidlake, one of the most influential cycling journalists at this time, wrote a column in the *Cyclists' Touring Club Gazette and Record* called 'Currente Calamo' (later anglicised as 'Current Comments'). In his column for December 1902 Bidlake stated that Pellant had written to him the year before, saying he had completed drawings for a 3-speed hub with a higher and lower than normal gear and a freewheel on all three. Pellant told Bidlake that he was working with William Reilly, so the gear in question was probably the one described in Archer's patent GB 15,638 of 1901.

Pellant's role in the early development of the 'Archer' gear was primarily entrepreneurial rather than technological. He used his reputation and contacts to try to get the gear put into production, his personal ambition being a lucrative agency. Without Pellant the 'Archer' gear

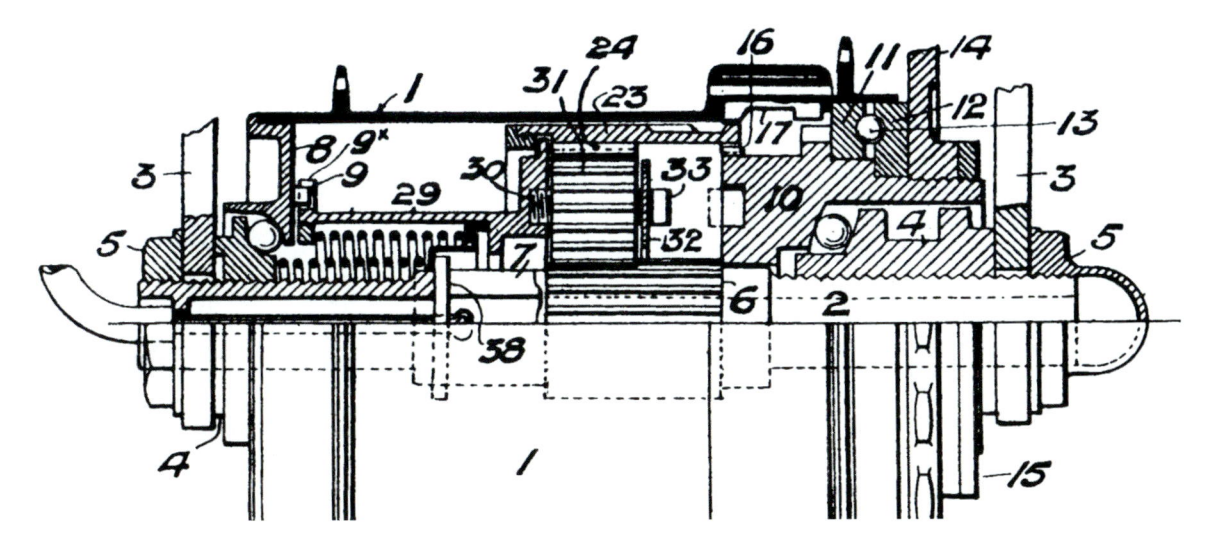

Fig. 3.3. The 'Archer' 3-speed (patent drawing).

might never have seen the light of day: Reilly could hardly promote it himself because he had signed his rights away, and Archer was unknown in cycling circles. But Pellant was a record-breaking cyclist, a well-known cycle dealer and London representative of Reilly's erstwhile employers, the Hub Two-Speed Gear Company.

## Reilly briefly breaks cover

In April 1902 Reilly surprisingly made a patent application in his own name (GB 8916 of 1902) for 'Velocipede etc., driving gear'. Perhaps he was testing the waters to see whether the Hub company reacted to the bait. Whatever the reason, this patent was declared 'void or abandoned' before publication.

Reilly made a further application in July (GB 15,986 of 1902). This time he gave his address as 57 Vere Street, Salford, further west than his previous abode but still within easy cycling distance of the Royce works. This patent related particularly to GB 519 of 1902 – the improvements to the 'Archer' gear. It dealt with a means of obtaining fixed or freewheel at will, while riding or stationary. But this modification was never put into production: in the *Cyclist* editorial of 19 June 1901 Staner had concluded that such a feature was an impracticable ideal. (However, in 1936 BSA introduced the DP or Dual Purpose hub, which was a 2-speed with selectable fixed or freewheel.)

## Bowden's quest for wider ratios

1899 saw the creation of the fourth limited liability Raleigh company in a financially tumultuous decade: Frank Bowden was its managing director. In a desperately competitive market, finding better change-speed gearing for Raleigh's safety bicycles was high on his list of priorities.

Bowden offered the Hub 2-speed on some Raleighs but he really wanted something that offered a wider range of gearing. As a keen cyclist himself he appreciated the value of variable gearing and kept abreast of new developments. These included John Fagan's 2-speed hub, later marketed by Eadie, but it was similar to the Hub and did not offer much advantage over it.

Fig. 3.4. Frank Bowden in later life (DDRN 6-20-3).

## Sharp's continuously variable hub gear

Bowden was particularly interested in a continuously variable hub gear designed by Archibald Sharp, the London-based engineer, patent agent and author of the classic text *Bicycles & Tricycles*. Sharp filed a patent for his gear in December 1900 (GB 22,574 of 1900) and made an arrangement with Bowden for Raleigh to manufacture it.

Unlike most internally geared change-speed hubs, Sharp's was not epicyclic. It was 'an apparatus for varying the speed ratio of two shafts continuously between certain limits.' Jim Papadopoulos, contributor to MIT Press's *Bicycling Science*, explains how it worked:

> In Sharp's hub gear, the sprocket drives the hub shell via four hub-mounted push rods that can ratchet relative to the sprocket bore. Hub speed increase is obtained by lowering the sprocket centre relative to the hub axle. When the sprocket is low, the topmost rod effectively connects the sprocket bore to a small hub radius. Thus the given sprocket rotational speed creates a greater hub speed. The bottom-most rod, and all the other rods, effectively representing larger hub radii [all marked L on the drawing], would tend to drive the hub slowly. But instead of holding the hub back, they simply 'click' as ratchets, traveling faster than the sprocket bore. Only the topmost rod drives the hub. By offsetting the sprocket to the maximum extent permitted by the rod dimensions, a speed increase of 39% is achieved. That is like installing an 18 tooth sprocket, and having the hub convert it to a 13 tooth sprocket, with nearly infinite variability.

Frank Bowden was all set to make Sharp's gear. But in May 1901 the Raleigh board was worried that Alexander Gray of Sutton in Surrey might have anticipated Sharp's patent. Frank Bowden met Gray whose terms for a licence were prohibitive but Bowden discovered that a German patent by Hoffbauer had probably anticipated Gray's invention. Sharp's patent

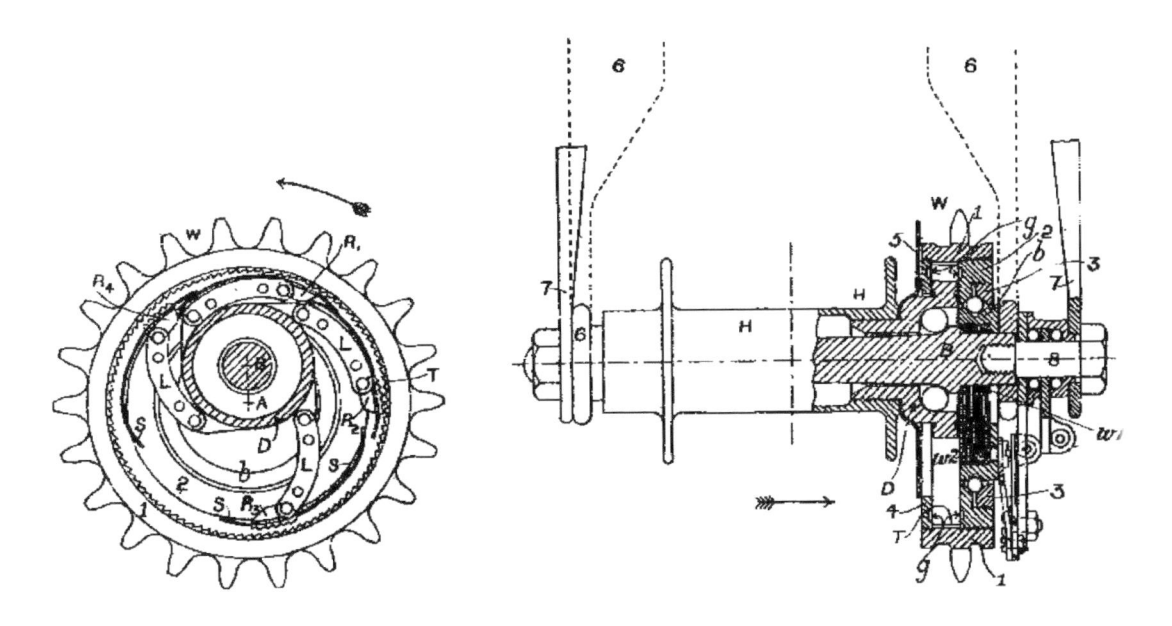

Fig. 3.5. Sharp's hub gear (patent drawings).

acknowledged Hoffbauer's work, so this ceased to be an issue. That was the good news: the bad news was that Raleigh's chief engineer, the record-breaking cyclist George Pilkington Mills, had tested a sample of Sharp's gear and found it deficient.

In July 1901 Sharp therefore visited Mills who pointed out defects in the gear. Modifications were agreed but a revised version also proved unsatisfactory. In December Bowden was authorised to release Raleigh from its undertaking to make Sharp's gear and, if necessary, to pay Sharp 'a sum not exceeding £100' (£10,000 today). Sharp settled for £50, agreeing to give Raleigh first offer of his gear 'if he made a success of it'. He never did and meanwhile Bowden turned to Henry Sturmey.

# Chapter 4

# Sturmey's contribution

### Sturmey patents his own 3-speed hub

### Henry Sturmey

John James Henry Sturmey was the son of a Merchant Navy captain and was born on 28 February 1857 in the village of Norton-sub-Hamdon, Somerset. He rode his first bicycle in 1872 while living in Weymouth. As a young man he became assistant master at Brixton Hill College but left at the age of 20. He wrote the highly successful annual *Indispensable Bicyclist's Handbook*, the *Tricyclist's Indispensable Annual* and *The Indispensable Handbook to the Safety Bicycle*.

Sturmey also had some bicycles built for retail but failed to make this a commercial success. So he continued his career as a schoolmaster, specialising in maths and science at Brynavor Hall College in North Wales but spending his vacations in Coventry and other centres of the bicycle industry.

While on one of these trips he met the famous publisher William Iliffe on a train. This led to the launch in 1879 of *The Cyclist* magazine with the 22-year-old Sturmey as its first editor, for which he received a third of the profits. He moved to Coventry but continued to mix his scholastic and journalistic careers, taking a tutorial post with a school in King Street. He was also chief consul of the Bicycle Touring Club, predecessor of the Cyclists' Touring Club. Sturmey had little interest in track racing, preferring touring and the 'political' aspects of club life.

Sturmey was involved with a number of magazines apart from *The Cyclist*, including *The Motor Cycle, Bicycling News* and *The Autocar,* but he eventually gave up journalism to concentrate on commercial projects, principally relating to cars and motor accessories. He was one of the first directors of the Daimler Motor Company and a promoter of the first major road trial for cars in Britain. He demonstrated that the motor car was more than just a novelty; the *Automobile Club Journal* described him as 'the first living authority on the British Motor Industry'. An obituarist wrote, 'He was not what is termed a successful business man, possibly because his enthusiasm for novelty in design caused his mind to diverge from the path that leads to wealth.' But Henry Sturmey never lost his interest in cycling.

### Sturmey's 3-speed

At the beginning of the twentieth century Sturmey was still deeply involved in journalism. As noted in the previous chapter, in the summer of 1901 Sturmey's magazine *The Cyclist* carried an editorial advocating the idea of a 3-speed hub gear. This was just five days after James Archer, on behalf of William Reilly, made an abortive patent application for a bicycle gear, details of which do not survive. Six weeks later Archer filed a patent for a 3-speed hub designed by Reilly.

Henry Sturmey, then living at Middleborough Road, Coventry, filed his own 3-speed patent eleven days after Archer's, in August 1901. It was entitled 'Improvements in or relating to Variable Speed Gears for Bicycles and other Machinery' (GB 16,221 of 1901). Sturmey began test riding his new gear in January 1902 and his patent was accepted seven months later.

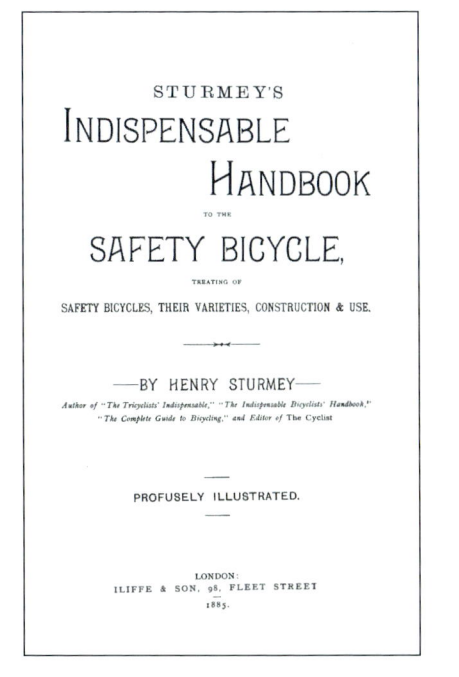

Fig. 4.1. Sturmey's 'Indispensable Handbook to the Safety Bicycle'.

Fig. 4.2. Henry Sturmey.

## Sturmey's paper

Sturmey presented a paper entitled 'Variable Gearing' to the Cycle Engineers' Institute on 29 May 1902 at the Queen's Hotel in Coventry. He started by looking at the need for variable gearing. Why depart from the simplicity of single-speed transmission? Sturmey answered that we are dealing with the human body and not with a steam engine. The body gets tired and it has a brain which makes it feel worse. He pointed out that even a motor car works better 'when its efforts are more frequent and less nearly approaching the limit of its powers'. Variable gearing simply enables riders 'to suit their gearing to the circumstances of the moment, and that's all there is in it'.

Sturmey felt confident that, when the advantages of variable gearing became generally known, few riders would fail to adopt it. He then went on to survey the 1902 cycling scene and concluded that 'seven marketable gears are known here'. Excluding foreign products that had made little impact, there were four 2-speeds, two 3-speeds and a 7-speed.

Henry Sturmey was exceptionally well acquainted with epicyclic gearing theory. He demonstrated a model of a Crypto type gear and showed that, from one simple epicyclic gear train, seven speeds could be obtained. In Sturmey's model the gear ring had three times as many teeth as the sun. The planet pinions were held in a cage. As a matter of convenience and practicality, the planet pinions were the same size as the sun but this had no bearing on the various speeds obtained. The table below, based on Sturmey's original, shows the seven possible output speeds relative to 100 input revolutions:

Fig. 4.3. 'The Cyclist' magazine, edited by Henry Sturmey.

| Speed | Driving (input) | Stationary | Driven (output) | Revolutions |
|-------|-----------------|------------|-----------------|-------------|
| 1 | | All locked together | | 100 forwards |
| 2 | Sun | Gear ring | Planet cage | 25 forwards |
| 3 | Gear ring | Sun | Planet cage | 75 forwards |
| 4 | Planet cage | Gear ring | Sun | 400 forwards |
| 5 | Planet cage | Sun | Gear ring | 133⅓ forwards |
| 6 | Sun | Planet cage | Gear ring | 33⅓ backwards |
| 7 | Gear ring | Planet cage | Sun | 300 backwards |

Sturmey pointed out that to obtain all seven speeds would be too complicated for practical purposes. Obviously gears 4, 6 and 7 would be of little practical use and gear 2 is rather low. However, gears 1, 3 and 5, between them, gave direct drive and a drop of 25% or a rise of 33⅓% – exactly the same as the classic Sturmey-Archer AW wide-ratio 3-speed.

Henry Sturmey continued his lecture by reviewing the gears then on the British market. These were the Collier 2-speed bracket gear; the New Protean/Whippet 2-speed derailleur; the Garrard 2-speed screw-on hub gear, the inventor of which was in the audience; the Hub

2-speed, which Sturmey praised for its lightness, compactness, ease of fitting and choice of ratios; Hodgkinson's Gradient 3-speed derailleur; and 'probably the most interesting of all', the Paradox 7-speed expanding chainwheel gear.

### Sturmey's 3-speed revealed

During the review Sturmey produced a bicycle fitted with his own 3-speed hub gear. This gave a 25% reduction and a 33⅓% increase and weighed 2 lb 10 oz (1.19 kg). The demonstration bicycle was geared to give 66, 88 and 117". The tendency towards high gearing then prevalent was aided by the long cranks then customary: the crank length in inches was usually one tenth of the normal gear, e.g. 8½" cranks for an 85" gear.

Sturmey stated that the gear would probably be on the market in a few weeks' time and that it would be produced by a syndicate. The commercial version was likely to be lighter and the ratios changed to give a drop of 20% and a rise of 25%.

### A general discussion – hybrids and an automatic

After Sturmey had presented his paper there was a general discussion. During this Mr C.R. Garrard pointed out the disadvantages of bracket gears: as the chain drive of a bicycle gears up (rather than down as with motor driven vehicles) the pressure at the hub is about one third of that at the cranks and therefore the components in a hub gear can be that much smaller and lighter.

He described the Garrard gear, designed by his son C.G. Garrard, who was also present. This ingenious 2-speed was a very compact epicyclic made small enough to screw onto any hub having the Cycle Engineers' standard thread. It weighed 17 oz (480 gm) to which, for purposes of comparison, should be added the weight of the single-speed hub.

Garrard pointed out that one of his gears screwed onto a Sturmey hub would give a 6-speed transmission. He went on to list other hybrid possibilities, including a Garrard-Sturmey with a Paradox expanding chainwheel gear, which would give 42 gears. This was greeted by laughter but the engineers were clearly aware of the possibilities offered by hybrid gearing even before the Sturmey-Archer hub commenced production.

H.W. Staner, assistant editor of *The Cyclist*, said that Sturmey's gear met the attributes postulated a year earlier in that magazine. At that time they were 'regarded as almost impossible'. Staner recommended that gear changing should be controlled from the handlebars and Sturmey agreed.

There was also some discussion of the relative merits of fixed-wheels and freewheels. Sturmey concluded that any gear should be either all one or the other and not a mixture of fixed and free like later versions of the Hub 2-speed gear.

The Dieterich automatic gear, produced in the USA by the Pope Manufacturing Company, was also discussed. Sturmey had corresponded with its inventor; it had been a commercial failure, principally because it weighed 4½ lb (2.04 kg). It was a completely automatic gearless and continuously variable transmission system, the subject of GB patent 17,911 of 1899. The mechanism was a variable eccentricity lever drive housed in an oversized bottom bracket.

### The coming thing

Although Sturmey's lecture was delivered more than a century ago, it is intriguing how many gearing concepts were discussed: derailleurs, expanding chainwheels, automatic transmission and hybrid gearing were all known to the Cycle Engineers' Institute in 1901. Douglas

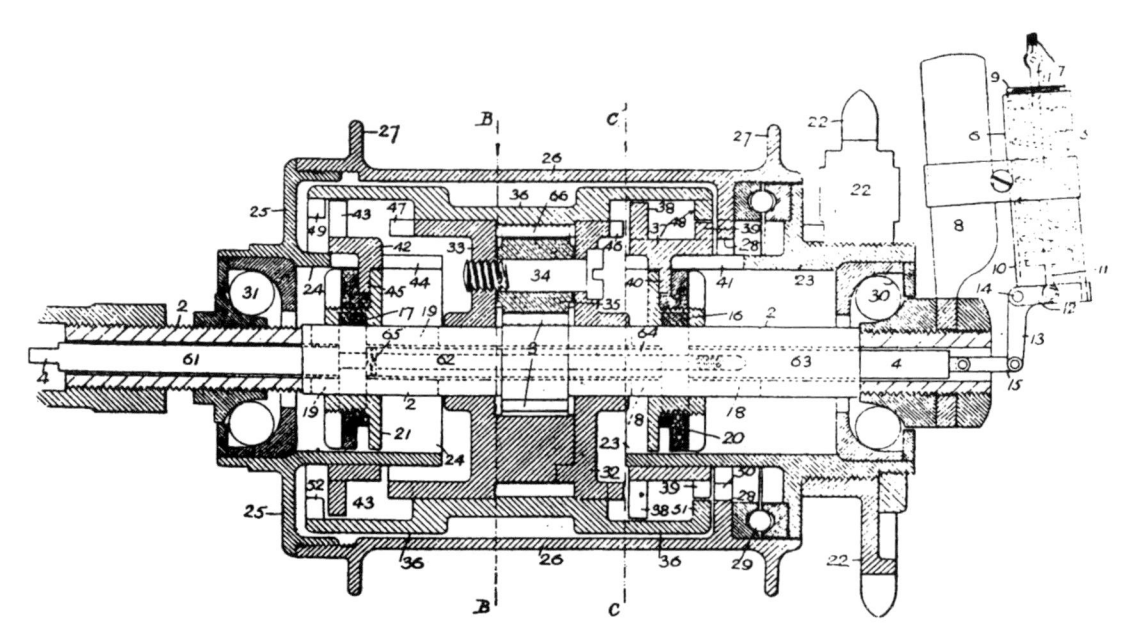

Fig. 4.4. Section through Sturmey's 3-speed hub (patent drawing).

Leechman, reporting Sturmey's lecture in the *Cyclists' Touring Club Gazette and Record*, stated that Sturmey's gear 'is after all the most logical arrangement'. He added: 'If such a gear is put upon the market, as it seems likely to be, it should meet with great success.'

So by mid 1902 Reilly (in the guise of Archer) and Sturmey both had feasible hub gears ready for production. What both designers needed now was an entrepreneur to set the wheels in motion.

# Chapter 5
# The 'Sturmey-Archer-Reilly-Mills-Pellant' gear

### Bowden buys the rival rights

### Bidlake's claim
The famous cycling journalist F.T. Bidlake claimed the honour for bringing Archer and Sturmey together. In his 'Currente Calamo' column in the December 1902 edition of the *Cyclists' Touring Club Gazette and Record*, Bidlake reported the launch of the Sturmey-Archer gear: 'At last the realisation of an ideal is available in the matter of change-speed gears, for a 3-speed hub is now on the market, manufactured by the Raleigh Company, but not exclusively for use on Raleigh cycles.'

Alfred Pellant had written to Bidlake the year before, saying that he was working with William Reilly on a 3-speed hub gear. Then Bidlake heard from Sturmey that he also had a 3-speed, which Sturmey thought was unique. The two designs were to be separately syndicated but Bidlake brought both to the attention of Frank Bowden, managing director of Raleigh. In Bidlake's own words, Bowden 'was after Sturmey, who was joined with Mr Archer, and a federation resulted, and of course when Mr Bowden got hold of it, and the Raleigh Company made it, and G.P. Mills put his reconstructive ability into it, success was completed. It is the Sturmey-cum-Archer-cum-Reilly-cum-Mills-cum-Pellant gear, and we need not worry about the priority of each man's claim, for they are all consolidated.'

Thus began the myth that Sturmey and Archer collaborated in the design of the first Sturmey-Archer hub gear. The reality was rather different.

### Bowden buys the rights to both 3-speeds
On 20 March 1902, nine months before launch of the Sturmey-Archer 3-speed, Frank Bowden informed the Raleigh board 'that he had secured an option for the sole right to manufacture Sturmey's patent 3-speed gear. Mr Sturmey would meet the Board on Thursday next prepared to enter into an agreement.'

A week later Henry Sturmey attended the Raleigh board meeting, as the minutes report:

> Mr Bowden said that since the failure of Mr Sharp's gear last year, he had been on the lookout for something to take its place, and in the early autumn had heard that Mr Sturmey was experimenting with a gear which Mr Bowden arranged to see and test when ready, but not hearing anything further for some time he had after several communications with Mr Sturmey secured an option on the gear which he had ridden and found satisfactory. Mr Sturmey … agreed to extend the option to 25 April in order to give the company time to make a complete search as to the anticipation and validity of Mr Sturmey's patent, which the managing director was instructed to have done.

While Raleigh had the patent search made, Frank Bowden announced to the directors on 17 April 1902 that

1. MR. H. STURMEY. 2. MR. A. PELLANT. 3. MR. G. P. MILLS.
4. MR. J. ARCHER. 5. MR. W. REILLY.

Fig. 5.1. Persons involved to varying extents in the creation of the Sturmey-Archer 3-speed (DDRN 4-10-12-1).

a 3-speed gear, the invention of Mr Reilly, one of the patentees of the Hub 2-speed gear, was now in the hands of Mr A Pellant of London, who was endeavouring to form a syndicate. As this gear was lighter, and had other features rendering it a formidable competitor with Sturmey's gear, Mr Bowden suggested that it would be well for the Raleigh company to obtain control of it ... Mr Pellant attended and the matter was discussed.

The minutes of a special meeting of the Raleigh board on Monday 28 April 1902, reveal the 'skin of the teeth' way in which Frank Bowden secured the rights to Reilly's gear:

After considerable discussion Mr Pellant agreed to submit terms to his syndicate ... for the Raleigh company to make and push the gear on a royalty ... making all the hubs required by the syndicate for the trade at 20% upon cost including labour, material, lead charges and depreciation of tooling. Mr Bowden attended Mr Pellant's office in the afternoon when Mr Pellant said that they were not prepared to grant the above terms and submitted others ... which Mr Bowden found ridiculous. He thereupon saw Mr Pellant and another member of the syndicate, and finding that Messrs Humber and Co were likely to get hold of the gear – respecting which they were telephoning and telegraphing at the moment – and seeing no other way of securing the before mentioned satisfactory terms for the company, he proposed that provided Mr Pellant granted these terms to the Raleigh company, he, Mr Bowden, would personally guarantee on his own private account the formation of the syndicate, the payment of the £2,000 cash down part of the amount required for the patents [£206,000 today] and the finding of the whole of the capital of £15,000 [£1,550,000 today], with the exception of £1,500 provided by Mr Pellant's friends.

Pellant accepted and three days later Bowden went to Manchester to see Wilson's, the patent agents dealing with the Reilly hub 'to see all the agreements between Reilly and the original inventor Archer, which he had found satisfactory.' Whereas the first reference in the minutes to Reilly made it quite clear he was the inventor, Raleigh now took great care to say that the inventor was Archer, lest the patents be invalidated. Bowden meanwhile started filing overseas patents where Pellant had not already done so, in countries such as Italy and Austria.

The Raleigh board minutes of 1 May 1902 record how Frank Bowden now dealt with Henry Sturmey: 'Mr Bowden had also seen Mr Sturmey and induced him to place his gear in the hands of the syndicate and so avoid competition and thereby also increase the manufacturing business of the Raleigh company. Mr Sturmey was disappointed that the Raleigh company were not taking up his gear and at first felt inclined to offer it to the Bowden Brake company.' (A company founded by E.M. Bowden who was not a relative of Frank Bowden.)

But despite his understandable disappointment Henry Sturmey played along with Frank Bowden and subsequently maintained to the world at large that he was the principal inventor of the original Sturmey-Archer gear. The story suited Raleigh's marketing nicely, Sturmey being a well-known personality at the cutting edge of technology and modernity, and he was to prove a very powerful propagandist for the new hub.

As noted in the previous chapter, in May 1902 Henry Sturmey presented his paper on variable gearing to the Cycle Engineers' Institute and demonstrated a bicycle fitted with his 3-speed hub gear. This was just a month after Bowden had told Sturmey that his gear would not now be put into production. Sturmey stated that the gear would probably be on the market in a few weeks' time and that a syndicate would produce it. He added that the commercial version was likely to be lighter, with closer ratios; this was because it would be the Reilly/Archer gear, though Sturmey did not reveal this.

## Gearing up for production

At the Raleigh board meeting of the 1 May 1902, Bowden revealed the proposed pricing and profit margin of the Reilly/Archer 3-speed:

> Mr Bowden said that the selling price of the 3-speed gear would, he thought, be £3 10s. 0d. retail [£360 today], about the same as that of the Hub 2-speed, and he hoped it could be produced for less than £1, which would leave a very handsome profit. He had confidence that the gear would be a great success and catch on with the public.

Why was Reilly's gear chosen in preference to Sturmey's? The Bowdens, father Frank and son Harold, were very cost conscious and 'eagle-eyed on every fraction of a penny', according to Israel Cohen. They therefore opted for the easiest and cheapest gear to produce, which also had the marketing advantage of being lighter. Examination of the patent drawings for the rival gears shows the difference. For instance, Reilly's solution to the gear shifting linkage at the end of the hub axle was a simple cord, whereas Sturmey used a bell-crank system. In production the familiar toggle chain and flared nut was used, as pioneered in the Hub: this was simpler, cheaper and more reliable.

George Pilkington Mills, a famous record-breaking cyclist and university-educated engineer head-hunted by Bowden from local rival Humber, was one of Raleigh's works managers and its chief engineer. He was initially responsible for setting up mass production

Fig. 5.2. The newly equipped 3-speed gear shop.

of the new gear. On 1 May 1902 Mills gave a rough estimate that £3,000 worth of extra plant (£310,000 today) would be needed to make 10,000 3-speed hubs. The board gave the go-ahead to obtain estimates for the necessary equipment. By the end of the month Frank Bowden had been authorised to buy the necessary equipment from Alfred Herbert Ltd or the Cleveland Steel Tool Company.

In July 1902 Mills test rode a sample of the 3-speed more than 850 miles in hilly Scottish terrain, including 1 in 7 gradients: it proved trouble-free. Frank Bowden and his son Harold also rode the hub in the pre-production period. Worrying news came the following month: the board heard that 'the patentees of the Hub Two Speed Gear company had filed an opposition to the sealing of the patent' for the Reilly gear. Fortunately for Raleigh, Reilly, Archer and Pellant, nothing came of this.

Henry Sturmey's opinion that the new hub would be available a few weeks after his May 1902 lecture proved wildly optimistic. In January 1903 Mills was asked by the Raleigh board when he could definitely promise deliveries of the 3-speed hub. He replied that he was 'quite convinced that the gears would be coming out from the factory in a month's time'. But Mills struggled with the initial set-up. Reilly's assistant Israel Cohen, who joined Sturmey-Archer in August 1906, wrote that, as what Mills 'knew about steel specifications and heat treatment would fill a book the size of a postage stamp, he made a mess of the job'. In July 1903 William Reilly was therefore placed in charge of the 3-speed shop. He brought in his old colleagues from Royce – James Archer and Tom White.

## The Three Speed Gear Syndicate

While Raleigh geared up to produce the new hub, the legal status of the new marketing syndicate and its relationship with Raleigh needed clarification. At the end of October 1902 the Raleigh directors therefore agreed 'that all correspondence, bookkeeping, storing, despatching, etc., be carried on by the Raleigh company on behalf of The Three Speed Gear Syndicate, the latter paying to the company 5% upon the sales other than to the Raleigh company, with a minimum of £100 per year [£10,300 today] for the first year'. The Three Speed Gear Syndicate of Faraday Road, Lenton, Nottingham was therefore established to produce the new hub with nominal capital of £15,000 (£1.55 million today) in £1 shares. Joseph Lazonby handled the company registration.

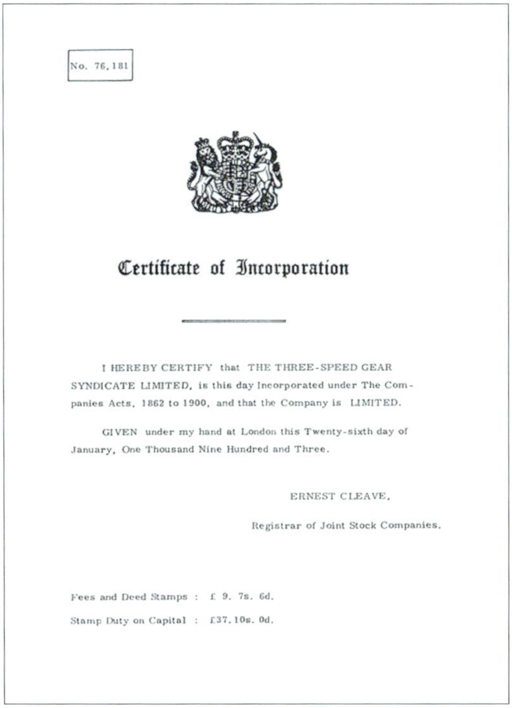

No. 76,181

Certificate of Incorporation

I HEREBY CERTIFY that THE THREE-SPEED GEAR SYNDICATE LIMITED, is this day Incorporated under The Companies Acts, 1862 to 1900, and that the Company is LIMITED.

GIVEN under my hand at London this Twenty-sixth day of January, One Thousand Nine Hundred and Three.

ERNEST CLEAVE,

Registrar of Joint Stock Companies.

Fees and Deed Stamps : £ 9. 7s. 6d.

Stamp Duty on Capital : £37. 10s. 0d.

Fig. 5.3. Certificate of Incorporation of The Three Speed Gear Syndicate as a limited company.

The background of Lazonby, the company secretary, was something of a mystery. Cohen, while admitting that most of his information was second-hand, concluded that Lazonby assisted Bowden 'in China when the latter was gathering wealth in land dealings. Either then or later when in England Lazonby became less wealthy and Bowden prospered. Bowden thereafter treated him like a poor relation, just keeping him alive. Why, we can only guess.' These comments were made in a letter written in 1951 to Harold Karslake, who felt that Lazonby's involvement 'looks terribly fishy business'.

The share subscribers listed in the registration documentation of 22 January 1903 were: Frank Bowden of Mapperley Road, Nottingham; Edward Charles Farrow of Baker Street, Nottingham; George Pilkington Mills of Beeston; Edmund Hobson Pearce of Arundel Street, Nottingham; Thomas Long of Noel Street, Nottingham; John Walker of Cromwell Street, Beeston; and Frederick Charles Bush of Gedling Road, Carlton.

On 28 January 1903 two agreements were drawn up: the first between Alfred Pellant, Frank Bowden, William Reilly, James Archer and the syndicate; the second, between the syndicate and the Raleigh cycle company. Both agreements were formally approved at the syndicate's first board meeting on 10 March 1903.

The lawyers were busy on 28 January 1903, as this was also the day on which William Reilly and James Archer established the legal basis on which the syndicate would reward Archer for use of the patent registered in his name, while remunerating Reilly for having invented the gear. Archer, then living at 146 Moss Lane, East Manchester, signed an indenture whereby he sold to the syndicate the benefits of British patents 15,638 of 1901 and 519 of 1902 and all present or future patents, including foreign and colonial ones, for inventions or improvements in variable gears for cycles and motorcycles. The sale was for an unstated cash payment and a royalty of 1% on the wholesale price of all UK-manufactured hubs sold, excluding control mechanisms. The indenture states that 'James Archer hath bargained with the said William Reilly for the sale to him of all his rights in and to the said royalty', that Reilly has paid him £200 (£20,400 today), and that all Archer's rights regarding the royalty are therefore transferred to William Reilly. So the syndicate had to pay the royalty to Reilly rather than Archer. Reilly was then living at 57 Vere Street, Manchester. Archer signed an almost identical indenture nearly three years later on 8 November 1905.

On 27 February 1903 there was a meeting of the signatories of the syndicate's memorandum of association; present were Frank Bowden, Edward Charles Farrow (Raleigh company secretary), George Pilkington Mills, Edmund Holson Pearce, Thomas Long, John Walker and Frederick Charles Bush (later general manager of Raleigh). It was carried unanimously that the directors should be Frank Bowden, William Reilly, Alfred Pellant, Joseph Lazonby (banker, solicitor and Raleigh director) and Harold Houston Bowden (Frank Bowden's son). It is significant that neither Sturmey nor Archer was a director whereas Reilly was.

At the first board meeting, on 10 March 1903, Alfred Pellant proposed Frank Bowden as chairman; William Reilly seconded this and the motion was carried. Reilly proposed and Pellant seconded Frank Bowden as managing director and (via a separate motion) that the syndicate should bank with Lloyds at Alfreton Road, Nottingham; both motions were carried.

There then followed an allotment of 5,500 shares: the first 1,000 went to Reilly, the next 1,000 to Pellant, 500 to the Rt Hon. Andrew Graham Murray, 2,250 (by far the largest holding) to Frank Bowden, 500 to Harold Bowden and 250 to Joseph Lazonby. It is again significant that neither Sturmey nor Archer was allocated shares but Reilly was. The directors' salaries were fixed at £50 per annum and Joseph Lazonby was appointed company secretary. Frank Bowden's salary as managing director was subsequently set at £100 a year (£10,000 today).

Alfred Pellant was appointed agent for an area 15 miles around Charing Cross and for the whole of England south of 'a line drawn from the south side of the Thames to the East of London boundary around it on the north side passing through Trowbridge, Wiltshire direct to the Bristol Channel'. Pellant, as wholesaler for that district, was to receive a discount of 33⅓%, plus 5% off the net cash retail price, plus 5% commission on all hubs ordered direct from the factory by customers in his district. But in March 1904 his area was pruned back to just Greater London.

At an extraordinary general meeting on 11 May 1908, The Three Speed Gear Syndicate was reformed as Sturmey-Archer Gears Limited.

### Henry Sturmey's exit

On 3 March 1904 Henry Sturmey attended a board meeting at which he assigned to the syndicate his patents for the United States of America, Germany, Belgium and France for a sum of £1,000 (£102,400 today); at the same meeting he was 'on the proposition of Mr Bowden seconded by Mr A. Pellant elected director'. However, the minutes of the annual general meeting held on 11 July 1904 report that 'Mr J.J.H. Sturmey not having qualified, was not proposed for re-election.'

His four-month period as a director marked the end of any significant involvement by Sturmey with the syndicate or its successor. Cohen wrote that thereafter 'Sturmey never showed himself in Nottingham to the best of my knowledge.' Instead he turned his attentions more to the motor industry, setting up a company to produce Duryea cars in England. This became Sturmey Motors Limited, producers of the first specially-designed London taxi, the first motor hearse and a car for use in the Australian outback.

Nineteen years later, with Coventry engineer John William Peart and completely independently of Sturmey-Archer, Henry Sturmey filed a patent for the first 5-speed hub gear. This was tested successfully and weighed only a few ounces more than a 3-speed. But it was so far ahead of its time that it never went into production: the expert view in the UK was that very few people needed more than three speeds. It is deeply ironic and rather sad that no hub gear invented by Henry Sturmey was ever series-produced, least of all by Sturmey-Archer.

## Archer's later life

James Archer spent the rest of his career quietly at Raleigh. He fell seriously ill in May 1919 and never properly recovered. He was kept on the payroll and died 14 August 1920 aged 66, survived by at least 10 of his 13 children. Israel Cohen worked alongside James Archer after becoming Reilly's assistant in August 1906. Cohen stated that 'Archer was merely a good mechanic and never showed any signs of inventive ability'. This was not said vindictively: Cohen knew the Archer family and got on with them well. Before joining Sturmey-Archer, Cohen had been an apprentice at John Hetherington & Sons Limited of Manchester. One of James Archer's sons, Len (Henry Leonard) was a junior apprentice working under Cohen's supervision. When Cohen went to work in Nottingham, James Archer 'took a paternal interest' in him and introduced him to his family circle.

Fig. 5.4. Henry Sturmey in later life.

Cohen left Raleigh about two years before Archer's death; but that was not the last he saw of the Archer family. In the late 1920s and early 1930s Cohen worked at HMV with Archer's daughter Kate, unaware of her identity; and when he moved to Plessey in 1933, Cohen found himself working with another of Archer's sons, Will, whose granddaughter was a friend of Tony Hadland's mother.

## A persistent myth

For understandable legal and marketing reasons, the creation story of the first Sturmey-Archer gear was well and truly spun from the outset. Advertising and information fed to the press gave the impression that the new 3-speed hub was the product of a great collaborative effort, instigated by Frank Bowden, led by Henry Sturmey, with major assistance from James Archer and tweaking by George Mills, Alfred Pellant and William Reilly. This myth has been reinforced by repetition over the years and was still being reiterated in the early twenty-first century.

The truth is rather different and may be summarised thus. Neither Sturmey nor Archer invented the first Sturmey-Archer 3-speed. Sturmey and Archer did not collaborate in any meaningful way in the development of the first Sturmey-Archer 3-speed. Reilly invented the gear that was put into production. Sturmey independently invented a similar gear that was

Fig. 5.5. An example of the first Sturmey-Archer 3-speed hub.

heavier and more expensive to make, which Raleigh originally intended to manufacture but abandoned having acquired the rights to Reilly's gear. Archer's principal role was to sign patent applications declaring himself the inventor of Reilly's creations. This was to 'launder' them, because such inventions were *prima facie* the intellectual property of the Hub Two Speed Gear Co, later absorbed into BSA. Pellant was Reilly's front man who, while acting as agent for the Hub Two Speed Gear Company, was complicit in denying them the benefit of their legal (but arguably unfair) right to Reilly's inventions. Mills' contributions were limited to designing the handlebar-mounted gear changer, test riding and, rather ineffectively, starting to set up the production facilities.

But Henry Sturmey was one of the biggest names in cycling, and so he was given priority in the promotional drive. Mills and Pellant, because they were record-breaking cyclists, were also given more prominence than they deserved. The role of Archer, as the supposed co-inventor, was necessarily elevated in the creation myth, while Reilly's contribution was downplayed to that of a mere improver, tinkering at the edges.

## The Hub … only more so

The first Sturmey-Archer gear had no model number. It gave a 25% increase and a 20% decrease from normal and freewheeled automatically in all gears. It added about 18 oz (510 gm) to the weight of a single-speed bicycle; the cost was £3 10s. (£360 today) complete with all fittings. It was only marginally heavier and more expensive than the Hub 2-speed. Typical gears offered were 56, 70 and 88". Bidlake would have preferred slightly closer ratios but felt that 'the value of a change-speed gear grows on one till it becomes absolutely indispensable'. He described the first Sturmey-Archer as 'the Hub, only more so – much more so'. Inasmuch that William Reilly designed both, he could not have been nearer the truth.

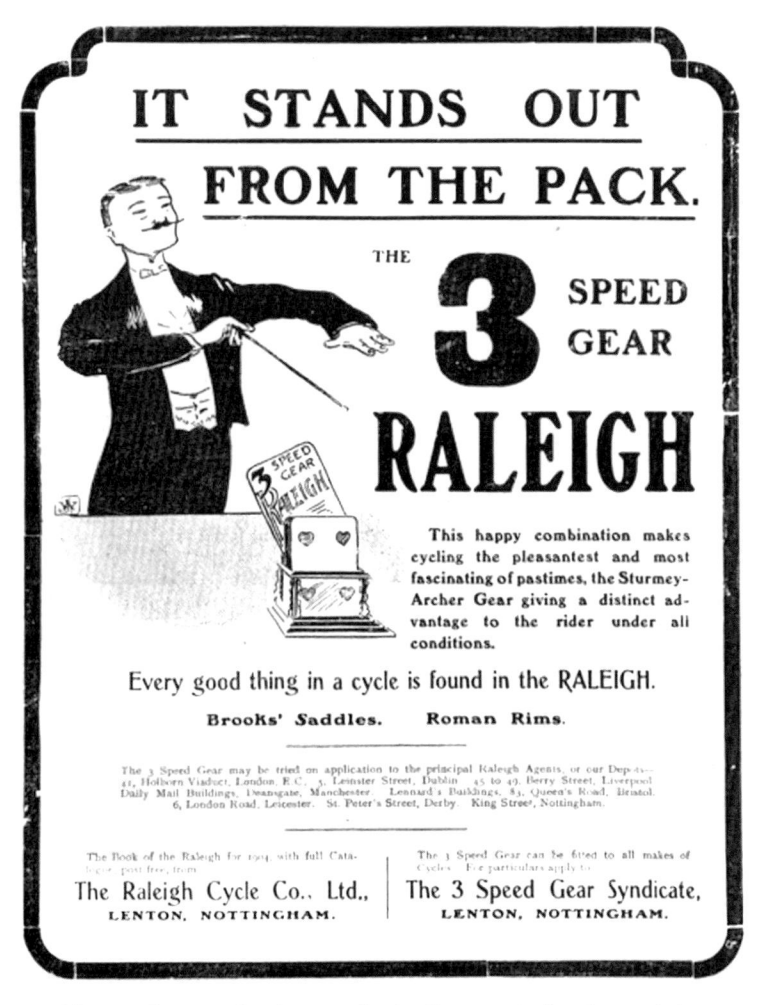

Fig. 5.6. A 1904 advertisement for the Sturmey-Archer 3-speed, the magician bearing a resemblance to James Archer.

## Chapter 6
# Reilly at Nottingham

### The 3-speed is launched and more hubs follow, 1903 to 1910

### The first Sturmey-Archer 3-speed

The first Sturmey-Archer 3-speed was enthusiastically received by the cycling press and by the public. It was launched late in 1902 and Sturmey's magazine *The Cyclist* contained one of the first detailed reviews, noting that the invention was 'the joint production of Mr Henry Sturmey, Mr James Archer, and Mr William Riley' and adding that certain improvements had been made by 'Mr Alfred Pellant and Mr G.P. Mills, AMICE, MIME, chief designer and constructor to the Raleigh Company'.

Having misspelled Reilly's name, *The Cyclist* then indulged in a little pro-Sturmey banner waving:

> It is only fair to point out that Mr Sturmey's gear as originally made was thoroughly successful, and the two or three trial hubs made by hand are still in daily and satisfactory use … so far as we can ascertain, the honour of being the first to invent and use a 3-speed hub belongs to Mr Sturmey.

The article proceeded to praise Frank Bowden who 'realised the benefits of the 3-speed gear directly it was brought to his notice' and who 'immediately made up his mind to fit it to the Raleigh best models as a standard.' Having distributed the credits, the review turned to the gear itself, first describing the gear lever. This had been patented by G.P. Mills and clipped onto the handlebar in a small cylindrical casing:

> To change to low gear from the normal, which is the middle notch, one pushes the lever forward with the thumb. To put it in the high gear one presses it back from the middle notch, and, as the Raleigh people claim, the operation is as simple as ringing the bell. As there is a freewheel on each gear, there is no fear of damaging gears in changing, as those who have not the knack of slightly easing the pedalling at the moment of change can cease entirely.

Mills had tested a prototype Sturmey-Archer 3-speed while cycle-touring in Scotland during the summer of 1902. This experience led him to design the control lever mechanism, which Logos believed to be the first application of a Bowden cable to a handlebar mounted gear control system. The patent for the lever (GB 22,086 of 1902) was filed in October 1902, only a few weeks before the first hubs were passed to the cycling press for review.

The Bowden cable, comprising a flexible cable moving back and forth in a hollow flexible sheath, was invented by Ernest Monnington Bowden, founder of E.M. Bowden's Patents Syndicate and E.M. Bowden's Brake Company. He was not related to Frank Bowden but in 1900 Frank and fellow Raleigh director Edward Harlow became members of the syndicate, giving Raleigh rights to adopt the Bowden mechanism.

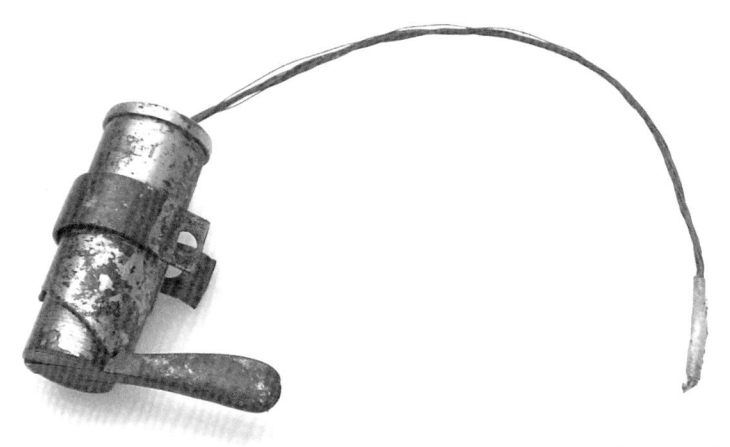

Fig. 6.1. The cylindrical control lever.

The body of the changer was a fixed cylinder, one end of which was

> formed as an inclined plane cam furnished with ratchet shaped teeth or stops ... located in such positions thereon as to correspond to the various position which the gear can assume.

The other end of the cylinder formed the abutment of the Bowden cable sheath. Within this cylinder was an inner sleeve with one end attached to the control cable and the other end connected to a lever 'pivoted transversely thereto'. This lever engaged with the inclined plane cam of the fixed cylinder, against which it was spring loaded. Hence operation of the lever caused the inner sleeve to move within the outer cylinder, tightening or slackening the control cable and causing the gear to change.

The article in *The Cyclist* noted that the gear gave a reduction of 20% and an increase of 25%. The reviewer would have preferred the wider ratios of Henry Sturmey's hub: 25% down and 33⅓% up. However, he pointed out that 'The Three Speed Gear Syndicate felt that the majority of the cycle world are not yet sufficiently educated in the use of multi-speed gears to comfortably accept such large variations'. Time was to prove Sturmey right: the majority of wide-ratio 3-speeds produced during the history of Sturmey-Archer have used his ratios.

The reviewer accurately predicted that

> as time goes on still greater variations will be given, and possibly more of them. In the meanwhile, the user of the variable gear will experience not only greater ease, but greater variety and pleasure in his riding.

*The Cyclist* article contained an explanation of how the gear worked. Unlike most later hub gears it had the toggle chain on the left but, in common with the classic AW 3-speed, a slack cable gave high gear. Apart from the freewheel mechanism, all the clutches in the hub were 'interlocking or jaw clutches'.

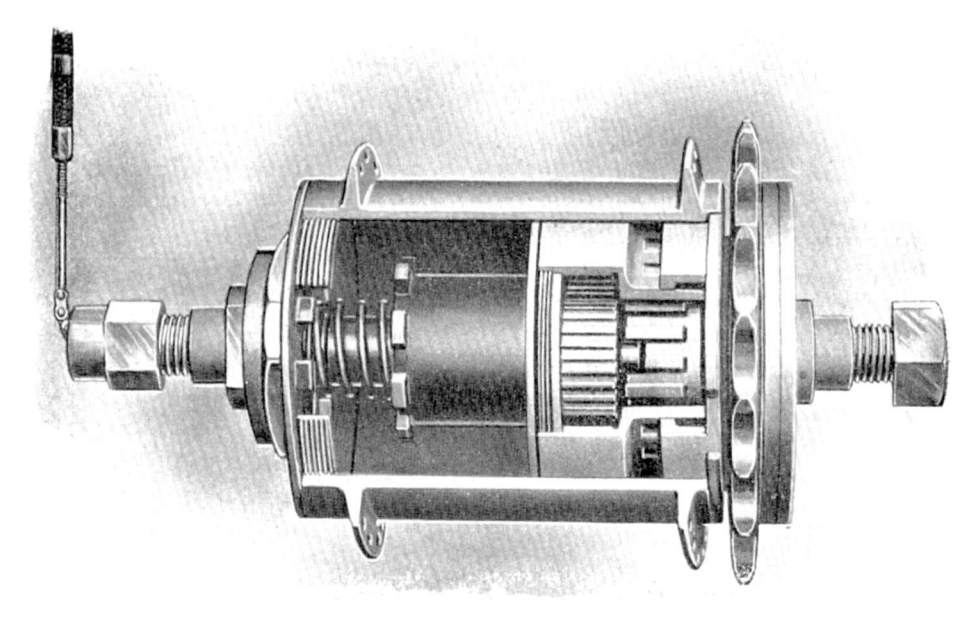

Fig. 6.2. Contemporary cutaway illustration of the 1902 3-speed (DDRN 4-10-12-1).

With the control cable tight, the driver (on which the sprocket was mounted) was clutched to the gear ring. Drive passed from the driver to the gear ring and through the epicyclic gears to the planet cage, which rotated at a reduced rate and fed the drive to the hub shell, giving low gear.

When the control cable was slackened to the middle position, the complete planet cage and gear ring assembly moved to the right, disengaging the planet cage from the shell and locking the shell and gear ring to the driver. Drive passed from the driver direct to the shell, bypassing the epicyclic gears and giving middle gear.

With the control cable fully slackened, the complete planet cage and gear ring assembly moved further right, freeing the hub shell from the driver and locking the driver to the planet cage. The gear ring remained locked to the shell, so drive passed from the driver to the planet cage, via the epicyclic gears to the gear ring and hence to the hub shell, giving high gear.

The gear incorporated a spring hold-off device that allowed downward gear changing with the bike stationary and caused 'a spring engagement to the clutches … when changing from high to normal and from normal to low'. This reduced the risk of damage to the clutches during clumsy gear changes. The freewheel was of the 'Micrometer type of silent springless clutch' which used unsprung crescent-shaped pawls.

*The Cyclist's* review stated that the gear was being made by Raleigh for The Three Speed Gear Syndicate 'who will shortly be able to supply it for fitting to all makes of cycles.' The price was £3 10s. (£357 today). In the *Cyclists' Touring Club Gazette and Record*, Archibald Sharp wrote that the 'Sturmey-Archer-Reilly-Pellant-Mills' 3-speed was one of the most noticeable exhibits at the trade shows. Sharp's article, like that in *The Cyclist*, was accompanied by a sectional drawing of the hub and he added: 'The sectional drawing may at first sight impress the reader that the device is rather complex and likely to get out of order, but this is an utterly mistaken notion. All the parts are thoroughly well protected and can be perfectly lubricated.'

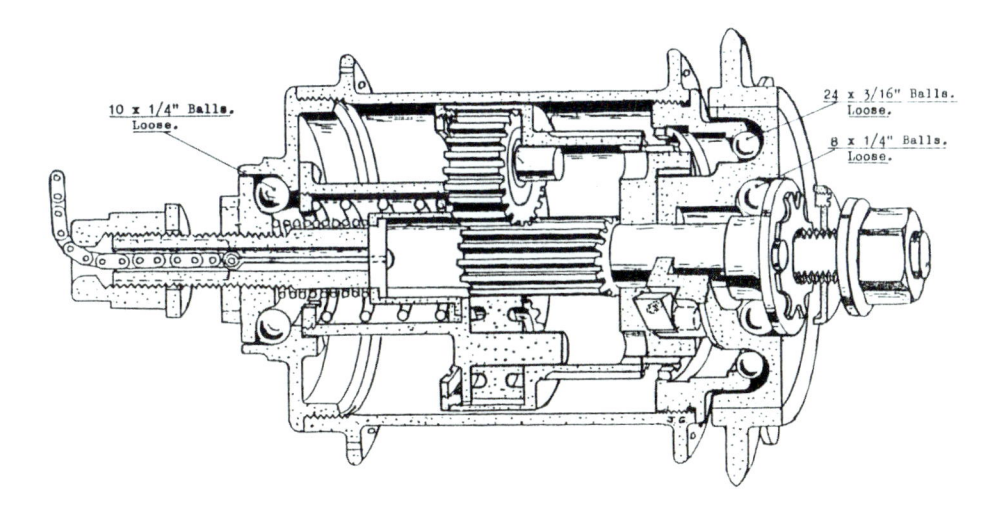

Fig. 6.3. Cutaway view of the 1902 3-speed by Jim Gill.

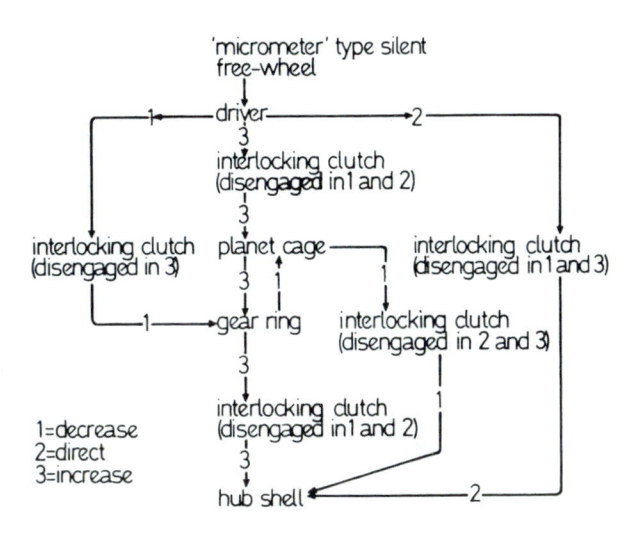

Fig. 6.4. Flowchart for the 1902 3-speed.

ORIGINAL STURMEY-ARCHER THREE-SPEED
Silent but two 'no drive' positions.

Not everyone today would agree with his comments on desirable gear ratios. He concluded that 50" and 80" were the outer limits and that 'if any gradient is so steep that it requires a lower gear than 50" to ride it comfortably, it is better still to dismount and walk'. However, it should be borne in mind that longer cranks giving greater leverage were normal at the time.

### Teething troubles
The new gear did have some teething problems. In January 1903 Raleigh works manager G.P. Mills had a letter published in *Cycling* about a modification of the clutch design to prevent the gear slipping when not in precise adjustment. A fortnight later *Cycling* published a letter

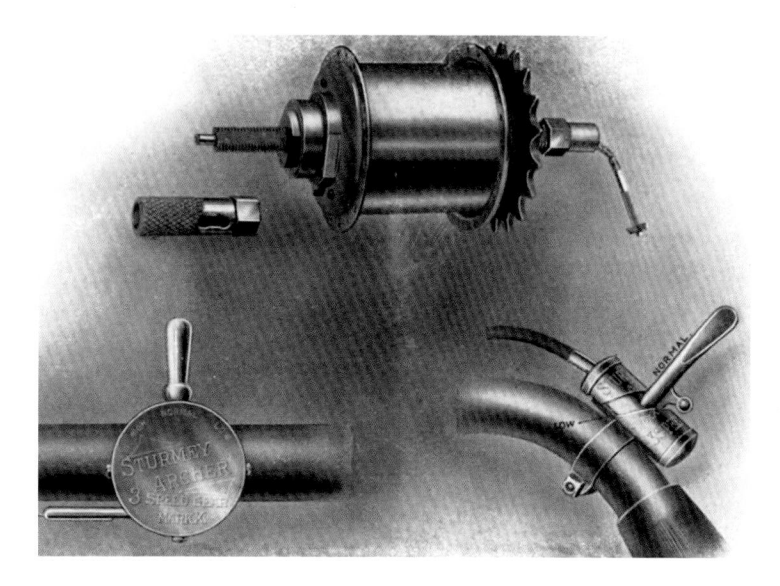

Fig. 6.5. The type X 3-speed and controls. This example was made after the formal adoption of the type X designation.

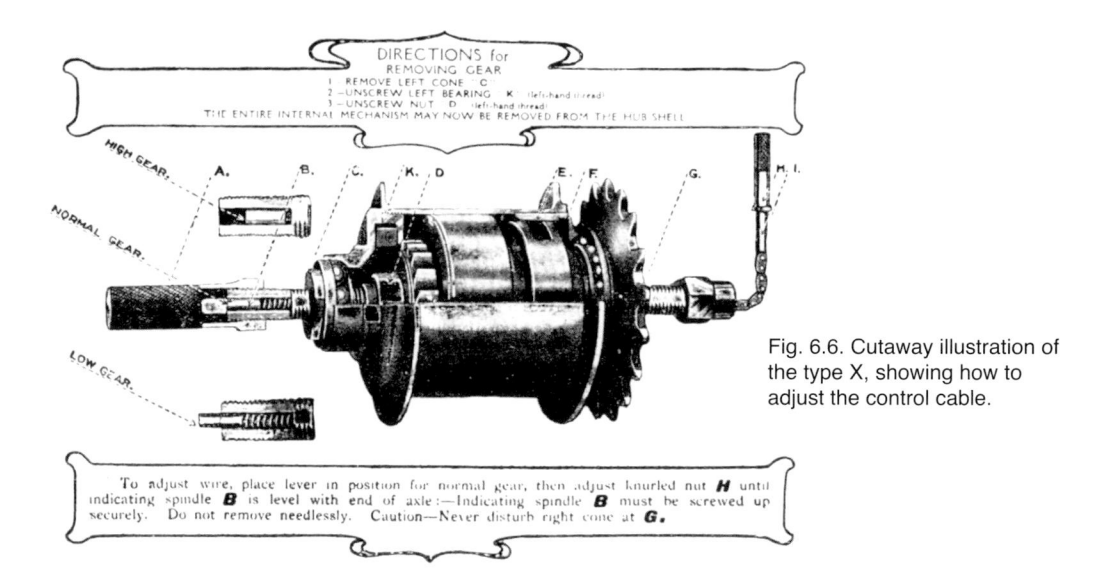

Fig. 6.6. Cutaway illustration of the type X, showing how to adjust the control cable.

from a reader offering constructive criticism of the internal support mechanism when operating in normal and high gears. The same edition, which featured a full-page advertisement proclaiming '1903 the year of the 3-speed gear', reported that deliveries would not be possible until the following month because of the decision to widen the clutches and make other alterations to render the gear as foolproof as possible.

In February 1903 *Cycling* printed a long letter raising questions concerning lubrication and the rider's weight being carried by the freewheel bearings. The same issue contained G.P. Mills' reply to these points. This obviously did not placate the questioner because a fortnight later another of his letters was printed, through which he expressed himself not wholly satisfied with Mills' reply.

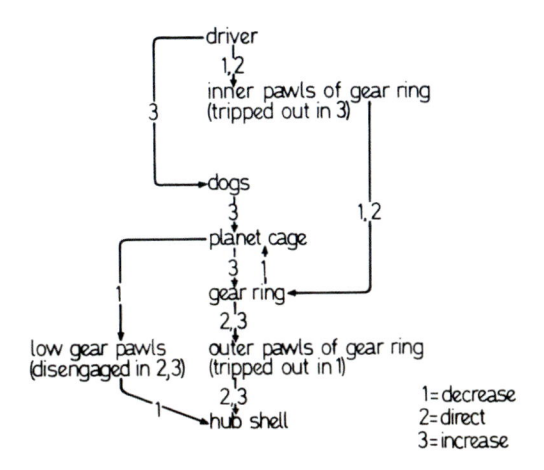

Fig. 6.7. Flowchart for the type X 3-speed.

TYPE X/BSA THREE-SPEED
No 'no drive' position, silent except when freewheeling.

After William Reilly was put in charge of 3-speed production in July 1903, reliability improved and the gear grew in popularity and reputation. Modifications introduced during 1903 included: widened clutches; replacement of the unsprung freewheel pawls by sprung pawls; modification of the driver for screwing on the sprocket rather than shrink fitting; changing the right-hand ball cup from a press fit to a threaded type; and folded shell flanges rather than solid.

## The reputation grows

In October 1903 *Cycling* contained a major article on variable speed gears. This described the Sturmey-Archer as the invention of Henry Sturmey and James Archer. Mills and Pellant no longer got any credit but Reilly was still mentioned as being responsible for improvements.

The Sturmey-Archer was described as the 'most interesting of the Crypto movements'. The author noted that there had been two minor causes of trouble but that these had now been completely overcome and the hub was 'perfectly sweet in running and quite easy in speed changing'.

## The unnamed type X

The Three Speed Gear Syndicate continued to develop their product and in January 1904 applied for GB patent 1,912 of 1904. This was also in Archer's name (still giving an address in Hulme) and referred back to earlier Archer/Reilly patents of 1901 and 1902. The new patent had a threefold aim: to simplify construction and assembly, to allow gear changing 'without disconnecting the pedals' and to allow the planet cage and gear ring to remain stationary when freewheeling.

This design eliminated the 'no-drive' positions between the gears by using unidirectional clutches (typically pawl and ratchet mechanisms) that could be tripped out of engagement or overrun, instead of relying solely on sliding jaw clutches that interlocked in both rotational directions. The improvements were incorporated into the Sturmey-Archer 3-speed and, according to Logos, the result was 'so greatly superior to its predecessor that it may be regarded as an entirely new invention'. A heavy duty version of the hub was prototyped, with some components made of nickel-chromium case-hardened steel, but it was not manufactured.

The toggle chain was transferred from the left to the right side of the hub: an advantage, because men's cycles of that period typically had an extended left-hand wheel nut to act as a mounting step. Transferring the toggle chain to the right got it out of the way of the step. A slack cable now gave low gear instead of high and, to facilitate accurate gear adjustment, an indicator rod was provided in the left of the hub axle.

This new version of the Sturmey-Archer 3-speed, like its predecessor, had no formal model number. It was an early version of the famous X type hub and offered slightly wider ratios than its predecessor: an increase of 31.25%, direct drive and a decrease of 23.8%. The new gear was first marketed in 1905 but was not widely available until February 1906.

The gear changes were effected by the whole epicyclic mechanism sliding along the axle, thereby engaging and disengaging the clutches. There were four of these:

- Low gear pawls mounted in the left-hand ball cup of the hub shell, which engaged with a ratchet track on a leftward extension of the planet cage.
- Pawls, also mounted in the gear ringRamped dogs on the right end-face of the planet cage, which engaged under the action of the gear change hold-off spring with ramped dogs on the left end-face of the driver. (In the early version the planet cage dogs were formed by the projecting chamfered ends of the planet pinion axles.)
- Pawls mounted in the gear ring assembly, which connected it to a ratchet track on the driver.
- Pawls, also mounted in the gear ring assembly, which connected it to the hub shell.

For low gear the control cable was slack and the epicyclic mechanism as far left as it would go. Drive passed from the driver via pawls C to the gear ring, through the epicyclic gears, and out of the planet cage via pawls A to the hub shell.

For middle gear the control cable pulled the epicyclic mechanism to its central position on the axle. Pawls D now engaged with their ratchet track. Drive passed from the driver via pawls C and D direct to the hub shell, bypassing the epicyclic gears and giving direct drive. In the event of any momentary simultaneous engagement of low and middle gears during the gear change, pawls A would overrun their ratchet track, preventing any damage; there was therefore no need for a 'no-drive' position between low and middle gears.

For high gear the control cable pulled the epicyclic mechanism as far right as it would go. The drive passed from the driver via dogs B to the planet cage, through the epicyclic gears and out via the gear ring and pawls D to the hub shell. If while shifting there was a momentary simultaneous engagement of middle and high gears, pawls C would overrun the driver, preventing any damage; there was again no need for a 'no-drive' position between middle and high gears.

## Peak performance and a round-the-world ride

In summer 1905 the Touring Club of France sponsored 'the greatest mountain climbing contest ever held'. The competing cyclists had to ride 'every foot of 149 miles' (240 km) of a tough Alpine mountain course near Chambéry within 28½ hours. The total elevation climbed was nearly 5 miles (8 km). Harold Bowden competed, using a Sturmey–Archer gear. Subsequent Sturmey-Archer catalogues were proud to declare that the official report of the Touring Club of France stated:

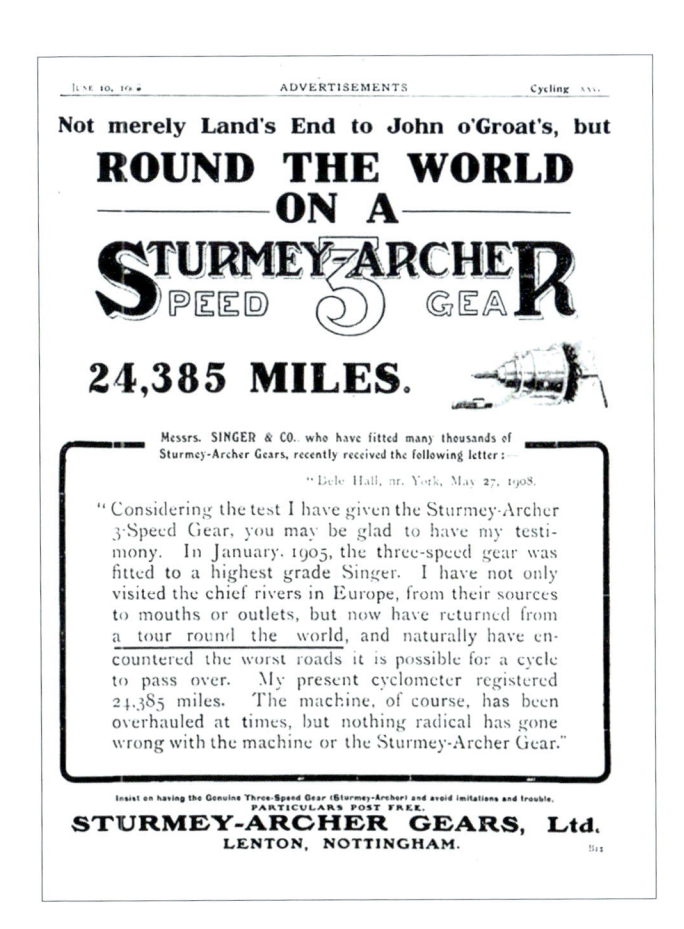

Fig. 6.8. A 1908 advertisement featuring the round the world ride.

Examination of the mechanism of the Sturmey-Archer 3-speed gear has not revealed any signs of wear. The changing arrangement on the handlebar is very simple and very easy to manipulate.

Early in 1905 a cyclist from Belle Hall near York had a Sturmey-Archer 3-speed fitted to 'a highest grade Singer' bicycle. In spring 1908 he wrote to the Singer company:

> I have not only visited the chief rivers in Europe, from their sources to mouths or outlets, but now have returned from a tour round the world, and naturally have encountered the worst roads it is possible for a cycle to pass over. My present cyclometer registered 24,385 miles [39,244 km]. The machine, of course, has been overhauled at times, but nothing radical has gone wrong with the machine or the Sturmey-Archer gear.

This was probably the first circumnavigation of the world on a hub-geared bicycle. The testimonial featured in a Sturmey-Archer advertisement in *Cycling* in June 1908. The rider remained anonymous but his achievement would have won the admiration of many contemporaries. Today it is possible to cycle round the world almost entirely on sealed road surfaces but it was a very different matter in the Edwardian era.

## Tricoaster
Following the launch in summer 1905 of the Eadie 2-speed coaster, the next Sturmey-Archer

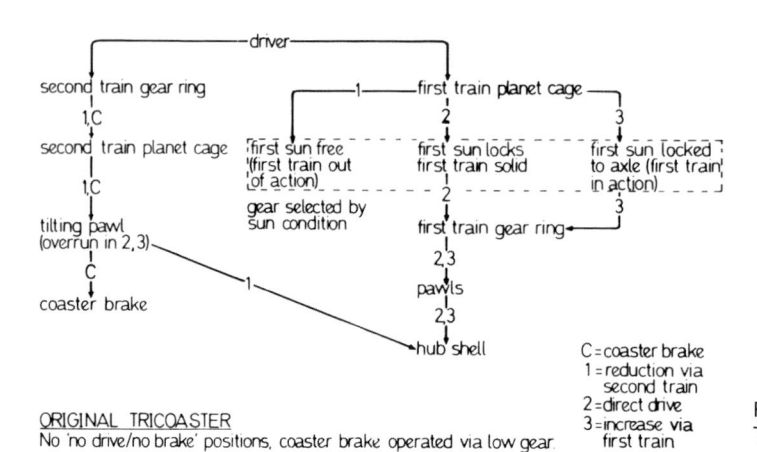

## The Hub of the Universe

```
                    ┌─── driver ───┐
                    │              │
second train gear ring    ┌─── first train planet cage ───┐
        │ 1,C              │ 2                         │ 3
second train planet cage   first sun free        first sun locks    first sun locked
        │ 1,C             (first train out      first train solid   to axle (first train)
tilting pawl              of action)                                 in action)
(overrun in 2,3)           │ 1                  │ 2                  │ 3
        │ C                gear selected by     first train gear ring ◄─┘
coaster brake              sun condition              │ 2,3
        │                                            pawls
        └─────────1──────────────────►               │ 2,3
                                       hub shell ◄───┘

                                        C = coaster brake
ORIGINAL TRICOASTER                     1 = reduction via    Fig. 6.9. Flowchart for the first
No 'no drive/no brake' positions, coaster brake operated via low gear.    second train        Tricoaster (type C).
                                        2 = direct drive
                                        3 = increase via
                                            first train
```

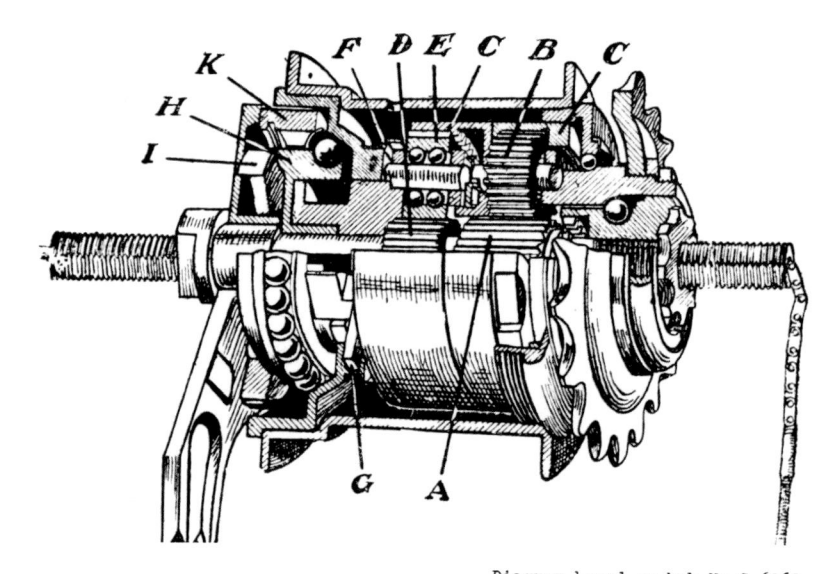

Fig. 6.10. Contemporary cutaway drawing of the type C Tricoaster. Note the planet pinions mounted on ball bearings.

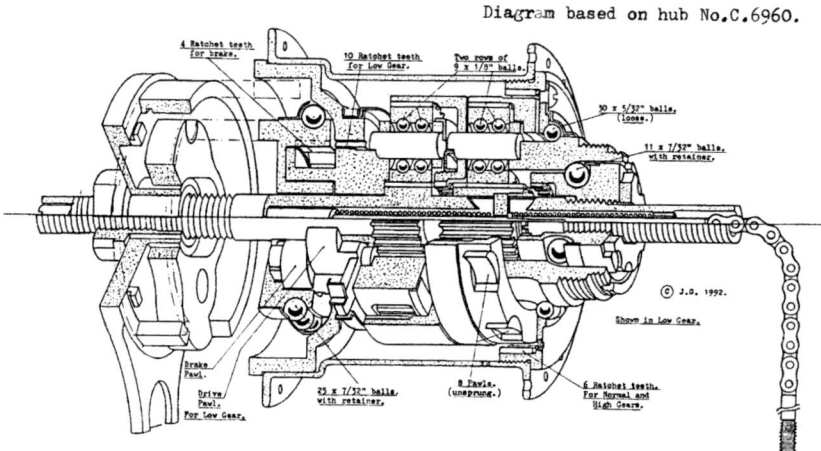

Fig. 6.11. Cutaway drawing of the type C by Jim Gill. Again, the planet pinion ball bearings are clearly depicted.

52

project was to create a 3-speed hub combined with a coaster brake. Consequently, a fortnight before Christmas 1905, James Archer (now of 35 Majors Road, Peterborough) and the Three Speed Gear Syndicate filed GB patent 25,799 of 1905.

This gear differed considerably from the original single-train Sturmey-Archer 3-speed. It might have been possible simply to combine a coaster brake with that gear but it would have been difficult to overcome two features that would have hampered braking: dead spots between the gears and different braking force depending on which gear was engaged. The new patent overcame both problems by using two epicyclic trains. As the specification put it:

Fig. 6.12. 1905 type C Tricoaster.

> Due to the double planetary gears the low gear is always in gear with the driver, and although overrun by the hub for the high and normal gears, it is always ready to take up the drive the moment the high and normal gears cease to act … With the brake always actuated through the low gear, the brake power is thus always the same.

The same patent contained a specification that covered a double epicyclic 3-speed without coaster brake but built on the same lines. One train gave high and normal, the other low gear, which was always in driving connection making it impossible for the drive to slip when changing gear. There was also a specification for a 2-speed combined with a coaster brake.

A week after filing this patent the same patentees applied for GB patent 26,406 of 1905. In the earlier patent a double-acting pawl, controlled by a drag friction ring, had been used for driving in low gear or applying the brake. In the new patent this was replaced by a sleeve or collar around a tubular part of the planet cage and running on a helical drive, the thread of which was known as a 'fast worm'. A drag friction device caused rotation of the sleeve to be retarded, resulting in it moving up or down the worm. Movement in one direction engaged the hub bush and gave drive; movement in the other direction engaged the brake bush and applied a steel-on-steel internal band brake.

A few months later an improved handlebar control was patented. GB patent 8,447 of 1906 was in the names of The Three Speed Gear Syndicate and James Archer, now of 76 Radford Boulevard, Nottingham. The aim was to produce a control that was easy and cheap to produce and that could overcome a problem inherent in the design of the combined 3-speed and coaster brake: the gears did not change in the normal sequence. A slack cable gave normal gear, intermediate tension gave low gear, and a tight cable gave high gear. The new control mechanism corrected the sequence to low–normal–high. The patent showed three possible arrangements, all using stampings and with the lever rotating in a slot cut in the wall of a

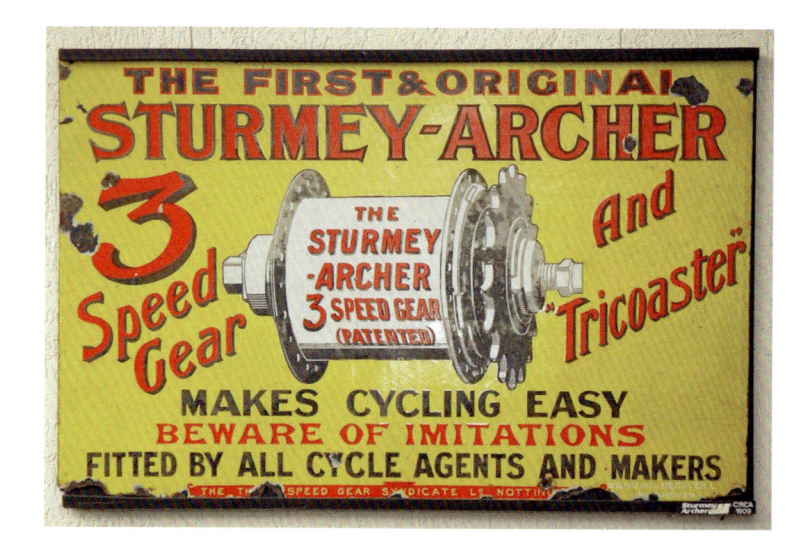

Fig. 6.13. Enamelled metal sign advertising the Sturmey-Archer 3-speed and Tricoaster

Fig. 6.14. Type N Tricoaster.

cylindrical housing. The control maintained a family resemblance with G.P. Mills' original handlebar lever.

## Ball bearing planet pinions

In July 1906 the same patentees filed GB patent 16,014 of 1906 (Archer reverting to his Peterborough address). This covered the mounting of the planet pinions on ball bearings and consequent modifications to the planet cage. The patent illustrations show two rows of balls per pinion. The specification states:

> With all the pinions similarly mounted the friction is greatly reduced, and the power exerted in driving a bicycle is used to better advantage. Moreover, by mounting and arranging the pinions and their axes in the manner described the manufacture of the parts is simplified and their durability increased.

A month later I.C. Cohen joined the firm as a tool designer and became William Reilly's assistant. Cohen was responsible, under Reilly's direction, for introducing ball bearings inside the planet pinions. Forty-six years later Cohen wrote:

> There was a double row of ⅛-inch … balls which ran in double grooves inside the pinions, but on a parallel pin carried by the planet carriers. This is opposed to current practice which insists on grooved bearing surfaces with a load-carrying capacity about five times as great. The result was that the balls acted on much the same lines as a pipe cutter and large numbers of hubs were returned where the planet pins had been cut up into three separate pieces. As soon as possible reversion was made to plain bearings. Possibly modern materials would have delayed the evil day, but the plain pin was unavoidable owing to assembly conditions.

Reilly was a great believer in ball-bearing pinions, as this account from Cohen reveals:

> Unknown to myself the 'innards' of my own hub were changed from plain to ball bearings just before one long weekend ride, and Reilly was much disappointed when, asked if I had found any difference in riding lately, I reported no perceptible difference and in turn asked him why he was curious.

Cohen also recalled Sturmey-Archer's tests on ball bearing planet pinions:

> I have vague memories of comparative tests which showed that the ball bearing pinions on top gear improved the efficiency from 95 to about 95.5 per cent, and on low gear from 97 to 97.3 per cent, but cannot vouch for the accuracy of the figures.

The disaster of the much-publicised ball-bearing planet pinions contributed greatly to Reilly's fall from grace.

## Tricoaster developments

One of Israel Cohen's first jobs was working on the combined 3-speed and coaster brake. The development continued for a further year. It seems that a few of the new hubs were released in September 1907, presumably for review by the cycling press and as trade samples. They incorporated the new ball bearing planet pinions and used separate pawls for low gear and brake operation. The combined 3-speed and coaster brake was christened the Tricoaster, which became the generic name for the company's 3-speed coaster combinations.

Pre-production Tricoasters apparently gave an increase of 25% above normal and a decrease of 20%. However, this would have entailed machining the main axle and sun pinion down to a size risking axle failure. Production hubs gave wider ratios: an increase of 31.25%, direct drive and a reduction of 23.8%.

An early review of the Tricoaster in *The Scottish Cyclist* shows a diagram of the epicyclic train: it has a 64 tooth gear ring, 20 tooth sun and 22 tooth planets. This gives the wider ratios of the production version. But the same article shows a cutaway drawing of a ball bearing planet pinion that appears to have 24 teeth. Assuming the same gear ring was used in both cases, the 24 tooth pinions would have needed a 16 tooth sun, thus giving the ratios of the pre-production version. What probably happened was that bigger planet pinions were originally considered necessary to accommodate ball bearings but it was later found that ball bearing planet pinions could be made smaller, allowing a bigger sun, resulting in wider ratios and a stronger axle.

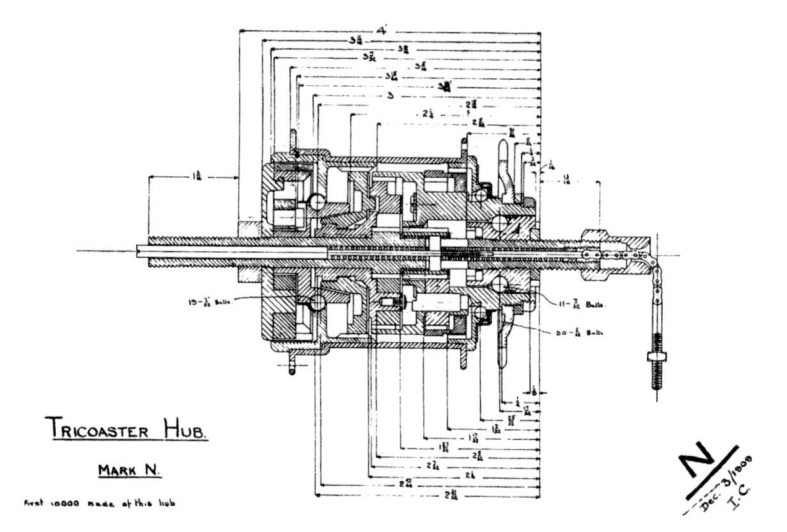

Fig. 6.15. Type N sectional drawing by Israel Cohen, bearing his initials.

The production Tricoaster used a double-acting pawl in place of separate low gear and brake pawls. The hub had a stepped shell and incorporated one fixed and one sliding sun. The toggle chain was on the right and there was an indicator rod in the left end of the hub axle.

Logos' book *Variable Gears* was published soon after the Tricoaster's introduction. Logos described the Tricoaster as the first 3-speed and coaster combination to be patented; but he also pointed out that a rival product from Crabbe was on sale before it. He added that 'Mr Archer, the inventor, is entitled to unlimited praise for the ingenuity he has exercised' in designing the Tricoaster. In reality Archer had little or nothing to do with the hub: Reilly was the principal designer. The new hub was displayed at the Stanley Show in autumn 1907 and by early 1908 the cycling press were enthusing over the new hub.

The first production Tricoaster became known as the type C and had serial numbers prefixed by that letter. At the time of its launch it was merely described as the Tricoaster. The hub weighed 3 lb 6 oz (1.53 kg) and cost £2 5s. (£226 today). The weight was criticised by some as excessive but, as C.W. Brown pointed out in the January 1909 *Cyclists' Touring Club Gazette and Record*, the critics failed 'to deduct from the hub the weight necessary with brakes of the ordinary class'.

The earliest Tricoasters were machined by the Birmingham-based ammunition maker Kynoch, with hardening, grinding and assembly by Raleigh. According to Cohen, Kynoch charged 10 shillings (£50 today) for each set of parts; when Sturmey-Archer could produce the parts in-house for 9 shillings, Kynoch lost the job.

The syndicate had used Kynoch's services as early as 1906 to make complete Sturmey-Archer hubs (presumably the unnamed type X). At least 600 Kynoch-made Sturmey-Archer hubs were sent out to the trade during the first half of 1906 and Kynoch produced more than 5,000 of these hubs before June 1906, when Reilly refused to accept further deliveries. The problem was Kynoch's apparent inability to master the hardening processes; no doubt this was the reason why they only did the machining for the Tricoaster.

In 1908 the Tricoaster was slightly modified. The right-hand gear ring (for low gear) originally had eight unsprung crescent-shaped pawls: these were now replaced by four similar pawls with spring assistance.

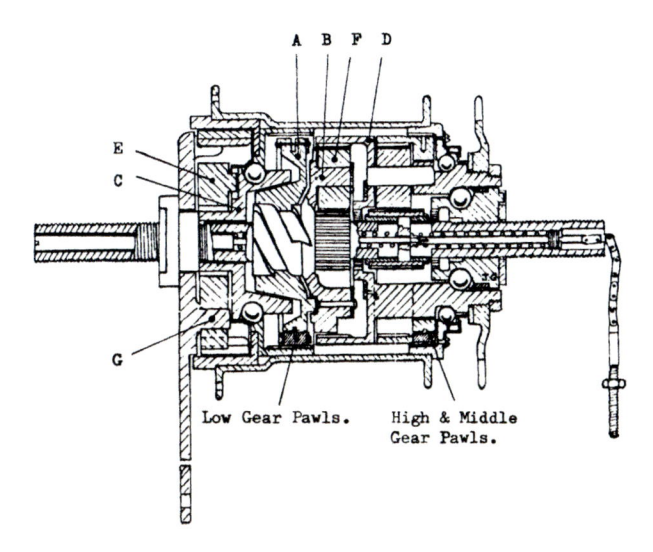

Fig. 6.16. Type N section by Jim Gill.

Low Gear Pawls.    High & Middle Gear Pawls.

## Type N Tricoaster

The original type C Tricoaster was replaced in 1910 by the broadly similar type N. The double-acting pawl was replaced by separate sprung crescent-shaped pawls for low gear, and by a helical drive and actuating cone for the brake (as described in GB patent 26,406 of 1905). The high gear pawls were fitted with flat springs in place of the coil type. About the same time the ball bearing planet pinions were replaced by planets with plain bearings and the original steel brake band was superseded by a phosphor-bronze band on a steel liner.

The abandonment of ball bearing planet pinions was kept very quiet. Further modifications during production of the type N Tricoaster included: brake drum and low gear ratchet ring separated and screwed into the hub shell with opposing threads; straight wire springs fitted under Micrometer-type pawls; left-hand ball raceway becoming part of the low gear ratchet ring; main ball race altered; driver and low gear ring, hitherto one piece, divided; and left-hand ball raceway made part of the brake drum.

Between 1912 and 1914 Raleigh adopted a finer axle thread of 26 threads per inch (TPI), similar to that used on subsequent twentieth-century Sturmey-Archer gears. During the changeover period, Tricoasters with the new thread were identified as FNs, the prefix F standing for 'fine thread'; earlier hubs had a 20 TPI axle thread.

The type N Tricoaster was a successful design that enjoyed a good reputation. Although production ceased in 1921, parts were still freely available well into the 1930s.

## Type N coaster

The earliest Sturmey-Archer single-speed coaster was based on the brake section of the type N Tricoaster. A prototype was produced in 1912 and small numbers were manufactured to gauge dealer and user reaction. The hub was not advertised and production appears to have ceased temporarily in 1913.

## Continuing success

During its early years The Three Speed Gear Syndicate enjoyed considerable success, despite intense competition. In the first three years the syndicate sold about 10,000 original pattern Sturmey-Archer 3-speeds. In 1904–5 it sold 6,562 hubs; the following year it sold 14,384 on the open market, 4,955 to Raleigh and held 620 in stock – a total of 19,353 representing a trebling of production in a year. Profits during the period 1904 to 1907 were good, share dividends being in the order of 11% to 70% before tax.

In February 1907 the syndicate raised additional capital of £2,000 (£200,000 today) by issuing further shares to Frank Bowden. More capital was raised in the autumn when 4,425 additional shares were issued to Bowden and he loaned the company £3,000 (£300,000 today) at 6% interest.

Much of this money was invested in new machinery that featured in a Three Speed Gear Syndicate brochure, according to which the Sturmey-Archer machine shop contained 'over £6,000 [£600,000 today] worth of the latest automatic machinery specially designed for making Sturmey-Archer 3-speed hubs under the direction of Mr W. Reilly, the sole inventor of the Hub 2-speed gear'.

## BSA 3-speed

By the end of 1907 the Birmingham Small Arms Company (BSA) was desperate to produce a 3-speed hub gear. It had recently merged with Eadie and had acquired the rights of the Hub Two-Speed Gear Company. BSA could therefore produce four 2-speed hubs – the Hub, the BSA Mk 2, the Fagan/Eadie, and the Eadie 2-speed coaster. But demand for 2-speeds was now much reduced, whereas the market for 3-speeds was almost insatiable.

The Hub Company had patented a 3-speed (GB 22,306 of 1903) but BSA were not interested in making it. Instead they approached The Three Speed Gear Syndicate requesting permission to build the Sturmey-Archer 3-speed under licence. The syndicate was unable to cope with demand in 1907 and therefore granted a licence to BSA.

The BSA 3-speed was essentially the early but unnamed X type. It was modified by I.C. Cohen to incorporate ball bearing planet pinions and, as Logos reported, 'a separate bearing for the sprocket sleeve [driver], with the object apparently of obviating any rocking movement'. The BSA 3-speed went on sale early in 1908. BSA advertising referred to it as 'the original 3-speed with a single train of pinions', thereby trading on its common ancestry with the Sturmey-Archer hub.

As BSA had acquired the rights of the Hub Two-Speed Gear Company, strictly speaking they owned all Reilly's developments in bicycle gearing. However, they were clearly in no position to quibble: they were more interested in making the Sturmey-Archer gear than fighting the Bowdens. As Cohen wrote later: 'When I designed the first BSA 3-speed hub their representative was in Reilly's office next to mine and I understood that part of the contract was that no legal proceedings should be taken against Reilly for his breach of contract with The Hub Two-Speed Gear Syndicate.' According to Logos, another aspect of the agreement concerned the Tricoaster: the coaster brake element was identical to that of the Eadie, 'reciprocal arrangements having recently been made between the BSA company and the Three Speed [Gear] Syndicate'.

The BSA 3-speed was acclaimed by *Cycling* for its 'virtues of extreme simplicity'. Like the Sturmey-Archer hubs of that time, it gave a 31.25% increase and a 23.8% reduction on direct drive. Typical gears were 49, 64 and 85" and the hub weighed 2 lb 13 oz (1.28 kg).

By the time the BSA 3-speed came on the market, the Sturmey-Archer version had also been fitted with ball bearing planet pinions; so for a short time both products were almost identical, apart from the lack of a driver bearing in the Sturmey-Archer version, which was therefore slightly lighter. In 1909 Sturmey-Archer altered the driver of the type X to bear on

Fig. 6.17. BSA 3-speeds, early and late examples.

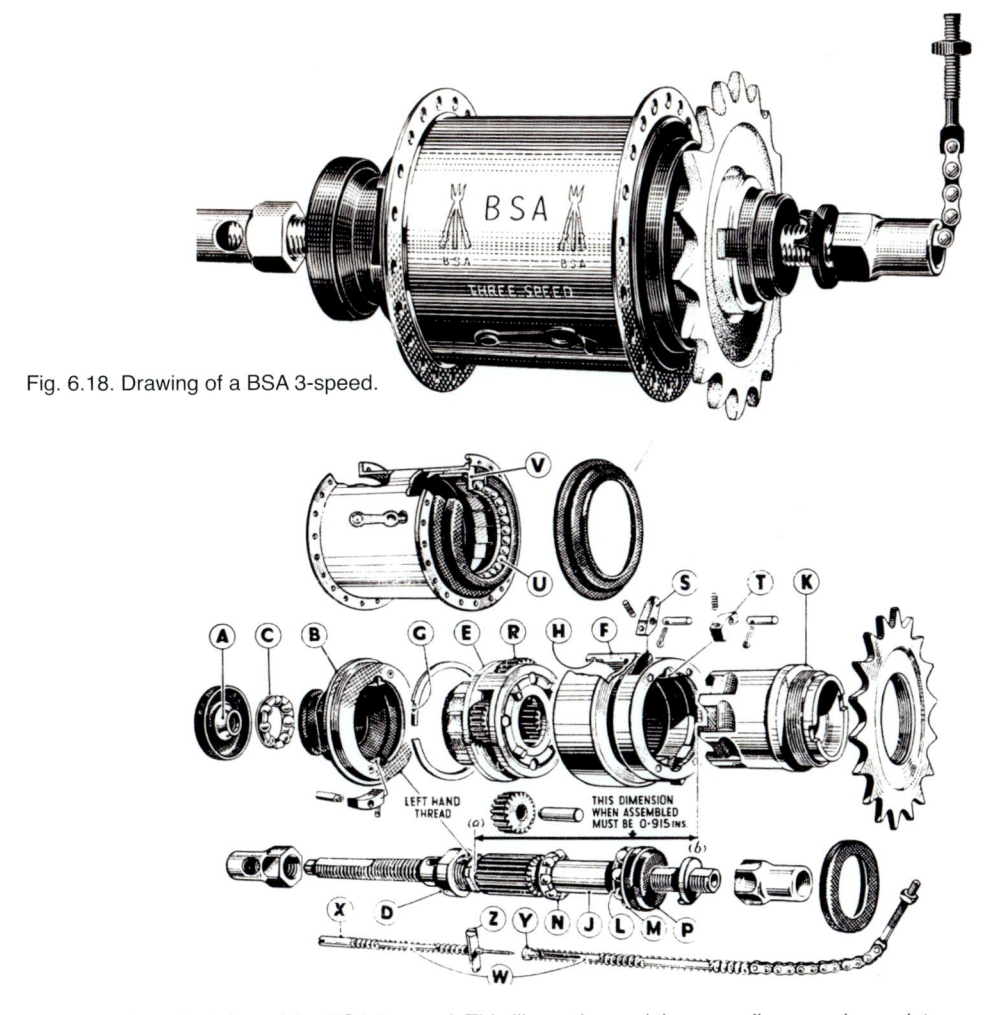

Fig. 6.18. Drawing of a BSA 3-speed.

Fig. 6.19. Exploded view of the BSA 3-speed. This illustration and the preceding one show a late 1940s example, which was very similar to the original, apart from the lack of ball bearings for the planet pinions.

59

Fig. 6.20. Front of the 1908 Sturmey-Archer catalogue, with the strapline 'The Hub of the Universe'.

the wheel axle rather than the sun but with a plain bearing rather than the ball bearing used in the BSA.

### Differing views on ball bearing planet pinions
The introduction of ball bearing planet pinions was widely publicised by both gear makers. The syndicate claimed that the ball bearing planets saved 60% of friction. Their advertising hammered the message home in a way that could easily be construed to mean the effort required to propel a bicycle fitted with the new gear would be reduced by the same amount; whereas the friction referred to was merely that in the planet pinions.

According to the first edition of Whitt & Wilson's *Bicycling Science* (MIT Press), the losses in a hub gear due to plain bearing planet pinions would be in the order of 2% of input power at high torque levels. If the friction at the pinions was reduced by 60%, then a total saving of about 1.2% of input power could be expected. As noted above, Cohen's recollection was a measured saving of 0.3 to 0.5%. During 1982 Sturmey-Archer carried out efficiency tests on an experimental AW 3-speed fitted with roller bearing planet pinions: the average results were 91% for low gear, 98% for normal and 93% for high gear. The average results for six new standard AWs were 93.8% for low, 96.3% for normal and 92.5% for high gear: thus the experimental hub was found to be 1.7 percentage points more efficient in normal, 0.5 percentage points more efficient in high but surprisingly 2.8 percentage points less efficient in low gear.

The Edwardian cycling press was divided over the subject of ball bearing planet pinions. In the January 1908 *Cyclists' Touring Club Gazette and Record*, F.T. Bidlake described them as 'most desirable' and C.W. Brown wrote: 'I think that in a very short time every gear of this class will be constructed with ball bearings for the planet wheels.'

The author of *Cycling's* 1908 annual review of gears was less enthusiastic. He commented that the friction thus eliminated was very small; he was also concerned by the added weight of the ball bearings. He thought that more attention could be given to the shaping and manufacture of the pinion teeth and concluded: 'It is a matter which the manufacturer's reputation will settle satisfactorily, for the most successful gears have succeeded because they were well made.'

### Manufacturing techniques
In spring 1908 *Cycling* ran an article by The Owl entitled 'How Variable Gears are made'. The author had visited a number of manufacturers and was particularly interested in the use of ball bearing planet pinions. He observed that Sturmey-Archer used 'a very ingenious little tool' to scoop out the pinion ball races. He had been asked not to describe it but was able to relate how Sturmey-Archer smeared the centres of their pinions with petroleum jelly and dipped the pinions into the balls, which then adhered. Thereafter the pinions were put in the planet cage and the studs (pinion axles) pushed through.

The Owl revealed that BSA used a slightly different technique. Their pinions were slipped over the studs and the balls dropped in forming two rows, with a washer between. There were 18 balls per pinion.

Other production processes were described by The Owl, such as the milling of pinion teeth, the manufacture of hub axles and the heat treatment of highly stressed components. Armstrong's axle test sounded impressive: every spindle was held securely by each end in a small steel frame while the ball races and sun pinion were tested with a file, to ensure that it

Fig. 6.21. Harry 'Goss' Green breaks the Land's End to John O'Groats record (DDRN 4-10-1-25).

would not mark them. Then the centre of the spindle was struck with a heavy mallet: if faulty it would snap but if satisfactory it would usually bend slightly and then be trued up.

## Record breakers and racers

In July 1904 an anonymous member of the North Road Cycling Club used a Sturmey-Archer 3-speed to ride unpaced from Land's End to John O'Groats: it took 4 days, 7 hours and 25 minutes. Four years later both Sturmey-Archer and BSA were keen to demonstrate the efficiency and reliability of their new hubs. In July 1908 Tom Peck broke the Land's End to John O'Groats record using a BSA 3-speed. He was the first rider to complete the run in under 3 days, taking 2 days, 22 hours and 42 minutes, which was 6 hours and 38 minutes faster than the previous record.

A week later the record was broken again, this time by Harry 'Goss' Green, most of the time riding a Raleigh fitted with the Sturmey-Archer Tricoaster. His time was 2 days, 19 hours and 50 minutes. Green's machine had a normal gear of 94" and hence his top and bottom gears would have been 123" and 72'" respectively. Later in the ride he had the sprocket changed to give an 80" normal. For the cobbled roads of Lancashire he changed to a heavy roadster and for the Cumbrian mountain Shap he rode a 63" single-speed light path racer.

Green was not enthusiastic about variable gearing and allegedly confided that he used a single-speed disguised as a Tricoaster throughout the ride. Frank Urry, an official observer on the ride, supported the claim that Green rode a camouflaged hub and later said that Green would use nothing but a single-speed. But there was no need to tamper with a Tricoaster to turn it into a single-speed: Green only needed to leave it in normal. He may have ridden single-speed throughout the ride but the hub may nonetheless have been a fully functional Tricoaster.

Sturmey-Archer followed Green's success with full page advertising. Without mentioning BSA by name, they pointed out that the previous record was achieved 'using a 3-speed gear with ball-bearing pinions (S-A licence)'. The advertisement warned prospective purchasers to 'refuse imitations with plain bearing pinions'.

In 1913 a Sturmey-Archer 3-speed was used in the Tour de France at a time when change-speed gearing was rare in the race. The rider was Lucien Petit-Breton (real name Lucien Georges Mazan), the first rider to win Le Tour twice. He had subsequently failed to finish five years running but, using the hub gear, he got considerably further than in any of his other uncompleted Tours.

Fig. 6.22. Petit-Breton rides a Sturmey-Archer 3-speed in the 1913 Tour de France.

### Relyabull 3-speeds
A few Sturmey-Archer hub gears were sold circa 1910 branded as Relyabull products. The Relyabull name was used by the Nottingham Factoring Co. Ltd, a cycle accessory company owned by Frank Bowden and based in Faraday Road, Nottingham.

### Type V 3-Speed
In 1908 Sturmey-Archer abandoned the single train epicyclic formula on which their success had been built. The new type V wide-ratio 3-speed was essentially a Tricoaster without the back-pedal brake (as in GB patent 25,799A of 1905). The type V had a stepped shell like the Tricoaster but with the large diameter on the right rather than the left. Two versions of the shell were produced: one with sharp steps, the other with rounded ones.

Most of Sturmey-Archer's competitors were now using two epicyclic trains in their 3-speed hubs. This, and the fact that the End-to-End record had been broken using the Tricoaster, may have encouraged Sturmey-Archer to follow suit. Perhaps they also wished to differentiate their product from BSA's. But the sharing of many common parts with the Tricoaster made production cheaper and this was probably the deciding factor.

Despite the double epicyclic trains, the new gear appears to have been a little lighter than its predecessor; according to *Cycling's* 1909 Penny Handbook *Variable Gears and all about them*, it weighed 2 lb 10 oz (1.19 kg) with top tube control and only slightly more with handlebar control.

But the type V was not well received. The normally supportive Bidlake wrote:

Late last year the Sturmey-Archer people introduced a new pattern, but candidly it does not come up to the type it displaced and, although a new move can be expected before long I sadly feel that the change must have meant a vast cash loss as well as a fall in prestige of the premier triple gear firm.

Fig. 6.23. Type V 3-speed.

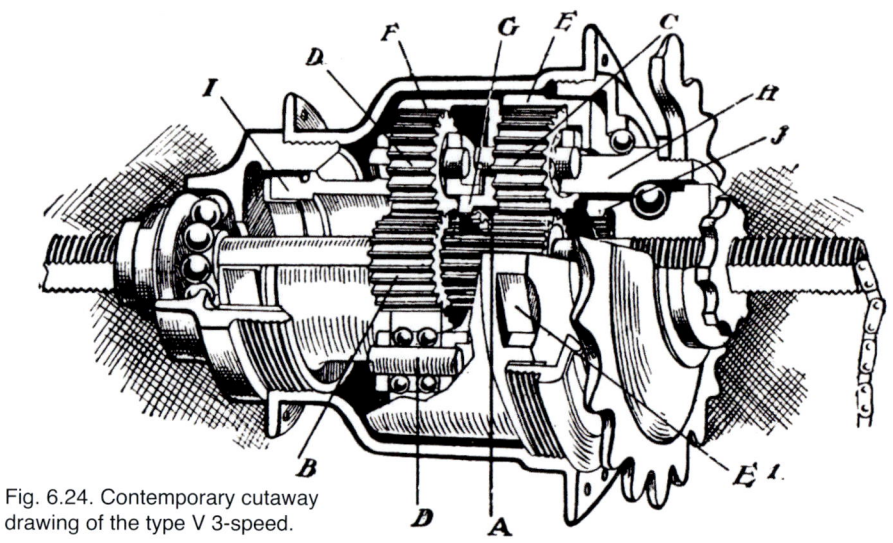

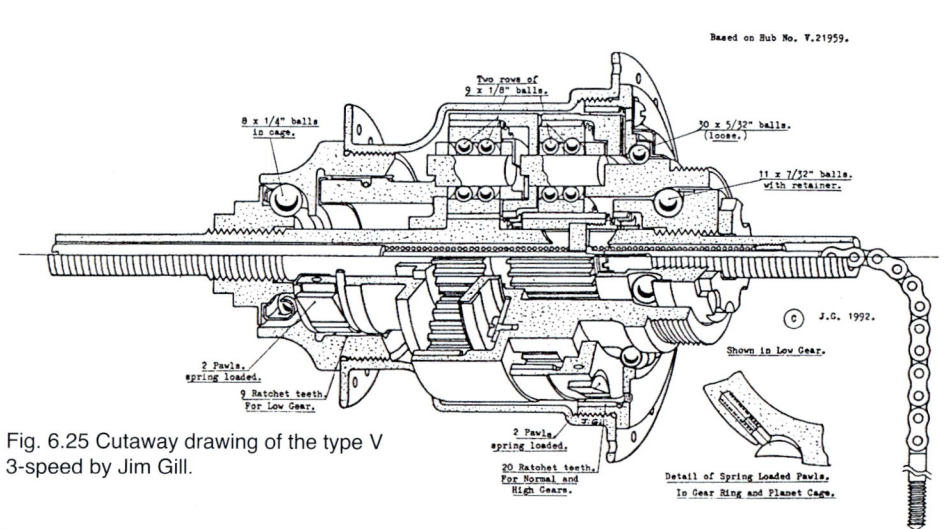

Fig. 6.24. Contemporary cutaway drawing of the type V 3-speed.

Fig. 6.25 Cutaway drawing of the type V 3-speed by Jim Gill.

On the other hand, he was enthusiastic about the BSA gear which 'embodies the early design of the Sturmey-Archer plus the improvement of ball races to the planet pinions … a splendid piece of work … which runs with equal smoothness on all gears'. He also praised the fact that, when the cable was slack, the hub was in low gear.

Serious production problems with the type V were encountered from the start. In October 1908 Reilly was relieved of his responsibility for overseeing production: this passed to William Raven of Raleigh and in December Raleigh took control of the Sturmey-Archer manufacturing plant. Reilly was relegated to designing hubs and tool making. An annoyed Reilly then claimed an additional £750 (£74,000 today) for inventing the Tricoaster, a claim that the board referred to Douglas Leechman as arbitrator and who ruled against Reilly. The board meeting of 9 June 1909 was attended only by the Bowdens and company secretary Lazonby. At this meeting a letter from Reilly was read out which withdrew all claims in connection with the Tricoaster except for royalties. The meeting then went on to discuss the disastrous new hub.

It was calculated that by 1 November 1909 there would be 27,000 unsatisfactory type Vs in stock. The board resolved to scrap parts amounting to 15,000 hubs and to alter the rest, which Raleigh would adopt for 1910. (This may explain the two styles of stepped shell found on V type hubs.) The loss involved was estimated at £6,000 (£600,000 today). The board decided to revert to the type X for 1910: 'Thus the syndicate would be able to start 1910 with a saleable article.'

At the same meeting it was decided that management and organisation of the 3-speed department would be placed in Raven's hands. William Henry Raven, known to some as Billy, was born in Foleshill near Coventry in 1872. At the age of 19 he was a fitter in a cycle works; a decade later he was a cycle works manager, living in Smethwick with his wife and three small children. In 1907 Frank Bowden recruited him from the New Hudson cycle company. No shrinking violet, Raven claimed to be able to raise Raleigh's output from 17,000 a year to 1,000 a week while saving £10,000 in wages (£1 million today) if Bowden would support him.

What was the problem with manufacture of the type V hub? In the 1990s engineer and leading hub gear expert Jim Gill analysed many types of Sturmey-Archer hub gears in considerable detail. He could not find any reason why the type V was a failure. He concluded: 'This hub was said to have been a failure. However, the C, N, FN and A range of hubs were all manufactured for many years without any reports of problems. These latter hubs all used the same two gear trains as the V, so it cannot have been the gears that caused the troubles. Looking at the left-hand end, the V has two pawls engaging nine ratchet teeth. There is thus an eccentric load on the planet cage. But again, the N and FN have three pawls engaging twenty ratchets so again there is an eccentric resultant. The A hubs have two pawls engaging twenty ratchets which means a balanced load on the planet cage, yet these hubs were fitted with two rows of balls to support the cage. I have not solved this enigma.'

But failures due to the pipe-cutting action of the ball bearing planet pinions were probably the main factor. Frank Whitt reported seeing what he thought was an early 1909 Sturmey-Archer hub with the planet pinions on brass sleeves instead of ball bearings. The planet pinions of late type V hubs probably ran on sleeves rather than balls. BSA continued using ball bearing planets for a little longer than Sturmey-Archer but eventually also adopted plain bearings.

Fig. 6.26. A 1907 type X 3-speed.

## Type X returns

In September 1909 Bidlake was delighted to report that Sturmey-Archer were reverting to the earlier pattern of single epicyclic 3-speed. He regretted that 'apparently the designers have ceased to regard the ball race for the secondary pinions as a valuable feature.' He noted that BSA still had them and added: 'I believe that it has been absolutely proved that the employment of such bearings decidedly discounts the added friction of variable gear mechanisms.'

The 'new' Sturmey-Archer 3-speed was a re-launch of the unnamed model that had formed the basis of the BSA hub. Now officially known as the type X, it continued in production until late 1914. Jim Gill concluded that ball bearing planet pinions were fitted until about 1910. Shortly before the type X went out of production, the finer 26 TPI axle thread was adopted, hubs with the new thread being designated FX.

The validity of the type X design was demonstrated by the very similar BSA 3-speed, which continued in production virtually unchanged until 1955, when BSA's bicycle interests were taken over by Raleigh.

## Reilly's departure

By 1909 relations between the Bowdens and William Reilly had deteriorated greatly. Not only was there the matter of the defective type V hubs but also an issue regarding Reilly's brother, A.H. (Harry) Reilly, who had recently helped set up the rival Armstrong-Triplex Three-Speed Gear Company. Harry Reilly had worked at Raleigh and I.C. Cohen believed that the first Armstrong gear was a discarded William Reilly design that Harry had appropriated. The Bowdens accused William Reilly of complicity and from thereon it was downhill all the way.

At the board meeting of 20 July 1910 William Reilly's resignation as director was accepted. It was agreed that his rights would be purchased for £2,500 (£240,000 today) and 925 shares belonging to Reilly were transferred to Frank Bowden's son Harold. Reilly left the company and, according to Cohen, 'he took with him most of the parts of a new type of 3-speed hub and got a Manchester friend named Rose to patent it. Nothing commercial ever ensued.' The Manchester friend's name was actually Ross and the new 3-speed was designed for motorcycle use (see Chapter 7).

In 1921 William Reilly's son, a draughtsman called William Henry Reilly, was granted a patent for improvements to 3-speed hubs. This looks suspiciously like a design by his father being laundered. The patent was GB 167,230 and referred to existing 3-speed hubs containing a sliding clutch between the driver and the planet cage that controlled the movement of pawls carried by the gear ring to couple and uncouple the driver and planet cage. The patent aimed at easier, cheaper manufacture and more reliable operation but nothing came of it.

The Raleigh organisation now tried to expunge, or at least play down, the memory of William Reilly and continued to do so for many decades. Harold 'Oily' Karslake was librarian of the Association of Pioneer Motor-Cyclists. During 1949–51 he was involved in private correspondence with I.C. Cohen concerning the history of hub gears for bicycles and motorcycles. In 1951 Karslake was permitted to read Sir Harold Bowden's personal history. This contained the incredible statement: 'It is improbable that it will ever be established who was the actual inventor of the Sturmey Three-Speed Gear.' Karslake stated that this could only be interpreted in one way: 'Someone has the evidence and has either destroyed it or has hidden it away and has no intention of making any disclosures. The staff adopt the same attitude, no doubt under instructions.'

This was more than 40 years after Reilly's departure from Sturmey–Archer. In December 1952 Cohen sent his own history of Sturmey-Archer to H.H. England, then editor of *Cycling*. England replied that he had read the document 'with great interest' and that he would 'preserve it carefully until such time as it can be brought to light'. But it never has been and the whereabouts of the document are unknown.

The proof that Reilly's true role was still perfectly well understood by Raleigh's senior management is revealed by this note in the board minutes for 16 September 1947: 'A pension of £2 per week [£66 today], as from 1 August 1947, to Mr W. Reilly the inventor of the Sturmey-Archer gear, was authorised.' The late awarding of a modest pension to the octogenarian engineer shows that someone on the Raleigh board was prepared to acknowledge Reilly's key role in the establishment of Sturmey-Archer, albeit in a very private manner. That person was probably George Wilson, who rose from Sturmey-Archer sales representative to president of the Raleigh group, and who was noted for his gentlemanly behaviour and fair dealing.

But the octogenarian William Reilly benefited for little more than two years from this small windfall. He was living in Hazel Grove near Stockport, working for a small engineering firm, despite being in his early 80s. In a letter to *The Classic Motor Cycle* magazine (June 1987) Norman Brooke wrote of working with 'Bill' Reilly who did most of the company's machining, on one occasion even turning a square hole with a lathe by using an accessory he had made himself. Reilly told Brooke how he had invented the Sturmey-Archer gear and claimed that he had been cheated out of the patent rights. He also showed blueprints which he said were the original drawings.

Brooke revealed that, in autumn 1949 while cycling to work, Reilly felt ill. Standing his bicycle against the kerb, he sat down in the doorway of a shop and died.

# Chapter 7
# A motorcycle excursion

## Gears and engines for motorcycles, 1909 to 1935

### New name, new market

At an extraordinary general meeting on 11 May 1908, The Three Speed Gear Syndicate changed its name to Sturmey-Archer Gears Limited. The products had always been branded Sturmey-Archer but the first patent in that name was GB 2,013 of 1911. It was for a motorcycle hub gear designed by Israel Cohen.

Cohen produced the prototype in 1909. It had two similar epicyclic trains with a common sun, and gave three speeds: direct drive and two lower gears. The middle gear drove through the first train only, whereas bottom gear drove both trains in series: a compound arrangement involving a reduction of a reduction. The gear also incorporated a multi-plate clutch. There were two driving members, one each side of the hub; one was driven by the pedal crank, the other by the motor.

### How Cohen's motorcycle hub gear worked

Drive was fed to the gear ring of the first epicyclic train. Gear changing was effected by a clutch that could slide along the axle while enclosing the epicyclic trains. For high gear the clutch locked the hub shell to the first train gear ring, giving direct drive. For middle gear the clutch locked the shell to the combined first train planet cage and second train gear ring. And for low gear the clutch locked the shell to the second train planet cage.

The patent was amended to include a statement that the patentees were aware of a somewhat similar proposal that involved a disc clutch outside the hub. This may have been in one of the many patents of Manchester engineer Arthur Alltree. According to Cohen:

> This Alltree had the knack of inventing impossible hub gears and waiting until some designer licked them into shape, then claiming royalties. I believe he trapped several manufacturers, though none of his gears would work as invented … The fact remains that probably due to the ingenious wording of his patent claims he was able to levy toll on practically all users of double train epicyclic gears.

### Raven's motorcycle hub gear

Raleigh filed another patent for a 3-speed motorcycle hub, GB 21,386 of 1911. This was in the name of Frank Bowden, trading as the Raleigh Cycle Company, and

Fig. 7.1. William Raven.

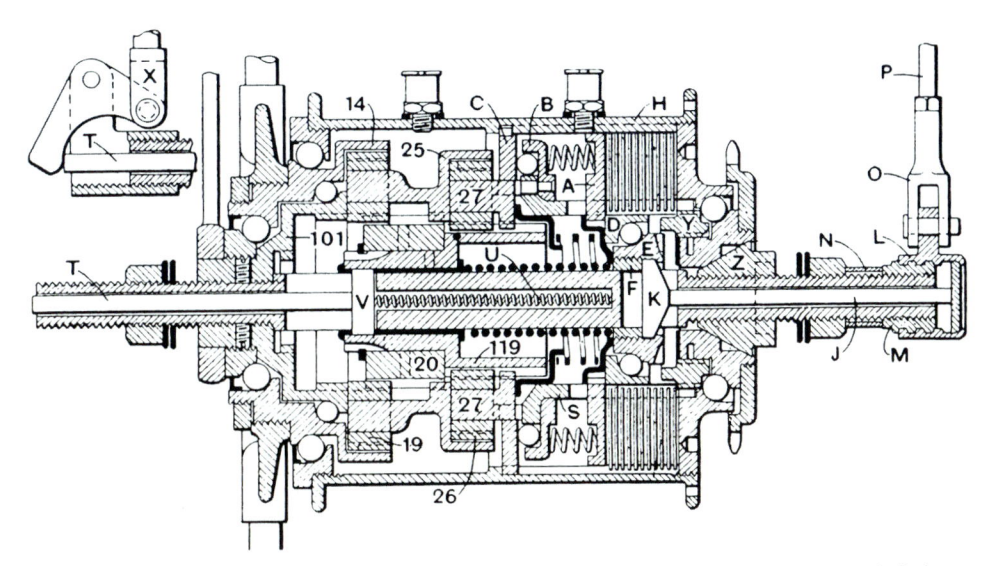

Fig. 7.2. Sectional drawing of Raven's motorcycle hub gear.

William Henry Raven, works manager. The minutes of the board meeting of 8 March 1912 noted that 'the Raleigh Cycle Company being the owners of a patent for a 3 speed gear for motorcycles, it has been arranged with them that this company should market the gear under the name of Sturmey-Archer'.

At first sight this gear looks similar in concept to Cohen's. It had two epicyclic trains and a friction clutch. High gear was direct drive, middle gear used the first epicyclic train, and low gear was a compound reduction using both first and second trains. However, the changing mechanism was different: Raven's gear had a pair of suns, one larger than the other, that could be moved along the axle to engage with various components, thereby changing gear.

### How Raven's motorcycle hub gear worked

For high gear both suns were clutched to their respective planet cages but were free to rotate on the axle, making both epicyclic trains inoperative. Direct drive passed from the primary gear ring to the combined primary planet cage and secondary gear ring, then to the secondary planet cage, and finally via the friction clutch to the hub shell.

For middle gear the suns were moved to the right along the axle. The sun of the secondary train remained locked to its planet cage while free to rotate but the sun of the primary train was locked to the axle. Thus the primary train came into action to give a reduction in gearing. Drive passed from the primary gear ring through the primary epicyclic train and out via the combined primary planet cage/secondary gear ring giving a reduction in gearing, then direct to the secondary planet cage without reduction, and finally via the friction clutch to the hub shell.

For low gear the suns moved further right along the axle. This locked the secondary sun to the axle but freed it from its planet cage; the primary sun remained clutched to the axle. Thus the drive passed from the primary gear ring through the primary epicyclic train and out via the combined primary planet cage/secondary gear ring giving a reduction in gearing, then through the secondary epicyclic train and out via the secondary planet cage giving a further reduction, and finally via the friction clutch to the hub shell.

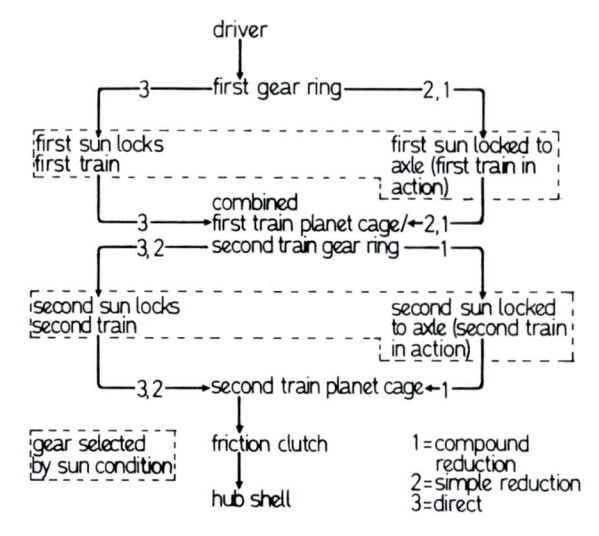

Fig. 7.3. Flowchart for the Raven motorcycle hub gear.

The Raven gear's sliding sun system did away with the need for the rather cumbersome all-encircling clutch member used in Cohen's motorcycle hub.

## Friction between Cohen and Raven

It is a mystery why the two motorcycle hub gear patents were filed under different names. Perhaps Frank Bowden was encouraging inter-departmental rivalry or trying to confuse his rivals. More likely it was because of the natures of the patentees. William Raven and Israel Cohen did not like each other. Years later Cohen wrote that Raven 'hated me like poison whilst I worked for him, then did his utmost to regain my favour in later years.' He added:

> Raven imported all his pals from Birmingham and planted them in strategic positions throughout the works. The Gestapo hadn't much they could teach him ... and even when I left the firm for the first time Raven wanted to search my belongings.

Cohen's account of the early history of the Sturmey-Archer motorcycle hub gear sheds further light on the mystery:

> Mr Raven, the works manager, came to me one day with a so-called design of his own, or rather an axle made up surreptitiously by one Cooper, a relative, and told me to design a hub gear round it. This I did and samples were circulated round the trade. Later Humbers [Humber Limited, the bicycle and motorcycle manufacturer] wanted to enter the six-day trials, so I redesigned the hub with wider gear ratios. Later I saw some papers that showed royalties were being paid to both Raven and Alltree.

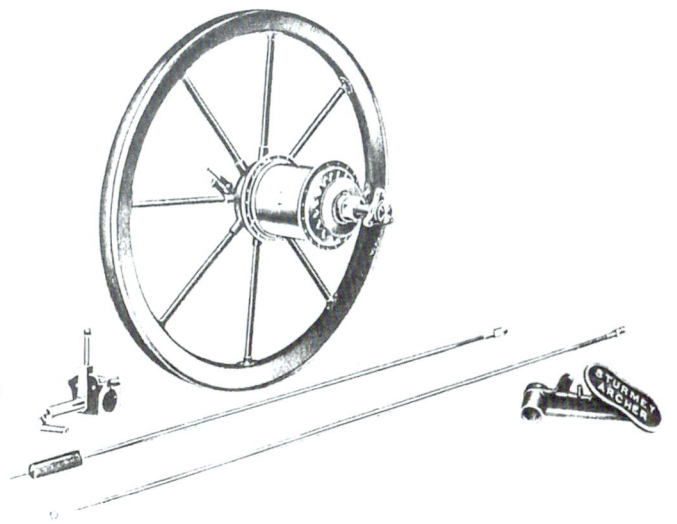

Fig. 7.4. Sturmey-Archer motorcycle hub gear, showing the necessarily large drive belt drum (pulley).

## Initial success

The Sturmey-Archer motorcycle hub gear was reviewed in *Motor Cycling*. The reviewer stated: 'The hub is so strong that on one occasion, when subjected to the test of having the clutch let in suddenly, when the engine was racing, it refused to give way, though the fork ends of the motorcycle frame were bent right round.' Needless to say, this endorsement found its way into Sturmey-Archer's product literature.

Raven's hub gave direct drive and reductions of 36% and 59%. The clutch consisted of tiny plates of steel acting against others of bronze. Hubs produced circa 1914 had the wider ratios referred to by Cohen, with direct drive and reductions of 46% and 76% and all-steel clutch plates.

At least sixteen manufacturers fitted the early Sturmey-Archer hub gear to their motorcycles, including Triumph, Excelsior and Humber. It enjoyed some racing success, being used by the Triumph team that won the 1913 Italian 1,000 km Time Trial. In 1914 George Brough, on one of his own 3½ hp machines fitted with a Sturmey-Archer hub gear, was the only winner of a gold medal in the Bristol Motor Cycle Club Open 18 Hours Trial.

## Cyclecar gears

Not content with patenting a hub containing three speeds and a friction clutch, Sturmey-Archer went a step further by adding a reverse gear. The hub covered by GB patent 273 of 1913 was intended chiefly for cyclecars – lightweight vehicles based on motorcycle technology. The patent was in the names of Frank Bowden and Israel Cohen.

Although a hub gear, the patent suggests an alternative use in a countershaft position between the crank axle and driven wheel, an arrangement often used in tricycles. The gear is not built into a wheel but held in a cradle between the bottom bracket and the rear wheel axle. Drive from the crank is fed by chain to the sprocket on the driver of the gear; the output from the gear is fed from an extra sprocket on the gear shell, via a second chain, to a sprocket on the rear wheel axle. The earliest known Sturmey-Archer 3-speed hub adapted for countershaft use is on a Raleigh X-frame tricycle made about 1906. This adaptation is undocumented and may not have been made by Sturmey-Archer.

Although the specification in GB patent 273 of 1913 showed the gear as a 3-speed similar

Fig. 7.5. 1913 advertisement for Sturmey-Archer motorcycle 3-speed.

to Raven's, the patent allowed for additional speeds by way of extra epicyclic trains. The reverse gear was obtained by bodily moving one of the gear trains which thereby clutched in such a way that the final driven member ran backwards.

Three days after filing this patent the same patentees applied for GB patent 451 of 1914 which covered a 'Combined Variable Epicyclic and Differential Gear for Motor Road Vehicles'. It was a unit for use with cyclecars, with the differential built around the gearbox (preferably of the Raven type) and fitted in a countershaft position with belt or chain drives to the wheels.

Neither of these cyclecar gears was ever marketed but the specification for patent 451 of 1913 contains an interesting and possibly telling statement: 'The pinions may be either of the frictional type engaging a frictional surface on the outer wheels, or they may be toothed pinions, spur or bevel.'

## No future for motorcycle hub gears

Why the suggestion of frictional pinions? It seems likely they were a protective measure to allow internal slippage between the pinions and gear rings when the hub was highly stressed. As motorcycle engines rapidly increased in power it became apparent that the hub was the wrong place for a motorcycle gear. A petrol engine must be geared down for torque at the expense of speed, the opposite of what happens in a pedal cycle. The wheel hub of a motorcycle is therefore the most highly stressed and unsuitable end of the drive to place variable gears.

Both Sturmey-Archer and their rivals Armstrong produced motorcycle hub gears. This is how Cohen summed them up:

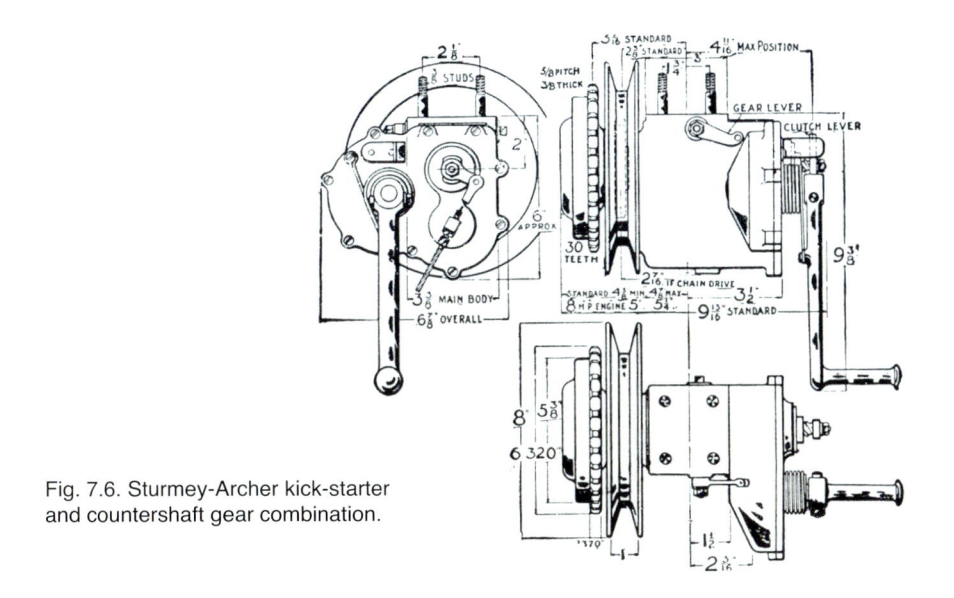

Fig. 7.6. Sturmey-Archer kick-starter and countershaft gear combination.

The early Armstrong gears cracked up wholesale. Most of the Sturmeys didn't, though they were never designed for the powers that were used. Actually, the original Sturmey hub gear was for making the 2 hp Humber suitable for riding by sedate people as against men who could do a run and jump mount and also run alongside up hill. We only used the 3 hp Raleigh, my 3½ Triumph, a Bradbury and sundry Nortons to get a margin of safety. What killed the hub gear was the use of smooth running twin engines that gave the lubricant no chance of returning to the bearings under pressure.

### William Reilly's motorcycle hub gear

By the time he left Sturmey-Archer even William Reilly had been seduced by the idea of motorcycle hub gears. The 3-speed design he took with him was such a gear and he got it patented a fortnight before his former assistant, Cohen, filed the first Sturmey-Archer motorcycle hub gear patent.

Reilly's motorcycle hub gear was the subject of GB patent 819 of 1909, in the name of machinist James Edwin Ross of 361 City Road, Old Trafford, Manchester. Like Cohen's original design, it was a two-train epicyclic with a common fixed sun pinion; but in this case direct drive was middle gear, one epicyclic train giving the high gear, the other low. The hub incorporated a coaster brake and a spring-controlled plate clutch but was never produced commercially.

### Motorcycle hub gears abandoned

The first Sturmey-Archer motorcycle gear patent completely to abandon the hub gear principle was GB 563 of 1913. This was another Bowden/Raven application. It retained the compound double epicyclic system and was similar in operation to Raven's earlier motorcycle hub gear. The most significant difference was that the mechanism was encased in a separate gearbox for mounting in a countershaft position.

Although this gear did not go into production, Sturmey-Archer were moving inexorably towards countershaft gears and in 1914 they launched what would now be regarded as a fairly conventional motorcycle gear. It was a 3-speed box with enclosed kick-starter and a cork-

Fig. 7.7. 1915 550cc Triumph model H.

inset clutch, suitable for motorcycles from 3 to 8 hp. This new gear was a great success and was adopted by the British army, particularly for use by despatch-riders. Triumph produced over 30,000 motorcycles during the First World War and most were fitted with the Sturmey-Archer countershaft gear. During the war Sturmey-Archer's motorcycle gear sales earned £267,000 (£17 million today).

### Raven's countershaft gear
Raleigh's GB patent 112,388 of 1918 covered a 4-speed motorcycle gear 'of simple and efficient construction' designed by William Raven. In this gear the driven (output) shaft was hollow and revolved on the drive (input) shaft. Pinions on these coaxial shafts were clutchable to either shaft and meshed with other pinions on a parallel layshaft.

### Countershaft gears in the interwar years
Many motorcycle and cyclecar makers fitted Sturmey-Archer gearboxes: they included Acme, Ariel, Cotton, Coventry-Eagle, Diamond, Dunelt, Mars, Matchless, Montgomery, Nestoria, New Hudson, Norton, NUT, Phelon & Moore, Rovin, Royal Enfield, Sarolea, Sheffield-Simplex, Soyer, Sun, Tamplin, Triumph, Victoria and Zenith. The gearboxes evolved to keep pace with the development of more powerful engines and the increased use of side-cars. They had various designations – LE, HW, LS, BS, BW and FW. British patents relating to these designs included numbers 180,925; 198,142; 207,922; 202,158; 204,571; 224,663; 261,124 and 261,127. Most of these were jointly in the names of the Raleigh company and William Wilkie.

All production of Sturmey-Archer countershaft gears ceased in l935, following the worldwide economic slump and Raleigh's withdrawal from motorcycle production.

### Barratt's infinitely variable gear
An infinitely variable transmission with direct drive on all gears was offered to Raleigh in summer 1921. Its co-inventor was Arthur Garfield Barratt, a British citizen living in Johannesburg, who submitted it to Raleigh on behalf of a South African syndicate. A similar

Fig. 7.8. Sectional drawing from the 1921 Sturmey-Archer motorcycle countershaft gear catalogue.

Fig. 7.9. LS kick-starter and gearbox combination.

device was offered to Raleigh by a Mr Fenn but not taken up.

Barratt's gear involved a link between an input shaft and an output shaft, both on the same axis. The link comprised a worm (a short revolving cylinder bearing a screw thread) on the output shaft and a worm wheel (a pinion with teeth shaped to be driven by a worm) on the input shaft. The pitch of the worm was such that, if the worm wheel was held stationary, the worm rotated on its own axis while rotating in a cage around the worm wheel.

The worm had an auxiliary drive from a friction wheel travelling in a circular path, the radius of which was controlled by the user via a cable linkage. When the friction wheel's circular path was at its smallest, axial rotation of the worm was very slow, and gearbox output speed was almost the same as the input speed, because the worm and worm wheel were acting

75

Fig. 7.10. A 1928 advertisement for Sturmey-Archer motorcycle 3-speed.

almost as a solid dog clutch. At the other extreme of adjustment, when the friction wheel's path was at its maximum, axial rotation of the worm was at its fastest, and gearbox output speed was at its slowest, being much reduced by the spinning of the worm. So the auxiliary friction drive merely controlled the speed of rotation of the worm and was not directly involved in transmitting power from the engine to the road wheels. But in summer 1922 tests of the gear proved unsuccessful and Raleigh abandoned the project.

### Raven and Cohen depart

Sir Frank Bowden, who had headhunted Raven, died in April 1921. His son Harold succeeded him as chairman of Raleigh and Sturmey-Archer and inherited the Bowden baronetcy. Raven soon decided he could not work under Sir Harold, who was constantly complaining about slacking. In January 1922 Raven left Raleigh very suddenly; Cohen left later in the year. Raven subsequently established a rival cycle firm, Ray Cycles, close to the Raleigh works and was joined by most of Raleigh's senior sales staff.

### Sturmey-Archer motorcycle engines

Raleigh motorcycle engines were produced in many variations and in the interwar years were sold to other companies under the Sturmey-Archer name. The first was a flat twin designed by William Comery, manager of Raleigh's motorcycle division at the time.

In the mid 1920s some Sturmey-Archer engines were combined with gearboxes and sold as 'units'. The 1929 tri-lingual Sturmey-Archer motorcycle engine catalogue lists 198, 248 and 298 cc side-valve engines and 348, 496 and 598 cc overhead-valve engines. The gearbox range continued to develop as motorcycles became more refined and powerful: the 1929 LS type was suitable for engines up to 1,000 cc.

### Winding down

In 1931 the management committee decided that production of motorcycle gears was no longer profitable and all development work on engines was abandoned. The following year Raleigh rejected an offer to make milking machines. They were also offered a chance to manufacture an agricultural device called the Rototiller but negotiations broke down.

Early in 1933 a meeting was held with Mr Smith of Norton Motors Ltd. It was proposed

Fig. 7.11. Sturmey-Archer motorcycle gearboxes at the 1929 Olympia Motorcycle Show.

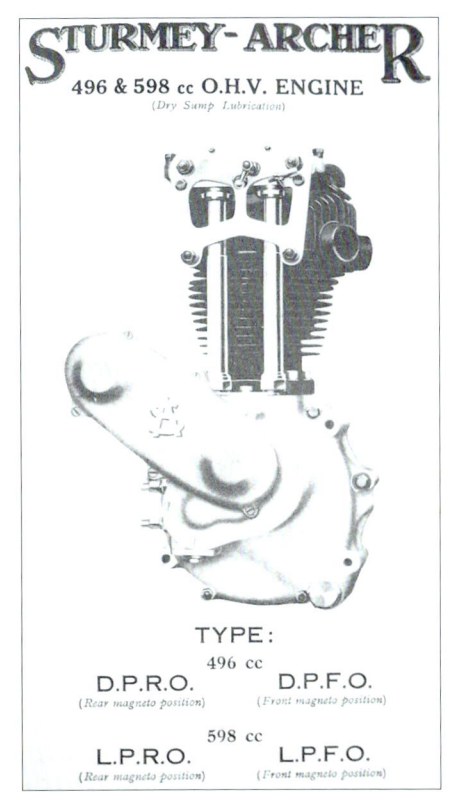

Fig. 7.12 Sturmey-Archer 496cc & 598cc OHV engine (from a 1929 tri-lingual brochure).

that Sturmey-Archer supply all Norton's requirements for gearboxes until the end of the 1934 season. The Raleigh board hoped this would give Norton time to consider making their own gearboxes for the 1935 season and possibly to take over manufacture of Sturmey-Archer gearboxes.

During 1933 Norton, Victoria and Protto placed orders for their 1934 engine requirements; the committee then decided that no further engine orders should be accepted. In 1934 negotiations with Burman to make Sturmey-Archer countershaft gears broke down; the committee agreed that gear spares with a retail value of £34,000 (£2 million today) would be made for the next five years as part of the exit strategy.

But Sturmey-Archer engines were still manufactured under licence. Negotiations concluded in 1935 led to an arrangement whereby Ransomes, Sims & Jefferies of Ipswich, makers of agricultural machinery, continued to make Sturmey-Archer engines for their own use after Raleigh ceased to.

## The German subsidiary
Sturmey-Archer exported many motorcycle engines and gearboxes to Belgium, Scandinavia and particularly to Germany. In the late 1920s the German government imposed heavy import duties and Sturmey-Archer sought ways around this.

In 1927 Raleigh directors visited German cycle and motorcycle manufacturers to study

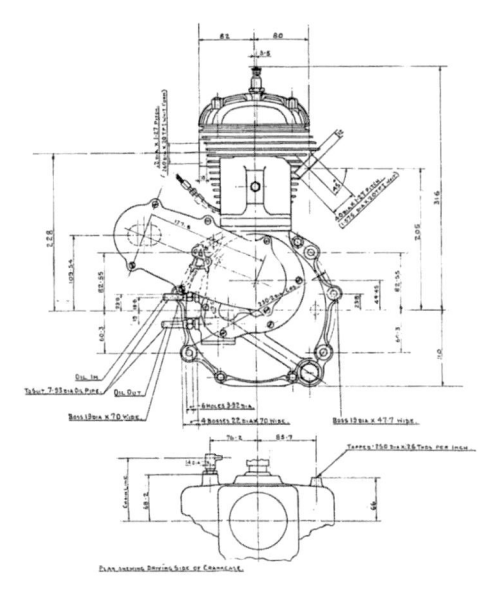

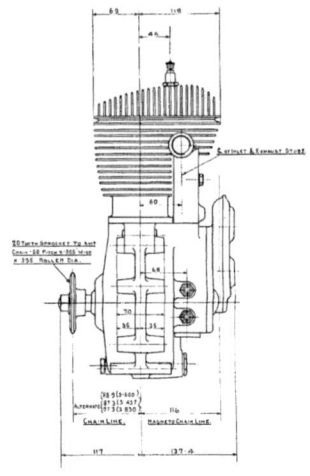

Fig. 7.13. Drawing of the 1931 Sturmey-Archer 348cc SV engine.

Fig. 7.14. 1932 advertisement citing Norton's use of Sturmey-Archer motorcycle gears.

their production methods, including four companies in Nürnberg: Elite, Wanderer, Victoria Werke and Triumphwerke. This led to collaboration with Victoria Werke, including the adoption by Raleigh of Victoria's patented liquid brazing method. Meanwhile the German firm Montan started assembling Sturmey-Archer gearboxes in Berlin. Following complaints about Montan's quality, Nordesta took over assembly and distribution in Germany for a while.

Collaboration with Victoria Werke continued and in 1929 an engine and gearbox assembly factory in Nürnberg was established, run jointly by Sturmey-Archer and Victoria. The following year Raleigh set up a German subsidiary with a capital of 25,000 Reichmarks (£500,000 today). It seemed a good move, as at the time about half the new motorcycles in Germany were fitted with Sturmey-Archer engines and gears. But the operation was not successful and made heavy losses. It was virtually abandoned in 1932 and sold off four years later.

# Chapter 8

# Competition and conflict

### Hub gears and munitions work, 1902 to 1918

### The market in 1902
When the Sturmey-Archer 3-speed was launched in 1902, the future of cycle gearing was in the melting pot. On the UK market there were epicyclic bracket gears, epicyclic 2-speed hubs, an expanding chainwheel and a couple of early derailleurs. In the recent past in the USA there had even been a fully automatic gearless transmission. But by the end of the First World War the choice of variable gears for most British cyclists lay between 3-speed hubs by Sturmey-Archer or BSA.

From the turn of the century until the outbreak of the war, there was intense competition between many British gear manufacturers. Expanding chainwheels and derailleurs disappeared fairly quickly but bracket gears maintained a following for some time. The hardest struggle involved the various makers of epicyclic 2-speed and 3-speed hubs.

Henry Sturmey, in his 1902 lecture to the Cycle Engineers' Institute, reviewed the main bicycle change-speed systems then on the market. There were the New Protean and Hodgkinson's Gradient derailleurs; the Collier bracket gear; the Paradox expanding chainwheel gear; the Garrard 2-speed epicyclic screw-on hub gear; and Reilly's 2-speed epicyclic Hub.

Shortly thereafter the Sturmey-Archer 3-speed was launched and it was an instant success. Other inventors and manufacturers lost no time in turning their attention to this new and expanding market.

### 'The Variable Gear Movement'
In October 1903 *Cycling* printed a major review of change-speed gearing systems. So great was public interest that the magazine wrote of 'the variable gear movement'. In addition to the gears reviewed by Henry Sturmey the previous year, there were a number of newcomers. These included the Sunbeam 2-speed epicyclic bracket gear and the beautifully simple Eadie 2-speed hub gear, designed by John Fagan of Dublin.

Two new 3-speeds were in the experimental stage: the Pedersen and the ultra-wide-ratio Peart, which like the 2-speed Garrard was designed to screw onto a standard hub. Other variable gear developments were noted in Belgium and the USA. Of the British gears described, only the Garrard was available with a coaster brake.

### Increasing competition
The next few years saw the introduction of many new gears, some of very original design. The Boon chainwheel gear of 1904 used pivoted teeth to vary the effective diameter of the chainwheel but was not commercially successful. The following year a coaster version of the Eadie 2-speed was launched. In 1906 the Humber-Cordner 3-speed was introduced. By then Crabbe was making 2-speed and 3-speed hubs, both available with a coaster brake, and the

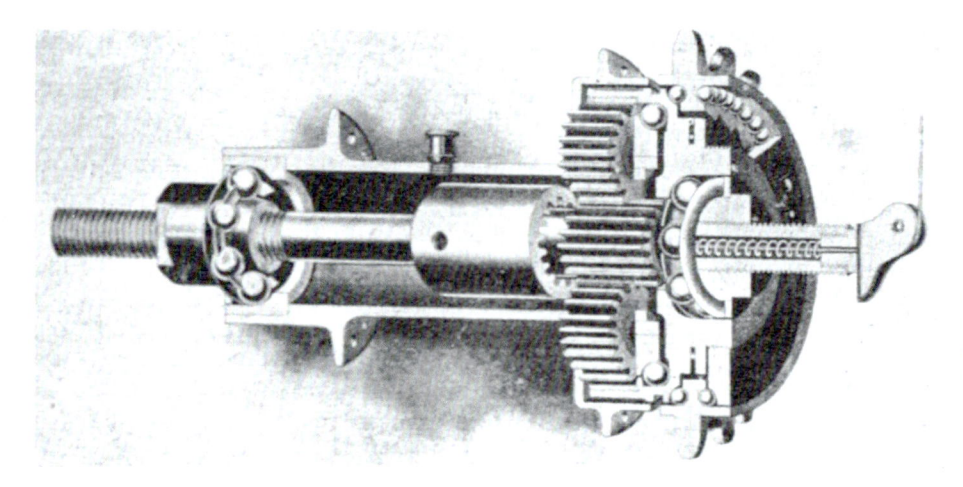

Fig. 8.1. Cutaway illustration of the Eadie 2-speed, designed by John Fagan.

Dursley-Pedersen 3-speed hub had also been launched.

*Cycling's* 1907 review of variable gears described 29 change-speed systems. Seven 2-speed hubs offered direct drive and a lower gear. These were the Manchester Hub (as Reilly's 2-speed was now known), the Crabbe, the Eadie (Fagan), the Simplex, the BSA Mk 2, the Stanley and the Griffin. Most offered a reduction in the order of 20% to 25%. There were three 2-speed hubs that gave direct drive and a higher gear: the Pedersen, the Villiers and the Micrometer. The Garrard seems to have disappeared from the market by then.

Three 2-speed hubs were offered with a coaster brake: the Eadie, Crabbe and New Departure. The Triumph 2-speed gear and hub brake was in a class of its own, being the only gear combined with a cable-operated band brake. It comprised a Manchester Hub combined with a Triumph freewheel and band brake.

Although the Collier was no longer mentioned, there were still some bracket gears in production: the Sunbeam, which geared up and could only be supplied fitted to Sunbeam bicycles; the Centaur, which geared down and could only be supplied fitted to Centaurs; and the James, which gave similar gears to the Centaur. There was only one 3-speed bracket gear, the Allen. It was still in the experimental stage and was a twin epicyclic, driving direct in low gear.

## Three-speed competitors in 1907

The Sturmey-Archer was pre-eminent amongst the 3-speed hubs but by 1907 there was competition from six other makers.

The Sunbeam had two sun pinions mounted on ball bearings. Locking one gave high gear, locking the other gave low. Releasing both gave direct drive; if the cable broke the hub remained in middle gear. There was no 'no-drive' position. Sunbeam's full page advertisement in *Cycling* quoted Bidlake as saying 'A beautifully-made article – more expensively produced than most gears.' Much was made of the fact that the pinions were cut rather than pressed. The Sunbeam hub was specially made for the company's bicycles and was not supplied separately. The Seabrook worked on a similar principle and was described as 'extremely simple' and 'worth close inspection'.

The Pedersen offered very wide ratios and reviewers of the period were divided as to whether or not it was an epicyclic gear. The hub shell had a projecting hinged cover over a layshaft carrying three planet pinions. Pedersen also made a 2-speed version. Although the internals of both Pedersen gears looked very different from other epicyclics, having an extra

Fig. 8.2. The Pedersen 3-speed with casing removed.

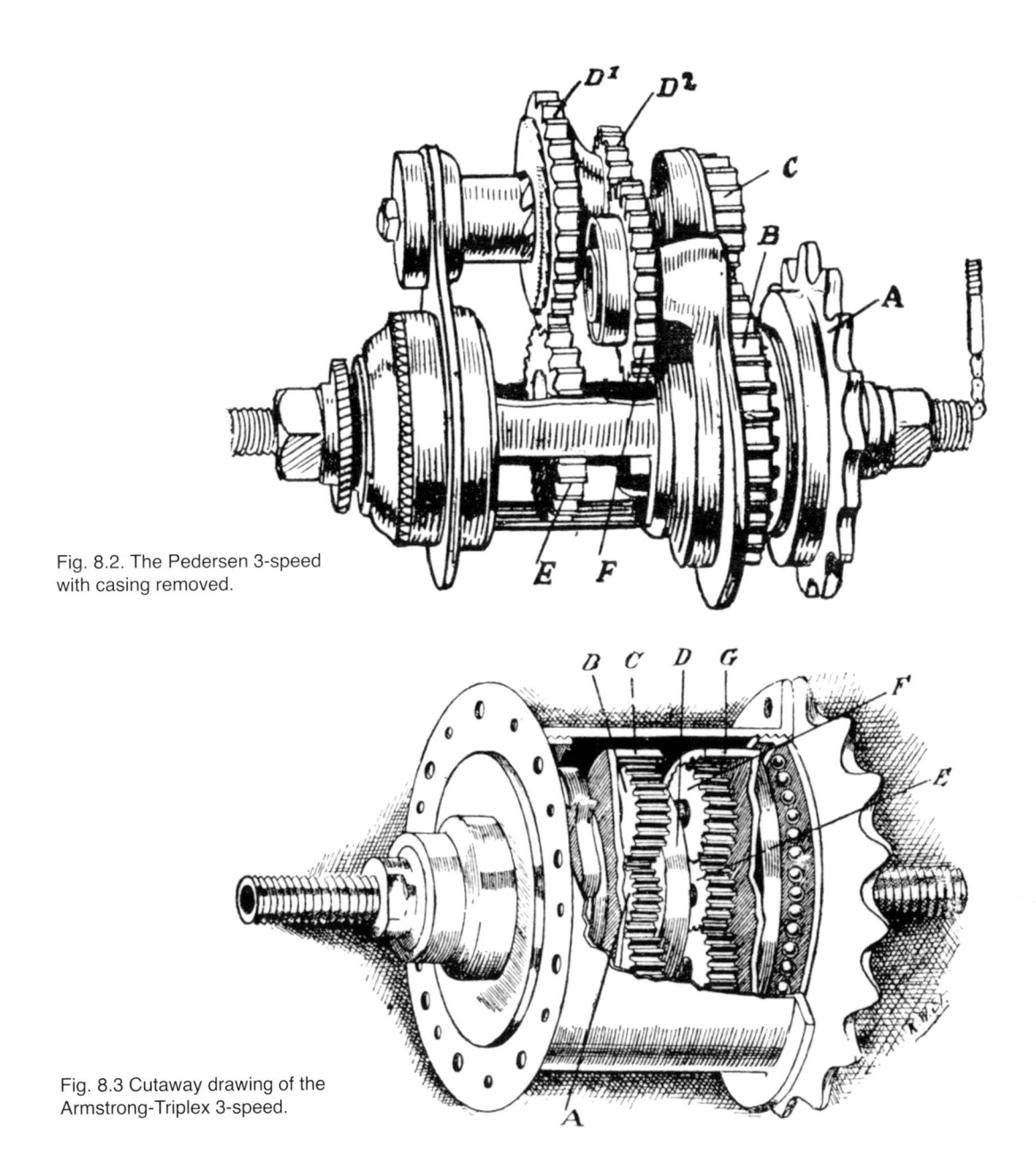

Fig. 8.3 Cutaway drawing of the Armstrong-Triplex 3-speed.

sun instead of a gear ring, they were certainly planetary motion mechanisms.

The Armstrong-Triplex 3-speed was a twin epicyclic gear, allegedly a discarded Sturmey-Archer prototype designed by William Reilly and pirated by his brother A.H. (Harry) Reilly. The Humber-Cordner was also a twin epicyclic. Like the Sunbeam, it gave middle gear (direct drive) if the cable snapped. It was fitted to Humber bicycles and was also made by another firm who offered it in fixed or freewheel versions.

The Optimus 3-speed hub was new in 1907 and offered closer ratios than the other gears. It was a twin epicyclic but, unlike the others, direct drive was the lowest gear. The Crabbe

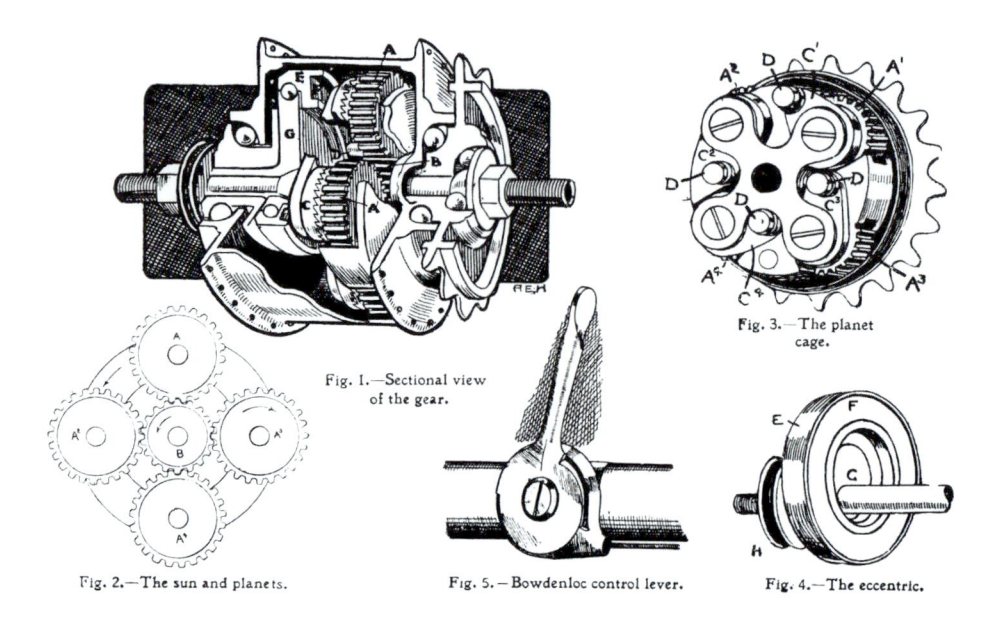

Fig. 8.4. The All-Speed continuously variable hub gear.

was another twin epicyclic hub and the Crabbe Coaster was the only 3-speed and coaster brake combination.

## The All-Speed
The most ingenious gear described in the 1907 article was the All-Speed. It was based on patents held by G.F. Taylor of Birmingham and was expected to be on the market very soon. The All-Speed had a twist-grip control and was continuously variable between direct drive and 50% increase. The planet pinions were mounted in such a way that an adjustable cam plate could give them additional rotary motion, thus simulating the effect of an increasingly large sun pinion.

## The gear for a guinea
The Three Speed Gear Syndicate fought back against the competition with hard-hitting advertising, comprehensive technical information and price cutting. Their *Hints to Users of the Sturmey-Archer 3-Speed Gear* included a diagram of the hub's constituent parts and listed all the options. These included 9 tooth sprockets for 1" pitch chains, 18 tooth for ½" and 14 tooth for ⅝". Chain widths of ⅛", 3/16" and ¼" could all be accommodated, as could any chainline from 1½" to 2". The hub shell was only available with 40 spoke hole drilling but the gear could be supplied 'for any width of back jaw down to four inches'. ('Back jaw' width equated to 'over locknut dimension'.)

The gear came down in price from £3 10s. (£360 today) in 1903 to £1 15s. in 1908 (£175 today). By the end of the Edwardian era the Sturmey-Archer 3-speed was 'the gear for a guinea' (a guinea being 21 shillings or £1 1s.) at less than a third of its launch price. But this considerably reduced price still represented perhaps two-thirds of a week's wages to most working men.

## Fourteen 3-speeds

By 1909 there were still seven 2-speed hubs that geared down from direct drive: the Centaur, Crabbe, Eadie, Griffin, James, Simplex and Stanley; the Crabbe and the Eadie were also available combined with coaster brakes. The Centaur and James were newcomers but BSA had discontinued production of their Mk 2 and the Manchester Hub since absorbing Eadie. The Villiers was the only remaining 2-speed hub to gear up from direct drive.

The James, Centaur and Sunbeam 2-speed bracket gears were still available. The Sunbeam had been modified for tricycle use by Abingdon-Ecco Limited and in this form was sold as an Abingdon gear. Sunbeam also advocated using their bracket gears together with 2-speed or 3-speed hubs to give 4-speed or 6-speed systems. The Allen 3-speed bracket gear seems to have disappeared, its place being taken by a 3-speed version of the James, although there is some doubt whether this was ever mass produced.

The chain-shifter systems had completely disappeared from the UK market by 1909 and were viewed with derision by most British cycle gear experts. In 1911 *Cycling* commented on a pair of French derailleur gears:

> To the Britisher, accustomed to the epicyclic system of gearing with all the mechanism hidden within the hub shell, the crude methods of obtaining increase and reduction adopted by the French appear ridiculous.

The All-Speed Gear was still undergoing development in 1909 but there is some doubt whether this gear ever went on general sale. Only two examples are known to exist: one found in France, the other in Britain.

The rest of the gears on the market in 1909 were all 3-speed hubs, fourteen in all. Four of these were Sturmey-Archer designs; the Sturmey-Archer 3-speed (later known as the type X), the type C Tricoaster, the licence-built BSA and the Triumph, which by this time was a Sturmey-Archer 3-speed combined with a Triumph external band brake. The other ten 3-speeds were the Crabbe-Simplex (a single epicyclic replacement for the earlier Crabbe), Crabbe Coaster, Armstrong-Triplex, Seabrook, Stanley, Sunbeam, Humber-Cordner, Micrometer, Pedersen and Optimus.

Sturmey-Archer's 3-speed hub production reached 100,000 per annum by 1913. The following year Raleigh bought the Armstrong-Triplex Three Speed Company for £6,000 (£550,000 today) – another competitor out of the way.

## Competition from Germany

In 1912 Bidlake wrote in the *Cyclists' Touring Club Gazette and Record*, 'The cult of variable gearing shows no sign of diminishing.' He went on to describe the Fichtel & Sachs Universal Torpedo, a 4-speed hub gear combined with a coaster brake.

The German firm Fichtel & Sachs was founded in 1895. Ernst Sachs had patented a ball bearing hub for bicycle wheels that used four rows of ball bearings and adjustable spherical cones (GB patent 25,164 of 1894). He had worked in a bike shop in Schweinfurt am Main while recovering from a fall during a cycle race. While in Schweinfurt he met Karl Fichtel and a partnership was born. The enterprise started in a barn donated by Fichtel's parents. Karl Fichtel was the businessman, and Ernst Sachs the inventor, works manager and mechanic. Initially they employed just one other worker.

Fichtel & Sachs then went through an intense period of coaster brake development that

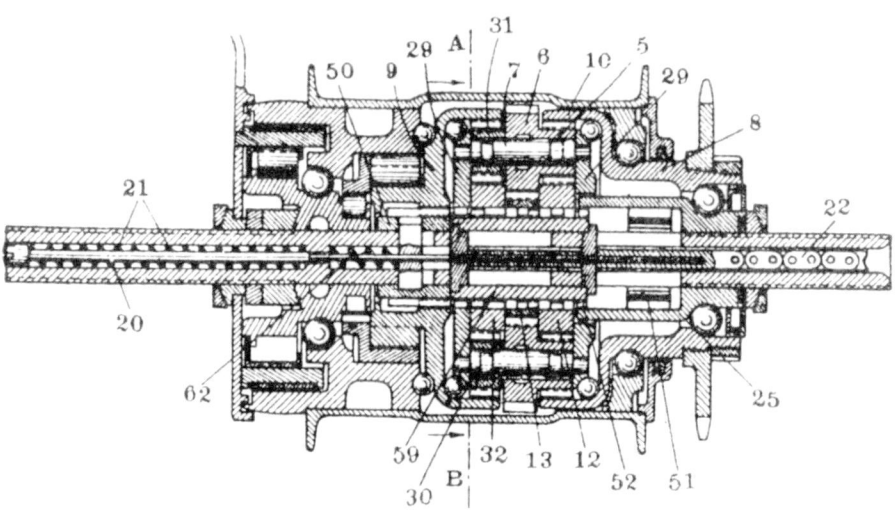

Fig. 8.5. Sectional drawing of the Fichtel & Sachs Universal Torpedo 4-speed coaster hub (patent drawing).

paralleled the simultaneous work on hub gears in England. According to the company's marketing literature, various systems and types of friction materials were tested until, dissatisfied with progress, Sachs ceased all work on existing designs and disappeared to the Alps with his development engineers. He returned in 1904 with the first Torpedo coaster brake. It was simple, compact, reliable and the basis of many modern back-pedal brakes.

But just as the genesis story of Sturmey-Archer is riddled with spin, so is that of Fichtel & Sachs. The actual inventor of the first Torpedo coaster brake was Johann Modler, Sachs' engineer. Sachs patented the coaster in his own name (German patent 216,985 of 1903) and denied a 2 per cent royalty to Modler, who consequently left Fichtel & Sachs, emigrated to the USA and was airbrushed out of the company history.

By 1912 Fichtel & Sachs employed a workforce of 2,000 in a model factory producing ball bearings and cycle hubs. The Universal Torpedo, launched that year, was a coaster brake combined with a 4-speed hub. This was a quarter of a century before Sturmey-Archer first marketed a 4-speed. Bidlake reported that the Universal Torpedo was 'devised on the customary sun and planet principle but with two suns and the usual sliding control operating through a hollow axle. Virtually it is a 3-speed hub with an additional very low bottom speed.' Like the later Sturmey-Archer FW, direct drive was third gear. A typical range thus offered was 40, 51, 68 and 90". Bidlake thought the 4-speed Universal Torpedo would 'best appeal to pass-stormers'. He remained a believer in 'the sufficiency of a 3-speed contrivance giving a generally used normal and two emergency gears as limiting extremes'.

The combination of attitudes like Bidlake's, the outbreak of war in 1914, and intense price competition from better-known British products did not bode well for the Universal Torpedo on the UK market. But the probable main reason for Fichtel & Sach's lack of success here is less obvious: in spring 1912 the board of Sturmey-Archer decided to accept an offer of £3,250 (£306,000 in 2017) from Fichtel & Sachs for Sturmey-Archer's German, Austrian and Swiss patents. The agreement included a price maintenance scheme and probably placed restrictions on Fichtel & Sachs' activities in the United Kingdom.

Fichtel & Sachs gained a considerable market in Germany and some other northern

Fig. 8.6. The type S hub was a type FN Tricoaster licence-built for Sears Roebuck.

European countries. But they never earned a major position in the British market, their principal successes in the UK being modest and involving 2-speed coasters. During the mid 1930s Fichtel & Sachs marketed a Torpedo cable-operated 2-speed combined with a coaster brake; this did not compete directly with any Sturmey-Archer product. In the mid 1960s their cable-free Torpedo Duomatic 2-speed coaster, which also had no competition from Sturmey-Archer, was adopted by Alex Moulton for his Stowaway bikes. Moulton used a later version of the same gear on some of his spaceframe bikes, introduced in 1983.

### Foreign patents

The Three Speed Gear Syndicate kept a watchful eye on the patent applications of their rivals. The board meeting minutes of 7 February 1905 show that the syndicate employed a patent agent to contest the application by the Hub Two-Speed Gear Company for GB patent 22,306 of 1903 which covered a 3-speed hub gear. The patent was consequently amended to include the statement:

> we declare that we are well aware that variable gear has been constructed with … three speeds, one lower and one higher than the normal and having planetary gear incapable of endwise movement, and we do not claim such constructions per se.

While jealously guarding their British patent rights, Sturmey-Archer sought to capitalise on their overseas patents. During 1905 Frank Bowden negotiated with Messrs Dubied of France and the Aachen Company of Germany: arrangements with both firms were approved by the Sturmey-Archer board in November of that year. Seven years later Bowden went to Paris to negotiate the sale of patents to Monsieur C. Lomcot. In the same year the German firm Wanderer placed an advertisement in the *Berliner Tageblatt* newspaper announcing a district court ruling that Sturmey-Archer had violated Wanderer's patent rights for hub gears.

Sturmey-Archer were particularly keen to take advantage of their US patents. In summer 1910 the board agreed to accept an offer of £1,250 (£120,000 today) from C.P. Norris for these

Fig. 8.7. This Sturmey-Archer advertisement, published in May 1914, depicts a peaceful world soon to be shattered by war.

rights. This agreement may have fallen through, because in autumn 1912 terms were offered to Morris Russell & Company. In spring 1914 an agreement was made with Sears Roebuck & Company of Chicago; they were to pay £500 (£46,000 today) for use of Sturmey-Archer's US patents, plus a royalty for every hub sold. The board expected this to be a very profitable arrangement.

## World War 1

On 4 August 1914 Germany invaded Belgium and Britain declared war on Germany. The conflict lasted more than four years and directly caused the deaths of an estimated nine million military personnel and seven million civilians.

Production of the type FX Sturmey-Archer 3-speed ceased soon after the war began. The type A replaced it and was essentially an improved type V, with a gear mechanism based on that of the type N Tricoaster. This rationalisation helped Frank Bowden devote Sturmey-Archer production facilities to munitions manufacture. His cooperation with the government led to him being awarded a baronetcy (a hereditary knighthood) less than a year after the war started.

Fig. 8.8. Type A 3-speed

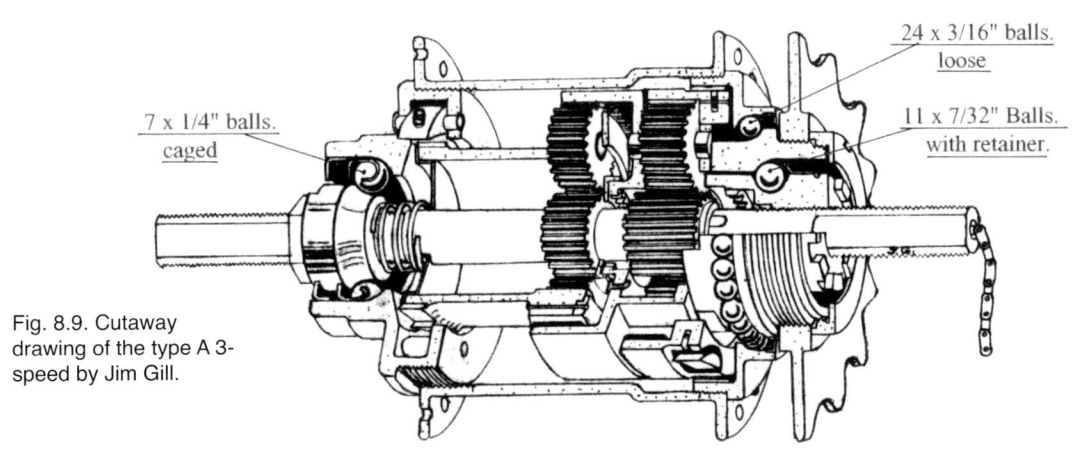

Fig. 8.9. Cutaway drawing of the type A 3-speed by Jim Gill.

24 x 3/16" balls. loose

11 x 7/32" Balls. with retainer.

7 x 1/4" balls. caged

Above diagram shows hub fitted with End Cap K.45 and Spring K46, also later type Cone.

By the end of 1915 demand for munitions was so high that Sturmey-Archer's mass production of bicycle hub gears ceased. But the company's motorcycle gears continued to be produced in large numbers and the Raleigh group became one of the largest munitions makers in the country, with a workforce of 5,000 and munitions sales of £2,285,803 (£147 million today).

It proved relatively simple to convert the existing plant for war use. Automatic machinery was easily modified for making shell cases and fuzes. It was also straightforward to adapt the big presses for making the circular magazine pans of the Lewis gun, a light machine gun designed by the American Colonel Isaac Newton Lewis.

In the first two years of the war considerable effort went into making the Gaines Relais artillery shell fuze. Its manufacture involved the following precision operations: milling lower inner and outside threads on heads; drilling and tapping top inside threads of heads; facing and recessing fuze heads; drilling screw holes in heads; pressing, tinning and soldering bouchons and queues; annealing bodies and bouchons; pressing and gauging bodies; gauging heads; assembling; resistance testing of bodies, vacuum testing and final inspection.

Another of the munitions made by Raleigh was the No.106 direct-action percussion fuze.

Fig. 8.10. Women making parts for Gaines Relais fuzes. Note the young boy in the right-hand foreground.

Fig. 8.11. Women and girls making fuze components.

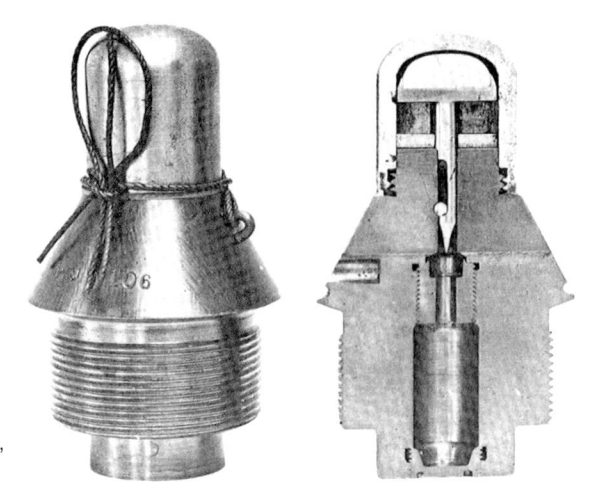

Fig. 8.12. Two views of the No.106 fuze, including a section through the highly sensitive detonation section.

Fig. 8.13. A 1917 advertisement aiming for Sturmey-Archer post-war sales.

This was the first British instant-impact fuze and was put into service early in 1917. Instead of driving deep into the ground before detonating, it fired on contact, even if it hit a lightweight object, such as a wire fence. This meant that high-explosive shells could be used to clear barbed wire, without creating deep craters that impeded advancing troops. It also made shrapnel shells obsolete, as an artillery shell exploding just above ground level was more effective as an anti-personnel device.

Fig. 8.14. A 1919 advertisement citing Sturmey-Archer's contribution to the war effort in a pitch for post-war civilian sales.

Advertising continued throughout the conflict, sometimes making the link between wartime use of Raleigh products and future peacetime use. In 1917 a Sturmey-Archer advertisement read 'On national service today. At your service after the war.'

## Victory

Even before the outbreak of hostilities, Sturmey-Archer had won the decade-long struggle against a host of competitors. The disruption caused by the war was to hasten the end of many of their rivals. The demobbed British soldier in search of a new 3-speed was likely to be faced with a simple choice – a Sturmey-Archer hub or a BSA, designed by Sturmey-Archer.

# Chapter 9

# Conservative consolidation

### The first half of the interwar years, from 1919 to 1929

The interwar years were a golden era for Sturmey-Archer, already Britain's leading cycle gear maker. This chapter covers the company's output during the first decade of the post-war period, in which there were major management changes resulting from the death of Sir Frank Bowden in 1921 and the passing on to his son Harold of the Bowden baronetcy and leadership of the Raleigh empire.

### Post-war supply and demand problems

Demand for 3-speeds was so high just after the war that night shifts were occasionally worked. Sturmey-Archer resumed type N Tricoaster production by outsourcing it to the King Sewing Machine Company in the USA. Samples received in spring 1919 seemed satisfactory, as did the first delivery of 5,000 Tricoasters a few months later. But subsequent American hubs proved so poorly made that the committee decided to bring production back in house. King tried to blame the problems on the design of the hub; unsuccessful attempts to get recompense dragged on until autumn 1920. The remaining unreliable American hubs were set aside and most internal parts were scrapped at the end of 1923.

At the 1919 National Cycle Show complaints were received about poor service from two companies authorised to provide spare parts and service for Sturmey-Archer hubs – Cromwell Engineering and County Engineering. The committee therefore decided to make all spare parts at Nottingham and to advertise that Sturmey-Archer accepted no responsibility for repairs or replacements executed elsewhere.

Coated inner wire for hub gear controls was in short supply in 1920, so an order was placed for 200,000 feet from Funke of New York. Raven meanwhile devised a method for enamelling seven-strand wire in-house to provide a satisfactory back-up. But once the backlog of demand for hubs created by wartime shortages was satisfied, demand fell away. Trade became so depressed that the 3-speed works were closed for several weeks in 1921.

### A new factory

Production of hub gear components was highly mechanised but final assembly involved skilled manual work. To increase efficiency and boost output a new gear factory was opened in Cycle Road early in 1921. It was a two-storey building, 411 feet (126 metres) long, with a floor area of more than 36,000 square feet (3,345 square metres). When the cycle trade revived in 1923 and 1924, Sturmey-Archer was able to supply large numbers of hub gears to Raleigh's competitors, such as Humber, Royal Enfield, Challenger and Rudge-Whitworth.

In spring 1923 major problems were found with Sturmey-Archer's steel hardening department. Many components had not been heated adequately and pyrometers were installed to ensure the correct temperature. All 3-speed and Tricoaster hubs in stock at Nottingham were dismantled and the parts re-heated. Raleigh sent workmen to Rudge-Whitworth and Enfield to replace defective parts in hubs supplied to those companies and

Fig. 9.1. A press advertisement from 1920 targeting female customers.

replacement parts were sent to the Humber and Challenger cycle companies for their own people to install.

## Exports and product range

During the 1920s Sturmey-Archer continued to increase their overseas interests. Trademarks were registered or renewed in Australia, France, Germany, Japan and China. In 1921 an order for 500 Tricoasters and 1,000 ordinary 3-speeds was received from Japan, and Comiot of Paris ordered 3,000 3-speeds.

Sturmey-Archer made a great many freewheels. Weekly output was raised to 3,000 in 1919 and the following spring an order for 100,000 was received from Japan. But demand from Raleigh's chief freewheel markets, Italy and France, died away due to unfavourable exchange rates. And BSA started selling freewheels at a much lower price than Raleigh, who cut their prices to compete even though they were unable to reduce the cost of manufacture.

From 1924 and for the rest of the decade there was no significant change in the Sturmey-Archer product range for bicycles: it merely comprised the K 3-speed, the KC Tricoaster and the CC single-speed coaster hub, all of which are described in more detail below.

## Relationship with BSA

The only other hub gear maker of any significance on the British market was BSA, with whom Raleigh made price agreements. In 1923 Raleigh proposed that BSA should stop making 3-speeds and instead buy from Sturmey-Archer at a special rate. In return Sturmey-Archer would stop making coasters and instead buy Eadie coasters from BSA on preferential terms. BSA rejected the proposal but in 1927 a major agreement was reached between the two companies. Under this BSA gave up manufacture of 3-speed hubs except for their own bicycles. In return Sturmey-Archer paid BSA commission of 5% on any increased business obtained.

9.2 An early type K 3-speed.

The two firms also agreed to share technological and costing information. Sturmey-Archer then increased the weekly production of the K 3-speed to a minimum of 3,000 and Raleigh ordered nearly £500 (£28,000 today) worth of gear cutting and shaping machines from BSA. In autumn 1927 more than £1,500 (£84,000) was spent by Raleigh on BSA automatic lathes and three months later a BSA centreless grinder was ordered at a cost of £650 (£37,000 today).

## Advertising
Promotional material in the 1920s stressed that no bicycle was complete without a Sturmey-Archer 3-speed. A 1924 advertisement headed 'The progress of cycling' said, 'First it was the Safety Bicycle, then the pneumatic tyre and then the Sturmey-Archer 3-speed gear.' Durability was also stressed: a 1923 advertisement highlighted J.J. Whitaker's report that his Sturmey-Archer hub 'has run 33,000 miles [53,100 km] without a fault or trouble of any sort'.

Between 1923 and 1930 Sturmey-Archer products accounted for between 7% and 13% of Raleigh's factory sales.

## K 3-speed
Production of type A 3-speeds resumed soon after the armistice and continued until spring 1922. An undocumented example of a type A hub combined with a drum brake exists. It appears to have been an abandoned prototype made about 1918.

The type A was only a stopgap. Sturmey-Archer took advantage of the wartime years to create a simpler 3-speed, the type K. By summer 1919 William Raven considered the hub good enough to use for the following season. In the autumn he produced a version that he claimed was lighter, better and cheaper to manufacture and which the board approved.

Fifty samples were made in spring 1920 for the trade and testing. That summer sufficient steel was ordered to produce 100,000 type K hubs. The committee decided no public announcement would be made about the new hub until after the 1920 cycle show 'as the knowledge might be useful to our competitors.' Demand for 3-speeds was 'very flat' and the committee chose to finish making type A hubs before promoting the new hub. The A was still being advertised in 1921 and the first Ks did not leave the factory until late spring. Complaints were received about rattles, so a spring-loaded cup was fitted inside the hub 'to obviate to a very great extent the chief cause of complaint'. Early in 1922 the committee decided that volume production of the new gear could no longer be delayed: within a year output reached 2,500 a week.

Fig. 9.3. Sectional drawing of the type K 3-speed.

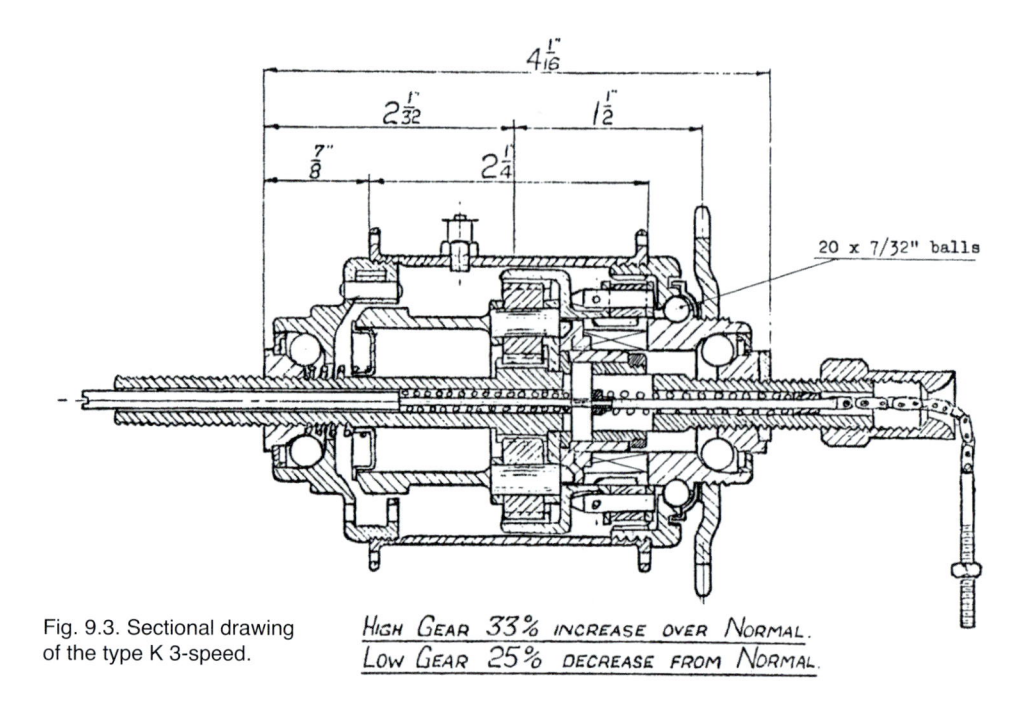

HIGH GEAR 33% INCREASE OVER NORMAL.
LOW GEAR 25% DECREASE FROM NORMAL.

Why did Sturmey-Archer introduce a new model instead of reverting to the type X? According to I.C. Cohen, it was 'all because it worked out ½d. or so cheaper.' The K was a much less sophisticated gear than the X but it was lighter and simpler; it did not use a sliding epicyclic mechanism, it had one less set of pawls and was generally easier to service.

But the X almost made a comeback more than once. In spring 1923 when it was hoped that Sturmey-Archer would take over BSA's hub gear production, the committee considered reintroducing the type X, of which the BSA 3-speed was a licence-built version. Works manager Albert Holland reported that production could resume at 9d. more per hub than a type K. But after the negotiations failed the committee decided to continue with the type K hub, albeit with improvements.

In autumn 1923 it was decided to spend the huge sum of £3,000 (£161,000 today) promoting the K, following the bad publicity caused by problems with hardening of components. In 1924 and 1925 the external finish of the K was improved, following unfavourable comparison with the BSA 3-speed.

In autumn 1924 the committee learned that 'many of those most intimately connected with Sturmey-Archer business' recommended reintroduction of the type X. The matter arose again early in 1926 but was finally dropped in spring that year after the committee decided that 'the present pattern should be improved in every possible respect, even to the extent of slight additional cost, in order to remove the disparity which exists between our own manufacture and that produced by a well-known competitor'. By spring 1928 production of K hubs exceeded 4,000 a week and the weekly output target was raised to 5,000.

## How the type K worked
Gear changes were effected by a six-arm sliding clutch that ran between the six prongs of the driver. The gear used three sets of unidirectional clutches:

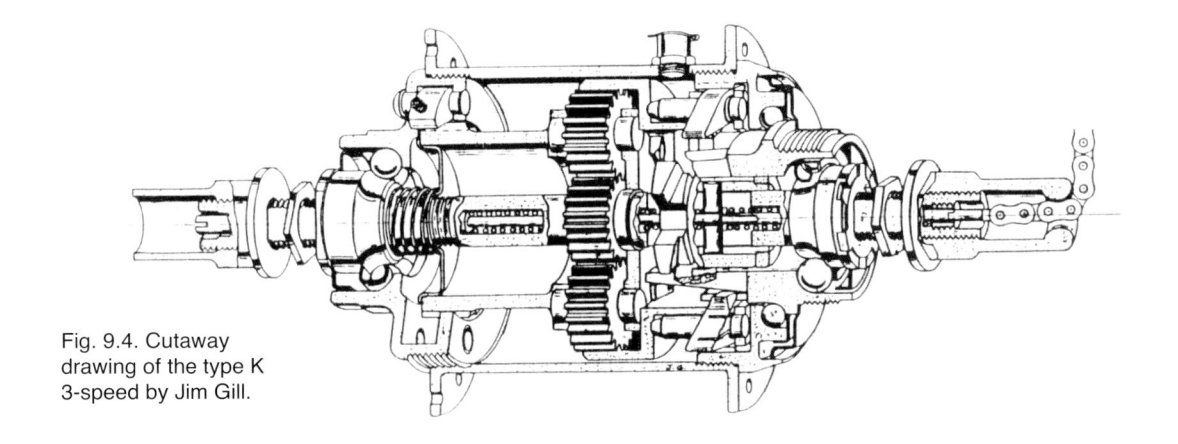

Fig. 9.4. Cutaway drawing of the type K 3-speed by Jim Gill.

a. Low gear pawls mounted in the left hand ball cup of the hub shell. These fed drive from a ratchet track on the planet cage to the hub shell.
b. Ramped dogs on the arms of the sliding clutch. Under the spring action provided by the gear change hold-off spring, these engaged with dogs on the inside of the gear ring assembly.
c. High gear pawls in the gear ring assembly, which connected it to a ratchet track in the hub shell.

For high gear the control cable was slack and the sliding clutch as far left as it would go. Its arms therefore engaged with dogs on the face of the planet cage. Drive passed from the driver via the sliding clutch to the planet cage, through the epicyclic gears and out of the gear ring via pawls C to the hub shell. Pawls A were overrun.

For middle gear the control cable pulled the sliding clutch to its central position, disengaging it from the planet cage dogs and engaging its ramped dogs with the gear ring dogs. Drive passed from the driver via the sliding clutch to the gear ring and out via pawls C to the hub shell, bypassing the epicyclic system to give direct drive. Pawls A were overrun. The ramped dogs B allowed the gear ring to overrun the spring loaded clutch during any momentary simultaneous engagement of high and middle gear: there was no need for a 'no-drive' position between high and middle gear. But after modifications made in 1935 a 'no-drive' position was introduced.

For low gear the control cable pulled the sliding clutch as far right as it would go. The clutch remained dogged to the gear ring but its arms tripped the tails of pawls C, disconnecting the gear ring from the shell. Drive passed from the driver via the clutch to the gear ring, through the epicyclic gears and out of the planet cage via pawls A to the hub shell. Until the moment pawls C were tripped out of action, pawls A were overrun: hence it was impossible simultaneously to engage middle and low gear, and a 'no-drive' position was unnecessary between these gears.

The type K provided an increase of 33⅓% over direct drive and a reduction of 25%. It weighed 2 lb 6 oz (1.08 kg). Top tube control added 3 oz (90 gm) whereas handlebar control added 6 oz (170 gm). The gear could be ordered with axle lengths of 6" (152 mm) or 6 5/16" (160 mm). The shell was drilled for either 40 or 36 spokes which could be up to 13 gauge.

The sprockets were dished and screwed onto the driver. They were available with 16, 17, 18, 19, 20 or 22 teeth, for either ⅛" or 3/16" chains. The chainline could be varied between 1½" (38 mm) and 1¾" (44.5 mm) by altering the positions of two 1/16" (1.6 mm) spacing

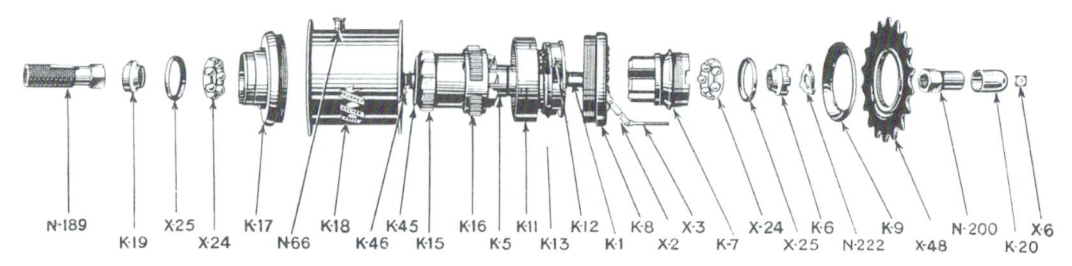

Fig. 9.5 Exploded view of the type K 3-speed.

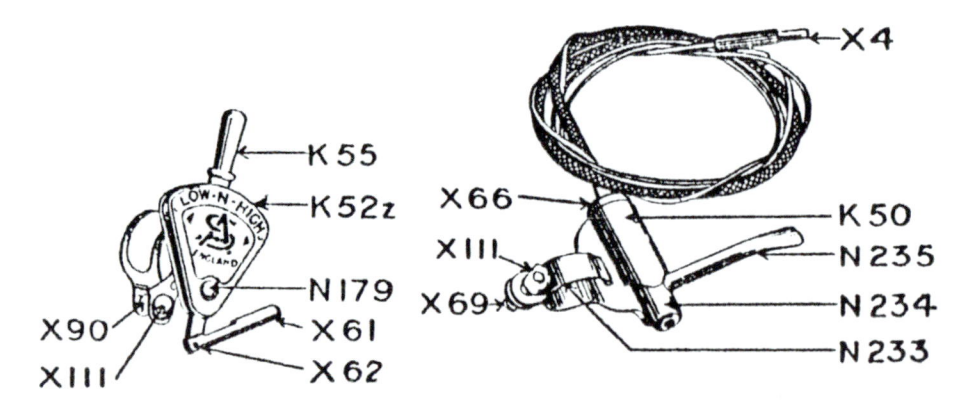

Fig. 9.6. Control options for the type K.

washers and reversing the dished sprocket.

The toggle chain was on the right of the hub and there was an indicator rod in the left end of the axle. In middle gear the end of the indicator rod was level with the end of the axle.

## Later modifications to the type K
Although this chapter focuses on the period 1919 to 1929, for completeness and convenience later developments of the type K hub are also covered here. In 1933 a new right-hand ball ring was introduced to enable a redesigned clutch to be dropped straight into the hub during assembly. In the same year the dogs on the planet cage were ramped and in 1934 the number of teeth on the left-hand low gear ratchet was reduced.

The type K originally had a No Intermediate Gear (NIG) feature, meaning there was no 'no-drive' position between high gear and normal. However, the gear could slip if the ramped dogs on the sliding clutch were badly worn. These dogs were subject to heavy wear if pedal pressure was not eased during changes from high to normal. From about 1935 the NIG feature was dispensed with by widening the gap between the planet cage dogs and the splines of the gear ring.

## An X Tricoaster?
In spring 1918 Sturmey-Archer and James Archer applied for GB patent 124,279, which was granted a year later. This was the first patent for some years to use Archer's name. It is possible that the patent covered an invention by Archer himself, though in view of his previous lack of form this seems improbable and Cohen would surely have mentioned it. It is more likely

Fig. 9.7. A pair of type KC Tricoasters.

that Archer's signature was used for marketing purposes. His profession was given as mechanic and his address as 32 Johnson Road, Lenton, Nottingham.

The new patent referred to the earlier one covering the type X hub (GB 1912 of 1904) and provided 'a method of and means for enabling the planetary gears to be moved bodily endwise, whilst maintaining a constant driving connection for the low speed with the hub or brake'. In other words, it provided a means for combining a hub such as the type X 3-speed with a coaster brake.

In the type X the planet cage moved along the axle, depending on the gear selected. But for a Tricoaster hub it is preferable to operate the coaster brake through low gear, regardless of the speed selected. This is difficult to achieve if the planet cage position is variable. The new patent proposed overcoming this problem by introducing a separate member to carry the low gear pawls and the fast worm thread that operated the cone actuator of the coaster brake. This member was connected to the planet cage by a telescopic arrangement: pegs on the member were free to move axially within hollow planet pinion axles mounted in the planet cage. The patent implied that the member would therefore receive low gear drive at all times, in the same direction as the pedals were turning.

But a standard type X gear combined with a coaster brake in this way would not have worked: the unidirectional clutches would have prevented reverse drive from being delivered to the planet cage. That may be a reason why, when the type N was replaced in 1922, the new Tricoaster used a gear section based on the type K. Other reasons would have related to the economies of mass production.

## KC Tricoaster

The new Tricoaster was known as the KC (C denoting Coaster) and was approved by the management committee at the end of 1919. It had a stepped diameter shell and incorporated better dustproofing and waterproofing than the type N Tricoaster.

The gear section of the KC was based on that of the K, and had the same ratios. However, the KC had a narrower planet cage that also carried a helical drive for the coaster brake, and a low gear pawl ring which, like that of the type N, used sprung crescent-shaped pawls.

The coaster brake mechanism was similar to that of the type N. On the planet cage helical drive's fast worm ran a clutch nut, serrated for good grip against the brake cone: on pedalling

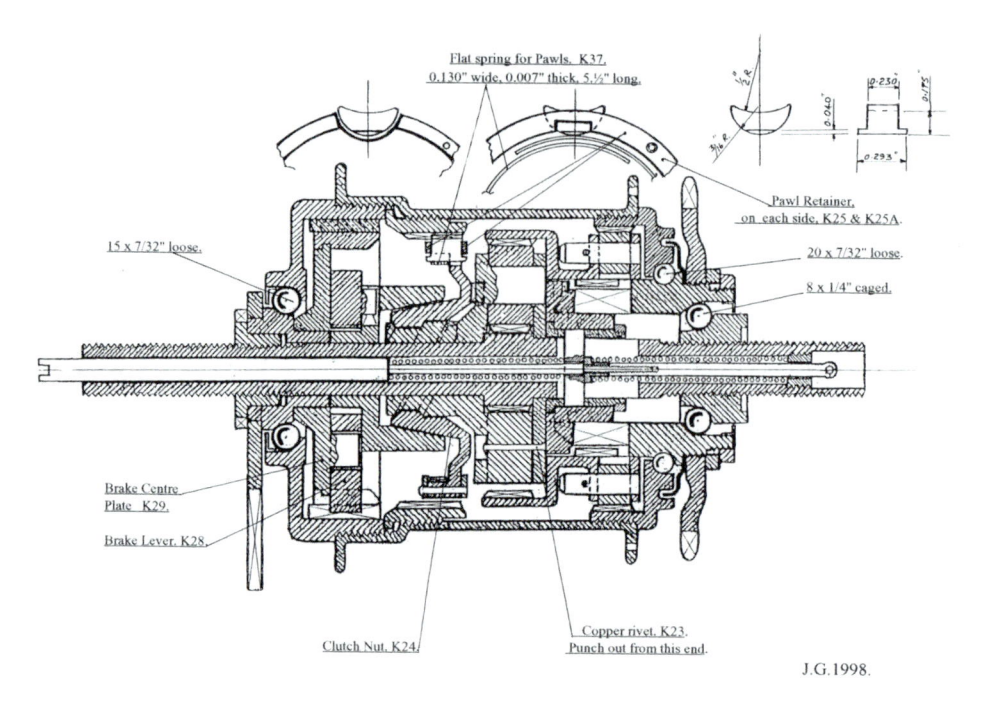

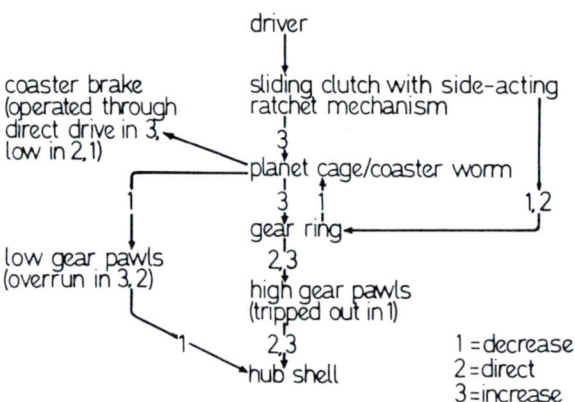

Fig. 9.8. Sectional drawing of the KC Tricoaster by Jim Gill.

Fig. 9.9. Flowchart for the KC Tricoaster.

TYPE KC TRICOASTER

backwards the clutch nut moved to the left into the hollow brake cone which it gripped, rotating it backwards; this operated the brake lever that forced the brake band to open against the lining of the brake drum. The brake band was available in bronze or steel.
But the KC was inferior to the type N inasmuch that the braking effort depended on the gear engaged: if the hub was in middle gear or low gear, the driver was connected to the gear ring, so the coaster was operated through low gear; if the hub was in high gear the driver was directly connected to the planet cage and the coaster was operated through direct drive, torque to the brake being reduced by 25%.

## KC production and reception
In summer 1920 the committee considered ceasing production of Tricoasters but Sir Frank

Bowden's view prevailed: if the new KC version were made in sufficient numbers, Sturmey-Archer would have a near monopoly on coaster hubs in the UK.

Early in 1922 works manager Albert Holland had to stop Tricoaster production because: 'The allowances made in the past for machining were altogether unreasonable and resulted in the assembled gear being totally unsatisfactory for use.' The gear tended to lock immediately after application of the brake. The problem was soon overcome but complaints were still being received in the autumn.

By spring 1922 Tricoaster production was reaching 500 a week. In the summer the Harda Trust ordered 1,000 Tricoasters for Japan and in the autumn a night shift was necessary to meet demand. But output dropped by spring 1924 to less than 200 a week. Later that year complaints were received about the ineffectiveness of braking when in high gear: experiments were conducted to overcome the problem.

In the run-up to Christmas 1924 an order for a further 500 Tricoasters was received from Japan and production soon rose to 560 in a week. Thereafter demand fluctuated: production targets sometimes reached 400 a week but at other times manufacture ceased altogether. In spring 1928 the committee resolved to let the KC 'die out' during the coming season. But two years later they decided that a further 10,000 KCs could be sold, which as far as possible would be produced in the slack season. The end finally came in spring 1933 when the last 2,000 KC hubs were assembled from spare parts. Sturmey-Archer did not produce another Tricoaster until 1952.

During its production run the KC Tricoaster was modified several times. About 1932 the fulcrum for the internal brake lever was modified. The 1933 changes noted above for the type K also affected the KC, though Jim Gill's analysis of old hubs suggests that the new driver may have been the 12-spline type (introduced in 1933 for the KS and KSW hubs) rather than a modified type K threaded driver with sprocket lock-ring.

## Return of the N single-speed coaster

In spring 1919 William Raven was instructed to resume making the type N single-speed coaster hub. Within four months 100 to 200 a week were being turned out – more than Raleigh could use. It was therefore decided to sell these in competition with Eadie, the market leader, but only to Raleigh agents.

## CC single-speed coaster

In spring 1921 Raven reported favourably on samples of a coaster by the German cycle company Schönebeck. A London firm, the Hertford Record Company, offered licensing rights. A sample was tested and found to be very good. Schönebeck wanted £300 (£12,700 today) and a royalty of 2 shillings on every hub sold (£4.20 today). This was too much for the committee, so Raven was instructed to get round the patent – he had already produced two copies of the hub – and it appears that Schönebeck eventually assigned the patent to Raleigh.

By early 1922 Raven had left Raleigh but his successor Albert Holland was testing the prototypes. The CC hub was known within Sturmey-Archer as the 'German coaster' because it was a Schönebeck design. A retail price was set at £1 (£50 today) and there was a choice of steel or rolled bronze brake bands. The CC was claimed to be the lightest single-speed coaster yet.

In spring 1922 Raleigh started fitting the hub to some of their machines and production reached 250 a week by summer. Good feedback was soon received from South Africa and an order of 100 was placed for Japan; Canada and France also showed interest. Negotiations

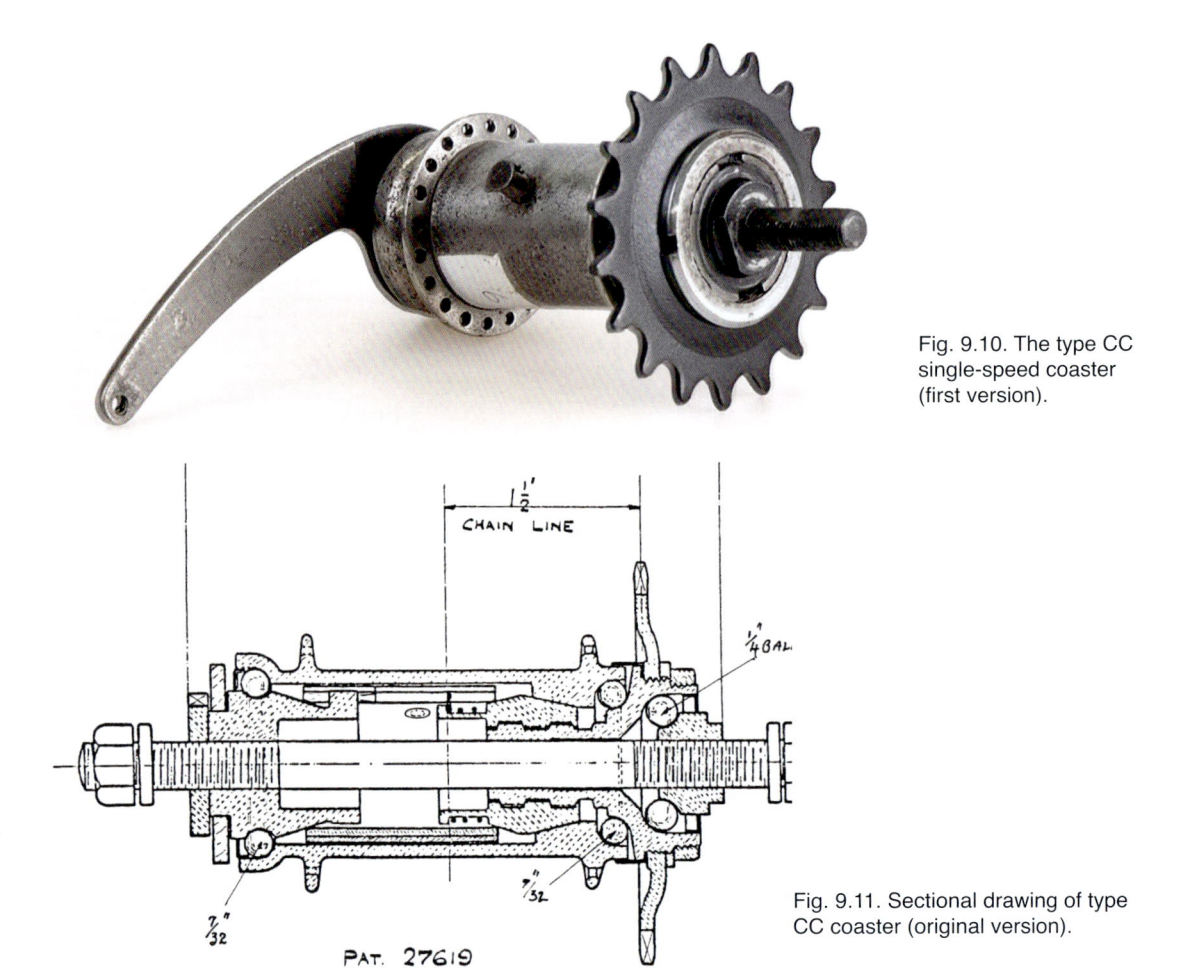

Fig. 9.10. The type CC single-speed coaster (first version).

Fig. 9.11. Sectional drawing of type CC coaster (original version).

began with Société Industrielle D'Albert, holders of the French patent, but they wanted more than Raleigh was prepared to pay. Early in 1923 the committee decided to increase output to 600 a week. To put this in perspective, BSA were thought to be making 8,000 coasters a week.

The CC used a helical drive with a fast worm thread on the driver: on this thread ran a brake-actuating and forward-drive clutch nut, with a drag spring. Pedalling forwards moved the nut to the right, clutching the driver to the hub shell; in the original version this was merely by means of a friction fit but, as noted below, this proved unsatisfactory and was later changed to a positive drive. Pedalling backwards caused the nut to move to the left, forcing the brake band to expand against the hardened cast steel hub shell. If the pedals were stationary the clutch nut rested between the drive and brake positions, providing a freewheel action.

## The international coaster market

Despite initial positive feedback about the CC, by early 1924 slipping drive was causing big problems. Raleigh's Japanese agents asked for the old pattern coaster to be fitted to cycles exported to them. The coaster market in South Africa was lost to a competitor, Raleigh's Bermuda agents refused to take delivery of the hubs and the Irish agent was not happy either. This stung Raleigh into action and by the end of the month, works manager Albert Holland

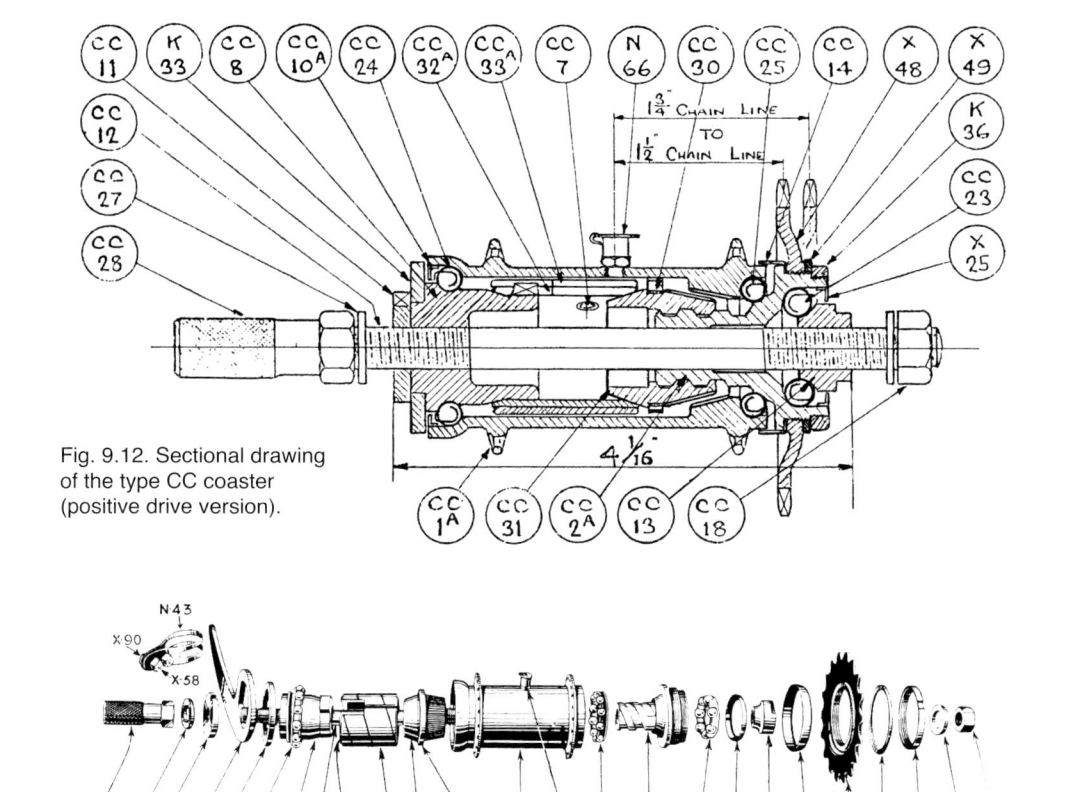

Fig. 9.12. Sectional drawing of the type CC coaster (positive drive version).

Fig. 9.13. Exploded view of the positive drive type CC coaster.

had a prototype positive drive coaster on test and another under development.

The first redesign proved unsuccessful but the second worked well and used mostly the same parts as the friction drive original. It had teeth on the clutch nut and the hub shell which locked together, rather than merely relying on friction. Twenty-five samples were made and fitted to machines owned by staff: feedback was good. Production of the positive drive type CC soon began and by the summer 1,000 a week were being produced.

Production reached 1,250 a week in January 1925 but complaints from the Continent revealed a preference for the Fichtel & Sachs Torpedo coaster rather than the Sturmey-Archer CC. This was because the Torpedo had a quicker braking action: there was less lost motion of the cranks before the brake started to work. Experiments were made to address the complaint but by spring 1925 demand for coasters had fallen so much that assembly was discontinued for a while.

The committee realised there was tough competition, especially on the Continent, and that no large increase in business could be expected in the near future. Suggestions for improvements from the Dutch Sturmey-Archer distributor Fongers were incorporated. By summer 1925 demand for CC coasters was less than one a day. By this time the lost motion had been minimised and positive brake action had been added to complement the positive drive feature. It was decided to modify all hubs in stock to incorporate these features and a heavy advertising campaign was sanctioned.

An order for 3,000 hubs was received from Canada in autumn 1925. These had to be specially made, as the order specified 36 spoke holes rather than the standard 40. Production was about 500 hubs a week by Christmas but soon ceased. The committee decided to let the CC 'gradually die out', with assembly only against special orders.

## The coaster that would not die

The CC refused to die: by spring 1927 demand was so high that the weekly target was raised to 750. Later in the year the committee considered making a copy of the Fichtel & Sachs Torpedo instead of the CC. Albert Holland was instructed to make a camouflaged Torpedo copy but nothing came of this. Meanwhile the mechanic at Raleigh's Sheffield depot suggested a minor improvement to the CC and was rewarded with £5 (£280 today).

In spring 1929 Hercules ordered 2,000 CC hubs. Less than a year later all type CCs being put into stock were chrome plated: this was the fashionable new finish for 'brightwork' cycle components that hitherto would have been nickel-plated as an alternative to black. In summer 1930 William Raven (now back at Raleigh) suggested copying the Eadie coaster, rather than continuing with the CC. He was dissuaded from this for fear of upsetting BSA and prompting them to compete with Sturmey-Archer. Sir Harold Bowden suggested instead copying the Swedish Novo coaster made by Husqvarna: Raven responded that it differed little from the CC.

A few months later Raven revealed that he had examined a coaster made by the German company Victoria Werke and found it very good. He intended altering the CC to incorporate certain features of the German hub. A prototype was made but proved unsatisfactory and the idea of a replacement coaster was then abandoned. Production of the CC continued uneventfully until 1934 when the last 2,500 hubs were sanctioned.

A Raleigh catalogue issued soon afterwards showed Raleigh cycles fitted with Eadie coaster hubs. It was to be nearly 30 years before Sturmey-Archer again featured a single-speed coaster in their product range.

During the 1920s Sturmey-Archer's only new British patent concerning bicycle hubs was GB 207,039, which covered a cheaper and more efficient drag spring – a simple but vital component of most coaster brakes.

## Henry Sturmey's 5-speed

After WW1 Henry Sturmey again turned his attention to the development of hub gears. In 1921 he applied for a patent for the first 5-speed hub gear. After several years of development Sturmey made the invention public in an article in *Cycling* in spring 1924. In this he traced the evolution of bicycle gearing and described the 3-speed hub as a development 'for which I myself was responsible'. He then noted that only the Sturmey-Archer, BSA and Pedersen 3-speeds were still available. He remarked that Sunbeam bicycles had been available with a 3-speed hub combined with a 2-speed bracket gear 'apparently giving a range of six speed ratios', adding that they actually only gave four speeds. (Sturmey was forgetting that a special wide-ratio version of the Sunbeam bottom bracket gear was used to ensure that the arrangement really did give six distinct speeds.) He also observed that:

> In France, especially in the Alpine districts, quite a number of somewhat quaint and crude devices are in use for the purpose of giving the rider more gears – in one case as many as seven.

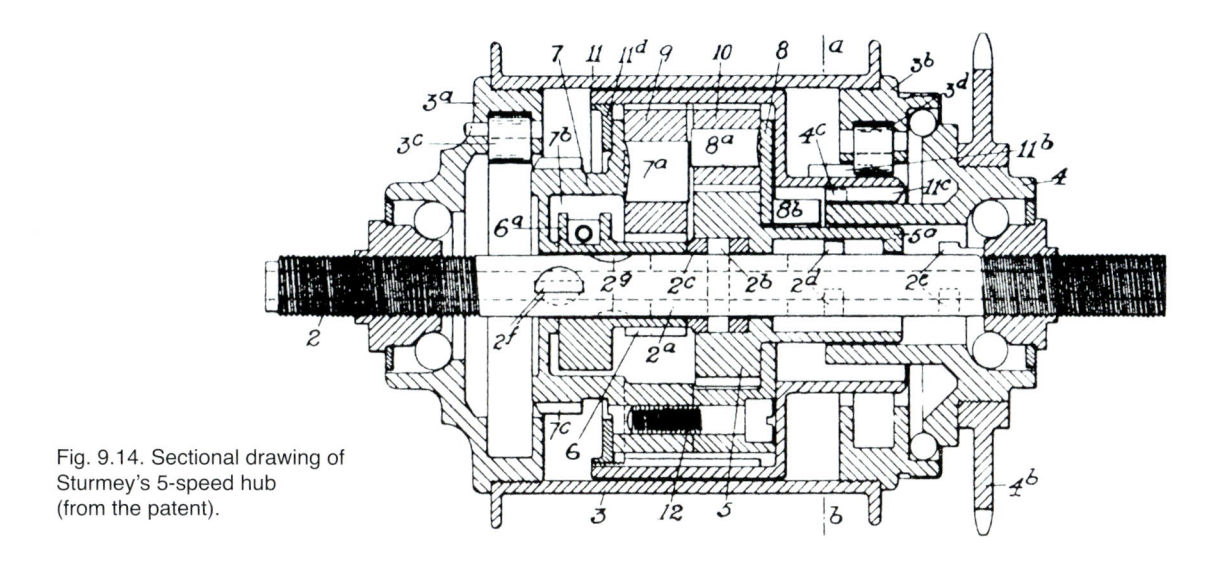

Fig. 9.14. Sectional drawing of Sturmey's 5-speed hub (from the patent).

Sturmey concluded that there was a demand for more than three speeds, as long as the increase in weight was marginal. He then described his 5-speed hub gear which added 'but two or three ounces to the weight.' What Sturmey believed would be the final model had

> been ridden by several expert and everyday riders about 2,000 miles without any trouble developing, so that it will probably become a purchasable production within the next few months.

Sturmey's 5-speed was the subject of GB patent 188,178, the application being also in the name of John Peart, an engineer of 6 Melville Road, Coventry. This was presumably the same John Peart who in 1903 had produced the prototype screw-on wide-ratio 3-speed mentioned previously.

### How Sturmey's 5-speed worked

The 5-speed contained two epicyclic trains, although it had only one gear ring. It had two sets of planet pinions and two slidably mounted suns of different sizes. The net effect was to produce a gear containing two 3-speeds: one wide-ratio and the other ultra-wide-ratio. Direct drive was obviously the same for both trains, hence five speeds were available. The ultra-wide-ratio train provided the highest and lowest gears (fifth and first), whereas the wide-ratio train provided fourth and second.

The whole epicyclic mechanism could slide along the wheel axle, and was so arranged 'that the requisite clutchings and declutchings with the required parts are made in the proper sequence in the course of its travel'. This enabled the use of a single cable and quadrant lever for all five gears.

Ultra low gear gave a reduction of 35.3%, low was a 21.5% reduction, normal was direct drive, high gave an increase of 27.2%, and ultra high an increase of 54.5%. Sturmey subscribed to the 10:1 theory of crank length/normal gear relationship: if you use a 6½" crank, you should use a 65" normal gear. He favoured 9" cranks for a normal gear of 90" and his new hub offered him gears of 57, 70, 90, 115 and 142".

## No takers

In a letter in the *CTC Gazette* in spring 1924 Sturmey stated that the 5-speed hub was unlikely to be available much before 1925. He added that it 'will not be a Sturmey-Archer production'. Thirteen months later, in another letter to the *CTC Gazette*, Sturmey revealed that he was having difficulty in getting the 5-speed manufactured. He wrote:

> The history of the three-speed gear is repeating itself with the five, because, when capital is sought to manufacture it, people who ride or sell bicycles are asked about it, and the reply given is more often than not: "You have got a low gear for uphill and a high gear for downhill; what more do you want?" What little imagination the average "man in the street" has!

## Reversible hubs and bracket gears

Despite the sad indifference to Sturmey's new gear, and despite increasing sales of the K 3-speed, many cyclists were interested in alternative gearing systems, although not necessarily with more speeds. As the editor of *Cycling* reported, while welcoming the prospective 5-speed, an increasing number of cyclists were fitting reversible hubs – single-speed hubs fitted with a different sized sprocket on each side, thus offering a choice of two speeds by removing the wheel and re-fixing it in the reversed position. He considered that the popularity of the reversible hub was

> proof that as a cyclist learns to ride in an intelligent manner and extract the most from himself and his mount, he not only attains greater deftness with a single gear, but also realizes that no single gear can be equally suitable for all purposes.

The editor cited the claimed advantages of the reversible hub as lightness, fewer moving parts, closer ratios, direct drive, quick-release and absence of noise. He felt that epicyclic gears should be developed in these directions. (The quick-release was generally achieved by using wing-nuts, although Chater-Lea introduced a skewer-type quick-release hub in the early 1920s.)

Other cyclists resurrected the idea of bracket gears but Henry Sturmey was quick to point out their disadvantages. In a letter published in the *CTC Gazette* in spring 1924 he took issue with his 'old friend' W.F. Grew, who had suggested that the bottom bracket was the best place for a variable gear. Sturmey reiterated the fact that the stress was greatest at the bottom bracket and that this necessitated a bracket gear being about two and a half times as strong and heavy as a hub gear. In the same letter Sturmey turned to a Mr Blake (presumably Vernon Blake, the gearing pioneer and polymath) who had expressed a dislike for the high gear of a 3-speed passing through the gear train; Blake would have preferred high gear to be direct drive. In reply Sturmey stated that in high gear there was no more than half the frictional loss experienced in low gear.

In the *CTC Gazette* in autumn 1926 Sturmey again attacked the bracket gear concept. This time the subject had been raised by A.H. Walker and F.W.R. Finch. Sturmey responded as 'the originator of the 3-speed gear' and, in reiterating the arguments against bracket gears, pointed out that the reverse argument applied to motorcycles. He commented that Sturmey-Archer had made a mistake when they adapted the 3-speed hub for motorcycle use.

Sturmey then proceeded to discuss why there seemed to be no further significant improvements in bicycle design, and concluded that it was 'largely a question of demand' and that any radical departure would be very expensive. He cited the Dursley-Pedersen and sprung-frame bicycles as examples of developments that had been thwarted. He concluded by stating:

> Undoubtedly there is room, and plenty of it, for further development in the bicycle; but, for it to be commercially successful, the public must be prepared to pay the necessary price during the earlier stages of development until universal popularity and production enable them to be supplied at competitive prices.

## Hub gears for tandems

Another matter that found its way into the columns of the *CTC Gazette* was the suitability of hub gears for tandem use. Much of it related to the X hubs, many of which were still in use. A member stated that his tandem had travelled nearly 9,000 miles (14,500 km) on a Sturmey-Archer X. Another tandemist had achieved 5,000 miles (8,050 km) using a BSA 3-speed. He felt that with medium weight riders there was no risk if care was taken on bumpy roads. He reiterated the advice of an earlier writer who had achieved 15,000 miles (24,100 km) on a BSA-geared tandem: never apply the drive while changing, keep the control wire accurately adjusted and lubricate correctly. A life member had ridden 4,000 to 5,000 miles (6,400 to 8,000 km) in hilly country on a second-hand tandem fitted with a Sturmey-Archer 3-speed. His only trouble had been a snapped control wire and that was on a level road. He considered that there was

> no phase of cycling in which a Sturmey-Archer is so appreciable as with a tandem. Fellow members … may have no fear whatever regarding the stability of the Sturmey-Archer.

However, T.H. Pettipher of Oxfordshire considered that 3-speeds when used in tandems were 'hardly up to the work'. He had experienced a fair amount of trouble during 15 years of their use. His best hub had been a custom-built Pedersen with an extra thick axle and widely-spaced bearings. This had run for 20,000 miles (32,200 km) with only a few small renewals of broken parts. Pettipher had also used a 1915 Sturmey-Archer type X that had needed repair three times in about 3,000 miles (4,830 km). He had recently tried a reversible hub with quick release and found it little inferior to the 3-speed.

## Trade mark registration

In 1923 Sturmey-Archer granted power of attorney to register its trade mark in Japan; this took longer than expected because of a major earthquake. The following year a firm was appointed to register the trade mark in Australia. In 1925 the board appointed an attorney to contest an application by a Japanese subject to use the words 'Sturmey-Archer' on non-company goods. In 1927 the company decided to renew its French trade mark and to register the Sturmey-Archer scroll device (as engraved on many hub shells) in Germany. And in 1929 the board decided to re-register the scroll device in China and register the S-A monogram in Britain and Japan.

## Complacency

The 1920s was a period in which Sturmey-Archer produced little in the way of original or new ideas. No new patents for bicycle gearing were taken out, and most of Raleigh's efforts went into the development of motorcycle gears. Sturmey-Archer's 3-speed hubs had swept

Fig. 9.15. Advertisements from 1928. The smoking flat-capped cyclist was called Archie and appeared for many years in Sturmey-Archer promotional material.

the board as far as utility riders and many touring cyclists were concerned and this success seems to have bred complacency at board level.

There were rumblings of discontent from serious cycle tourists and racers but there was little demand for more ratios. It is a sad fact that Henry Sturmey died in January 1930 without seeing his 5-speed marketed. No hub gear designed by Sturmey ever went into production but this is not to deny his considerable ingenuity and understanding of bicycle gearing.

A Frenchman called Lucien Juy had meanwhile patented what Sturmey would have described as another of those 'somewhat quaint and crude devices'. Juy was the founder of Simplex and inventor of the double pivot derailleur – one of the incremental refinements that slowly improved the hub gear's main rival.

Fig. 9.16. A 1928 poster by cartoonist George Studdy, creator of Bonzo the dog. Originally in black and white, the colour has been added later.

# Chapter 10

# Innovative diversification

## The product range expands in the 1930s

### The early 1930s

There had been little innovation by Sturmey-Archer during the 1920s, the company having settled complacently into a comfortable rut. The 1930s, however, were to be marked by considerable inventiveness. Meanwhile the brand continued to dominate the market in the UK and was strong in many other countries. The advertising strapline 'The Hub of the Universe', first used in the Edwardian era, seemed entirely appropriate.

As the new decade commenced, Sturmey-Archer still maintained a reasonable reputation in racing circles. In 1929 Jack Rossiter had broken the Land's End to John O'Groats record by more than 6 hours, using a standard K 3-speed: in 1930 he broke the 1,000 miles (1,610 km) record by 4 hours.

But there was an increasing challenge from other gearing systems and Sturmey-Archer were under pressure to produce lighter, quick-release hubs with closer ratios. Double-sided reversible hubs were increasingly popular and chain-shifter gears were being steadily improved. In the UK they were now known not only as chain gears but also increasingly by an anglicised version of the French name 'dérailleur'. An example of the confusion caused by ill-fated attempts to maintain the French pronunciation can be seen in the minutes of the Raleigh management committee meeting of October 1930, when 'dérailleur' was minuted as 'Deuryea', having been conflated with Duryea, the name of an American car maker.

 The minutes stated: 'The chief claim in favour of [the derailleur] is that it is specially suitable for use on tandem bicycles.' The minutes emphasised that Sturmey-Archer hubs were also strong enough for tandem use and Sturmey-Archer director George Wilson was instructed to distribute free samples to various makers for testing. A few months later the committee again discussed the derailleur, which Wilson said 'was enjoying some popularity in certain quarters.' So Sturmey-Archer bought a derailleur and briefly experimented with it.

Amongst utility riders the K 3-speed maintained its strong position, its main rival being the BSA 3-speed. Early in 1932 minor alterations were made to the K: the driver prongs were changed from parallel sided to tapered; the ball bearings in the right-hand ball cup were changed from 7/32" to 3/16"; the cones were fitted with built-in dust caps; and for the first time cone locknuts were supplied as standard. About this time Sturmey-Archer also introduced special wing-nuts that could be fitted to the type K hub to facilitate quick release of the rear wheel. These wing-nuts incorporated an integral anti-rotation washer, serrated for good grip and with a projection that slotted into the frame drop-out.

1932 was the first year that Sturmey-Archer dated each hub by use of a single number after the type code. Thus a hub stamped K2 was a type K made in 1932, and KS4 indicated a type KS manufactured in 1934. (See Appendix F for more on hub numbering and dating.) Sturmey-Archer sales literature in the first few years of the 1930s harked back to the early days of hub gears:

Fig. 10.1. The Perry-Sturmey 3-speed drum brake.

A little over thirty years ago, when cycling was a mixture of hiking and hard labour, the first Sturmey-Archer 3-speed gear was introduced, with such effect, that from that time people began to take up cycling for the pure pleasure of the thing ... Nowadays, so popular have these hubs become that they are recommended by all leading cycle manufacturers, and are universally fitted to all good machines.

The Sturmey-Archer hub was described as

lightest and strongest of all 3-speed gears . .... Taking the weight of an ordinary freewheel and hub at 1 lb 5 oz, the adoption of a Sturmey-Archer 3-speed hub will add approximately only 1 lb to a machine.

## Freewheels and handlebar controls
In summer 1930 Villiers offered Raleigh freewheels at 1s. 1d. each (£3 today), whereas it cost Raleigh 1s. 5¾d. to make them. Villiers undertook not to supply Hercules, Raleigh's main competitor, nor to quote a lower price to any other competitor. Consequently Raleigh decided to discontinue making their own freewheels as the Villiers were cheaper and better.

Early in 1932 the management committee agreed that handlebar controls should 'at the proper time' be offered at no extra charge over the standard top tube quadrant system. This was despite the handlebar controls costing about 4d. more (£1 today).

## Drum brakes
By the 1930s coaster brakes had lost much of the limited popularity they had enjoyed in Britain, but there was a significant demand for hand-operated drum brakes, as recently popularised by the British Hub Company. The heyday of the drum brake in the UK was the brief period 1933 to 1935.

## Perry-Sturmey 3-speed and drum brake
In spring 1931 Raleigh works manager William Raven announced that he was experimenting

Fig. 10.2. Type KB 3-speed drum brake.

Fig. 10.3. 1930s top tube and handlebar gear control levers

with 'an expanding brake' – a drum brake with internal brake shoes, operated by a rod or cable linkage. A few months later Raleigh granted a licence to Perry Brothers of Birmingham to combine a Perry drum brake with Sturmey-Archer type K 3-speed internals, a combination sold as the Perry-Sturmey hub. Perry Brothers had recently won a Cyclists' Touring Club award for their drum brakes.

The Perry-Sturmey was available in two versions. There was a standard type for a gents' cycle, with cable-operated handlebar brake lever and top tube gear control. The other was for gents' tandems and had a 3¾" (95 mm) brake drum operated by a cable-cum-rod system. Both versions were available in nickel, chrome or black, and in 1934 cost £1 11s. (£95 today).

## KB 3-speed and drum brake
Soon after granting the licence to Perry, Sturmey-Archer filed their first bicycle hub gear patent for over a decade. It was for a similar product to the Perry-Sturmey but with a slightly smaller brake drum and made entirely in-house. The hub became known as the KB, which stood for K-series Brake. An agreement was made with Perry whereby the price to cycle manufacturers was £1 2s. 6d. per hub, regardless of whether they bought the Perry-Sturmey or the KB.

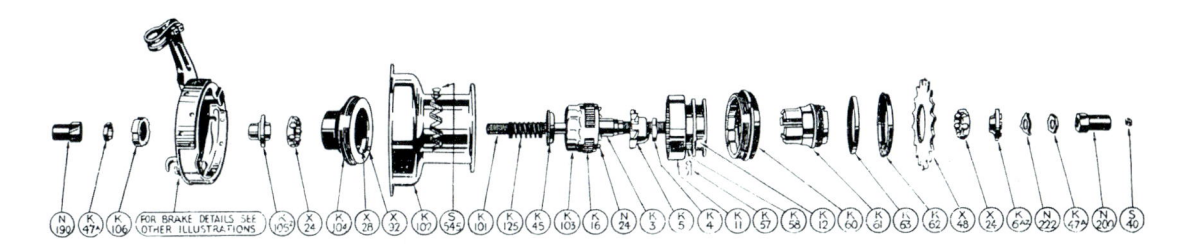

Fig. 10.4. Exploded view of the KB 3-speed drum brake.

Sturmey-Archer launched the KB in autumn 1931, production commencing early in 1932. The management committee decided that handlebar gear controls should be standard for this model but some manufacturers refused to take the hub unless supplied with a top tube lever. By spring 1932 the company had despatched 7,000 KBs and in summer 1933 target output was set at 3,000 a week.

The 1937 Raleigh cycle catalogue shows the KB as 'KBC'. The C suffix was added to indicate that the standard fitting was now for cable rather than rod operation. The same catalogue also describes the KBC as 'Sturmey or Perry'.

The patent covering the KB was GB 370,830 in the names of Sturmey-Archer and William Raven. The object was to provide an improved hub shell, a one-piece pressing with a large diameter at the left end to house the brake. The brake mechanism was mounted on a stationary end cover. The need was recognised to keep the gear section oil out of the brake drum: hence the stationary end cover was 'formed with ducts or channels and the like to pass any oil leaking from the gearing to the outside of the hub away from the braking surface'.

The gear section was based on the type K 3-speed but had a shorter planet cage to make space for the brake mechanism. Most of the brake parts were originally of aluminium but steel was substituted in 1936. The internal diameter of the drum was approximately 3½" (90 mm). The brake could be cable or rod operated. The rod operated linkage was modified in the mid 1930s to permit adjustment without the need for tools: a knurled nut at the brake end of the rods could be turned by hand.

Sturmey-Archer technical literature urged users to ensure that only Sturmey-Archer linings and shoes be used, and that the linings should be 'fitted at our works, to ensure efficient operation of the brake'.

The steel brake version of the KB weighed 3 lb 5 oz (1.5 kg), nearly a pound more than the standard type K 3-speed. Top tube gear control added 3 oz (85 gm) and handlebar gear control 6 oz (170 gm). A complete cable brake control system weighed 8 oz (227 gm).

The KB replaced the KC Tricoaster but both hubs were available concurrently for a while. The hub width across the locknuts and the chainline adjustments were identical to those of the type K. A special tool was produced to enable the left-hand ball cup to be unscrewed from the shell.

## LBR & LBF drum brakes

Dublin-born war hero George Wilson joined Sturmey-Archer in 1927 as a salesman; within two years he had become a director of the company. He went on to become successively managing director, chairman and president of Raleigh. When the KB hub was introduced

Fig. 10.5. The LBR and LBF drum brakes.

Wilson pressed for a front drum brake to complement it. Development was delayed because early samples proved 'too powerful'. Meanwhile Raleigh bought in front drum brakes from Perry.

In spring 1932 sanction was granted to make Sturmey-Archer's own front drum brake, the LBF, and a single-speed rear drum brake, the LBR. The first LBRs left the works in summer 1932. The brake sections of both were similar to that of the KB. Indeed, Sturmey-Archer literature described them as being 'fitted with the same internal-expanding hand-operated brake as used in our KB hub.' In spring 1933 arrangements were made to produce 10,000 pairs a week of LBF and LBR hubs.

The L prefix stood for 'lever-operated'. The prefix was dropped in 1936 when Sturmey-Archer ceased production of foot-operated coasters. The remaining initials stood for Brake Front and Brake Rear. The 1937 cycle catalogue added the suffix C to the drum brake names, indicating that the default fitting was now for cable operation rather than rod. So rather confusingly the rear brake was variously known as the LBR, BR or BRC, while the front brake was the LBF, BF or BFC.

The LBF front drum brake weighed 1 lb 13 oz (822 gm); the LBR single-speed rear drum brake was 9 oz (255 gm) heavier. Cable controls added 7 oz (198 gm) and 8 oz (227 gm) respectively. The hubs were advertised as being suitable for tandem use. The LBR could be fitted with a longer axle and distance piece to accommodate a derailleur gear.

The LBR, like the KB, was drilled with 40 or 36 spoke holes, whereas the LBF was available with 32 or 36 drillings. It was widespread and longstanding British practice to use 40 spokes in the rear wheel and 32 in the front: this reflected the typical load distribution pattern of a roadster, the rear wheel being more heavily laden than the front.

Attempts to sell brake hubs to Hercules were unsuccessful but BSA bought some in autumn 1933.

William Raven tried unsuccessfully in autumn 1936 to get Alphonse Kowalski of Montreal to visit Nottingham. Kowalski had filed a patent for a new type of drum brake containing a freely-rotating friction ring. Raleigh were very interested in this invention but nothing came of it. Meanwhile Raven was promoted from works manager to works director.

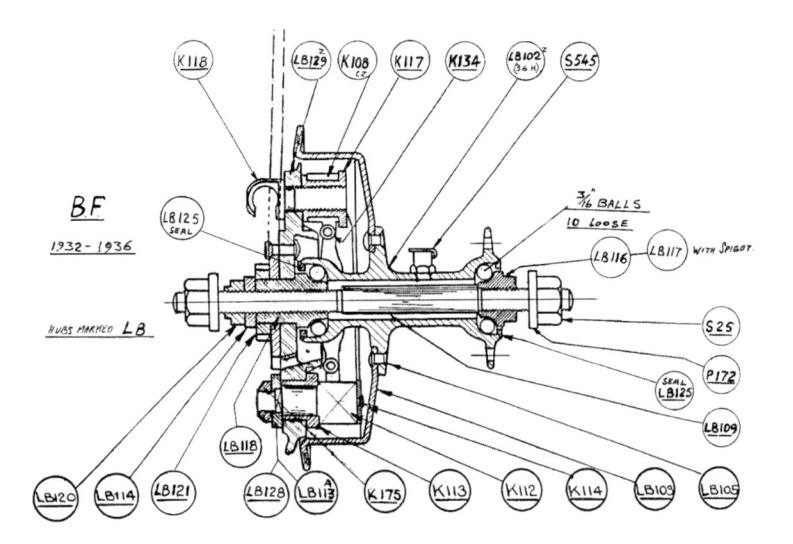

Fig. 10.6. Sectional drawing of an early LBF front drum brake.

Fig. 10.7. Sectional drawing of an early LBR rear drum brake.

Fig. 10.8. Exploded view of the LBR rear drum brake.

113

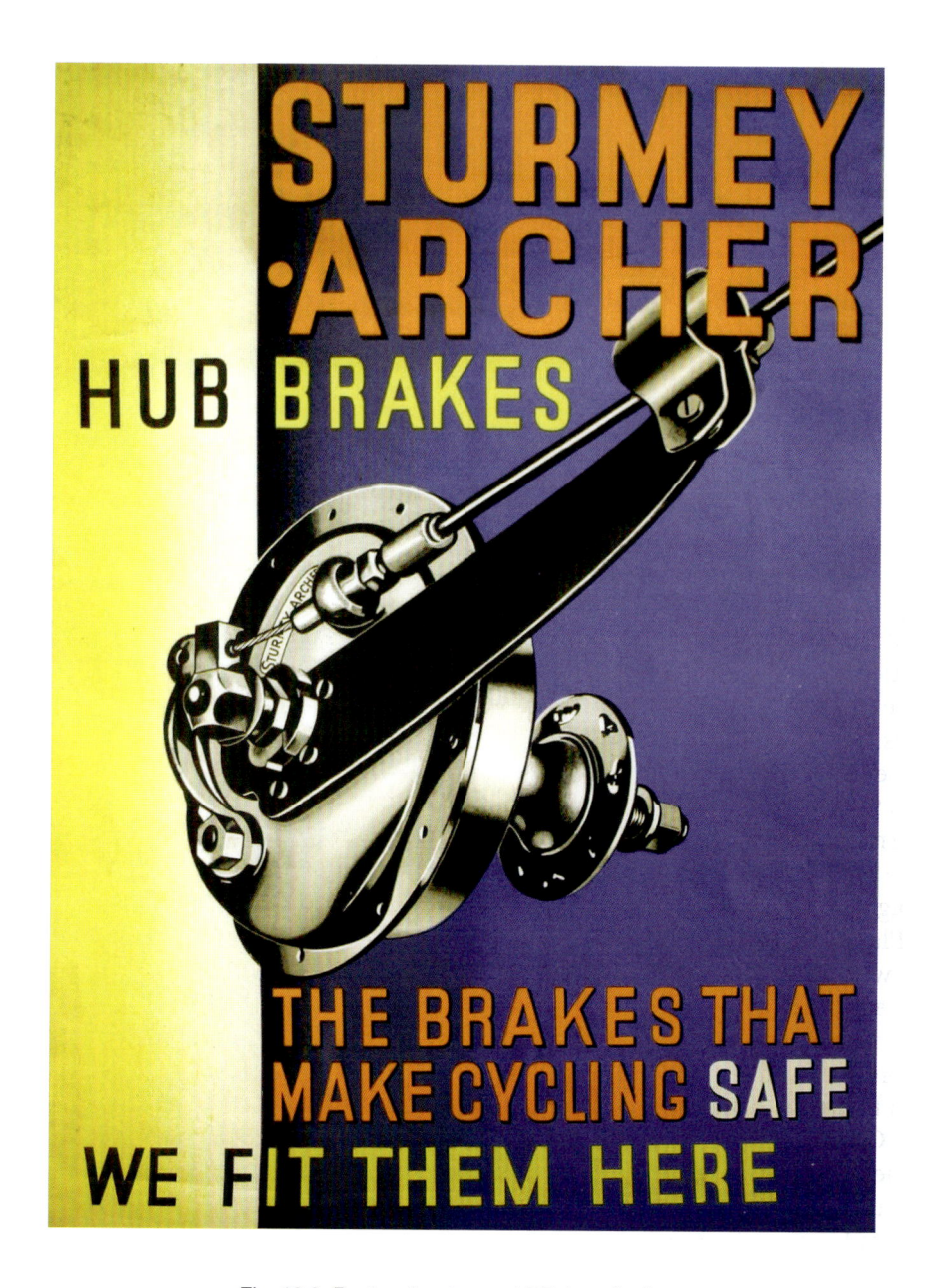

Fig. 10.9. Poster showing an LBF drum brake.

Sturmey-Archer described their drum brakes as 'particularly smooth yet powerful … not affected by wet weather as are rim brakes'. It is a tribute to their design quality that the brakes originally known as LBF and LBR were produced from the 1930s until the early twenty-first century. The initials varied from time to time, with prefixes and suffixes coming and going, but the core initials BF and BR endured. Over the years the hub body shape changed slightly and in the 1960s the asbestos linings were superseded by a safer material bonded to aluminium shoes, rather than drilled and riveted on. The elimination of drilling and riveting the linings had the added benefit of increasing their surface area, thus improving braking and allowing the later introduction of 70 mm drum brakes. Sturmey-Archer never made their own brake linings but bought them in from Ferodo. Owned since 1998 by Federal-Mogul, Ferodo is still Sturmey-Archer's brake lining supplier.

## KS close-ratio 3-speed

Early in 1932 Sir Harold Bowden (chairman of Raleigh and Sturmey-Archer) and Frederick Bush (general manager of Raleigh) rode a bike fitted with a prototype close-ratio 3-speed hub, the KS. Both were pleased with its performance, apart from some difficulty with the top tube quadrant control. The initials KS stood for K-series Sports. William Raven was given the task of looking into fitting handlebar control. Meanwhile, the test bike was sent for evaluation to cycling journalist F.T. Bidlake.

A few months later the management committee sanctioned production of the KS, advertised as 'The Hub designed for the Clubman.' It provided a 12.5% increase and an 11.1% decrease relative to direct drive. Typical gears thus offered were 46, 52 and 59" at one extreme and 83, 93 and 105" at the other.

Sturmey-Archer director George Wilson looked into whether a type KSB, combining the KS with a drum brake, would have a market. Feedback from manufacturers suggested it would be a 'big advance' but that 'the general public will require educating to the principle of close ratio'. Plans for this hub were abandoned in spring 1933.

Target weekly production for the KS in autumn 1933 was 250 but sales were disappointing and by early 1934 Sturmey-Archer had more than 10,000 KS hubs in stock. Production of a medium-ratio version of the KS known as the KSW (K-series Sports Wider-ratio) was sanctioned in summer 1934.

In a bid to boost sales KS and KSW hubs were offered to other cycle manufacturers at a rebate. George Wilson suggested that certain Raleigh and Humber Sports models be fitted with these hubs for the 1937 season to help popularise them and meet competition from derailleurs. So in summer 1936 the KS and KSW were reduced to the same price as the type K standard wide-ratio 3-speed.

The following brief but clear description of how the KS worked was published in *Engineering* in summer 1964:

> The difficulty with the simple epicyclic gear train is that to obtain a close ratio means keeping the diameter of the sun pinion small and using a large gear ring. This can be done up to certain ratios, but using the large gear ring entails increasing the size and also the weight of the hub. So in practice the minimum size of the sun pinion is the determining factor. The solution in the KS hub was to use compound planet pinions. The normal planet pinions were replaced by a pair of different diameter coupled together … The large diameter pinion ran on the sun pinion while the gear ring engaged the smaller pinions.

The Hub of the Universe

Fig. 10.10. The type KS close-ratio 3-speed.

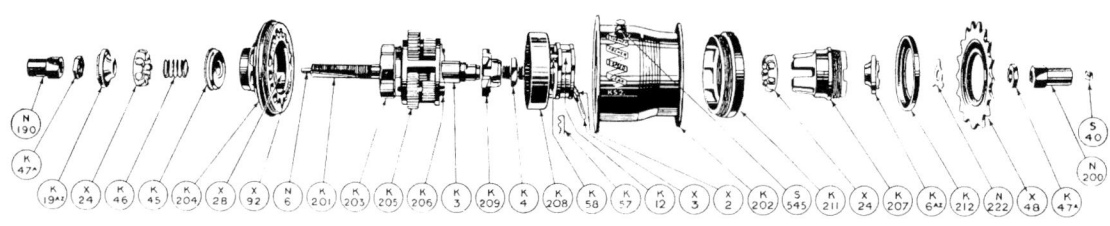

Fig. 10.11. Exploded view of the KS close-ratio 3-speed.

Fig. 10.12. Press advertisement for Tony Hadland's first bike, a Raleigh Speed Sports, which came with a KS gear. The Raleigh was 23-years old when he received it as a 'hand-me-down'.

To mesh properly with both the sun and gear ring, the compound pinions could only be fitted in one juxtaposition; failure to do so would result in a damaged hub and possibly a locked wheel. The three compound pinions therefore bore timing marks which had to be set so that the marked teeth pointed radially outwards from the centre of the wheel axle.

Early KS hubs had a six arm sliding clutch manufactured from nickel-chromium steel but by 1935 the standard type K clutch had been substituted. The early hubs also had specially lightened gear rings and planet cages that were drilled out and cutaway; later ones dispensed with these expensive refinements. The earliest KS hubs were fitted with threaded sprockets as used on the K and earlier Sturmey-Archer hub gears but this was soon changed to the 12-lugged system (see T series below) with locking ring to facilitate quick and easy sprocket changing.

When launched the KS was supplied with standard wheel nuts but quick-release wing-nuts were optional; by 1935 the wing-nuts were a standard feature. A quick-release connection was provided on the gear control cable. To operate this the gear lever was set to the high position, relaxing the cable; the nipple at the gear end of the cable could then be slipped out of a slot in the side of the connector without affecting gear adjustment. The gears were adjusted in the same way as for the K; for middle gear the toggle chain adjustment on the sprocket side was set so that the end of the indicator rod lined up with the end of the axle.

The chainline adjustment range and the over locknut width were the same as the K but there was a wider range of sprockets: from 14 to 20 tooth inclusive, and 22 tooth. To obtain sufficient chain clearance with 14 or 15 tooth sprockets a special right-hand ball ring was required; it was also necessary to omit the outer dust cap. Originally a 24 tooth sprocket was advertised but, if ever produced, it had been discontinued by 1935. The lugged sprockets were only available for use with ⅛" standard chain.

The KS had a slightly tapered 'milk bottle' shaped casing, with the larger diameter on the left. Despite the compound pinions, the weight was kept down to match that of the standard type K 3-speed.

Sturmey-Archer stated that the KS had been

> subjected to exhaustive tests before being placed on the market, and had proved to be thoroughly efficient. We have no hesitation in recommending it with every confidence to the rider who can appreciate a thoroughly good mechanical job which will enable him to obtain the very best return for the energy he puts into his bicycle.

### KSW medium-ratio 3-Speed

The KSW, a medium-ratio version of the KS, was launched in 1933. The somewhat confusing name KSW derived from the fact that this was a wider-ratio version of the close-ratio KS hub; KSW standing for K-series Sports Wide. It would have been simpler to have called it a KM (K-series Medium) and it is rumoured that the name KSM was considered.

The KSW was identical to the KS in almost every respect, except that the sun and compound planet pinions were differently sized from those of the KS. The KS had a 15 tooth sun and 30/15 tooth compound pinions; whereas the KSW had an 18 tooth sun and 27/15 tooth pinions. The KSW provided a 16.6% increase and a 14.3% decrease in gear ratios. Production was sanctioned in August 1934.

Fig. 10.13. The type KSW medium-ratio 3-speed, together with a spare driver fitted with twin sprockets for use with a derailleur as a 6-speed hybrid.

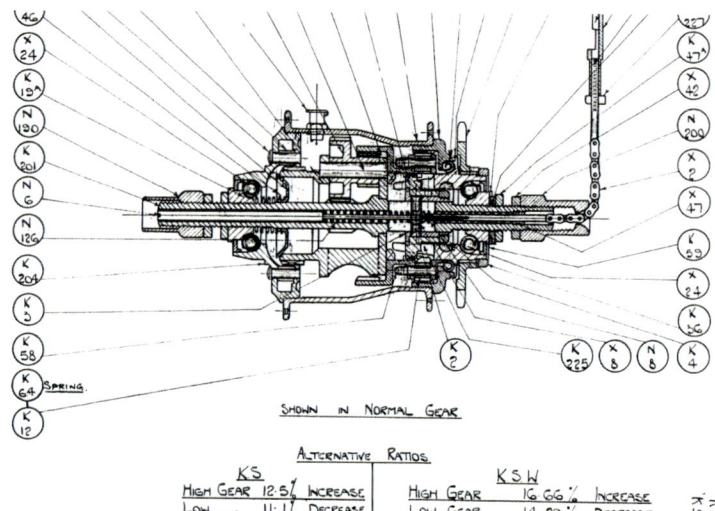

Fig. 10.14. Sectional drawing of the KS and KSW hubs.

## K series tools and prices

The type K special tools were used for the KS and KSW, and there was also a special spanner for the sprocket locking ring.

In 1934 the KS, KSW and KB sold for £1 11s. (£95 today) including controls, whereas the standard type K was a mere £1 2s. 6d. (£69 today). For an extra 1s. (£3 today) the K could be supplied complete with quick-release wing-nuts. At this time all four hubs were available in nickel, chrome or black finish; the nickel option was deleted about 1935 as chromium plating became the new standard for brightwork.

In common with all K series hubs, the KS and KSW incorporated integral freewheel mechanisms and a spring hold-off device intended to prevent drive slipping between gears. However, the comments in the second paragraph of the section of Chapter 9 headed 'Later modifications to the type K' also apply to the KS and KSW.

## K series tandem hubs

Sturmey-Archer's pocket manual for hub types K, KS and KSW stated on the cover that all

Fig. 10.15. The type KT 3-speed with 110 mm drum brake for tandem use.

three were 'Suitable for Solos or Tandems'. In spring 1932 Sturmey-Archer claimed that the KB was also suitable for tandem use but there must have been many who were unconvinced. To satisfy sceptical tandemists Sturmey-Archer designed a 3-speed and drum brake combination specifically for their use. In autumn 1934 works manager William Raven announced that he had developed tandem versions of the KB 3-speed with drum brake (type KT), the BR single-speed rear brake hub (type BRT) and the BF front brake hub (type BFT). The committee swiftly sanctioned manufacture of all three hubs.

### KT wide-ratio 3-speed and drum brake

The KT tandem hub was a wide-ratio 3-speed combined with a heavy duty hand-operated drum brake. The gear section was based on the type K but included a stronger nickel-chromium steel driver and planet pinions. The brake diameter was increased to 4⅜" (110 mm) and the drum was riveted to a standard plain diameter type K shell.

The KT weighed 4 lb 3 oz (1.9 kg); cable brake control added 9 oz (255 gm), whereas cable-cum-rod weighed 15 oz (425 gm). The KT used the same handlebar or top tube gear controls as the other hubs.

The hub width over the cones was 4⅞" (124 mm) for a 1½" (38 mm) chainline. If a 1¾" (44 mm) chainline was required, an axle ½" (13 mm) longer was used with a special packing piece. The hub used threaded sprockets: these were available with 16, 17, 18, 19, 20 and 22 teeth, and there were versions for ⅛" and 3/16" chains.

Special tools available from Sturmey-Archer for the KT hub comprised a screwdriver for the indicator rod, a cone spanner with a 'C' end for the left cone adjusting washer, and a spanner for the left cone and axle sleeve nut.

### BRT & BFT drum brakes

Just as the LBF and LBR drum brakes had been developed in parallel with the KB 3-speed drum brake, so the BRT and BFT tandem drum brakes were evolved alongside the KT hub. The BFT (Brake Front Tandem) weighed 2 lb 10½ oz (1.2 kg), cable control adding another 7½ oz (213 gm). The BRT (Brake Rear Tandem) was ½ oz. lighter than the BFT, but its necessarily longer cable control weighed 9 oz (255 gm). The BRT gave a 1¾" (44 mm) chainline and was advertised 'as suitable for the fitting of the Derailleur gear'. Both hubs were drilled for 40 spokes of up to 12 gauge.

Fig. 10.16. The type BFT tandem front drum brake.

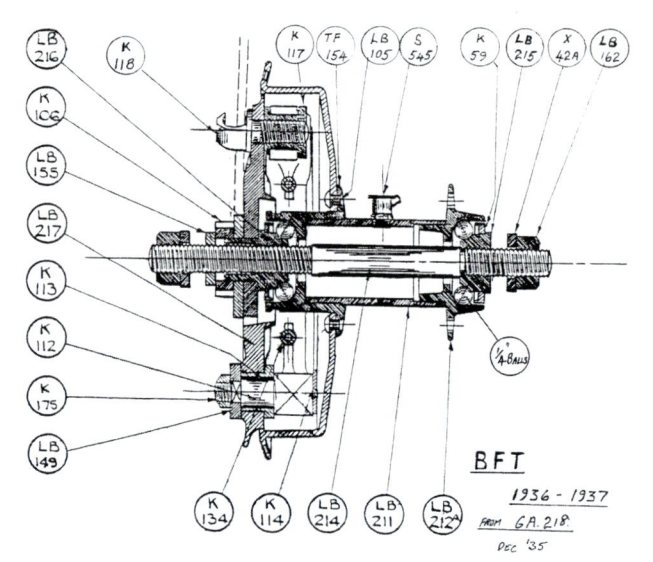

Fig. 10.17. Sectional drawing of an early BFT tandem front drum brake.

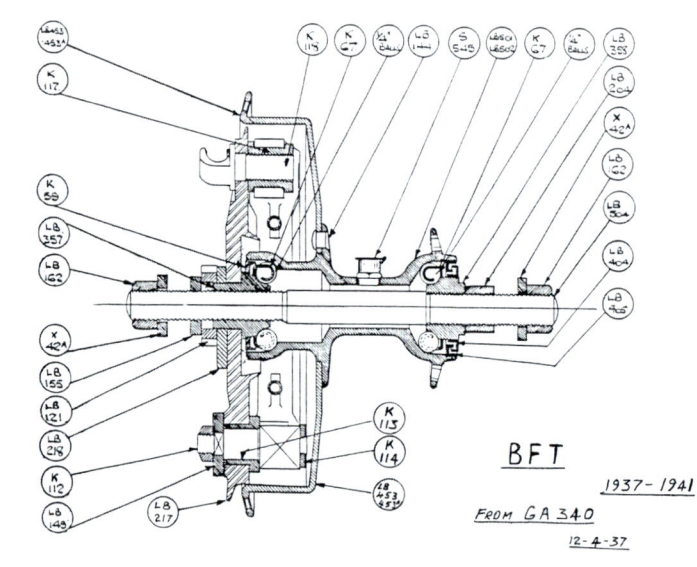

Fig. 10.18. Sectional drawing of a later BFT tandem front drum brake.

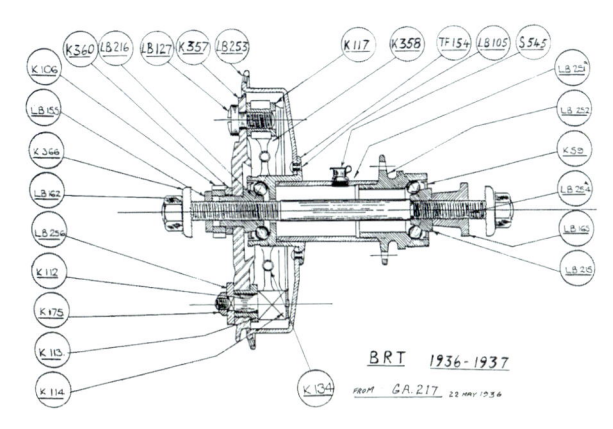

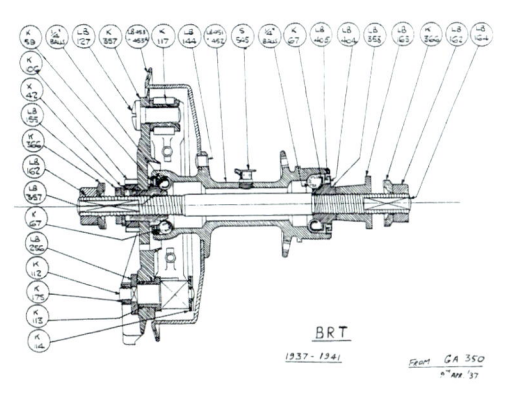

Fig. 10.19. Sectional drawing of an early BRT tandem rear drum brake.

Fig. 10.20. Sectional drawing of a later BRT tandem rear drum brake.

## Rivals galore

By the mid 1930s a number of improved derailleur gears were on sale in Britain and were gaining ground at Sturmey-Archer's expense. The Brown Brothers catalogue for 1934 showed a Pelissier available in 2-speed and 3-speed versions for solos or tandems, and 2-speed, 3-speed and 4-speed Cyclo derailleurs, including the Super Cyclo constructed of duralium. At this time both Pelissier and Cyclo were imported from France. Also in the catalogue was the British-made Trivelox 3-speed derailleur which optionally could be obtained combined with a drum brake. It differed from the other derailleurs in that it maintained a straight chainline while the sprockets moved sideways to change gear.

By 1935 several prestigious records, including the Land's End to John O' Groats, had been taken from Sturmey-Archer by riders using 3-speed Cyclo derailleur gears. The End-to-End was broken in 1934 by the Australian Hubert 'Oppie' Opperman; in the same year Frank Southall took most of the medium distance RRA records.

Sturmey-Archer had other rivals too. The 1934 Brown Brothers Catalogue featured Fichtel & Sach's 2-speed version of the Torpedo coaster brake. In spring 1936 The Cyclist reviewed the BSA DP (Dual Purpose) gear, a 2-speed hub that could be switched from freewheel to fixed while in use. Another rival was the Villiers 2-speed gear, reviewed as an 'entirely new type' in *The Cyclist* early in 1936. Low gear was direct drive but high gear was achieved via a second short chain that ran from the hub to a countershaft. The Villiers gear allowed an increase over direct drive of 10–36%, depending on the sprockets fitted, but was normally supplied equipped for a 24% rise. The gear was described as very popular and weather resistant. At only 15s. (£45 today) it was also relatively cheap.

The Frost gear, reviewed in *The Cyclist* in spring 1936, was built into a standard drum brake casing. Changing down necessitated freewheeling, followed by taking up the drive with a sharp flick of the pedals; changing back up to high gear also required freewheeling, followed by a gentle take-up of drive. *The Cyclist* also reviewed the German Adler 3-speed, a layshaft gear built into the bottom bracket. The reviewer felt unable to comment on its efficiency but the claimed advantages were 'more solid and frictionless drive through the substantial gearwheels on the shafts, and greater durability and freedom from trouble'. The Adler gave relatively close ratios: 12% increase, direct drive and 20% reduction. It was quite heavy and required a specially built bicycle frame. The expanding chainwheel also returned, this time in the form of the Nealeson 5-speed gear, designed by a team led by engineer W. Neale and intended to run in an oil-bath gearcase. According to *The Cyclist*, there was no immediate prospect of general availability.

At the Paris Salon in 1937 the Varlax 30-speed expanding chainwheel gear was displayed. It was produced from 1932 to 1938 but did not achieve great popularity. Another French chainwheel gear was the Milpat, introduced in 1935. It was housed in a casing, the chainwheel being internally toothed and driven by long ratchet arms from the eccentrically positioned crankshaft. The angle of the ratchet arms could be altered by means of a control with 12 settings: typical gears thus offered spanned 53 to 100 inches.

The above gears were by no means the only options available by the mid 1930s and it is clear that bicycle gearing was in a state of flux again. But Sturmey-Archer's main rivals were double-sided reversible hubs and increasingly refined derailleurs.

## T series 2-speeds

In spring 1933 GB patent 417,272 was filed by Raleigh and works manager William Raven. This covered a simple 2-speed hub, with a pressed metal shell, that gave direct drive and a lower gear. The mechanism was housed in a drum on the right hand side of the hub. The driver was integral with the gear ring, and the drum of the shell formed the planet cage. The sun was rotatable and slidable on the wheel axle. For high gear (direct drive) the sun was clutched into, and thereby locked to, the hub shell but was free to rotate on the axle. For low gear the sun slid sideways into a fixed sleeve on the wheel axle; this locked the sun to the axle which meant that the planet cage (the hub shell) rotated slower than the combined driver and gear ring.

The T series 2-speeds incorporated a spring hold-off mechanism that deferred gear changing until pedal pressure was eased. A slack control cable gave high gear and there was an indicator rod in the left end of the axle, the toggle chain being on the right. The patent stated: 'By this invention we are able to provide improved two speed gearing for use with pedal or motorcycle hubs in a very simple and convenient manner.' The patent's reference to motorcycle hubs is ironic, as the company had ceased production of motorcycle hub gears many years earlier.

This was Sturmey-Archer's first 2-speed hub. Their original success was largely due to their introduction of a reliable 3-speed at a time when others could only offer 2-speed hubs. It was a little ironic that the market now seemed to demand the reinvention of William Reilly's 2-speed Hub: Sturmey-Archer's new gear was remarkably similar in concept to that pioneering product.

Fixed wheels were back in vogue and, fitted with quick-release wing-nuts and a quick-release cable, the new hub could provide most of the advantages of a double-sided reversible hub while eliminating the need to remove and reverse the wheel each time a change of gear was required.

The new 2-speed was launched in the summer of 1933 as the TF (Two-speed Fixed). It gave direct drive and a 25% reduction. From spring 1935 the gear could also be supplied with a freewheel sprocket fitted to the driver; in this case it was known simply as the type T. William Raven offered samples of the new hub to the organisers of the international Brooklands cycle race and in return received favourable feedback. Sturmey-Archer technical literature described the T and TF hubs as 'designed expressly for the lightweight enthusiast, who requires a strong and reliable hub, which will provide the necessary variance of ratio'.

Fig. 10.21. Press advertisement for Sturmey-Archer's stand at the 1933 Cycle Show at Olympia in London. It includes the new 2-speeds.

Fig. 10.22. Type TF 2-speed.

The Hub of the Universe

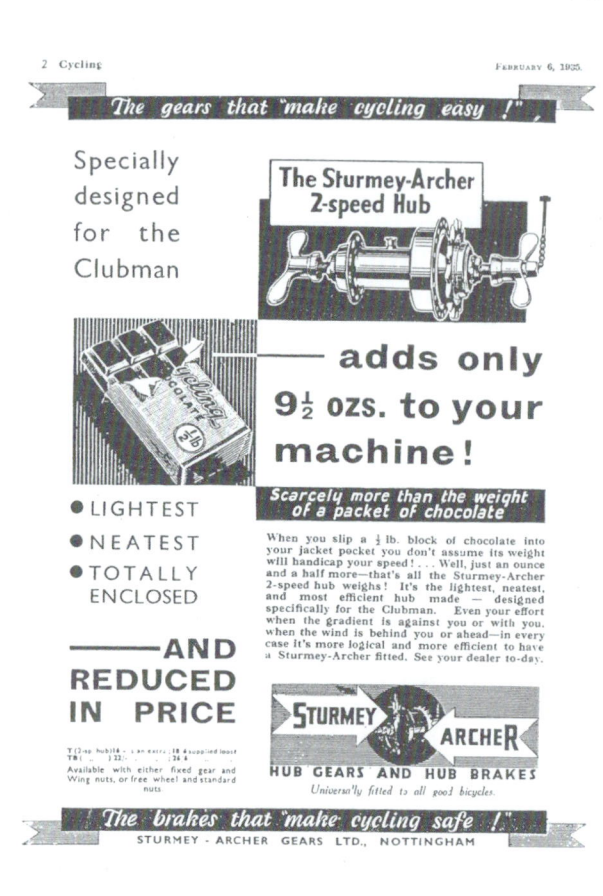

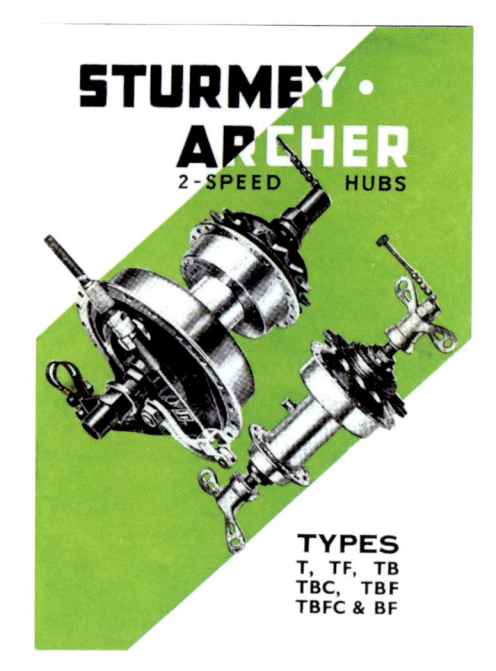

Fig. 10.25. T series leaflet.

Fig. 10.23. Press advertisement for the T series hubs.

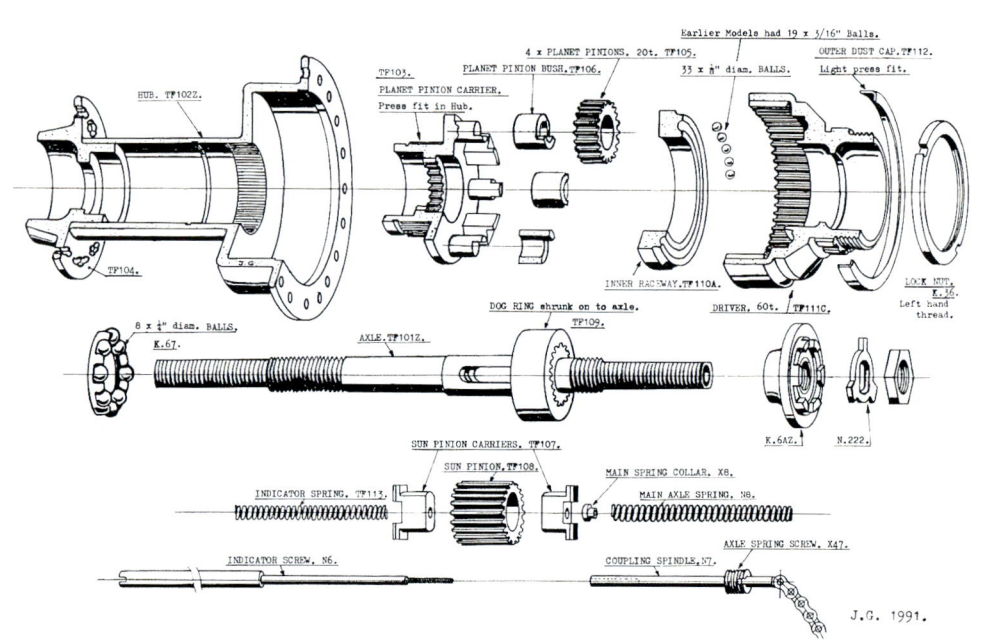

Fig. 10.24. Exploded cutaway drawing of the type T by Jim Gill.

The gears were certainly light, adding only a few ounces to the weight of a single-speed hub. The T version weighed 1 lb 12 oz (794 gm), and the TB weighed 2 lb 15 oz (1.33 kg). The fixed wheel versions were 3 oz (85 gm) lighter. The control systems were similar in design and weight to those for other contemporary Sturmey-Archer hubs.

In spring 1933 William Raven announced that he had in mind, at some time in the future, to do away with threaded drivers (the component on which the sprocket is mounted) and move to a splined design; 12-lug sprockets with a threaded locking ring were first used later that year on T series 2-speeds. These sprockets were available with 14–20 and 22 teeth; freewheels for the splined driver were supplied with 16–20 teeth. The spoke drilling options and the over locknut dimension were the same as for the type K.

An early modification to the design involved the inner ball race. Early hubs had nineteen 3/16" ball bearings 'perched' in place; by 1934 this had been changed to thirty-three ⅛" balls in a track, making assembly easier.

In 1939 the T and TF hubs cost 19s. 6d. (£54 today) each, supplied loose; they added 16s. 9d. (£46 today) to the cost of a new bike.

## T Series 2-speed and drum brake combinations

The drum brake design pioneered in the KB, LBF and LBR hubs, was wedded to the new 2-speed to produce the following variants:

TBF – 2-speed fixed wheel with rod-operated drum brake.
TB – 2-speed freewheel with rod-operated drum brake.
TBFC – 2-speed fixed wheel with cable-operated drum brake.
TBC – 2-speed freewheel with cable-operated drum brake.

## Raven tests derailleurs

At the management committee's behest, in spring 1935 William Raven agreed to produce a sample derailleur gear but there is no further mention of this in the minutes. But almost a year later he announced that 'he had tested the friction in the Derailleur or Trivelox as compared with our hub gear, and that in no case was the friction greater on a new S-A hub gear than on the other types, and [it] was certainly a great deal less after weather and wear had made their impression on both types'.

## TC close-ratio 2-speed

Early in 1936 Raven told the committee that he was working on a 2-speed close-ratio hub. George Wilson supported this idea which he thought would help combat competition. The resultant hub was called the TC (Two-speed Close-ratio), the subject of GB patent 473,205 applied for in spring 1936 by Sturmey-Archer and William Brown.

The construction and design of the TC had little in common with other hubs in the T series but it was included in that category because it was a 'sporting' gear. The TC's designer, William 'Jock' Brown, was an ingenious Scotsman who lived at 59 Orston Drive, Wollaton Park, Nottingham and who became manager of Sturmey-Archer's design and development section in 1935. He was to be responsible for some of the most successful hubs in Sturmey-Archer's history.

In spring 1936 samples were sent to the cycling papers for review. The TC became generally available in the summer and George Wilson received a letter of appreciation from

Fig. 10.26. The TBF 2-speed drum brake.

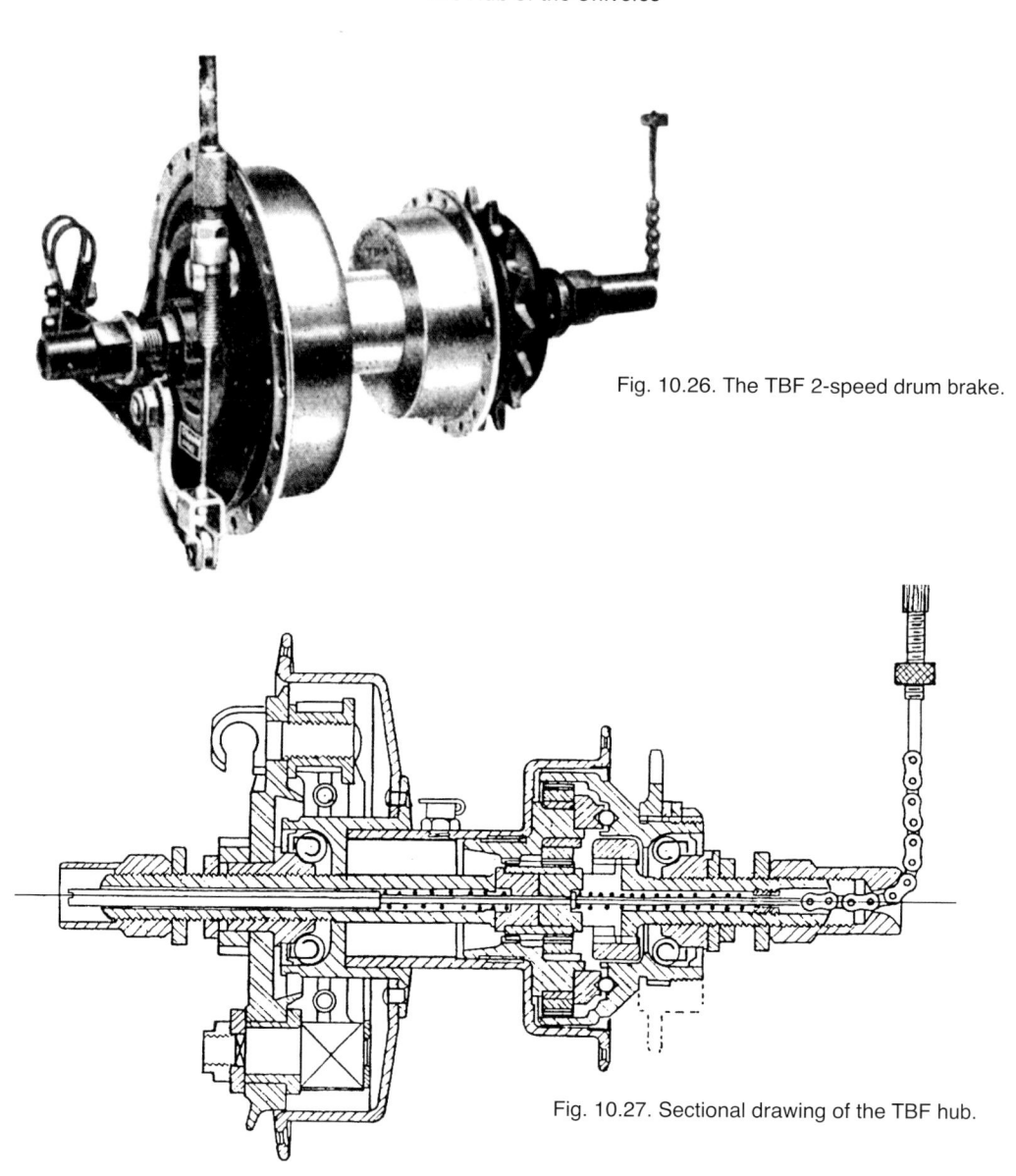

Fig. 10.27. Sectional drawing of the TBF hub.

a rider who used the new hub in the Isle of Man race.

The TC was a freewheel close-ratio 2-speed that gave direct drive and a drop of 13.46%. Typical gears offered were 64 and 55" or 90 and 78". Sturmey-Archer's literature described this as 'the equivalent to a sprocket difference of two teeth' and stated that 'the gear change is remarkably easy and rapid'. The TC had a fixed sun and, unlike other T series hubs, used compound planet pinions. In early hubs the axle and all pinions were of hardened and tempered nickel-chrome steel.

Unlike other hubs in the T series the shell of the TC was a simple cylinder. The chainline could be varied between 1½" (38 mm) and 1⅝" (44 mm) with a fixed wheel or 1½" (38 mm) and 1⅜" (41 mm) if a freewheel was fitted. However, a longer axle could be fitted to give an extra ¼" (6 mm) across the cones; in this case a 1¾" (44 mm) chainline was possible even

Fig. 10.28. Poster for the 1933 product range.

with a freewheel. The toggle chain and indicator arrangements were similar to those on the other T series hubs. The TC weighed 2 lb 5 oz (1.05 kg), and sold for the same price as the T and TF hubs.

GB patent 473,205 showed that a third gear could be obtained from a TC type gear by introducing a second sun engaged with the smaller steps of the compound planet pinions. Both suns would be in constant mesh but one or other could be clutched to the axle to give two different low gears; the gear would become a double epicyclic but with a single, shared gear ring. Top gear would be direct drive.

An alternative 3-speed configuration, outlined in the same patent, used triple compound pinions (three steps per pinion). In this variant the two suns were engaged with the two larger steps, the smaller step meshing solely with the gear ring. By this means the two lower gears could be even closer in ratio.

Fig. 10.29. 'Proved efficiency' advertisement, showing Raven's test rig.

Fig. 10.30 and Fig. 10.31. Two advertisements from 1936 promoting the KS 3-speed as superior to 'chain gears' (derailleurs).

Fig. 10.32. William Brown.

Fig. 10.33. The TC close-ratio 2-speed hub.

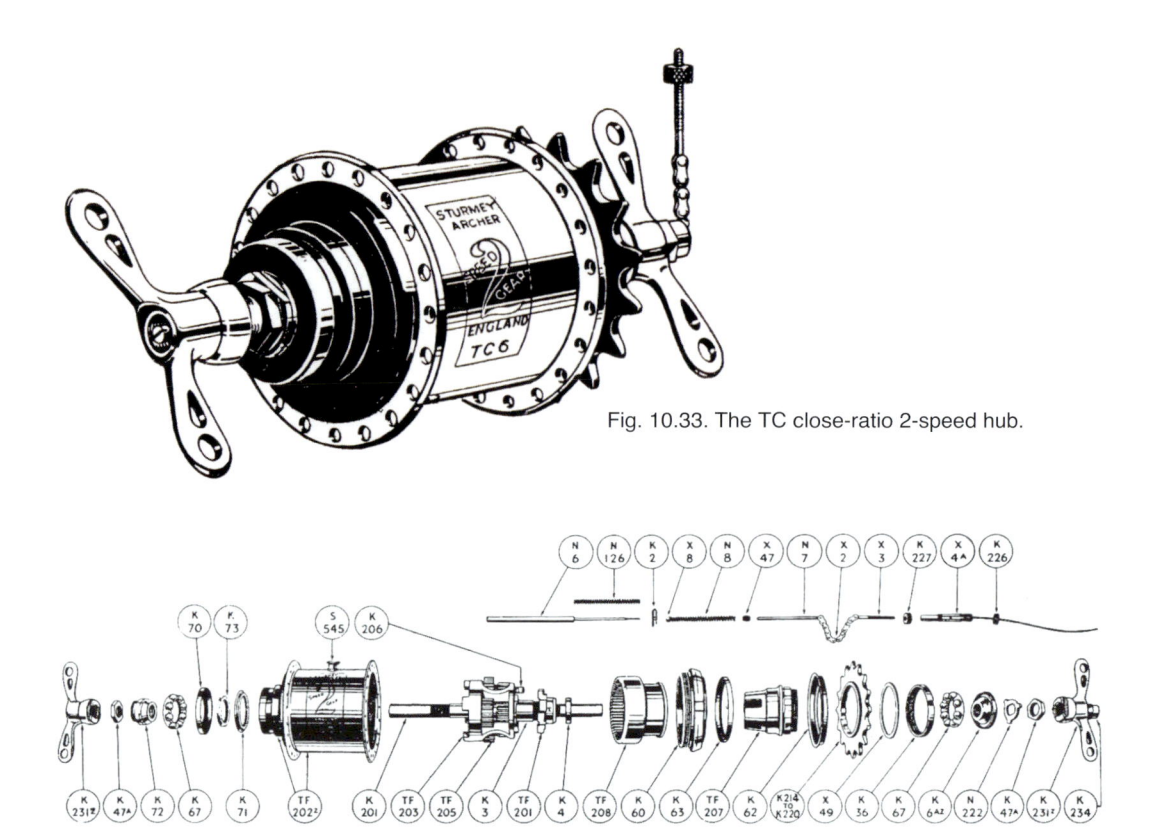

Fig. 10.34. Exploded view of the TC hub.

## AR ultra-close-ratio 3-speed

In autumn 1936 Sturmey-Archer and William Brown applied for GB patent 483,992 covering an ingenious ultra-close-ratio 3-speed. The aim was to produce a close-ratio gear capable of withstanding heavy stresses relative to its size. It was claimed to be especially durable because of the low relative speeds of its moving parts, its wide bearing surfaces and the large number of pinion teeth in mesh. The first of the A series hubs, it was designated the AR, the initials apparently standing for 'A-series Racing'.

The AR incorporated two epicyclic trains but combined them in a novel way. The secondary train gear ring was fixed to the left side of the primary train planet cage; the secondary planet cage was extended to the right, to form the sun of the primary train. The sun of the secondary train was fixed to the wheel axle.

The effect of this system was to rotate the sun of the first train in the direction of rotation of the driver. Rotating the sun the same way as the driver was equivalent to using a much smaller sun or a significantly larger gear ring in an ordinary wide-ratio 3-speed, without the practical disadvantages of added weight or mechanical weakness. The result was a much closer ratio 3-speed than hitherto, giving a 7.24% rise and a 6.76% drop relative to direct drive. Typical gears offered were 93, 100 and 107" and the hub had an integral freewheel.

The AR was advertised as 'designed expressly for fast road work' and being 'absolutely weather-proof, trouble-proof, and a revelation in easy and effortless gear changing. No other

Fig. 10.35. The type AR ultra-close-ratio 3-speed. Note the early pattern quick-release side entry cable connector.

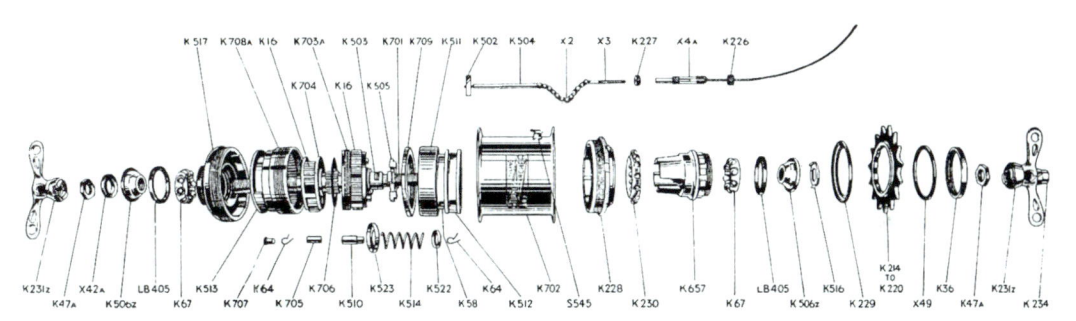

**TYPE AR 3-SPEED**
1936 - 1942 close ratio.
-6.76/direct/+7.24%

Fig. 10.36. Exploded view of the type AR hub.

gear can possibly give sweeter, easier, or more effortless riding.' It came complete with quick-release cable and wing-nuts and cost £1 9s. (£85 today) loose or £1 5s. 3d. (£74 today) when fitted to a new machine.

The AR weighed 4 oz (113 gm) more than the standard AW 3-speed (described below) but had the same dimensions over the cone locknuts and the same chainline options. It used the new 12-lugged sprockets. Early ARs had the toggle chain on the right with an indicator rod on the left; this was later modified to a combined indicator and toggle chain assembly on the right, as in the AW 3-speed. The AR was discontinued in 1942.

## AM medium-ratio 3-speed

In spring 1937 William Raven reported that tests on a replacement for the KSW hub had proved very satisfactory. In the summer it went into production as the type AM medium-ratio hub, the initials standing for 'A-series Medium-ratio'. That autumn Sid Ferris used the AM when he broke the 24-hour record on a Raleigh fitted with this hub. Weekly sales of AM hubs reached 2,000 by spring 1939: William Raven remarked that this 'must be affecting the position of the Derailleur gear'. According to Sturmey-Archer the new hub was: 'Designed to meet the exacting demands of the clubman and other enthusiastic sports riders. Particularly suited for massed start racing.'

Fig. 10.37. 1937 double-page spread advertising records gained by riders using the AR hub.

Fig. 10.38. Mid-1930s Sturmey-Archer oil can.

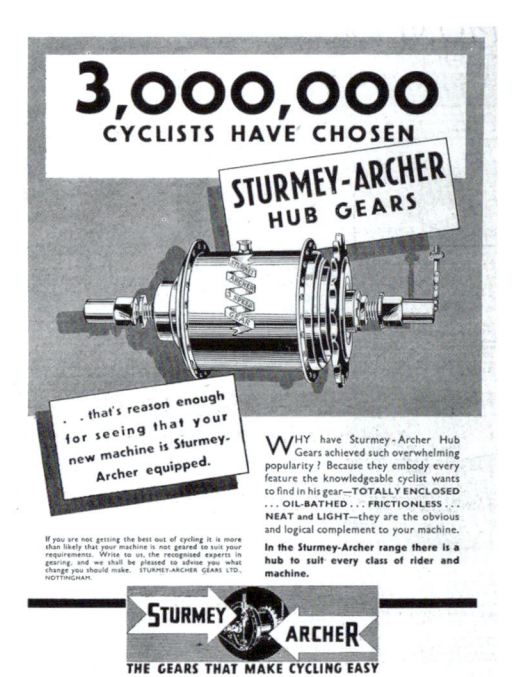

Fig. 10.39. 1936 press advertisement proclaiming sales of more than 3 million Sturmey-Archer hub gears.

Fig. 10.40. The AM medium-ratio 3-speed.

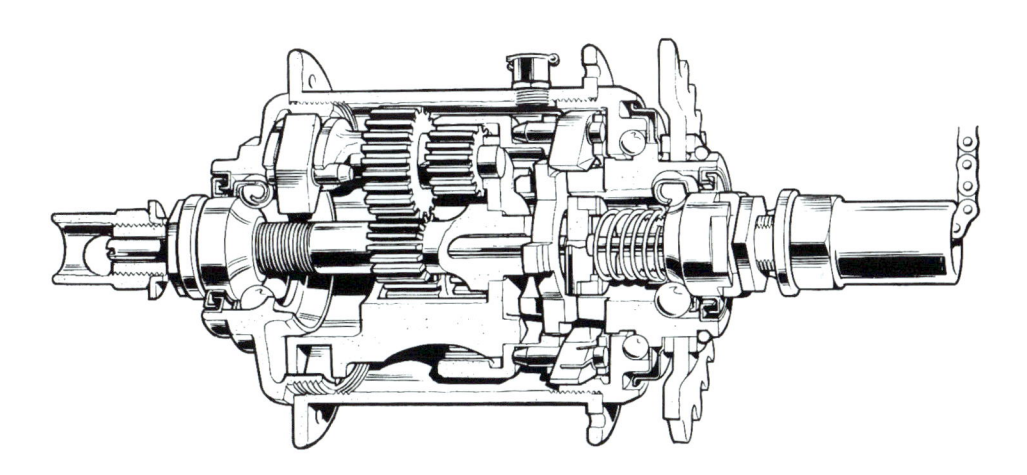

Fig. 10.41. Cutaway drawing of the AM hub.

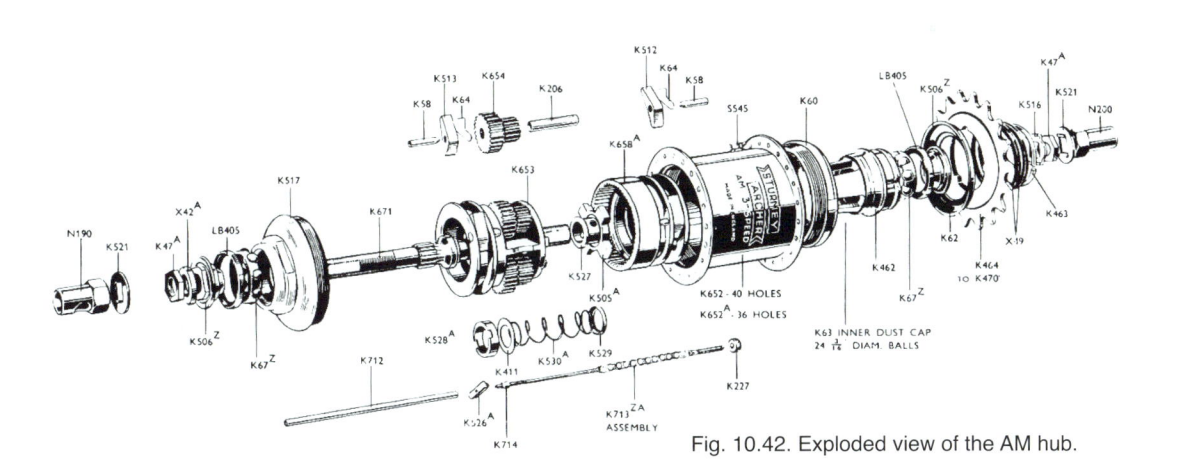

Fig. 10.42. Exploded view of the AM hub.

133

Fig. 10.43. A pair of AW 3-speeds: one with the original threaded driver, the other with the three-splined driver.

The AM was broadly similar in operation to a standard 3-speed but used compound pinions to narrow the ratios. It gave an increase over direct drive of 15.55% and a decrease of 13.46%; typical gears offered were in the order of 59, 68 and 79". The toggle chain was on the right and in early versions was combined with an indicator rod, as with the AW 3-speed. But in 1939 the design was modified slightly and a separate indicator rod was provided in the left of the axle: this was flush with the axle end when middle gear was selected.

The AM was fitted as standard with quick-release wing-nuts and a quick-release cable connection. It weighed 2 lb 6 oz (1.08 kg) and used the same range of splined sprockets as the AR. The hub was usually supplied with the standard over locknut dimension (4 5/16") but a longer axle was also available, in solo or tandem quality. In 1939 the AM cost £1 6s. (£72 today) supplied loose and added £1 3s. (£64 in 2017) to the cost of a new machine.

## AW wide-ratio 3-speed

In summer 1936 William Raven expressed his complete satisfaction with a new 3-speed hub. This became the AW (A-series Wide-ratio). The AW gave the same ratios as the K and was its successor. It was an outstandingly successful component: with many minor modifications over the years, and a brief break in the 1950s, it was produced until 2001.

The AW was cheaper to produce than the K, more durable and easier to service. By spring 1937 it was being fitted only to Raleigh bicycles: Sturmey-Archer intended supplying other manufacturers from the autumn onwards. But in the summer *Cycling* published a test of the type K, probably at Sturmey-Archer's instigation in a bid to clear stock. The AW was not widely available until 1938 and that summer *Cycling* featured a photograph of a disassembled AW that had been tested by Dunlop for 10,000 miles (16,100 km).

From the rider's point of view, the most noticeable difference between K hubs made before 1935 and the AW was the new hub's lack of a spring hold-off device to delay gear changing until pedal pressure was eased. As with late type Ks, there was a 'no-drive' position between second and third gears.

Sturmey-Archer literature referred to the AW as being of broadly similar pattern to the original Sturmey 3-speed Hub, which was true inasmuch as both were single train epicyclic 3-speed hub gears. It had the same ratios as the K: a decrease of 25% and an increase of 33⅓% relative to middle gear (direct drive). The new 3-speed was an ounce (28 gm) lighter than its predecessor and in 1939 sold for £1 3s. 9d. (£66 today). It added £1 1s. (£61 today) to the cost

Fig. 10.44. Sectional drawing of the AW 3-speed.

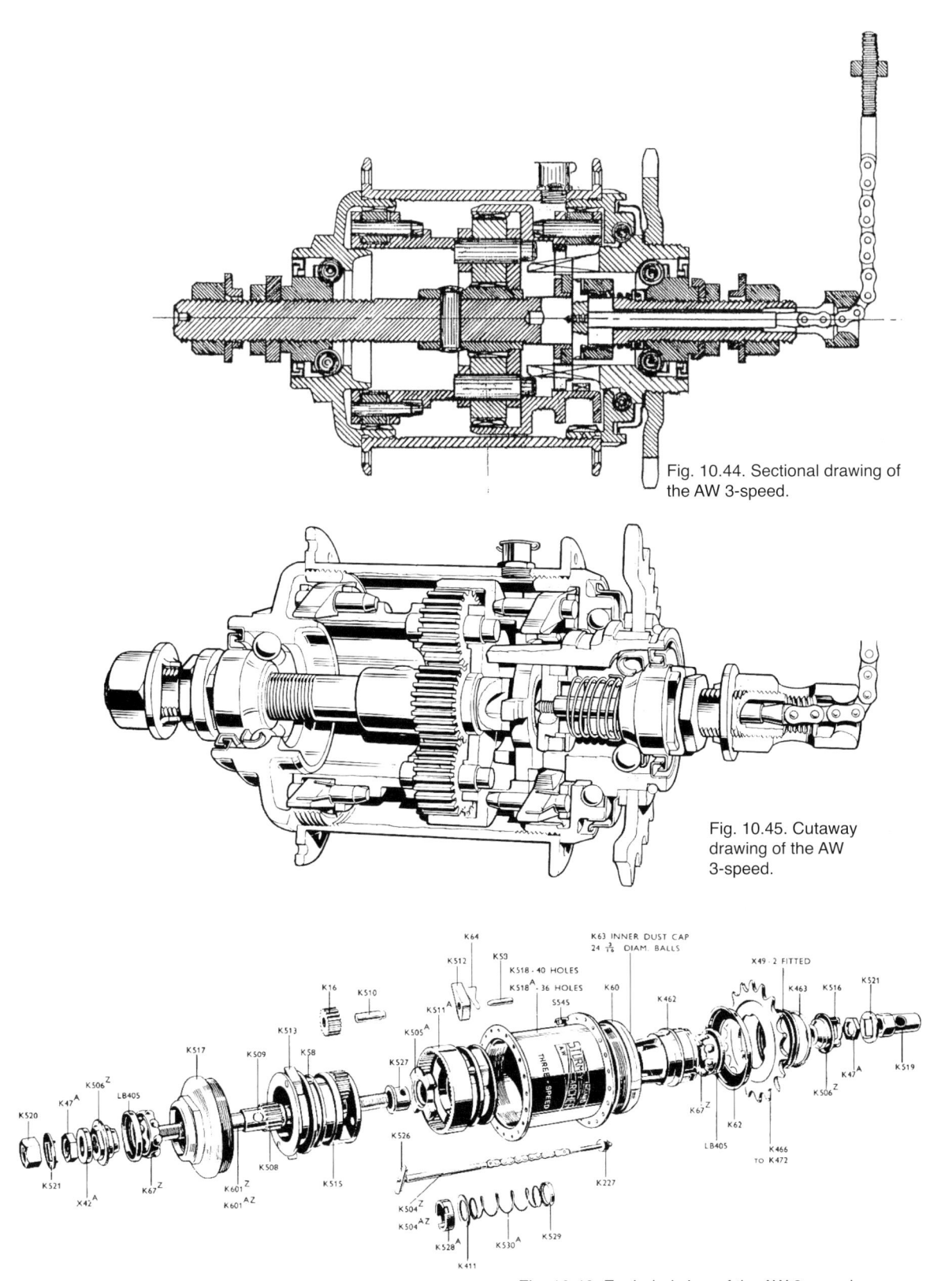

Fig. 10.45. Cutaway drawing of the AW 3-speed.

Fig. 10.46. Exploded view of the AW 3-speed.

Fig. 10.47. Flowchart for the AW 3-speed.

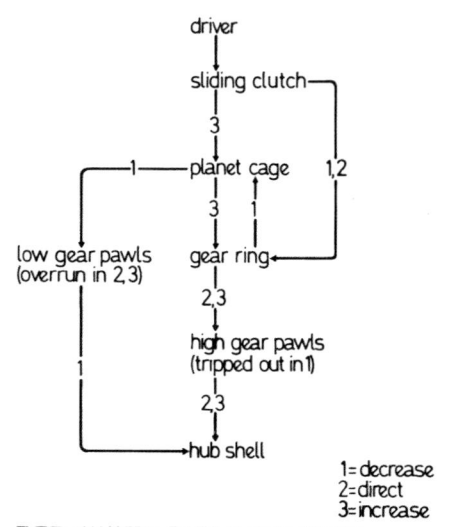

**TYPE AW WIDE-RATIO THREE-SPEED**
The AW has a simpler sliding clutch than the type K, more durable but necessitating a 'no drive' position between gears 2 and 3.

of a new bike, so it was still 'the gear for a guinea'.

The AW measured 4 5/16" (110 mm) across the cone locknuts but this could be reduced by ¼" (6 mm) by omitting the right-hand locknut and left packing washer. The chainline adjustment and sprocket range were similar to those of the type K. The AW was advertised as 'entirely dustproof' and 'suitable for tourist, sports and all types of roadster and tandem machines'.

The AW's four-prong driver was stronger than the six-prong K type. The use of the planet pins as drive dogs (where the K used specially formed dogs on the planet cage) made the

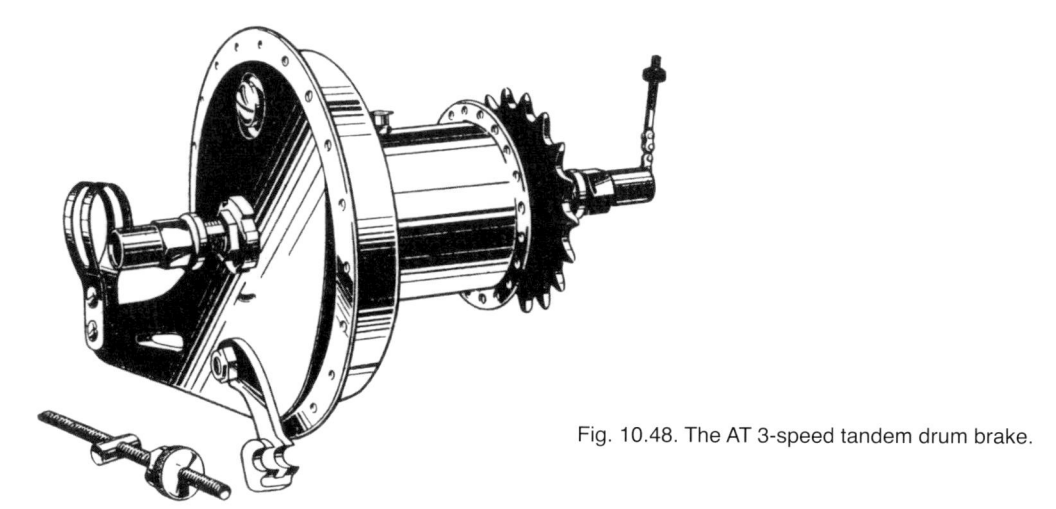

Fig. 10.48. The AT 3-speed tandem drum brake.

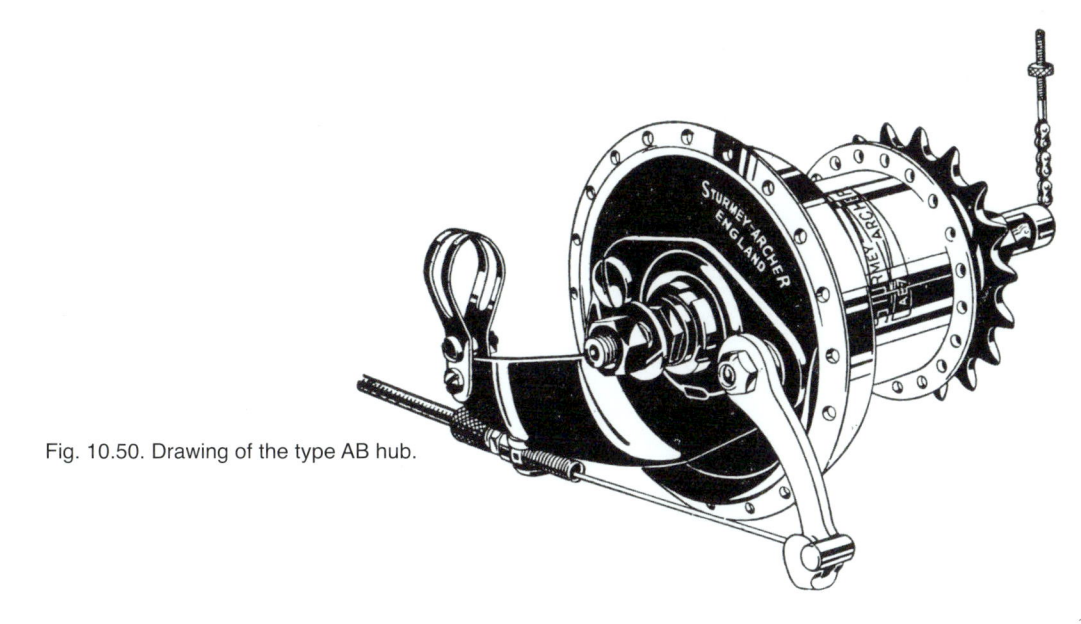

Fig. 10.49. The AB 3-speed drum brake and brochure.

need to replace the planet cage less likely. The low gear pawls were mounted on the planet cage assembly (rather than in the left-hand ball cup) and were therefore easier to replace.

The gear adjustment indicator was integral with the toggle chain assembly in the right-hand end of the axle and not, as with the K, a separate item in the left end.

### AT and ATC wide-ratio 3-speed tandem drum brakes
Tandem riders had the option of the AT and ATC hubs which combined the AW gear with a large diameter 4⅜" (110 mm) drum brake. They replaced the KT in 1938. Both new hubs

Fig. 10.50. Drawing of the type AB hub.

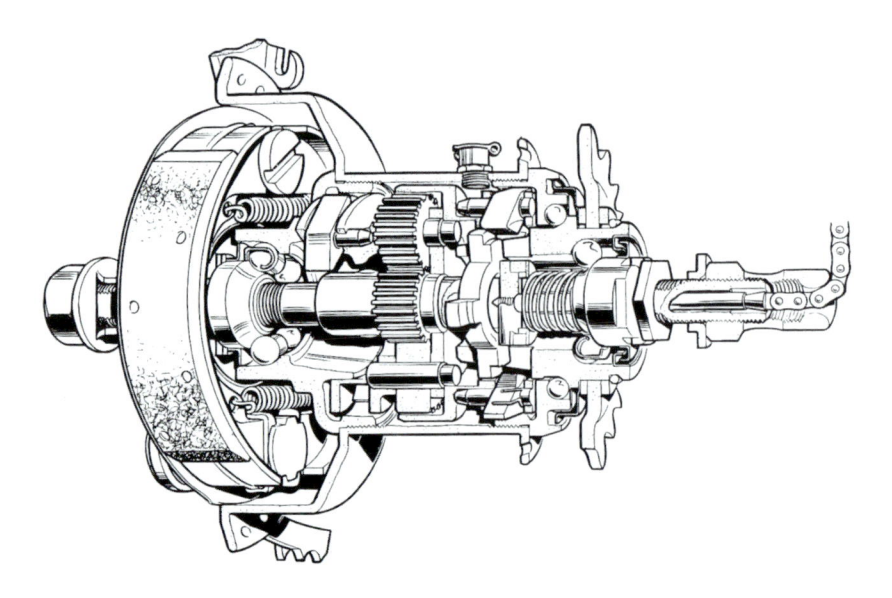

Fig. 10.51. Cutaway drawing of the AB 3-speed drum brake.

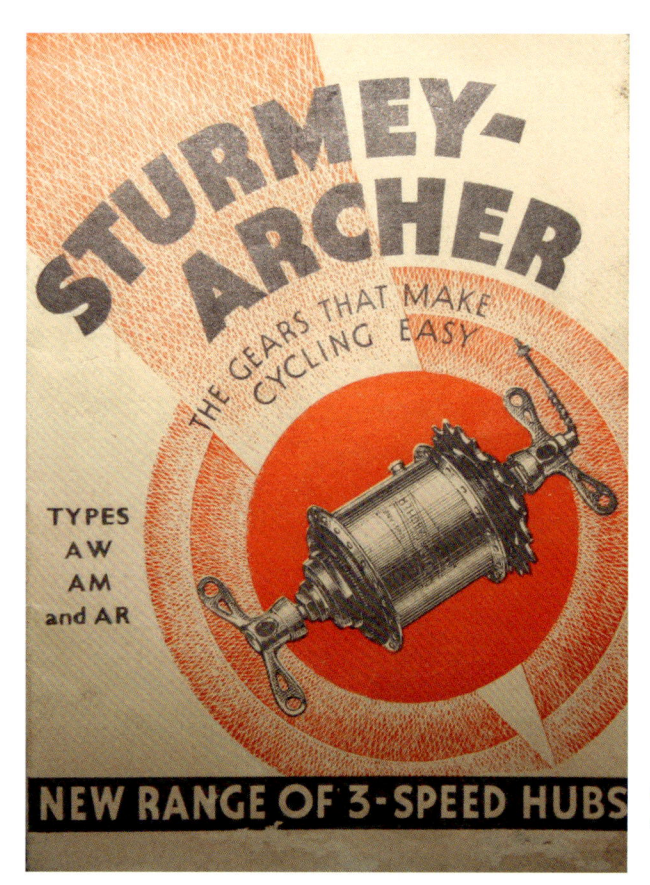

Fig. 10.52. Brochure for the new A-range of 3-speed hubs.

Fig. 10.53. Poster showing a comprehensive range of Sturmey-Archer hubs, six of them being drum brake variants.

had nickel-chromium sun and planet pinions for extra strength. The AT's brake was operated by a cable-cum-rod system whereas the ATC was an all-cable version. Sprocket and chainline options were the same as for the AW. In 1939 the AT and ATC each cost £ 15s. (£97 today) loose and added £1 8s. 6d. (£79 today) to the cost of a new tandem.

### AB and ABC wide-ratio 3-speed drum brakes
The new A range also catered for riders of solo machines who preferred drum brakes. The AB and ABC hubs replaced the KB in 1938: the AB was rod-operated, the ABC cable-controlled. The gear section was based on the AW but like the KB it had a narrow planet cage to make space for the brake mechanism, which was similar to the KB's. The 1939 price of the new brake hubs was £1 12s. 6d. (£90 today) and the added cost on a new cycle was £1 7s. 6d. (£76 today).

### Series A hub shells
With the exception of those versions incorporating a drum brake or hub dynamo, all series A hubs had plain cylindrical shells, many of which were interchangeable.

### Drum brakes continue
After Sturmey-Archer ceased to make coaster brakes (about 1936) lever-operated drum

Fig. 10.54. Advertisement for the Dynolamp (DDRN 4-11-13-20-1).

Fig. 10.55. Dynolamp advertisement, emphasising the reflector design.

brakes continued in production. The L prefix (for 'lever-operated') was dropped and the following designations were used for specific applications: BF – front drum brake, rod-operated; BFC – front drum brake, cable-operated; BR – rear drum brake, rod-operated; BRC – rear drum brake, cable-operated; BRD – rear drum brake, rod-operated, suitable for derailleur gears; BRCD – rear drum brake, cable-operated, suitable for derailleur gears; BFT – front drum brake for tandem; BRT – rear drum brake for tandem; BRTC – rear drum brake for tandem, suitable for derailleur gears. In 1939 the front brake hubs for solo machines cost 13s. 9d. (£38 today) loose; the rear hubs were 1s. 6d. (£4 today) dearer. The BFT cost 17s.

(£47 today) in 1939; the BRT was 18s. 6d. (£51 today).

## Dynolamps

In spring 1935 Raleigh and their employee Albert Victor Lafbery of Uplands, Coach Road, Wollaton, Nottingham applied successfully for a patent on a new type of dynamo (GB 452,940). Fixed rigidly to the seat stay was a dynamo casing, from which protruded a flexible drive shaft on which was a drive pulley to engage with the rear tyre. The pulley was fitted with a catch to enable it to be held clear of the tyre when the dynamo was not in use. The dynamo casing also housed a dry battery for use when stationary.

The GL1 Dynolamp, based on this patent, was a combined headlamp and dynamo launched by Raleigh in 1935 that fitted on the front fork. The tyre pulley was on the underside of the dynamo and output was 6 volts. In 1938 the more powerful 12 volt GL2 was introduced. The GL1 and GL2 both had 2.5 volt pilot bulbs. It was claimed that the Dynolamp gave 'a powerful light even at walking speed'. Raleigh registered the name Dynolamp as a trademark in autumn 1936 but cancelled the registration the following spring.

In February 1936 Raleigh entered into an agreement with H. Miller & Company of Birmingham and Frederick John Miller of Sutton Coldfield whereby Miller would make the Dynolamp for Raleigh. This was because of Miller's patent rights for electric lighting sets for cycles. It soon became apparent that these patent rights had been anticipated but Raleigh considered it politic to give Miller some orders nonetheless. Meanwhile, the committee decided to proceed with in-house manufacture of 5,000 Dynolamps.

It was agreed with Miller that Raleigh would accept all deliveries up to the end of March 1937 after which all outstanding deliveries would be regarded by both parties as cancelled. The 1937 Raleigh cycle catalogue featured the Dynolamp prominently.

By the end of 1937 Raleigh had 15,000 Dynolamps in stock. The committee wanted a special effort to sell these to clear the way for a new dynamo in the hub. This proved problematic because the agreement with Miller only allowed Raleigh to sell Dynolamps as original equipment. In spring 1938 Raleigh proposed an agreement whereby they could sell Dynolamps as separate items for a year at a royalty of 6d. per unit (£1.50 today). Miller did not respond for months and it is unclear whether this agreement was finalised. In autumn 1939 George Wilson negotiated with Currys for them to take the whole stock of Dynolamps at 8s. each (£22 today).

## Dynohubs

In autumn 1935 Raleigh and George William Rawlings of Willow Meer, Park Hill, Kenilworth, Warwickshire filed a patent for the hub dynamo concept (GB 468,065). Rawlings was an independent inventor responsible for a number of patents relating to dynamos. In summer 1936 he applied independently for GB patent 481,585, which covered improvements to magneto-electric machines, the primary objective being 'to provide a simple means of obtaining load voltage/speed regulation combined with high specific output in a small dynamo suitable for use in the electric lighting system of a cycle or motorcycle'.

While the Dynolamp was still evolving Raleigh started lengthy negotiations with Rawlings. These were not helped by the particularly complex situation regarding his various patents. In spring 1936 the committee decided to offer him £500 (£30,000 today) on account of the £2,250 (£135,000 today) due to him as a cash payment on signing of the proposed agreement with Raleigh. The committee decided to manufacture a hub dynamo regardless of the patent

Fig. 10.56. The Mk 1 Dynohub (12-volt).

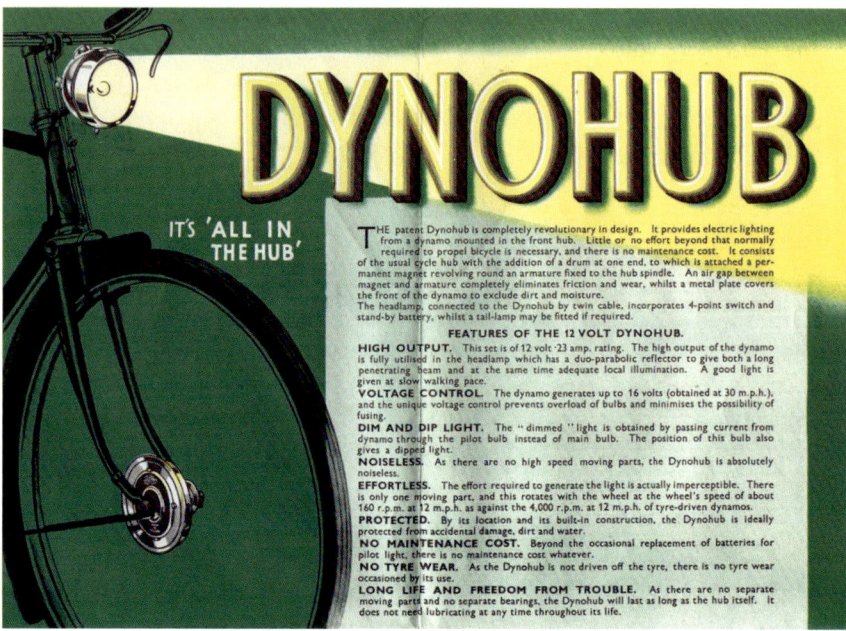

Fig. 10.57. An early Dynohub advertisement.

situation, as it would give Raleigh a year's start on its competitors. Soon Raleigh entered a formal agreement with Rawlings for a licence under five patents to manufacture a combined lamp and dynamo set.

In summer 1936 Raleigh started a 1,000-mile (1,600 km) test on a prototype hub dynamo, the product being given the name Dynohub (sometimes one word, two words or hyphenated). The committee sanctioned production that autumn. Raleigh chairman and managing director Sir Harold Bowden, works director William Raven and director George Wilson tested a sample of the hub in its final form. A Raleigh test rider, apparently Bert James, had a Dynohub fitted

Fig. 10.58. A pair of Mk 3 (8-volt) Dynohubs.

to a lightweight cycle and reported that he could not feel any appreciable drag when using it.

At the end of 1936 Rawlings agreed to spend four days at the works supervising production. The following month the committee debated whether to opt for a version of the Dynohub housed in the 4⅜" (110 mm) tandem brake drum shell or in the standard 3½" (90 mm) brake drum pressing. Raven and Rawlings agreed that it was not feasible to use the smaller shell, so the first Dynohubs were made to the larger size. Raven later complained of a lack of support from Rawlings and in spring 1937 took production out of his hands.

That year patents for Rawlings' specific 'magnet principle' were applied for in Australia, Belgium, Czechoslovakia, Denmark, France, Germany, India, the Irish Free State, Italy, Japan, the Netherlands, New Zealand, Sweden and Switzerland, and separate applications were instigated for the general principle of the hub dynamo in France, Japan and the Netherlands. Raleigh and Rawlings also applied for a patent in India covering improvements relating to magneto-electric machines.

In summer 1937 Raleigh formalised a supplementary agreement with Rawlings in connection with manufacture of a combined lamp and dynamo. This probably explains the cancellation of the Dynolamp trademark. Meanwhile Raven reported to the committee that a Philips representative had shown him a patented dynamo with much greater output than Rawlings' Dynohub. A further meeting was held with Philips but it later transpired that the improved output was largely due to a specific Philips bulb. When the bulb was fitted to the Dynohub it gave almost as good a light. Raleigh therefore initially ordered the expensive special Philips bulbs before switching to a much cheaper but satisfactory alternative from Survita.

As production of the Dynohub was initially limited, the committee decided that for the 1938 season only one Raleigh model would be fitted with it. Thereafter Raleigh would get preference for supplies but the hub would be offered to the trade as soon as possible. Meanwhile experiments were under way with a more compact Dynohub that could be housed in the smaller diameter brake drum pressing.

## Dynohub Mk 2

In autumn 1937 William Raven reported that the first 30 production Dynohubs had been completed. Soon Rawlings announced that his design had been improved to give a good light at much lower speed. Raven therefore decided to make the first 5,000 hubs to the original Mk 1 pattern, followed by 20,000 to the new Mk 2 pattern.

Rawlings made another independent patent application that autumn: this was for GB patent 504,800 which covered improvements to laminated magnetic elements. Sir Harold Bowden meanwhile received a request from Germany to build the Dynohub under licence. It was agreed that they could be made on the Continent on a royalty basis of 10%.

Early in 1938 it appeared that Rawlings' improvements, which involved a new armature design, constituted a new invention and so were not covered by his existing agreement with Raleigh. Rawlings was prepared to grant Raleigh the rights insofar as they applied only to bicycles. Raven was meanwhile authorised to produce tail lamps for the Dynohub.

There was more discussion of foreign royalties early in 1938 when target royalty figures were agreed for France, Germany, the USA and the rest of the world. George Wilson consulted with Raleigh's Continental representatives Baker, Fay & Baker. The directors resolved to offer Rawlings £500 (£28,000 today) and 10% royalties on turnover with a minimum of £2,000 (£114,000 today) per annum after the second year for his patent for all foreign countries except Germany, France and the United States. For France and Germany they offered £1,000 (£57,000 today) plus 10% on turnover with a minimum of £4,000 (£230,000 today) per annum after the second year; the terms for the United States were to be discussed later. Rawlings stood to make a fortune.

Raven felt that Raleigh and Humber cycles (which Raleigh now owned) should have exclusive UK use of the Dynohub for some considerable time, any surplus production being exported. George Wilson foresaw big overseas sales, particularly in Denmark, the Netherlands, Norway, Sweden and Switzerland.

## Dynohub Mk 3

The smaller Mk 3 Dynohub (8-volt rather than 12-volt) had meanwhile been successfully tested. By spring 1938 production of the Mk 2 Dynohub was about 550 a week; trouble was experienced magnetising the hub but Rawlings and Raven worked together to overcome the problem. Mk 2 production reached 1,000 a week in the summer and sanction was given to produce the lightweight Mk 3. That autumn George Wilson offered the German firm Haeckel a licence to make Dynohubs.

In 1938 Raleigh granted power of attorney to divide a Rawlings Japanese patent application into two separate patents. The Japan-based lawyer they chose was Walter Augustus de Havilland, father of the actresses Olivia de Havilland and Joan Fontaine and uncle of the aviation pioneer Sir Geoffrey de Havilland.

By the autumn 1938 more than 23,000 12-volt Dynohubs had been made and 94 of the new lightweight 8-volt units. Raleigh then discovered that Lucas were experimenting with their own hub dynamo. A propaganda coup came in October when Sid Ferris broke the 24-hour record using the Mk 3 Dynohub during hours of darkness; apparently the first British road race record broken using a dynamo.

## Legal tussles

Lucas and Miller showed their own hub dynamos at the national show in autumn 1938. Early

Fig. 10.59. Mid-1930s 'Good Fairy' poster advertising Sturmey-Archer hub gears and drum brakes.

## Cycling can be made more pleasant still

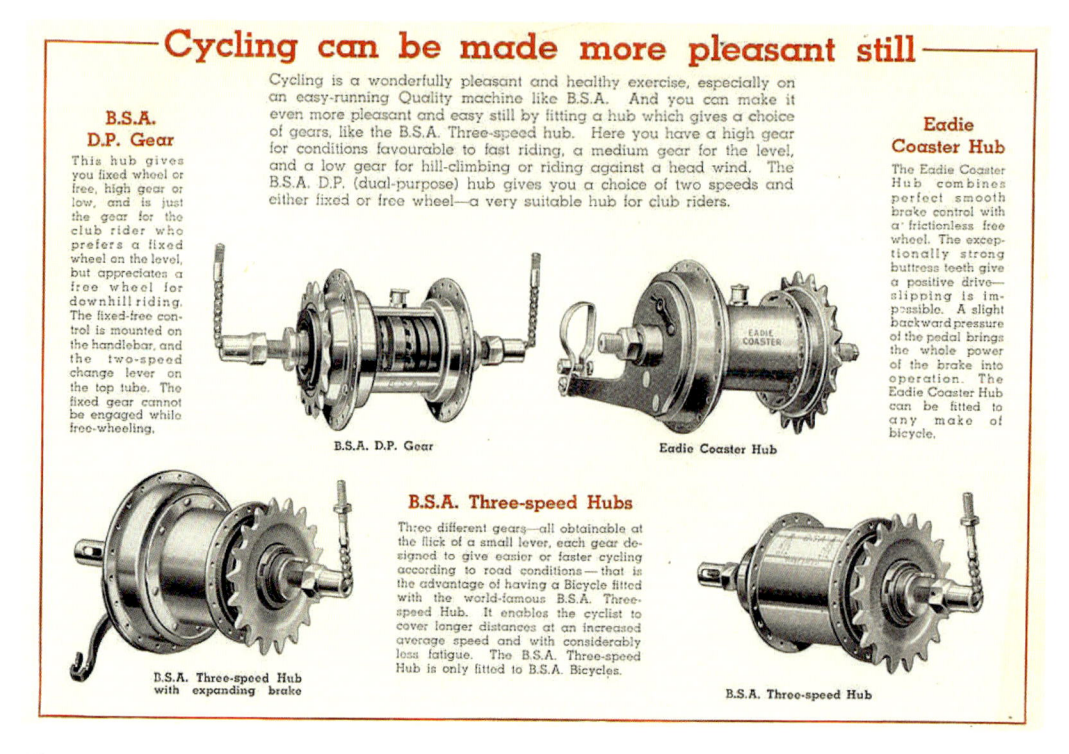

**B.S.A. D.P. Gear**
This hub gives you fixed wheel or free, high gear or low, and is just the gear for the club rider who prefers a fixed wheel on the level, but appreciates a free wheel for downhill riding. The fixed-free control is mounted on the handlebar, and the two-speed change lever on the top tube. The fixed gear cannot be engaged while free-wheeling.

Cycling is a wonderfully pleasant and healthy exercise, especially on an easy-running Quality machine like B.S.A. And you can make it even more pleasant and easy still by fitting a hub which gives a choice of gears, like the B.S.A. Three-speed hub. Here you have a high gear for conditions favourable to fast riding, a medium gear for the level, and a low gear for hill-climbing or riding against a head wind. The B.S.A. D.P. (dual-purpose) hub gives you a choice of two speeds and either fixed or free wheel—a very suitable hub for club riders.

**Eadie Coaster Hub**
The Eadie Coaster Hub combines perfect smooth brake control with a frictionless free wheel. The exceptionally strong buttress teeth give a positive drive—slipping is impossible. A slight backward pressure of the pedal brings the whole power of the brake into operation. The Eadie Coaster Hub can be fitted to any make of bicycle.

B.S.A. D.P. Gear            Eadie Coaster Hub

**B.S.A. Three-speed Hubs**
Three different gears—all obtainable at the flick of a small lever, each gear designed to give easier or faster cycling according to road conditions — that is the advantage of having a Bicycle fitted with the world-famous B.S.A. Three-speed Hub. It enables the cyclist to cover longer distances at an increased average speed and with considerably less fatigue. The B.S.A. Three-speed Hub is only fitted to B.S.A. Bicycles.

B.S.A. Three-speed Hub with expanding brake            B.S.A. Three-speed Hub

Fig. 10.60. BSA's range of hub gears and drum brakes in the late 1930s, including the DP, a 2-speed fixed-free hub. BSA was Sturmey-Archer's only serious competitor as a hub gear maker in the English-speaking world.

in 1939 Raleigh received counsel's opinion that they had a good case against Miller and Lucas for patent infringement. Both companies initially responded that they were prepared to fight. Lucas later declared that they no longer wished to make a hub dynamo but by the end of the year it became apparent that they had got round the patents. Although litigation continued beyond the main period covered by this chapter, it is convenient to describe it here.

Concentration on the war effort delayed resolution of the dispute with Miller for years. Early in 1943 Raleigh's solicitor wrote to Miller's lawyer notifying that legal action was proceeding and suggesting it be confined to the hub dynamo patent rather than also including the magnet patent. This was agreed and Raleigh offered a nominal licence to Miller for use of the magnet patent. But that autumn Raleigh's lawyer died and the dispute went into abeyance until after the war.

At the May 1948 Raleigh management committee meeting George Wilson reported that the House of Lords had granted permission for an appeal to be heard regarding an amendment to the key Dynohub patent, GB 468,065. This was heard by Mr Justice Vaisey, the outcome being described by Wilson as 'most satisfactory'. In the light of the Lords' decision Wilson had an off-the-record conversation with Mr Miller and the dispute appeared to be resolved.

In spring 1949 the matter was finally settled when the Court of Appeal amended GB patent 468,065 under Section 22 of the Patents and Designs Acts, 1946. The amendment meant that the general concept of the hub dynamo was not protected, only the specific design shown in

Fig. 10.61. Advertisement for the new trigger control.

Fig. 10.61a. Pre-production sample of a 3-speed 'flick' top tube control.

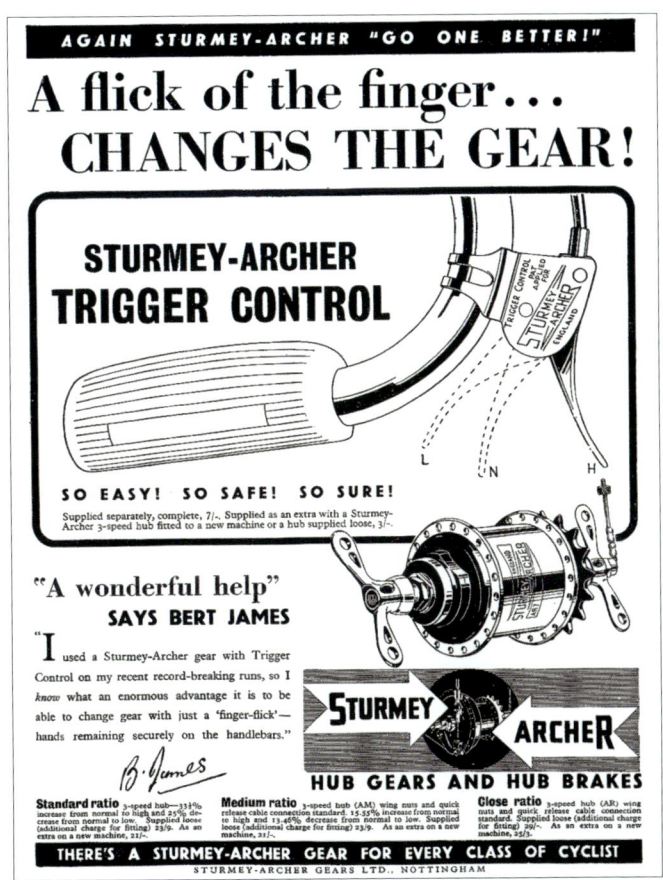

the patent. So other manufacturers were free to market rival products: the best known of these was the BSA Hublite which was offered in an alloy-shelled deluxe version. In 1952 the Patent Office granted an extension of six years on GB patent 468,065.

## Dynohub development continues

At the end of 1938 Rawlings made another solo patent application, this time for GB patent 522,749 covering improvements to the manufacture of overlapping laminated electro-magnetic elements. This related to one of his earlier patents, GB 504,800.

At the start of 1939 Raleigh and William Brown of Sturmey-Archer applied for a patent for a hub with two drums, one for an internally-expanding brake, the other for a hub dynamo. A prototype was produced but did not go into production. Not until the early twenty-first century did Sturmey-Archer market such a hub, by which time Raleigh no longer owned the company.

In spring 1939 Raleigh and George Rawlings made a further patent application, this time for improvements in apparatus for magnetising permanent magnets. The technique involved a very brief electrical surge from a direct current supply. In the summer Raleigh and William Raven applied for a patent for a combined lamp holder and switch, but this application does not appear to have been successful. The committee meanwhile decided to offer both the 12-volt and 8-volt Dynohubs in the 1940 catalogue. Soon in excess of 82,000 12-volt and more than 17,500 8-volt units had been made; they were selling exceptionally well.

In autumn 1940 the committee learned from Rawlings that a new steel developed by Philips could be used with the Dynohub, so that the 8-volt unit would give a better light than the 12-volt. The committee was divided over whether to continue building up a stock of Dynohubs for the post-war period (which was expected to be very difficult) or to keep supplying them loose and on new models. George Wilson, since 1938 managing director of Raleigh, took the former view, whereas director Alfred Simpson took the latter. Sir Harold Bowden, still chairman of Raleigh, left it to Wilson to decide in consultation with the other directors.

By spring 1942, when production ceased for the rest of the war, the total number of Dynohubs constructed was about 200,000. By 1943 Raleigh had fewer than 5,000 12-volt units in stock but almost 30,000 8-volt. They were running down the stock of 12-volt hubs first and holding onto the smaller-diameter 8-volt units. Sir Harold Bowden advised periodic testing of the stock to ensure that no deterioration had taken place.

Sturmey-Archer were meanwhile working on an electric bell, accumulator and concealed wiring for use in conjunction with Dynohubs. The bell never went into production but the accumulator eventually did. In autumn 1944 Cyril Clarkson reported that new experiments with the Dynohub had greatly increased its light output. But as far as the public were concerned there would be no news about these developments until after the war.

## Dimming circuits

In the 1930s cycle electrical lighting systems with a dimming facility were popular. Dimming was usually achieved by bringing into circuit one or more resistances, which wasted some of the available lighting power. In spring 1938 Raleigh and William Brown applied for GB patent 515,224 which concerned improved means of 'obtaining dimming in a novel and effective manner without … loss of efficiency'. It made use of the special qualities of dynamos with a 'high self-generated amperage limitation characteristic'. Instead of using additional and wasteful resistances, the new system used the differing resistances of bulbs of various voltage and amperage ratings. So a 2.5 volt, 0.3 amp pilot bulb would draw 0.75 watts, whereas a 12 volt, 0.23 amp main bulb would draw 2.76 watts. The new invention made use of this phenomenon in a suitably designed switching network.

## Improved lamps

Sturmey-Archer went further into lamp design than just the dimming circuitry: in summer 1936 they applied with William Brown for GB patent 532,205 which covered an improved form of 'vehicle lamp' construction. The glass front and attachment ring were permanently sealed together against moisture. A knob at the back of the lamp was connected to a threaded rod which could move the bulb holder assembly back and forth along the main axis of the lamp to produce the best beam.

## Trigger controls

In summer 1937 Sturmey-Archer and Charles Marshall filed GB patent 498,820 covering an improved handlebar-mounted control lever. (Marshall had been a noteworthy record breaking amateur rider and was involved in the adaptation of the type K hub for racing use.) The specification acknowledged that there were many known forms of control levers but noted that 'in most of them it is not impossible to pass an intermediate position and some skill or attention is required in their operation to avoid this'. The new design overcame this problem and was the basis of all Sturmey-Archer's subsequent triggers until 1985.

Early in 1938 William Raven announced that he was introducing the new trigger. It was agreed that an extra 1s. 6d. should be obtained from other manufacturers for the new control. That autumn Charles Marshall, who worked in Raleigh's cycle assembly section, was given an *ex gratia* payment of £75 (£4,300 today) for his work on the trigger and on Raleigh's special record-breaking cycles.

The new trigger was:

> A control lever mechanism comprising a stepped quadrant or like member, a pawl or stop engaging the steps of said member, and a lever … constrained in one direction of movement to move about a main pivot point and in the other direction of movement to move other than about such main pivot point whereby to effect relative disengagement of the pawl or stop and a step in the member.

This meant it was easier to use because, when going up through the gears, it could only flick from one gear to the next rather than sometimes jumping straight to the highest gear. The ergonomics had also been improved. The new trigger was available by spring 1938.

The familiar top tube control remained in production and like the trigger control underwent periodic cosmetic and minor detail changes. However, pre-production samples of 3- and 4-speed top tube controls based on the new trigger were produced and were mentioned in *Cycling* magazine early in 1940. A few pre-production examples exist but these designs were never put into mass production.

## Hub and derailleur hybrid gearing

After World War 1, the French cycle industry, centred at Saint-Étienne in a markedly more mountainous area than the English Midlands, took hybrid gearing seriously. In 1924 the Saint-Étienne cycle maker La Gauloise offered eight different ways of achieving six or more speeds via hybrid gearing arrangements. One of these combinations involved a 3-speed hub plus 2-speed or 3-speed rear derailleur, thus giving 6 or 9 speeds.

The Birmingham-based British Cyclo company was of French origin. In its 1935 catalogue Cyclo pointed out that an efficient 6-speed could be obtained with an existing 3-speed hub by two methods. If the existing sprocket was the screw-on type, simply replace it with a Cyclo screw-on twin-sprocket freewheel and fit a standard Cyclo rear derailleur mechanism. If the existing sprocket was the slide-on lugged type, a double chainwheel could be fitted and shifted via a Cyclo Rosa front derailleur mechanism.

In summer 1937 William Raven received a letter from the cycling writer Kuklos (W. Fitzwater Wray) suggesting that Raleigh sell a 2-speed derailleur to use in conjunction with a Sturmey-Archer 3-speed to give six speeds; Kuklos understood that BSA were to launch a similar device. The committee agreed that a derailleur converter could be exhibited at the annual show at Earls Court, London, if other firms did so. Raleigh considered approaching Cyclo to use one of their derailleurs but decided against it.

## Record breaking

While developing the various closer ratio hubs, Sturmey-Archer put together a racing team, the aim being to regain records lost to riders using other gearing systems. They signed up Sid Ferris, Bert James and Charles Holland: the combination of the new hubs and top riders proved potent. From June 1937 to October 1938 – a period of just 16 months – the team broke eight major records using the AM and AR 3-speeds.

Sid Ferris broke the Edinburgh–London record by 1½ hours, the Land's End–John O' Groats by nearly 2½ hours and the 1,000 mile record by more than 3 hours. The other winning margins were narrower but nonetheless impressive. Bert James took the London–Portsmouth–London, the Liverpool–London, the 12 hour, the London–York and the 100 mile record. Charlie Holland broke the Liverpool–Edinburgh and the Land's End–London records. Ferris, blind in one eye, used a Dynohub for the 15 hours of night riding involved in his successful Edinburgh to London ride.

The 1938 Isle of Man Tourist Trophy was won by a rider with a Sturmey-Archer hub. In 1939 Tommy Godwin used a Sturmey-Archer gear to break the year mileage record, with a total of 75,065 miles (120,805 km); he went on to cover 100,000 miles (160,900 km) in 499 days. Godwin's year record stood for almost 78 years until 2016 when American cyclist Kurt Searvogel exceeded it by just 11 miles (18 km). Godwin started his ride with a 3-speed Sturmey-Archer but soon switched to a 4-speed. According to a Sturmey-Archer advertisement published in 1940 the 4-speed enabled Godwin to increase his daily average mileage by a third, from 156 miles (250 km) a day to more than 200 miles (320 km).

### Advertising

Sturmey-Archer were quick to capitalise on their racing successes; their catalogues soon included enthusiastic comments from the record breakers. 'The frictionless running ensures maximum speed for minimum effort,' said Charles Holland of the AM gear. 'It's exactly what we racing men have always been looking for, a totally enclosed HUB gear with a really close ratio. I'll never ride without it,' said Sid Ferris of the AR.

The advertising men were also fond of unsolicited testimonials: the AR was 'a revelation in frictionless gearing', 'buying a bicycle without a Sturmey-Archer gear is like buying a car without a gearbox' and 'the drum brake has a wonderful silky feeling'. Not content with these accolades, the ad-men added their own: 'The rider who cycles for pleasure will find pleasure doubled, labour halved and speed increased.' The Sturmey-Archer gear could even reduce a girl's bill for hair setting lotion:

> If you watch … the girl who rides along with every hair in place and no streak of dishevelment … you will see on the handlebar or the top tube a little lever, and if you look very closely, you may observe that the hub of the back wheel is a little larger than usual.

### Fours and fives

As the decade drew to a close and the storm clouds of war brooded over Europe, Sturmey-Archer prepared to deliver what they hoped would be the *coup de grâce* in the battle of the gears. In autumn 1938 William Raven announced to the committee that Sturmey-Archer had developed a 4-speed hub: 'It embodies a very similar arrangement of gearing and selector mechanism and in much the same way provides close-ratio gearing, but it also embodies one or two additional ratios without additional gearing and provides also new characteristics and advantages.' This was the first product covered by GB patent 519,945 which Sturmey-Archer and William Brown filed the following month.

Fig. 10.62. The AF close-ratio 4-speed, shown here with a new type of quick-release cable connector.

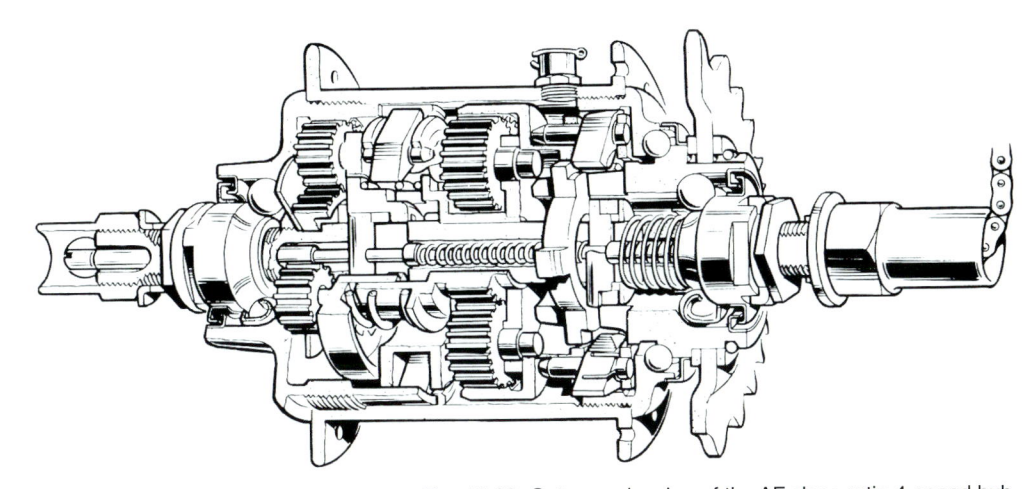

Fig. 10.63. Cutaway drawing of the AF close-ratio 4-speed hub.

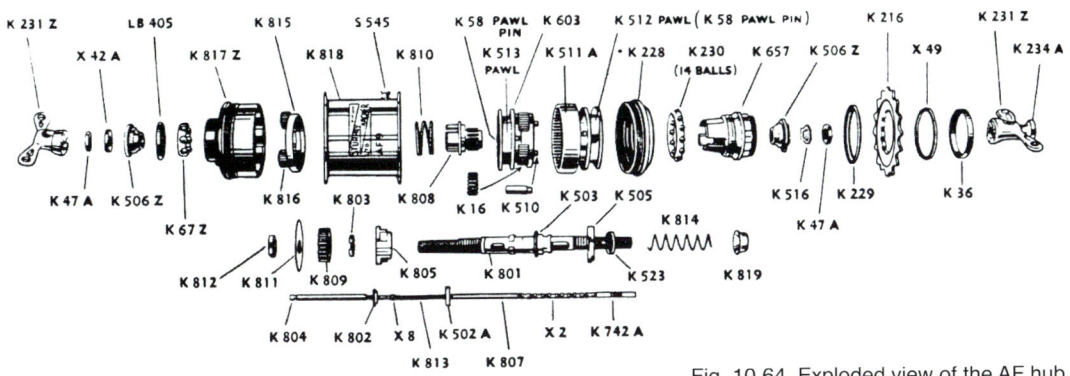

Fig. 10.64. Exploded view of the AF hub.

[Flowchart diagram with labels:]

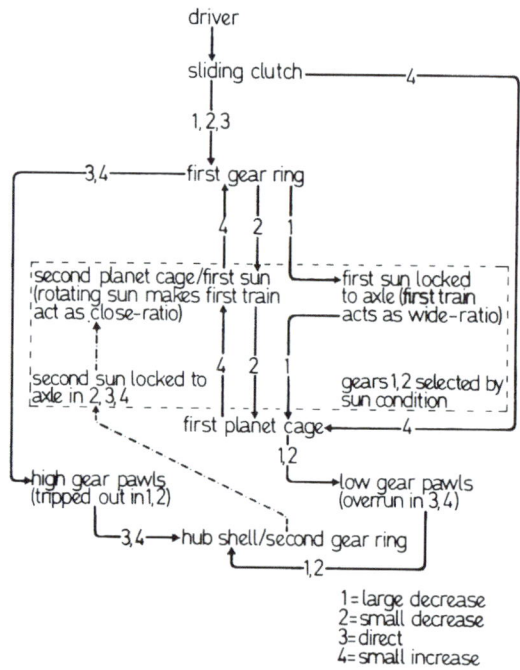

driver → sliding clutch → 1,2,3 → first gear ring

—3,4—

second planet cage/first sun (rotating sun makes first train act as close-ratio) → first sun locked to axle (first train acts as wide-ratio)

second sun locked to axle in 2,3,4

gears 1,2 selected by sun condition

first planet cage ← —4—

high gear pawls (tripped out in 1,2)

low gear pawls (overrun in 3,4)

—3,4→ hub shell/second gear ring ←—1,2—

1 = large decrease
2 = small decrease
3 = direct
4 = small increase

TYPE AF/FC CLOSE-RATIO FOUR-SPEED
The type AC ultra-close-ratio three-speed used a system based on gears 2, 3 and 4.

Fig. 10.65. Flowchart for AF close-ratio 4-speed.

## AF close-ratio 4-speed

Known as the AF (standing for A series Four-speed) and later as the FC (Four-speed Close-ratio), this gear fitted in the same shell as the AW and the AM. It was a close-ratio device to replace the AR 3-speed. William Brown was given an *ex gratia* payment of £120 (£6,600 today) for his development of this hub and the Dynolamp. In summer 1939 his salary was raised by £50 (£2,800 today) and he was offered a new employment agreement in recognition of his work on the A series hubs.

The AF was not ready for the 1938 national show but William Raven stated that in his view 'this hub would one day replace the existing type of 3-speed hub'. By early 1939 Raven considered it suitable for all sports models, hinting at a rationalisation of the Sturmey-Archer range. The committee promptly sanctioned manufacture.

In autumn 1939 Nimrod wrote in *Cycling* that his colleague The Speedman had 'suggested the ideal of a close-ratio 3-speed with a fourth lower gear for the bad pimples'. The top three gears of the AF were 9.1% increase, direct drive, and a reduction of 10%, almost as close as those of the AR, but there was also a substantially lower fall-back gear, giving a 25% decrease. The AF was advertised as being especially suitable for massed-start racing and time-trials, but also providing 'a very useful range of gears for the light tourist cycle'. Typical gears offered were 49, 59, 65 and 71" or 59, 71, 79 and 86."

The high, normal and low gears were obtained in the same way as in the standard 3-speed, except that the sun pinion of the main epicyclic gear train was rotated in the same direction as the driver by a secondary epicyclic train. This gave the effect of a smaller sun, resulting in

Fig. 10.66. The FM medium-ratio 4-speed.

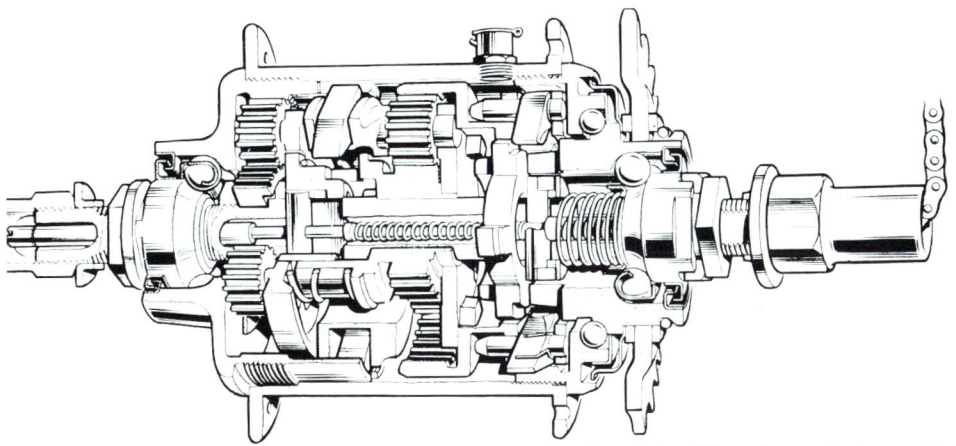

Fig. 10.67. Cutaway drawing of the FM medium-ratio 4-speed hub.

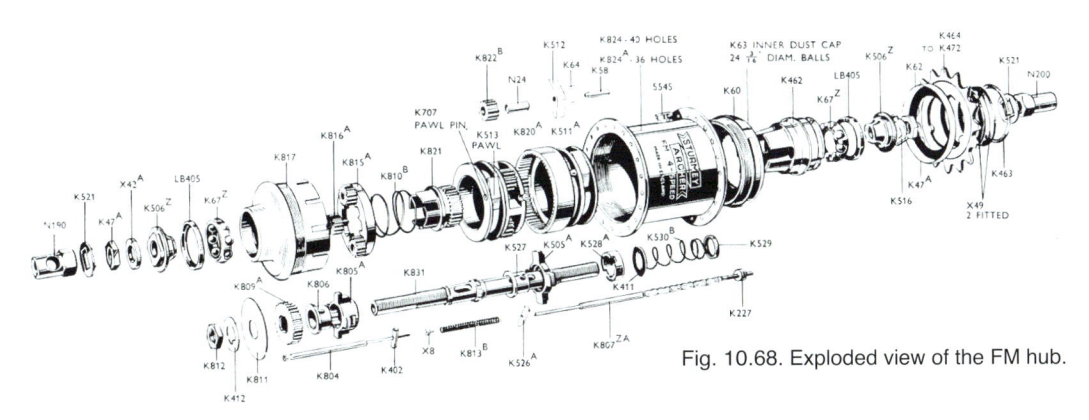

Fig. 10.68. Exploded view of the FM hub.

153

Fig. 10.69. The plaque awarded to Sturmey-Archer by the Cyclists' Touring Club in 1939 for developing 4-speed hub gears.

closer ratios for the top three gears, in much the same way as the AR 3-speed but with one important difference. The AF's secondary gear ring was fixed to the hub shell whereas that of the AR was fixed to the primary planet cage. Therefore in high gear the AF's secondary gear ring was moving faster than the AR's in its comparable gear, so the primary sun rotated faster giving the effect of a relatively smaller sun and therefore a closer spacing between high gear and direct drive. Conversely in second gear the AF's secondary gear ring was moving slower than the AR's in its comparable gear so the primary sun rotated slower, giving the effect of a relatively larger sun and therefore a wider spacing. For lowest gear the primary sun of the AF was declutched from the secondary planet cage and instead locked to the axle, giving a wider ratio.

The AF weighed 2 lb 5¼ oz (1.06 kg). Wing-nuts and an 18 tooth sprocket added 4¾ oz (135 gm) and the handlebar trigger control another 5½ oz (156 gm). The trigger was based on the new 'flick' control for the 3-speeds. An optional top tube lever was a derivative of the new handlebar trigger: it was illustrated and reviewed in an early 1940 edition of *Cycling*, which stated that 'marketing arrangements have been delayed by the war' but it was never mass produced. The manufacturers advised against making 'a practice of changing gear when stationary, as unless the dogs are in line an unfair load is placed on the control'.

The AF had the toggle chain on the right and an indicator rod in the left end of the axle. In second gear the end of the indicator was level with the end of the axle. The adjustment could also be checked in third; in this case a groove around the indicator rod had to be aligned with the end of the axle. The AF used the same 12-lugged range of sprockets as other close-ratio and medium-ratio gears. The shell was available with 40 or 36 holes in either 14 or 15 gauge drillings.

## Quick-release cable connector

About 1939 Sturmey-Archer introduced a new type of quick-release gear control cable connector. This was widely adopted by riders using the medium-ratio and close-ratio hubs. The connector could be 'broken' apart, simply by holding one section, and displacing the other out of line. The photograph of an AF hub (above) shows one of these new connectors partially disconnected.

## FM medium-ratio 4-speed

In spring 1939 William Raven informed the committee that he was working on a wide-ratio 4-speed. This was the type FW (Four-speed Wide-ratio) but the outbreak of war delayed its introduction until after the conflict. However, a couple of months into the war a medium-ratio version of the AF was launched, known as the FM (Four-speed Medium-ratio). Both hubs were fitted with quick-release wing-nuts and cable connections as standard.

The main differences between the AF and the FM were that the FM's main sun pinion had 30 teeth, whereas the AF's had 20, and the primary planet pinions of the FM had 14 teeth where the AF's had 20 teeth. Early AFs and FMs had 15 tooth secondary planet pinions, the theoretically correct number, but in 1940 this was changed to 14 teeth to allow use of a stronger tooth profile. The ratios were unaffected by this change.

The FM gave a 33.3% decrease, 14.3% decrease, direct drive and a 12.5% increase. Typical gears offered were 47, 60, 70 and 79" or 53, 69, 80 and 90". The gear went on sale in autumn 1939 and was advertised as suitable for touring in hilly districts and for tandem use.

The FM and AF both cost £1 19s. (£102 today) supplied loose, or £1 15s. (£97 today) when fitted to a new machine, although initially the FM was advertised at the premium price of £2 4s. 0d. (£122 today) supplied loose and £1 19s. 6d (£108 today) fitted to a new bike.

The AF and FM four-speeds were truly remarkable technical achievements – state of the art epicyclic gearing at the time. They were formally recognised as such by the award in 1939 of the Cyclists' Touring Club Plaque, which acknowledged 'the four-speed hub as being the greatest improvement in cycle design or equipment during the year'.

## More patents

In spring 1939 Sturmey-Archer and William Brown applied for three patents. The first, GB patent 527,629, covered simple and improved construction of hub gear parts, including a one piece planet cage. They also applied for GB patent 527,632 for an improved selector for gears covered by GB patent 483,992 such as the AR. This mechanism comprised 'a member having two or more alternative sets of internal selector splines or dogs, those of one set being circumferentially off-set in relation to those of the other set or sets'.

A further application, for GB patent 527,837, related to twin-train epicyclic gears such as those covered by GB patents 483,992 and 519,945. It showed two versions of a 4-speed gear with three closely-spaced upper ratios and a widely-spaced bottom gear. Typical percentage variations quoted were 20% decrease, 7.65% decrease, direct drive and a 9.2% increase; this could offer gears of 80, 92, 100 and 109" or 54, 63, 68 and 74". The patent illustrated an additional selector mechanism on the left of the hub for a 5-speed version of the gear. One version of the 5-speed had a widely-spaced top gear giving an increase of 25% and offering gears of 80, 92, 100, 109 and 125" or 54, 63, 68, 74 and 85". Another version gave wider percentage changes: 25% decrease, 10% decrease, direct drive, 11.1% increase and 33.3% increase, typical gears being in the order of 75, 90, 100, 111 and 133" or 45, 54, 60, 67 and 80". The planet pinions of either epicyclic train could be single or double (compound) depending on the desired ratios.

In autumn 1939 William Raven reported to the committee that a different 5-speed hub was being tested and that he would shortly be in a position to produce it. A patent for the hub was filed successfully the following spring (GB 541,332). The prototype was reviewed in *Cycling* but the 5-speed did not go into production for another 26 years.

## The end of a decade

The decade was all but over when Britain declared war on Germany in September 1939. But what a decade of inventiveness it had been and what a contrast with the previous decade. Apart from motorcycle countershaft gears, in 1930 Sturmey-Archer were marketing only the K wide-ratio 3-speed, the KC 3-speed coaster and the CC single-speed coaster. Yet by 1939 their range included wide-, medium- and ultra-close-ratio 3-speeds; wide- and close-ratio 2-speeds; medium- and close-ratio 4-speeds; and they had designs for a wide-ratio 4-speed and a wide-ratio 5-speed. There were also drum brakes for tandems and solos, including versions combined with wide-ratio 3-speeds – and there was the Dynohub.

Yet compared with the preceding decade the 1930s were unprofitable. Dividends during the 1920s had been reasonable: 10% in 1926, 15% in 1927. But for at least seven consecutive years during the 1930s Sturmey-Archer declared no dividend at all: according to the auditors the company merely broke even, making neither loss nor profit. In 1934 14,487 Sturmey-Archer shares had been transferred to the Raleigh Cycle Holdings Company, presumably to give added protection to shareholders during the Depression. Sturmey-Archer's overseas involvement had also been a source of economic concern during the 1930s: in 1936 the Board sold the German subsidiary.

Nonetheless, despite the difficult world-wide economic situation, Sturmey-Archer had fought off the challenge of rival gear systems and had regained their pre-eminence as gear makers to the record breakers. William Raven, William Brown and their colleagues had kept the derailleur at bay, at least for the time being.

# Chapter 11
# War and peace

**Sturmey-Archer in the 1940s**

## Initial effects of war
The United Kingdom entered World War 2 on 3 September 1939. Sales of Sturmey-Archer hubs had fallen significantly in the previous year: the night shift ceased and for a while most production facilities were put on a three-day week. But demand then grew steadily: by spring 1939 the weekly production target was 20,000 and the night shift resumed. That season almost 73,000 more hub gears were sold than in the previous year.

## Munitions
Supplies to civilian customers were heavily rationed as raw materials became scarcer in the first half of 1940. Raleigh became the largest commercial supplier of small shells, cases and fuzes to the Ministry of Supply, producing more than 382 million items during the war. After the conflict a book was published commemorating the company's contribution to the war effort. Entitled *Thus We Served* and written by Dudley Noble, it was illustrated by E. Boye Uden.

Munitions work increased the Raleigh workforce to about 10,000, of whom about a third were on the night shift. It is ironic that some of the most important machinery used by Raleigh to make munitions for World War 2 was built and installed by the people against whom it was used: the German firm Schütte was installing machinery at Nottingham for several years until the outbreak of war.

For nearly six years Raleigh Industries worked day and night, seven days a week, with 95% of its capacity producing munitions. The remaining 5% was devoted to bicycle manufacture, mostly for the armed forces. The Sturmey-Archer departments were experienced in producing component parts to low tolerances and their hub assembly lines were easily converted to fuze assembly and shell case manufacture, including for anti-aircraft gun shells and fighter plane ammunition. They also manufactured bulbs to hold DDT and carbon dioxide: each week 300,000 were made for killing mosquitos in the tropics. All hub gear manufacture ceased but research and development continued throughout the war.

## 4-speed and 5-speed developments during the war
In spring 1940 Sturmey-Archer and William Brown applied for GB patent 541,332. This related to the earlier GB patents 483,992 and 519,945. It was a further development of epicyclic gears embodying 'alternative ratchet and pawl drives, one of which is overrun when the other is operative and the other of which is tripped out when the other is operative'. The specification stated that the maximum number of useable speeds obtainable hitherto from a single train was three; the object of the new patent was to obtain one, two or more additional speeds without substantial modification of the design or components.

The patent described a new gear in 4-speed and 5-speed versions. It employed compound pinions, two suns and a gear ring that could be single or dual diameter. Soon after the patent was filed a 5-speed Sturmey-Archer prototype hub was reviewed in *Cycling*. It had a two-

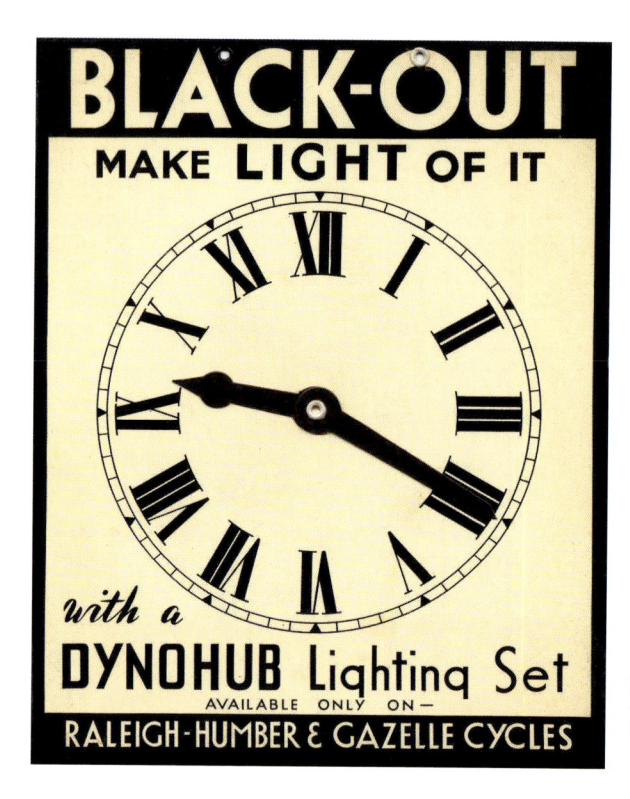

Fig. 11.1. The air-raid precautionary black-out provided a sales opportunity for the new Dynohub – but only on new bikes from brands owned by Raleigh (DDRN 4-72-8).

position lever on the top tube and a three-position trigger on the handlebars. The ratios were the same as those of the later S5 hub and, like that gear, it had a toggle chain on either side of the hub. But it was not put into production.

(The record-breaking cyclist and gearing expert Jack Lauterwasser told Tony Hadland about a chance encounter he had in 1940 while cycling in the London area. He met Harry England, editor of *Cycling*, who was testing a bicycle equipped with the prototype 5-speed hub. Lauterwasser subsequently became adept at converting Sturmey-Archer 4-speeds into 5-speeds, long before Sturmey-Archer marketed a 5-speed. He even converted FM hubs into medium-ratio 5-speeds.)

In the 5-speed described in GB patent 541,332 one or other of the suns could be brought into drive at any time, thus changing the gear from a wide-ratio 3-speed to a close-ratio 3-speed or vice versa. For this purpose there were two selector levers, as described in earlier Sturmey-Archer patents covering 5-speed hubs: one lever acted like a conventional 3-speed selector, the other selected wide or close ratio.

For the 4-speed version of the gear covered by GB patent 541,332, two systems of sun selection were described. In one version the suns were free to rotate on the wheel axle but could not slide along the axle; instead either could be clutched to the axle by a selector key inside the axle. Alternatively the suns could be slidably mounted on the axle with a second axle key controlling the sun selection. In the top three speeds this second axle key was held out of action by a compensator spring; but when the lever was pulled back to its furthest limit the additional force overcame the compensator spring and slid the suns to the right. This declutched the smaller sun and locked the larger one to the axle, giving the lowest gear. When engaging low gear, the lever was therefore pulling against three springs – the clutch spring,

Fig. 11.2. The 20 mm shell shop – by E. Boye Uden.

Fig. 11.3. Electrical furnaces annealing cartridge cases – E. Boye Uden.

Fig. 11.4. Hot forging shop – E. Boye Uden.

Fig. 11.5. Raleigh munitions workers, the vast majority being women (DDRN 6-20-4).

the compensator spring and the low gear spring. All three springs had to come from a matched set for the gear to operate properly.

## FW wide-ratio 4-speed

The sliding sun system described above was used in the FW wide-ratio 4-speed gear, FW standing for 'Four-speed Wide-ratio'. The new gear was reviewed in *The Bicycle* early in 1945; the war in Europe ended that summer and the FW became available the following year.

The FW gave an increase of 26.6%, direct drive and decreases of 21.1% and 33.3%. It was the most commercially successful 4-speed hub and formed the basis of the S5 5-speed, introduced two decades later. In the late 1940s the FW cost £2 3s. 3d. (£78 today) supplied loose with controls. When the FW was launched Sturmey-Archer stated: 'It will be of particular interest to those cyclists who consider that the high gear in the AW wide ratio 3-speed is too high, and the low gear not low enough.'

The FW gave 'four nicely spaced gears suitable for all normal purposes'. Among the merits claimed were 'neatness, lightness, weather-proof, reliability, durability' but most of all, unlike a derailleur, it was 'totally enclosed, with all the bearings running in oil, thus ensuring constant sweetness and silkiness in running'.

At first the FW was fitted with a threaded driver and the sprocket choice was limited to a range from 16 to 20 teeth. Hub width was 4 5/16" (110 mm) but could be reduced to 4 1/16" (103 mm) by removal of the left side spacing washer and the right side locknut washer. The hub, complete with 18 tooth sprocket, axle washers and nuts, weighed 2 lb 10 oz (1.19 kg), only 4 oz (113 gm) heavier than the AW 3-speed.

To make it easier to engage bottom gear the 'double square' dogs on the larger sun were soon replaced by dogs that were ramped off on the non-drive side for smoother changes; and weaker spring sets were introduced in 1950 to reduce the effort needed to engage bottom gear. But it still required a relatively hard pull to overcome the three springs when selecting lowest gear.

Fig. 11.6. Multi-spindle automatics producing Hispano cannon shells – E. Boye Uden.

Fig. 11.7. Precision tool making – E. Boye Uden.

Fig. 11.8. Section of press shop, cold pressing – E. Boye Uden.

*161*

Fig. 11.9. The FW wide-ratio 4-speed hub.

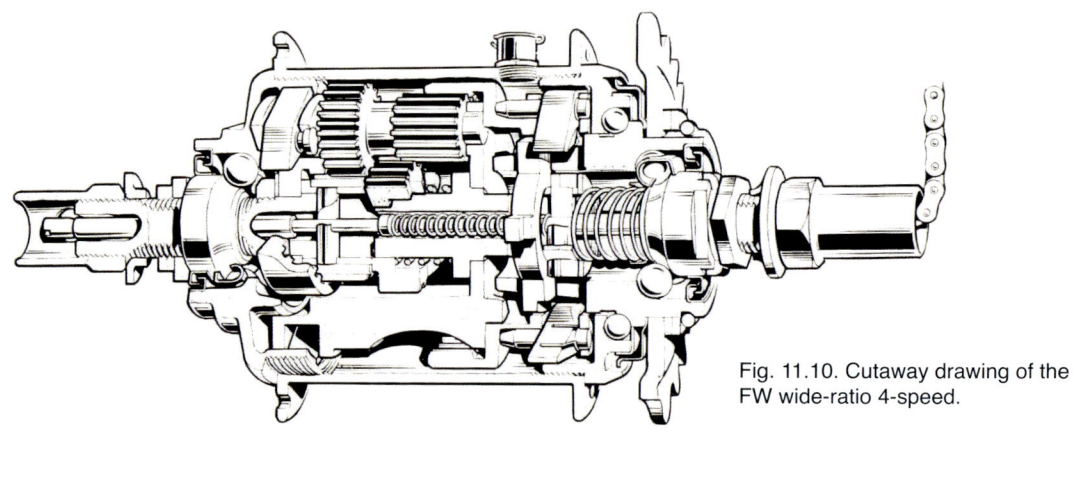

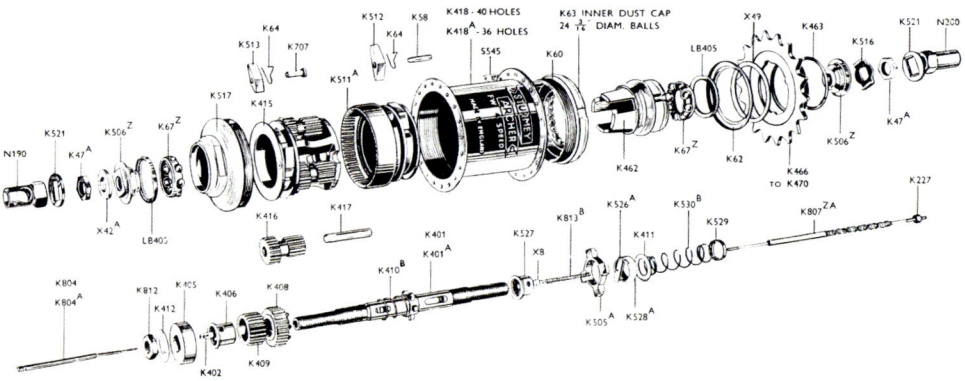

Fig. 11.10. Cutaway drawing of the FW wide-ratio 4-speed.

Fig. 11.11. Exploded view of the FW wide-ratio 4-speed.

The new gear incorporated a gear adjustment indicator rod similar to that in the AF and FM hubs. In common with other Sturmey-Archer hubs incorporating compound pinions (e.g. the KS, KSW, TC and AM) the FW's planets bore timing marks. When reassembling the gear it was necessary to arrange the planet pinions so that the marked teeth pointed radially outwards from the centre of the wheel axle. Recommended tools included the standard cone and nut spanner (now renumbered as X44A) and the DD5978 driver holder. A sprocket chain wrench, DD9l28, was also available.

### Dynohub maintenance
In summer 1941 *Motor Cycle and Cycle Trader* printed a three-page illustrated guide to 'The Servicing and Maintenance of the Raleigh Dynohub'. Raleigh later reprinted this article which contained their own trouble-shooting chart. The instructions related to the Mk 1, Mk 2 and Mk 3 Dynohubs and contained the warning that 'unless there is at hand a keeper ring for the magnet, it is essential that under no circumstances whatever should the armature be withdrawn from the magnet, otherwise demagnetisation will be caused, and the light afterwards will never be quite so bright as before until the magnet has been remagnetised'.

The keeper was merely a ring of soft iron over which the magnet was slipped and which was 'sold quite cheaply by the makers'. It was 'an essential item of equipment' for anyone contemplating servicing a Dynohub. As a later Sturmey-Archer *Cycle Maintenance Handbook* stated: 'At all times there must be iron within the magnet.'

### Swiss copies
In autumn 1942 the committee discovered that a Swiss company was contemplating making a 4-speed hub and that Raleigh had failed to patent their 4-speeds in Switzerland. The committee attempted unsuccessfully to negotiate with Scintilla AG of Switzerland to make Sturmey-Archer hubs under licence. Scintilla were already making poor quality unauthorised AW copies. Also, via Humber (now owned by Raleigh) the committee obtained samples of a 3-speed and a KB drum brake clone made by Vibo of Switzerland, construction of which was considered 'first class'. George Wilson meanwhile received a request from Arnold Schwinn of Chicago for co-operation in production of 3-speeds in the USA but this was held over until the end of the war.

### Close-ratio 3-speeds – GB patent 567,340
One of the most interesting wartime patents taken out by Sturmey-Archer and William Brown was GB 567,340. Filed early in 1943 and granted two years later, it covered a fixed-wheel modification to several previously patented Sturmey-Archer gear designs. On this occasion Brown gave his address as 130 Middleton Boulevard, Nottingham rather than following his usual practice of quoting the company address.

The patent briefly reviewed the basic hub gear configurations, including those using the revolving sun principle which it describes as 'arranged in cascade' or 'double-coupled'. It noted that:

> These arrangements and others not specifically mentioned, provide three, four, five or more speeds in a compact, strongly built, lightweight assembly, and offer a wide variety of ratios including close ratio and in some cases increases of ratio from normal which are less than the decreases from normal.

Fig. 11.12. Trigger of an unauthorised AW 3-speed copy made by Scintilla.

Fig. 11.13. The Scintilla X logo on the shell of an unauthorised AW copy.

Fig. 11.14. An unauthorised copy of an AW hub and trigger by Vibo.

The new invention involved use of either 'cascade' gears or of a compound epicyclic train: in either case there was to be a single positive (reversible) drive to the output member, thus giving the fixed-wheel effect. The invention could be embodied in the gears described in GB patents 483,992, 519,945, 527,837 and 541,332. This was done by omitting one of the alternative pawl and ratchet drives to the output member and converting the other to a positive drive:

> By so doing the total number of speeds obtainable with the gears is reduced slightly, but for those speeds which are obtainable, all the advantages of the earlier constructions are retained, and the presence of those advantages in a reversible gear justify the sacrifice of the speeds not obtainable.

The specification pointed out that if the gear in GB patent 541,332 was modified by omitting the ratchet drive from the gear ring, the speeds (other than direct drive) would be decreases;

Fig. 11.15. The ASC close-ratio fixed-wheel 3-speed.

whereas if the ratchet drive from the planet cage was omitted the speeds would be increases. If the gears in the other patents were modified, it was preferable to make only those modifications which involved removal of the ratchet drive from the gear ring. It was noted that in some cases the gears might not be in consecutive order.

### ASC close-ratio fixed-wheel 3-speed
The practical effect of GB patent 567,340 was the introduction of the ASC 3-speed fixed hub, reviewed in *Cycling* in summer 1945. The new hub's designatory letters ASC apparently stood for 'A-series Sports Close-ratio'.

The ASC used the 'cascade' (revolving sun) principle and gave direct drive and reductions of 10% and 25%. The gear was advertised as 'The only Three-speed FIXED Hub manufactured in the world today!' It was aimed at 'enthusiastic riders who prefer a fixed gear and who for years have longed for a 3-speed fixed'. It was also marketed as suitable for certain disabled riders 'who, through tragic circumstances, need a fixed hub'.

In the late 1940s the ASC cost £2 16s. 3d. (£87 today) supplied loose with all fittings. Early production was reserved for export. The ASC's British launch, complete with the new alloy shell that was to be offered on all Sturmey-Archer's sporting models, was deferred until the November 1948 Cycle and Motorcycle Show, the first since the end of the war.

### Planning for peacetime
George Wilson, Cyril Clarkson and William Brown met several times early in 1944 to agree Sturmey-Archer's post-war product range. Discussions were held in the autumn with Hercules about post-war conditions but no agreement was reached. By the following spring Wilson was negotiating a mutual trading agreement with BSA.

Early in 1945 Wilson asked Clarkson (works director since Raven's retirement in 1942) to establish an experimental shop to develop Sturmey-Archer gears and lighting systems. This was to be a small self-contained unit under the control of William Brown. The aim was to give Sturmey-Archer the edge in the fierce competition expected after the war. After further

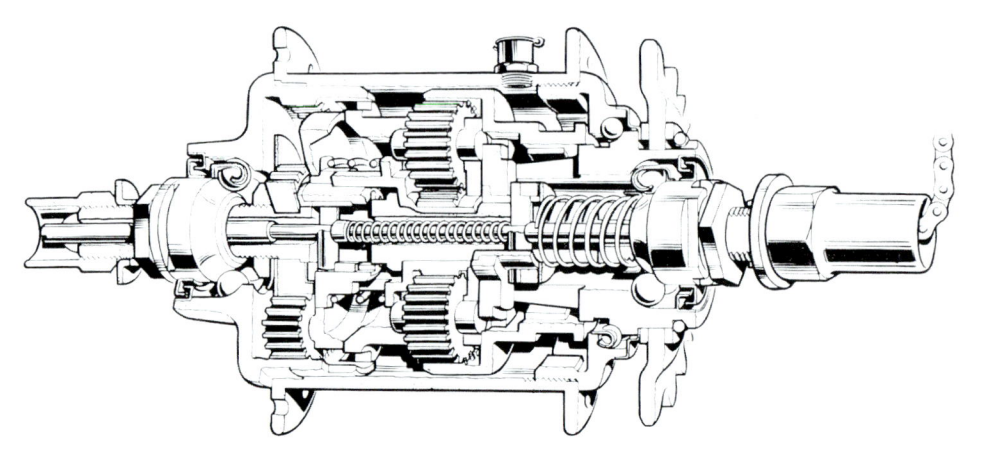

Fig. 11.16. Cutaway drawing of the ASC close-ratio fixed-wheel 3-speed.

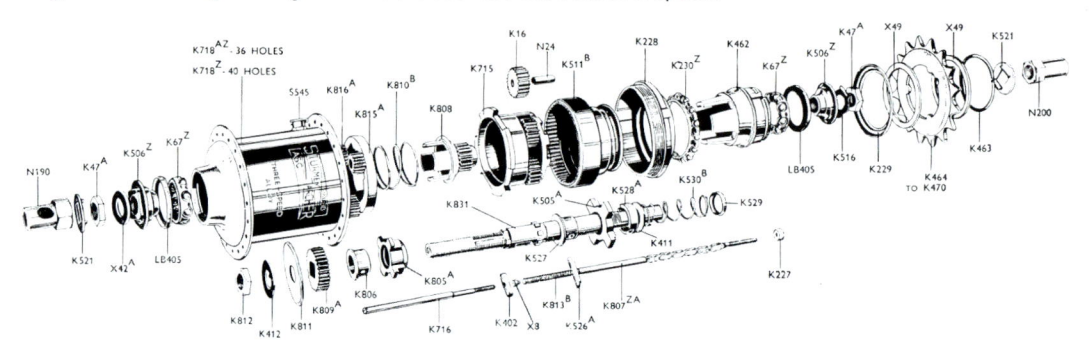

Fig. 11.17. Exploded view of the ASC close-ratio fixed-wheel 3-speed.

discussions it was agreed that this department should also address cycle development, the cycle side being controlled by Sidney Buxton.

## Shortages

In spring 1945 Sturmey-Archer production was well behind schedule, due to a shortage of labour. By the summer most of the stock of 3-speeds built up at the start of the war had gone but production was increasing and Clarkson hoped soon to be making 6,000 hubs a week.

The low stock situation inevitably led to frustration, as in autumn 1945 when sales director Alfred Simpson expressed his annoyance that trigger controls had been supplied to the Comrade Cycle Company, leaving Raleigh short of triggers for their own bikes. By spring 1946 Sturmey-Archer's production had risen to 6,900 hub gears a week. But in the autumn they had to stop making gears for a while because of a lack of materials and in the following spring a coal shortage seriously affected production.

## Putting on a show

Sturmey-Archer had an impressive display at the Raleigh Industries Fair at the Seymour Hall, Marylebone in autumn 1947. Nimrod, writing in *Cycling,* described the range of products on display as 'almost an exhibition on their own'. The Sturmey-Archer stand featured Archie the

Fig. 11.18. The FC close-ratio 4-speed.

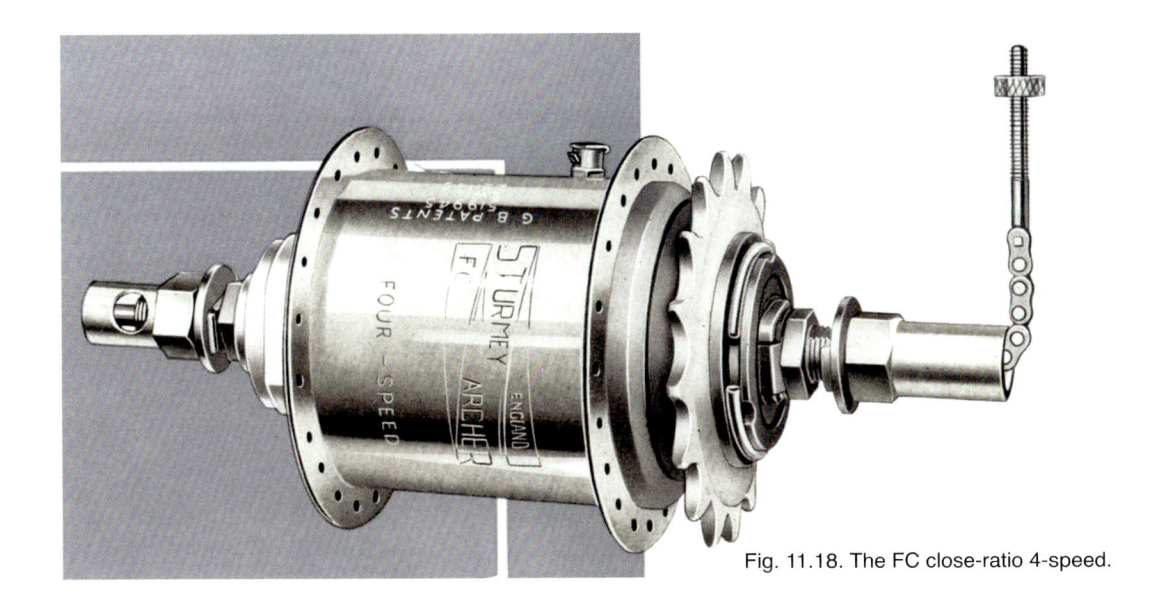

cycling robot. Dressed in loud plus-fours, wearing a flat cap and holding a cigarette, he pedalled a Raleigh-made Rudge-Whitworth cycle up an everlasting incline, pushed along by a winged Sturmey-Archer hub. The same character appeared in Sturmey-Archer adverts as far back as 1928.

## FC close-ratio 4-speed

Sturmey-Archer launched their FC close-ratio 4-speed in 1947. This was a reintroduction of the original AF with minor changes: a slightly different wheel axle, modifications at the low gear end and 14 tooth secondary planet pinions. The latter were of the same diameter as the original 15 tooth pinions fitted to the AF and hence provided a stronger tooth. A complete set of 14 tooth pinions could be substituted for the original l5 tooth set, the number of teeth on a planet pinion having no effect on the gear ratios.

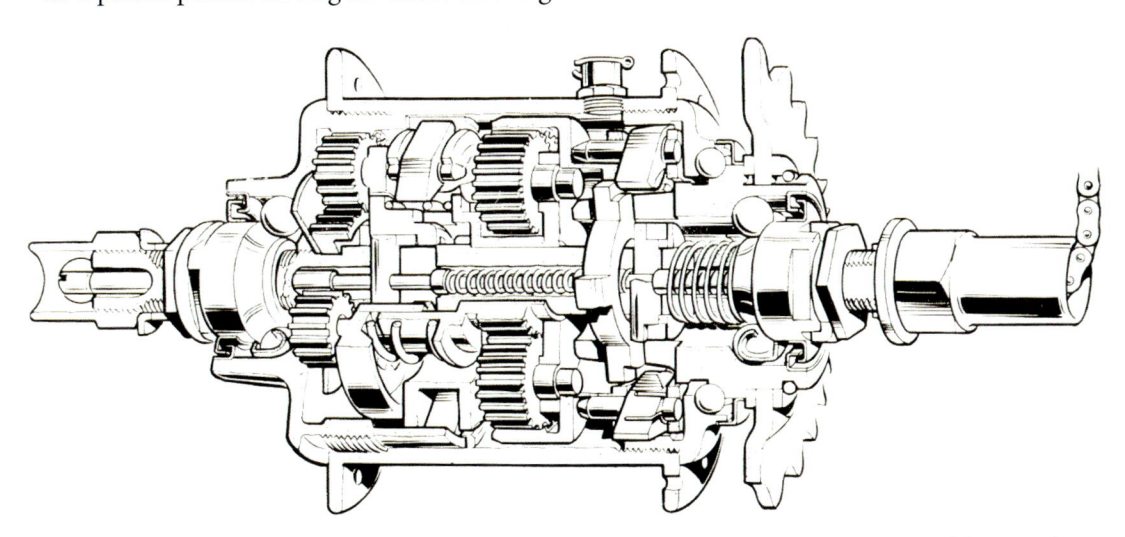

Fig. 11.19. Cutaway drawing of the FC 4-speed.

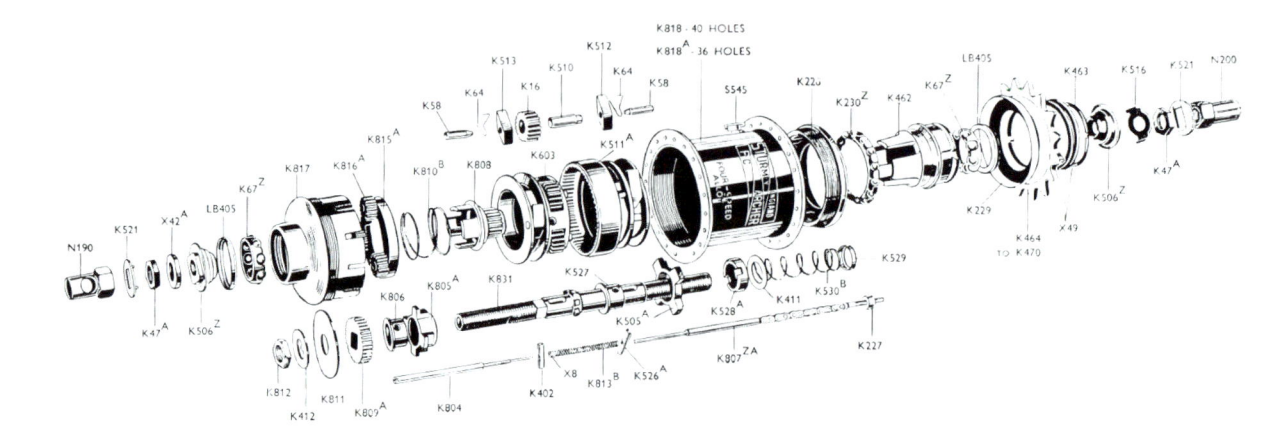

Fig. 11.20. Exploded view of the FC 4-speed.

Whereas the AF was housed in a steel shell, the new FC was available in either steel or alloy, the latter saving 4 oz (113 gm). In the late 1940s the FC sold for £2 14s. 6d. (£90 today) supplied loose with all fittings.

### Axle design changes
The detail changes that marked out the FC from the AF originated in 1940 in modifications to the FM 4-speed medium-ratio hub. Other changes instigated then included modified axle designs for the AW, AB/ABC and AM hubs; this was to accommodate new clutch spring and axle key arrangements, similar to those in post 1940 FMs and the FC. (The 3-speeds used a single axle key whereas the 4-speeds used two.) The main difference was that the original axle keys were square section whereas the later ones were round, necessitating different axle slots.

### Dynohub production
Dynohubs had been stockpiled in the early years of the war before production ceased. In autumn 1945 Raleigh had nearly 4,200 Mk 2 12-volt Dynohubs in stock and almost 27,000 Mk 3 8-volt hubs. By the following spring all 12-volt Dynohubs had left the factory and the stock of 8-volt hubs was down to about 11,000. In summer 1946 the committee noted that a new Dynohub factory in Faraday Road, Nottingham would enable production of up to 15,000 Dynohubs a week whereas the existing facilities could produce no more than 6,000. A construction licence was granted in summer 1947: the factory was operational by summer 1950 and by the autumn had taken on plating and hardening.

In 1950 the board decided to offer Dynohubs, hitherto reserved for Raleigh-owned bicycle brands, to the whole cycle industry. All the hub dynamos would be badged as Sturmey-Archer products and the spelling of Dynohub was standardised as one word.

### GH6 Dynohub
During the war Sturmey-Archer had continued development of the hub dynamo. In spring 1946 they commenced production of the classic GH6 Dynohub (GH6 standing for 'Generator Hub 6 volt'). This incorporated a 20 pole magnet with a stator having a continuous winding. It had a quoted output of 2.0 watts and ran a 0.3 amp headlamp and a 0.04 amp tail lamp.

Fig. 11.21. The GH6 Dynohub.

Various detail changes were made over the years, including the recommended bulb ratings, but the GH6 remained in production for almost four decades until withdrawn in 1984. The main external visual change was that early GH6s had black Bakelite armatures, whereas from about 1952 the armatures were steel.

The Dynohub faced competition from BSA, whose Hublite could be ordered with an alloy shell, something Sturmey-Archer never offered for the GH6.

Over the years, various alloys were used for Dynohub magnets, including AlNiCO, High Nickel and later a modified AlNi. The quoted output was downrated to 1.8 watts at some stage, possibly in the early 1970s. This may have been because of a change of magnet material, coil winding or output measurement technique.

Early GH6 Dynohubs generally had 32 hole spoke drillings but were also available with 36 holes. In the mid 1960s 28 hole drillings were made available for use with small-wheeled bicycles. The early GH6 had a more elegant shell than later versions; the diameter between the flanges was smaller and the finish was better. The shell also had an oiling point, a commendable feature that was later discontinued.

The GH6 achieved its rated output when a bicycle with standard-sized wheels reached a speed of about 12 miles per hour (19 km/h). According to the service manual 'the design prevents the output rising seriously beyond this at any higher speed'. If the correct bulbs were fitted a usable light was produced at brisk walking pace.

Headlamps type HF63 and HF62 were introduced for use with the GH6. These were

Fig. 11.22. Cutaway drawing of the GH6 Dynohub.Fig.

11.23. Exploded view of the GH6 Dynohub.

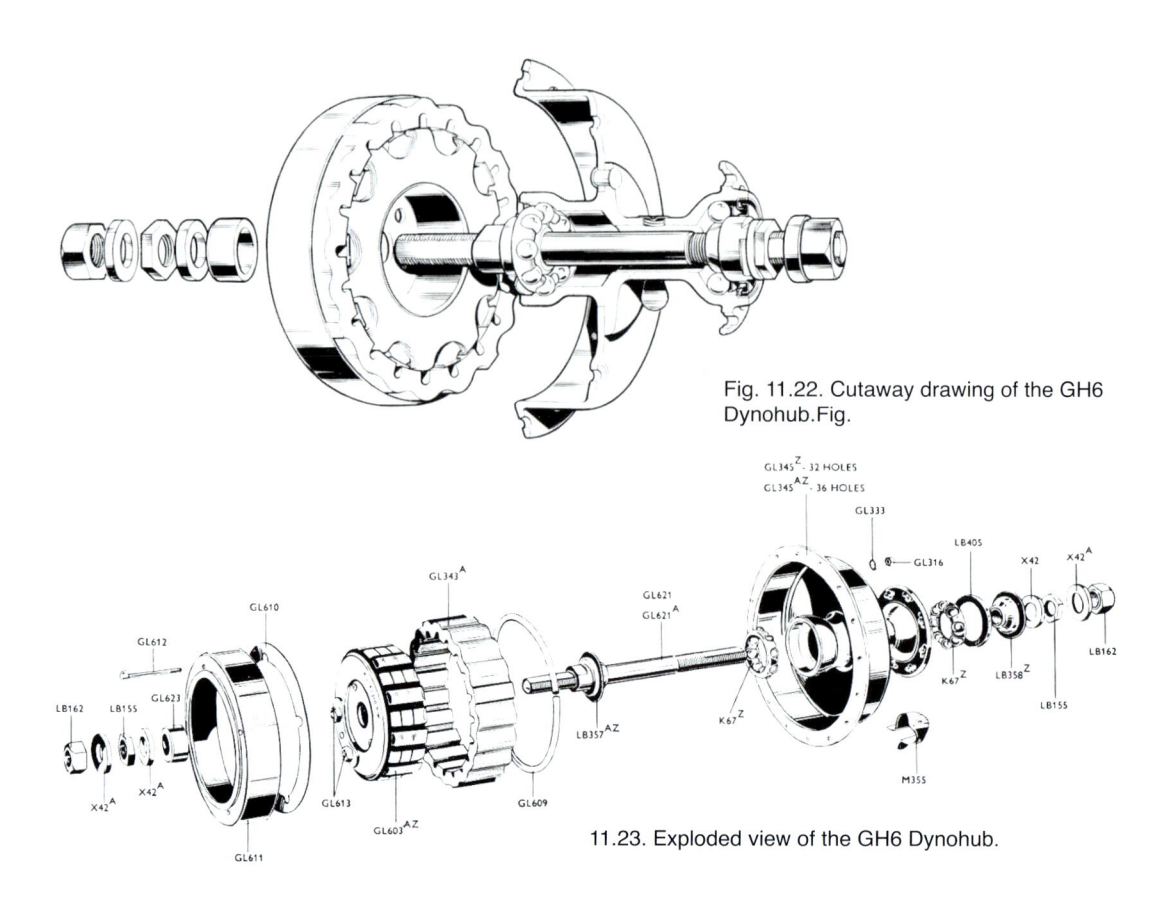

focussed by turning a sunken screw at the rear of the lamp; it seems their design was based on GB patent 532,205. Sturmey-Archer and William Brown applied for this in summer 1936 bu it was not accepted until 1941.

## Dry Accumulator Unit

Another Dynohub accessory was the short-lived Dry Accumulator Unit (DAU) launched just after the war. This was a tubular container fixed to the seat tube and containing three 2-volt RTU dry accumulator cells and a rectifier unit for charging the cells from the hub dynamo. The DAU provided a backup to the Dynohub: if while using the Dynohub the cyclist came to a halt, the DAU automatically cut in to maintain illumination.

Use of the DAU required headlamp HF62 fitted with a 0.2 amp bulb instead of the usual 0.3 amp. (The similar HF63 was used for Dynohubs without the DAU.)

Each of the three dry accumulator cells had to be topped up with distilled water, 'once a fortnight in summer and once a month in winter'. They were normally charged by the Dynohub, Raleigh's *Cycle Maintenance Handbook* advising that 'it is necessary to cover twice the period of time of riding with lights off to that with lights on in order to keep accumulators fully charged'. They could also be charged by a free-standing charger: Sturmey-Archer marketed two versions, one for AC mains and another for DC.

Problems were encountered with the batteries, a point raised by Raleigh chairman Sir Harold Bowden at a committee meeting in autumn 1946. The fluid-filled 'dry' cells could

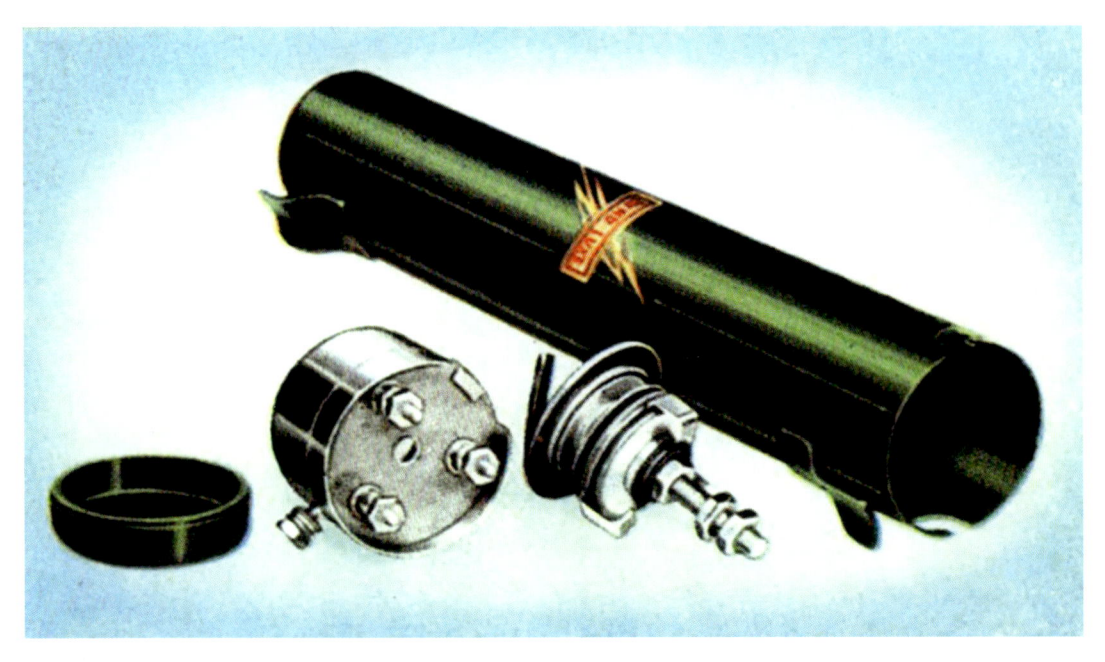

Fig. 11.24. The Dry Accumulator Unit.

easily leak in real world usage. Managing director George Wilson reassured Sir Harold that everything possible was being done to cure earlier problems but that 'one of our great troubles was the fact that few cycle riders were electrically minded'. Sturmey-Archer were soon considering switching to disposable dry batteries.

It was probably about this time that Sturmey-Archer produced quick-release wing-nuts for the Dynohub and for front drum brakes. These rarely seen items were similar to the rear hub wing-nuts but necessarily had a different thread and, in some cases, spigots adapted to front fork ends.

### AG Dynothree wide-ratio 3-Speed and Dynohub
In 1946 a combined 3-speed and Dynohub was introduced. This was the AG (standing for 'A-series Generator'), sometimes referred to as the Dynothree. It combined a narrow planet cage version of the AW 3-speed (as used in the AB/ABC hub) with a GH6 Dynohub. The shell was stepped and of one-piece construction. The AG was a successful design that remained in production until 1984. The Dyno-Luxe outfit combined the AG and the Dry Accumulator Unit.

### FG Dynofour wide-ratio 4-speed and Dynohub
The AG was soon followed by a 4-speed and Dynohub combination, the FG (FG standing for 'Four-speed Generator'). This hub was sometimes referred to as the Dynofour and until

The Hub of the Universe

Fig. 11.25. The AG 3-speed hub dynamo.

Fig. 11.26. Cutaway drawing of the AG 3-speed hub dynamo.

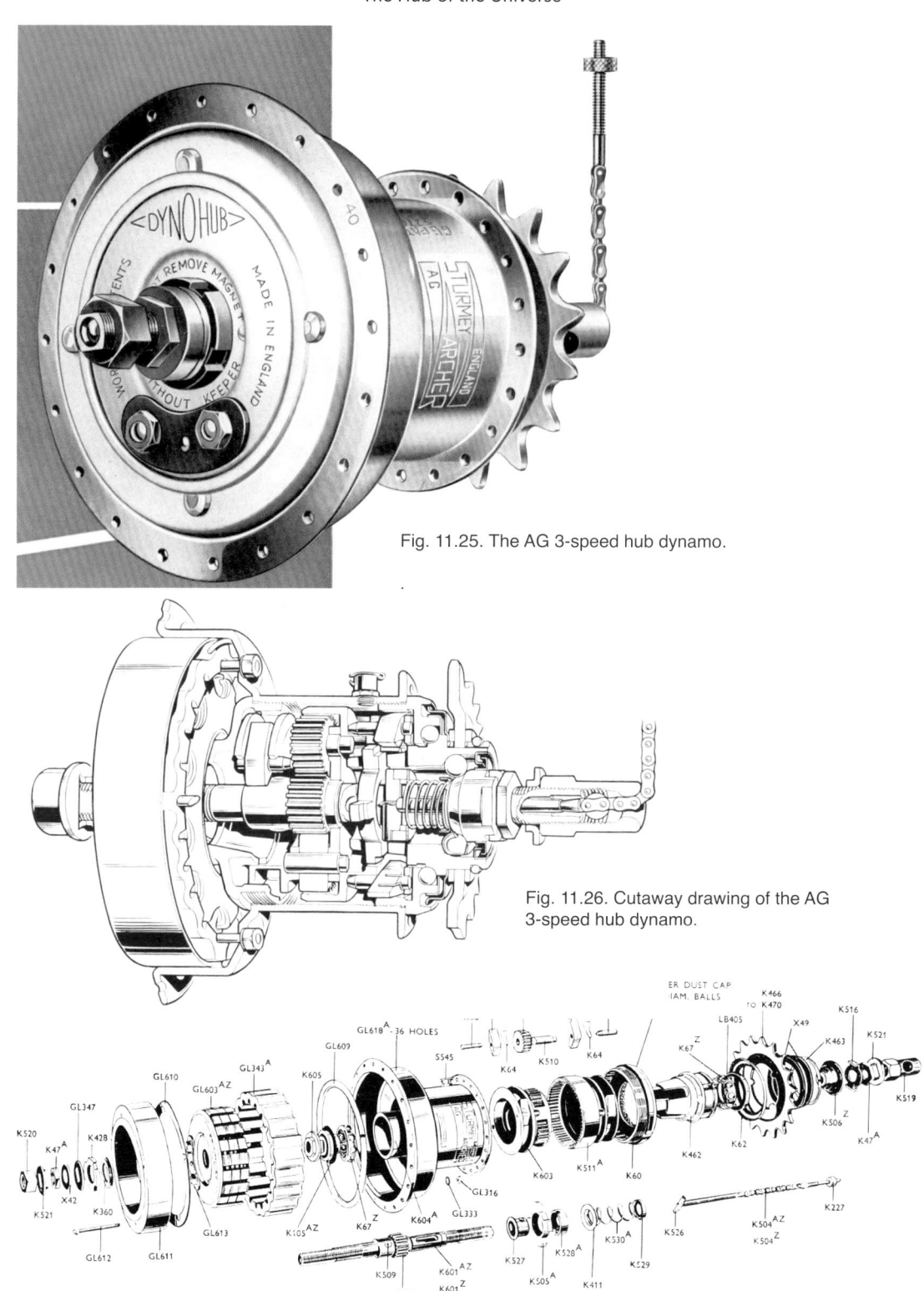

Fig. 11.27. Exploded view of the AG 3-speed hub dynamo

172

Fig. 11.28. The FG 4-speed hub dynamo.

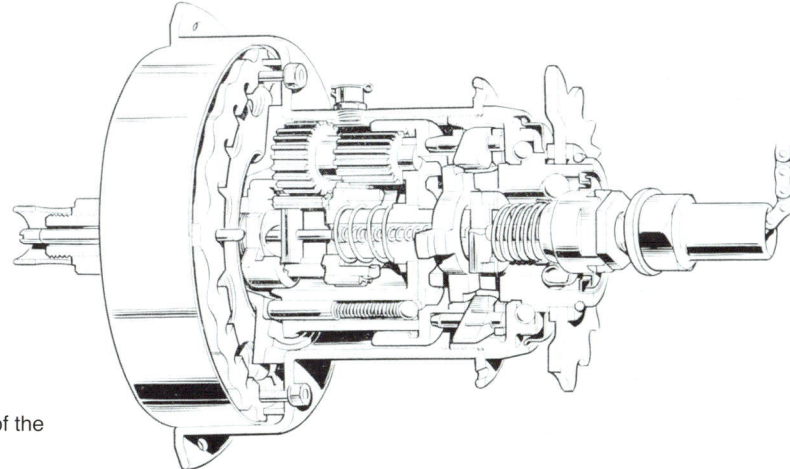

Fig. 11.29. Cutaway drawing of the FG 4-speed hub dynamo.

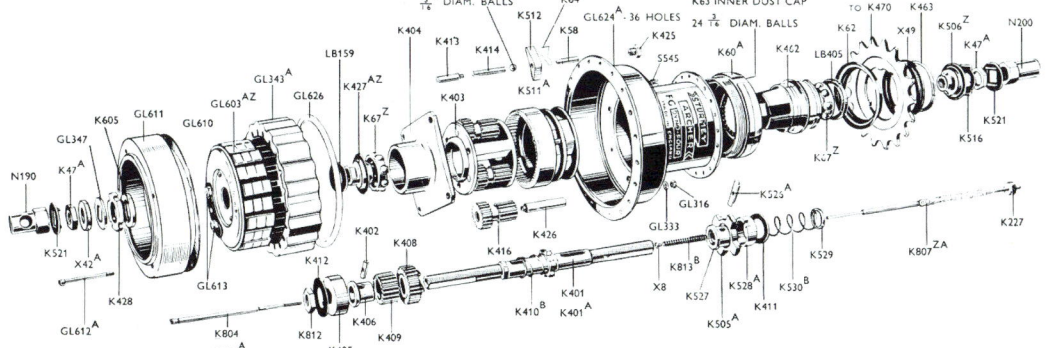

Fig. 11.30. Exploded view of the FG 4-speed hub dynamo.

Fig. 11.31. 1947 poster for the 'Original and Unrivalled' Sturmey-Archer range of hub gears and drum brakes.

Fig. 11.32. The AC ultra-close-ratio 3-speed.

1950 it was only fitted to Raleigh bicycles. The gear was based on the FW wide-ratio 4-speed but incorporated cylindrical plunger type pawls within the planet cage; these acted horizontally against a ratchet formed in the left-hand ball cup. In both the AG and the FG the armature of the generator was black Bakelite (as with the AG and the GH6) until about 1952; thereafter it was steel.

With both the FG and the AG the makers recommended use of a less powerful front bulb (0.25 amp) than for the GH6 front wheel Dynohub 'because, owing to the greater amount of metal within the hub shell, there is some slight magnetic loss'.

## FB 4-speed drum brake

The FG gear mechanism was also used in the FB hub, combined with the 3½" (90 mm) drum brake mechanism used in the AB/ABC 3-speed and drum brake combination. The FB was launched in 1949 but was never popular: only 439 were sold and it was withdrawn in 1952.

## AC ultra-close-ratio 3-speed

The 1949 Cycle and Motorcycle Show saw what Sturmey-Archer claimed was the reintroduction of the hub 'known prior to the last war as model AR' and which had 'enjoyed a ready sale amongst riders who use a variable [gear] in time trials'. The ultra-close-ratio 3-speed was now called the AC (standing for A-series Close-ratio). Although similar in concept to the AR, the AC was more like a closer ratio FC without the lowest gear: percentage shifts were plus 6.66% and minus 7.7% whereas the AR provided an increase of 7.24% and a decrease of 6.76%.

The AC could be supplied in the new alloy shell, fitted with wing-nuts and quick-release cable connection. The hub used 12-lugged sprockets and sold loose for £2 14s. (£81 today) including all fittings.

## The alloy shell

The Sturmey-Archer alloy shell, introduced in 1948, was a mere third of the weight of its steel counterpart and was well received. A year or so after its introduction the company

Fig. 11.33. Cutaway drawing of the AC ultra-close-ratio 3-speed.

Fig. 11.34. Exploded view of the AC ultra-close-ratio 3-speed.

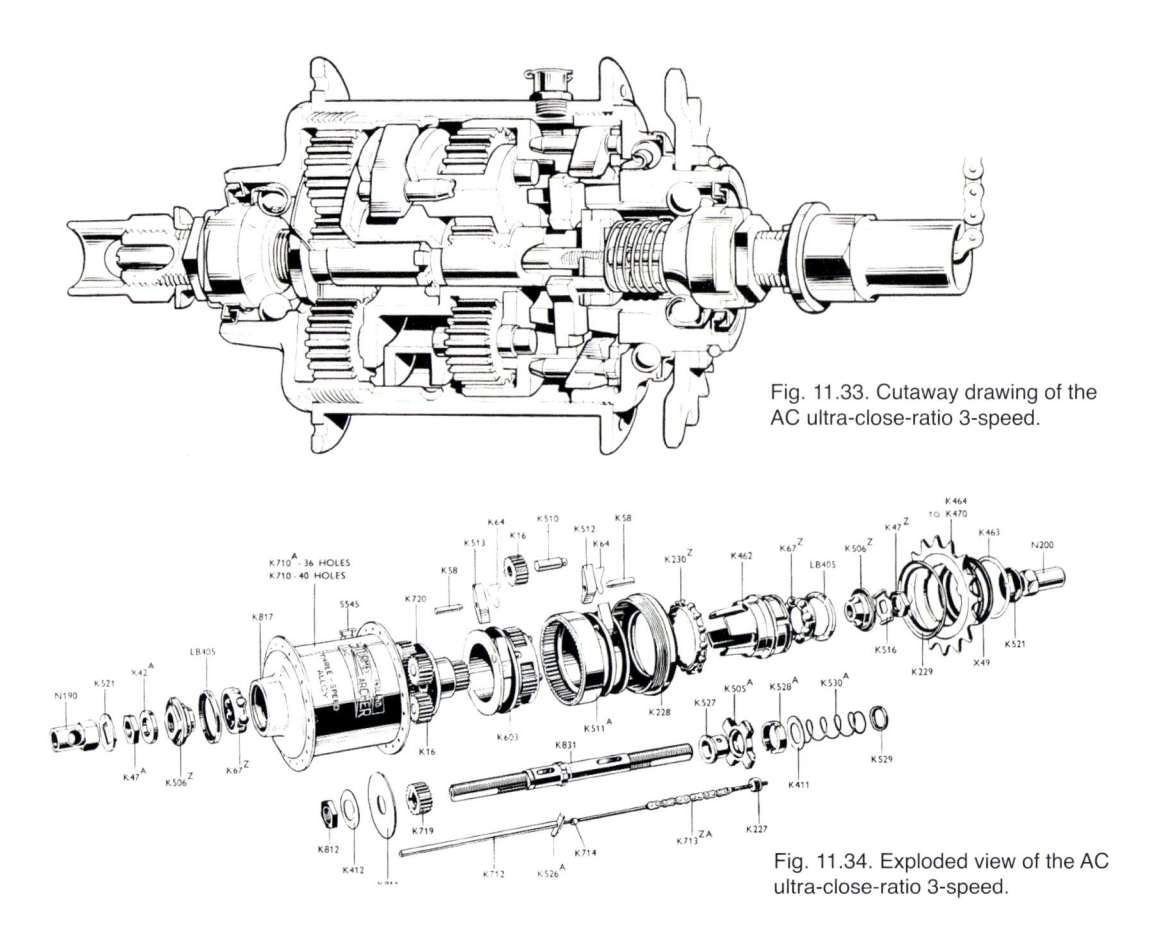

decided to supply it with all medium-, close- and ultra-close-ratio gears. Later the alloy shell was also offered with the FW wide-ratio 4-speed.

### An improved trigger

GB patent 649,009, filed by Sturmey-Archer and William Brown in April 1948, concerned improvements to the 'flick' trigger control. It referred back to GB patent 498,820; the main intention was to eliminate rattle and make the trigger easier and cheaper to manufacture. The restyled trigger, with its 'new luxurious finish', was launched about 1948 and incorporated an 'at a glance' visual gear indication – a circular opening in the fascia of the control that displayed figures engraved on the trigger. Depending on the position of the trigger, L, N or H would be shown, indicating Low, Normal or High. The restyled trigger, like its predecessor, was labelled on the assumption that it would hang below the handlebars rather than stand above like later triggers of similar design.

By about this time the trigger was supplied as standard with all the company's gears but a traditional top tube control could be ordered with AW and AB/ABC hubs.

For more on trigger development, see Appendix G.

## Miscellaneous lighting patents

William Brown, together with Raleigh, took out a number of other patents during the 1940s. GB 594,413, filed late in 1944, concerned a generator based on the Dynohub but for use with internal combustion engines. GB patent 611,032, filed early in 1945, proposed a headlamp with an annular lens adapted to surround a light bulb, the lens 'having a common principal focal point at which the filament of the bulb may be located'. This design permitted use of a conical metal reflector that was easier to manufacture than a parabolic type. The claimed advantages of the lamp included reduced size, less dazzle, a totally enclosed and easily cleaned optical system, and focussing over a wider range than with parabolic reflectors. The specification stated that 'the proposed system projects twice the light of a normal parabola'.

Brown's interest in electrics showed itself in patent GB 632,237. This was filed in spring 1947 and concerned improvements in electric relay switches. Of more relevance to cyclists was GB 636,526, submitted late in 1946, which concerned improvements in tyre-driven dynamos. Its intentions were to simplify construction and manufacture, at the same time reducing manufacturing errors of concentricity of the rotor and stator, and enabling a dynamo to be made smaller and lighter.

## Brown's 'No Intermediate Gear' 3-speed

In spring 1948 Sturmey-Archer and William Brown applied for GB patent 644,179. This covered a means of eliminating the intermediate gear (no-drive or neutral spot) between high and middle gears in hubs such as the AW 3-speed.

In such hubs the high gear is selected by clutching the driver to the planet cage; whereas in middle gear the driver is clutched to the gear ring which drives the hub shell via pawls. The specification noted that the neutral position was necessary to prevent any possibility of simultaneously engaging both speeds while changing gear and thus wrecking the hub. No such problem exists between low and middle gears because the change to low is effected by tripping out the pawls which otherwise drive the hub shell.

The new specification replaced the gear ring dogs with 'at least one pawl serving only such function and adapted to be tripped by lateral abutment with, or to over-ride the selector'. The advantage was that there was 'no possibility of damage due to chance engagement of the selector with the pawls while engaged with the dogs of the planet carrier'.

The new 'no intermediate gear' design also permitted a shorter mechanism and needed less travel in the control system. The basic principle was by no means new: William Reilly had incorporated it in early Sturmey-Archer gears and consequently the BSA 3-speed had a similar system. Sturmey-Archer nonetheless managed to obtain a patent for their latest variation on the NIG theme but the gear was not put into production.

## An improved freewheel hub

William Brown was not the only personally named patentee at Sturmey-Archer during this period. In autumn 1948 George Harold Neale was named as joint patentee of an improved freewheel hub. Like many other hubs, this had the sprocket carrier and the hub shell separately mounted on ball bearings. Neale's innovation was that both sets of bearings could be adjusted simultaneously from either end of the axle.

Between the wheel and sprocket carrier was a double cone which was slidably mounted on a splined portion of the wheel axle. Tightening either the left (wheel) cone or the right (sprocket carrier) cone would pull up the double cone so that any remaining play was shared

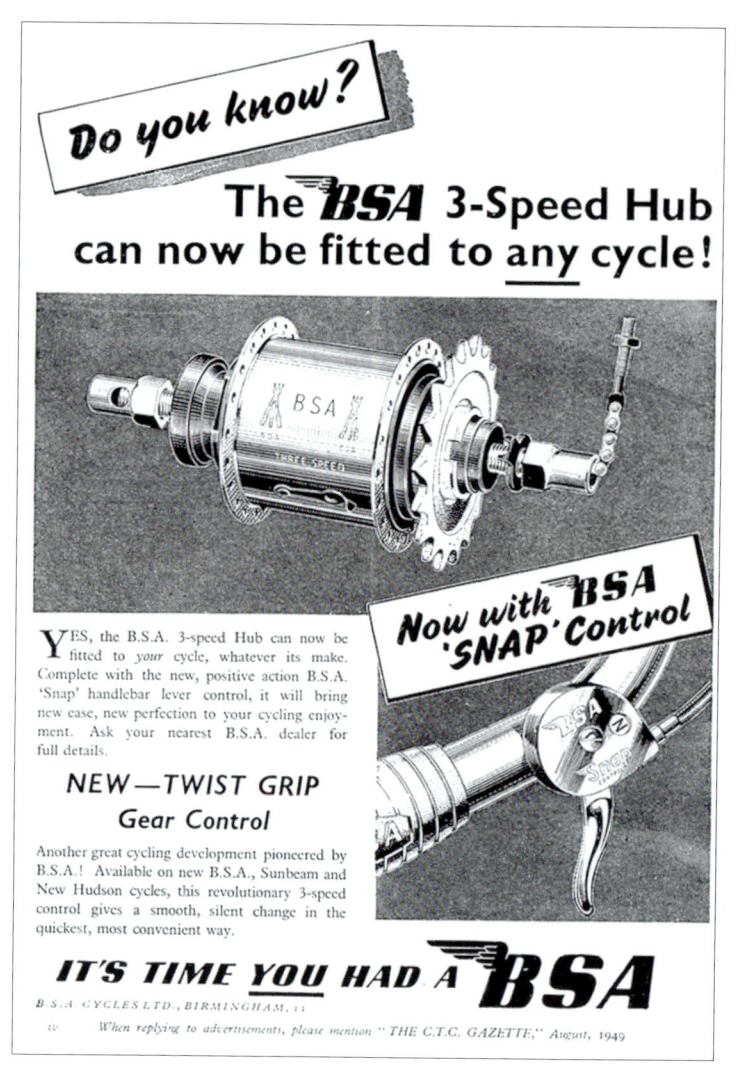

Fig. 11.35. A 1949 press advertisement for BSA's 3-speed, now with a 'snap' trigger to rival Sturmey-Archer's 'flick' trigger.

equally between the wheel and sprocket carrier.

## Product literature

The immediate post-war period saw a change in Sturmey-Archer technical literature. Before the war many of their pamphlets were of small, vertical format: typically 4⅜" by 6" (111 mm by 152 mm). These slim pocket books, which often contained about 16 pages, combined the functions of sales brochures, maintenance instructions and parts lists. After the war these functions tended to be separated.

The sales brochures became fold-out sheets, brightly coloured in Raleigh red and yellow and profusely illustrated with photographs. The trade was provided with large, horizontal format, staple-bound parts lists and service manuals. These were 10½" by 8¼" (267 mm by 210 mm), well written and clearly illustrated.

Bridging the gap between sales literature and trade service manuals were publications such as the 76-page *Cycle Maintenance Handbook*, first published in spring 1946. It contained descriptions and photographs of the flora and fauna that keen cyclists might see on their travels, hints and tips on cleaning the bike, safety hints, instructions for maintenance of the bicycle and its components, and a section on touring by lake, hill or sea, complete with route maps. All this cost just one shilling (£1.80 today).

## The opposition

During the 1940s there was relatively little development of derailleurs but towards the end of the decade the number of derailleur manufacturers increased to about fifty. Most derailleur freewheels offered three or four sprockets and stiff ⅛" chains were still the norm. Shifting was generally poor but derailleurs were improving and gaining in popularity: in 1949 French maker Simplex produced 1.5 million.

In the 1948 Cycle and Motorcycle Show at Earls Court more than a dozen British derailleur makers displayed their products. They included British Cyclo, BSA, Constrictor-Osgear, Hercules, Phillips, Resilion and Tri-Velox. There were 145 derailleur-equipped bicycles on display, not one of them produced by the Raleigh group of companies. In the world of hub gears, BSA were still producing their 3-speed, designed by Sturmey-Archer in the Edwardian era, while Hercules made an unauthorised copy of the Sturmey-Archer AW.

## AW copies

In autumn 1945 George Wilson reported to the committee that a sample of a new Hercules 3-speed had been obtained and dismantled. It was 'well made and of good quality'. It was an exact copy of the Sturmey-Archer AW. Raleigh therefore decided that all genuine Sturmey-Archer spares should henceforth be stamped with the Sturmey-Archer mark.

In copying the AW hub so exactly, Hercules infringed a Sturmey-Archer patent. This was filed in spring 1939 and covered a refinement to the forming of gear selector splines. Raleigh served a writ on Hercules and the Hercules AW copy was then modified to avoid infringing the patent. No other aspect of the AW design was protected by patent.

Another company that copied the AW was Brampton. Their 3-speed trigger had a distinctive stepped body like later Hercules triggers. This was not surprising, as later Hercules AW copies ('B type') seem to have been made by Brampton, which became a sister company of Hercules within TI's British Cycle Corporation.

In spring 1949 George Wilson reported that he was negotiating with Herr Frei of the Scintilla company in Switzerland. Wilson sought the rights to Scintilla's X hub, a copy of the AW. The deal involved Sturmey-Archer buying Scintilla's entire stock of about 80,000 hubs, which also included copies of the ABC and BFC drum brakes. The purchase price would enable Sturmey-Archer to make a profit on selling the hubs in Switzerland and give them 90% of the Swiss hub gear market. A new Sturmey-Archer company would be established in Switzerland and the Bank of England gave Raleigh permission to obtain the necessary Swiss francs for this purpose.

Raleigh formed the company Trix SA in the Swiss city of Biel in summer 1949, with a capital of 50,000 Swiss francs that cost Raleigh £2,883 (£87,000 today). The British Board of Trade allowed Raleigh to omit mention of the company and the names of its directors in Raleigh's annual accounts. Unfortunately the pound was devalued in autumn 1949 whereas the Swiss franc remained strong. So instead of making a profit, Sturmey-Archer stood to lose some £12,000 (£361,000 today).

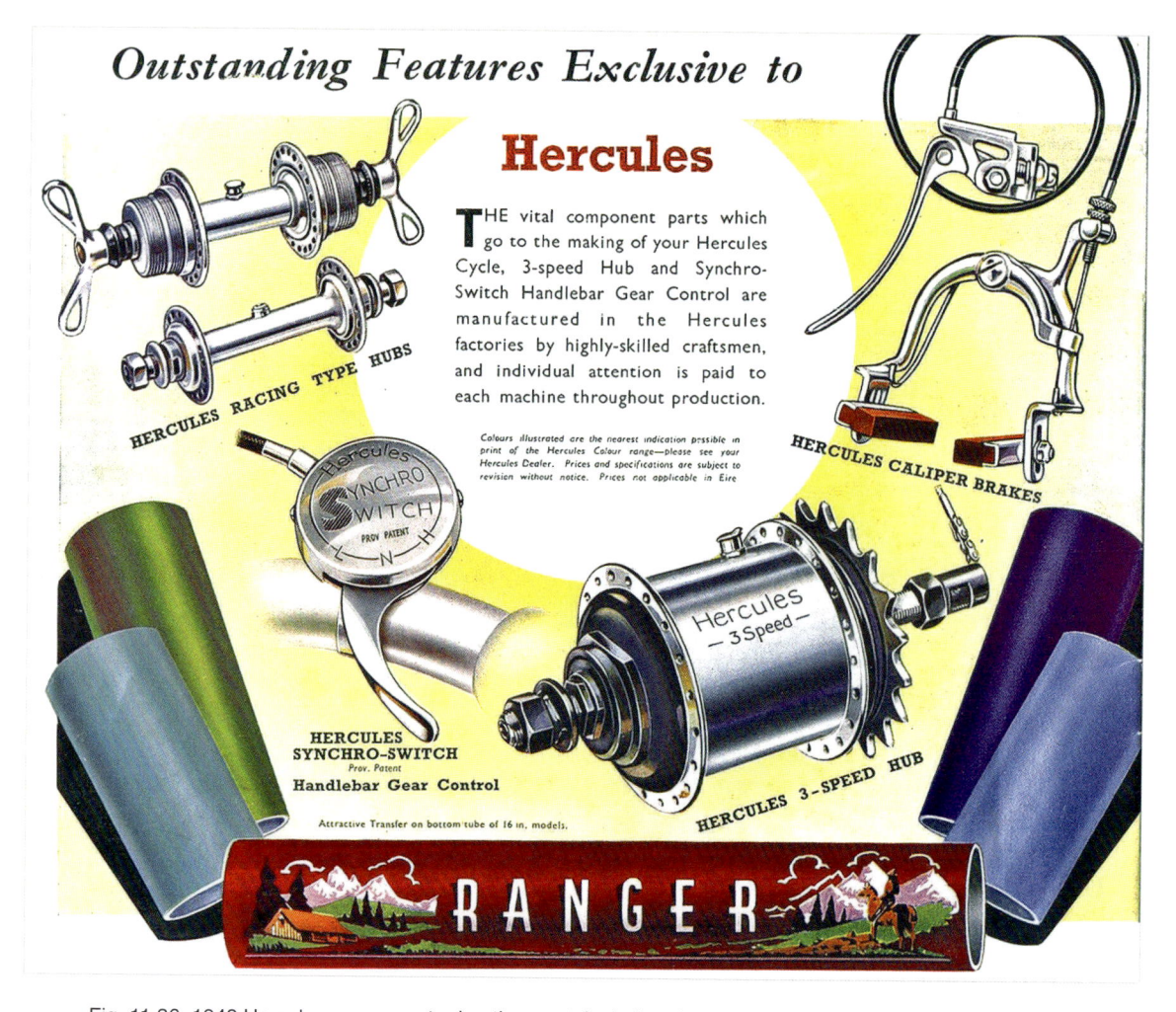

Fig. 11.36. 1948 Hercules component advertisement, including the AW copy with its new 'Synchro' switch.

## Production increases

The war had many adverse effects on the bicycle industry but there were compensations. For example, the flowline mass production techniques adopted for munitions manufacture encouraged similar practices in peacetime.

By the end of the 1940s Sturmey-Archer's product range was expanding again and almost half the output was exported. Production was up by about 50% on the pre-war figure. The country was pulling out of a long period of post-war austerity and heading for a balance of payments surplus. In the words of historian John Burke, 'It was a time for a modicum of rejoicing' – and Sturmey-Archer was heading for its golden jubilee.

# Chapter 12
# From jubilation to rationalisation

### Sturmey-Archer in the 1950s

### National recovery, shortages and fluctuating demand
The 1950s began with preparations for the Festival of Britain, intended 'to demonstrate to the world the recovery of the United Kingdom from the effects of war in the moral, cultural, spiritual and material fields'. The festival took place in Battersea Park, London during the summer of 1951 and also celebrated the centenary of Prince Albert's Great Exhibition. John Burke wrote: 'Eight and a half million people visited the festival … and were exhilarated by the achievements of which the country showed itself still capable.'

Sturmey-Archer was still coping with shortages of materials and fluctuations of demand following World War 2. In 1950 the board decided to offer Dynohubs, hitherto reserved for Raleigh-owned bicycle brands, to the whole cycle industry. The trade reacted favourably and by early 1951 weekly output of Dynohubs was 12,000. Production would have been higher but for a shortage of magnets. A 60% cut in supply was threatened but Raleigh negotiated with the Mond Nickel Company through whose 'good offices' the cut was limited to 20%. By spring 1951 Dynohub output was down to 9,000 a week: there was a serious shortage of strip steel, as well as magnets, and the factory was put on short time. Two years later Dynohub production was only 7,000 a week, well below the budgeted 12,000 a week maximum capacity.

### The product range in the early 1950s
Notwithstanding the materials shortages and fluctuating demand, the prevailing attitude at Sturmey-Archer reflected the national spirit of post-war optimism. At the start of the decade they were marketing a wide range of hubs.

There were six 3-speeds: the AW standard wide-ratio, the AB/ABC wide-ratio and drum brake combination, the AG wide-ratio with Dynohub, the AM medium-ratio, the ASC close-ratio fixed-wheel and the AC ultra-close-ratio. There were five 4-speeds: the standard FW wide-ratio, the FB/FBC wide-ratio and drum brake combination, the FG wide-ratio with Dynohub, the FM medium-ratio and the FC close-ratio. There were also the BF/BFC front drum brake, the BR/BRC rear drum brake and the GH6 front Dynohub.

In autumn 1951 prices ranged from £1 8s. 3d. (£42 today) for a front drum brake to £4 5s. 0d. (£126 today) for the FG 4-speed Dynohub. The standard AW 3-speed cost £1 19s. 3d. (£58 today).

### The derailleur threat looms larger
In the early 1950s Sturmey-Archer still had some following among the racing fraternity. This was bolstered by Reg Harris, World Professional Sprint Champion in 1949, 1950 and 1951. Harris appeared in the company's advertisements proclaiming: 'I use and recommend Sturmey-Archer, without doubt the finest range of cycle gears available today.' And as a Sturmey-Archer brochure put it: 'It is interesting to note that Reg Harris … considers the Sturmey-Archer FM (4-speed medium ratio gear) the best all-round gear for club use.'

Fig. 12.1. 'Since the early days' advertisement from 1951.

Fig. 12.2. The Sturmey-Archer range circa 1952.

The FM was certainly popular with many clubmen and is fondly remembered. However, it did suffer from reliability problems. The ratchet in the left ball cup had a tendency to fail, resulting in a low gear pawl bursting through the alloy shell. Examination of FM hub internals reveals that at least three different versions of this ratchet were manufactured. One version used a traditional ramped ratchet; the others were merely slots cut into a cylindrical projection of the ball cup. The slotted versions were the most suspect. Bearing in mind the assembly tolerance between the shell and the ratchet cylinder part of the ball cup, all the force of the low gear pawl was taken by one end of the ratchet 'tooth'. There could be no effective load sharing by either the rest of the ratchet ring or the hub shell acting as a compression ring.

In 1950 Raleigh sales representative Jack Lauterwasser, the former Olympic cyclist and record breaker, converted an FM into a medium-ratio 5-speed hub. Eventually Sturmey-Archer requested that he keep the 5-speed under wraps. This he did until 1966, when the company finally marketed a 5-speed. Had Sturmey-Archer marketed a medium-ratio 5-speed hub in the 1950s, the company might have maintained a larger following among club riders for longer.

Meanwhile, despite the support of Reg Harris, the derailleur threat was increasing; so much so that Sturmey-Archer took out two patents for derailleur mechanisms. Both covered designs by Henry Oxley. The first patent, GB 682,235, was filed in 1949. This covered a rear derailleur mechanism that offered 'the provision of means which will enable the chain-shifting fork to

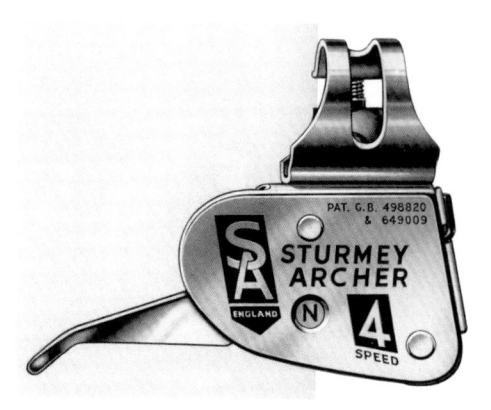

Fig. 12.3. Mid 1950s 3-speed trigger.

Fig. 12.4. Exploded view of the mid 1950s 3-speed trigger.

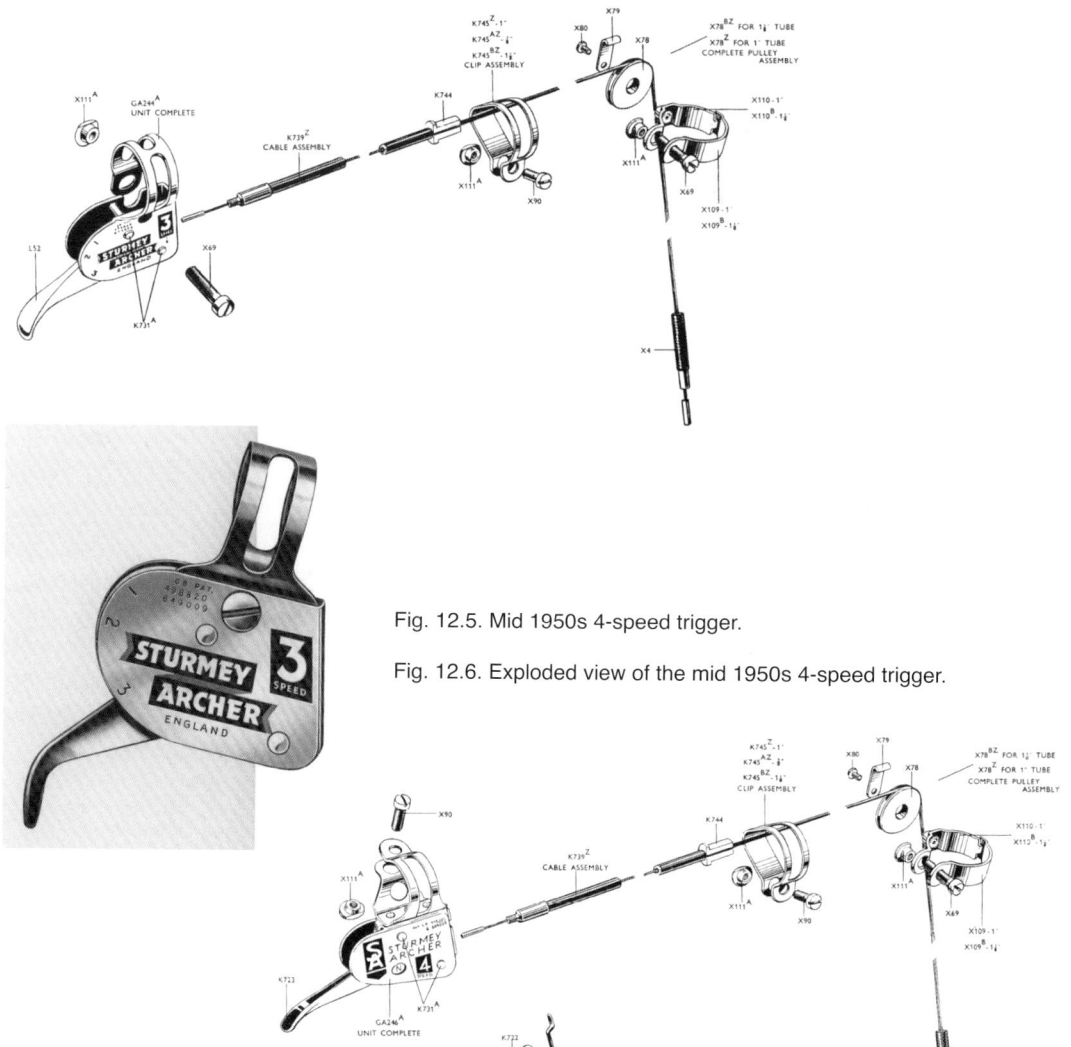

Fig. 12.5. Mid 1950s 4-speed trigger.

Fig. 12.6. Exploded view of the mid 1950s 4-speed trigger.

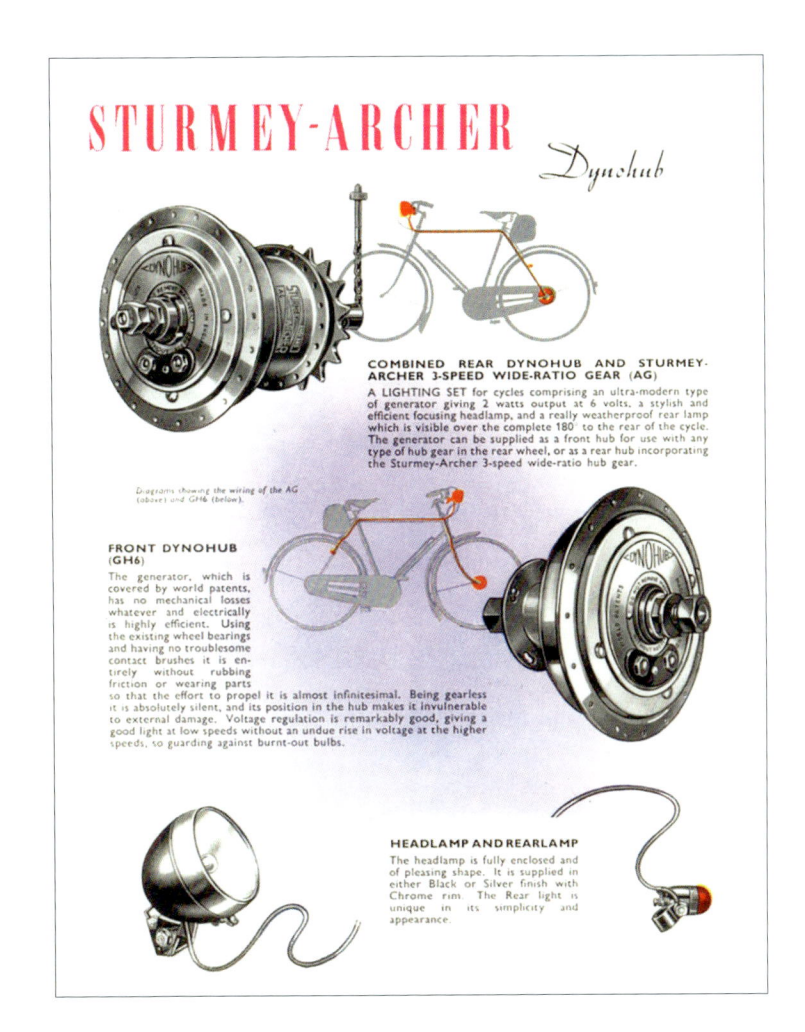

Fig. 12.7. 1952 Dynohub advertisement.

be located quite close to the group of sprockets without impeding removal of the back wheel'. Two versions were illustrated and each required a separate chain tension arm fixed to the chain stay. The second patent, GB 695,961, was filed in summer 1950 and covered a more modern-looking rear mechanism with a sprung double pulley assembly in place of the separate tension arm. These patents were a form of insurance, neither mechanism being put into production.

## Another change of sprockets
Sturmey-Archer announced that from 1951 all hub gear sprockets would be of the 3-lugged type, retained by a circlip. The new sprockets replaced the hitherto standard threaded sprockets for roadsters and the 12-lugged 'club' type. The 3-lugged type was adopted by rival hub gear and coaster manufacturers, such as Shimano and Fichtel & Sachs.

It took some time for the new sprockets to reach the trade; the 1952 Brown Brothers catalogue stated that they were not yet available. At first they were supplied only in sizes from 14 to 20 tooth inclusive. The 14 and 15 tooth sprockets could not be used with the AW, AB/ABC or FW if a 1½" (38 mm) chainline was required. To achieve this necessitated fitting a different ball ring, ball cage and dust cover, otherwise the chain would foul the dust cover.

## An ultra-close-ratio fixed-wheel 3-speed

In spring 1951 *The Bicycle* magazine carried an article about gearing. This prompted J.E. Harrisson, Sturmey-Archer's general sales manager, to write to the editor. His letter revealed that 'such a gear as *The Bicycle* suggests is possible and your readers may be interested to learn that a prototype ultra-close-ratio fixed 3-speed racing hub is at present under test'.

A week later Peter Bryan wrote to *The Bicycle* as 'the seventh to share the secret' of this new gear. He reported that Harrisson had half-jokingly taunted William Brown in 1949, saying:

> I bet that you cannot make a 3-speed ultra-close-ratio fixed hub gear with the direct drive on the normal gear, and the equivalent of one tooth up and down for top and bottom ratios.

Bryan was enthusiastic about the new gear and hinted it was very light. But when asked about production the company answered: 'No definite date, we are heavily committed with export orders.'

A few weeks later Sturmey-Archer and William Brown applied for GB patent 768,342 which covered the ultra-close-ratio hub referred to in Harrisson's letter to *The Bicycle*.

## Principles covered by GB patent 768,342

This complex patent covers gears with primary and secondary epicyclic trains 'coupled to provide alternative ratios between input and output members and in which one member of each train is permanently coupled to an output member'. The versions shown in the patent drawings had gear rings permanently coupled to the hub shell.

In one version the secondary planet cage housed two separate sets of planets of different size. The first set meshed with the gear ring and the second set of planets. The second set meshed with the secondary sun, which was rotatable on the axle; the primary train sun was also rotatable and could be clutched to any of the free members of the secondary compound train (e.g. the secondary planet cage or secondary sun). Another version used compound pinions in the secondary planet cage, again with a rotatable sun. Yet another incorporated a means of locking either sun to the stationary member to obtain further gears.

The feeling of insecurity within Sturmey-Archer instilled by the progress of the derailleur gear showed itself in this patent; when describing the ratios offered by the new fixed-wheel hubs, the patentees related some of them to derailleur sprocket tooth differences. One version offered a decrease of 8.6%, direct drive and an increase of 6.7% – equivalent to single tooth derailleur steps using 15, 16 and 17 tooth sprockets. Gears thus obtained could have been in the order of 62, 68 and 73" or 73, 80 and 85".

Another version offered direct drive, a 1% increase (practically impossible with a derailleur and arguably pointless), a 5.5% increase (a single tooth step) and an 18.6% increase (a further rise of about two teeth). This could have provided gears of 68, 69, 72 and 81".

A third version offered direct drive, a 7.4% increase, 8.6% increase and 33.3% increase; in other words, an ultra-close-ratio 3-speed with a wide-ratio fourth gear (e.g. for 'power driving' down hills). Gears obtainable from this hub could have been in the order of 68, 73, 74 and 91" or 60, 64, 65 and 80". All these were fixed-wheel hubs but none of them were marketed.

## Drum brakes

By autumn 1951 the rare FB/FBC wide-ratio 4-speed drum brake had been deleted. About this time the brake shoes and plates of the AB/ABC, BF and BR hubs were re-designed to

Fig. 12.8. The BF and BR internally expanding drum brakes. The following drawings show the brakes in their mid 1950s versions. Rod linkage was still an option, although Bowden cable control was becoming more common.

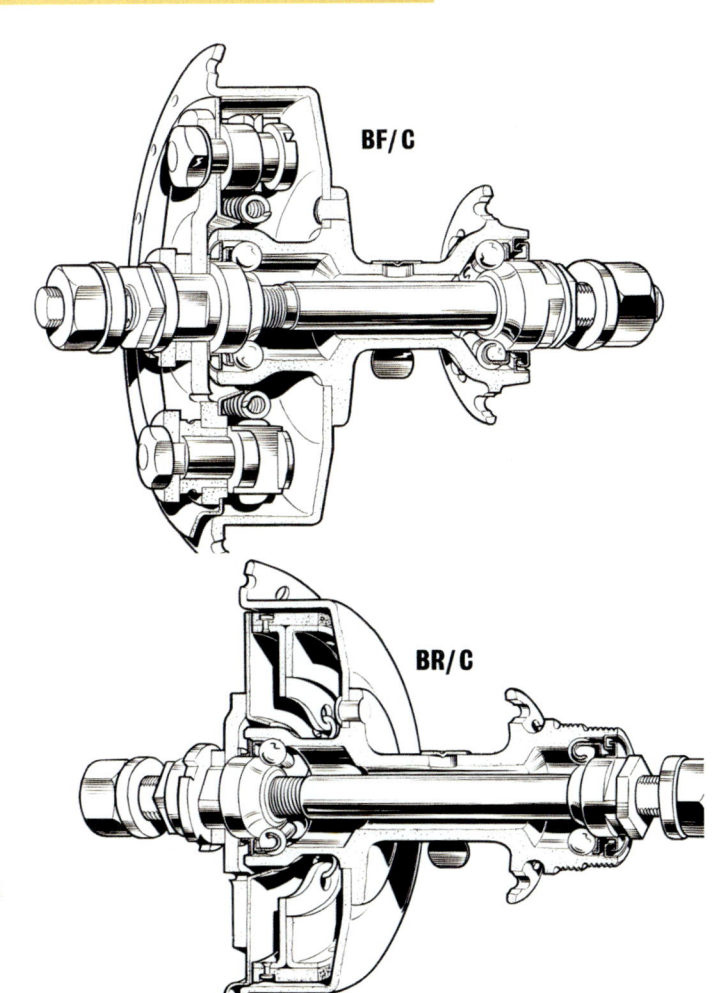

Fig. 12.9. Cutaway drawing of the BF drum brake.

Fig. 12.10. Cutaway drawing of the BR drum brake.

187

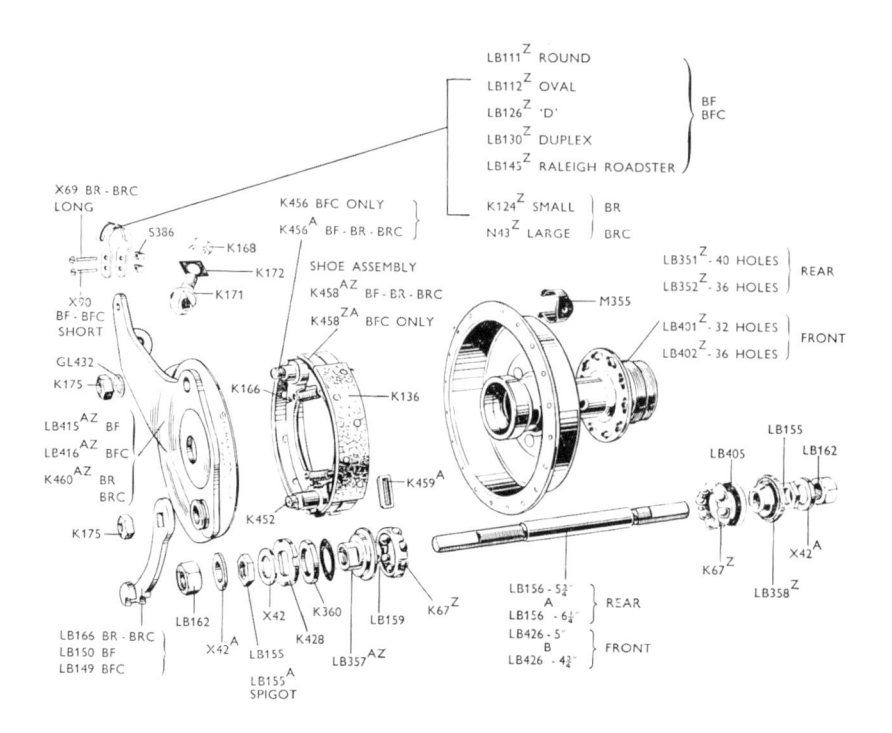

Fig. 12.11. Exploded view of the BF drum brake.

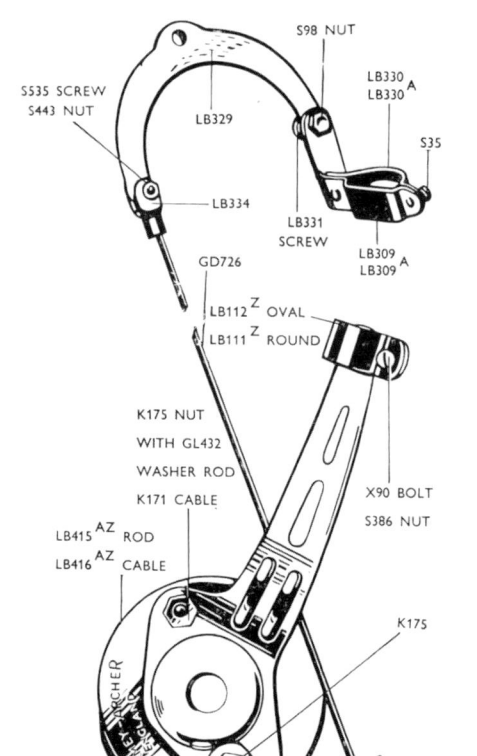

Fig. 12.12. Rod linkage for the BF front drum brake.

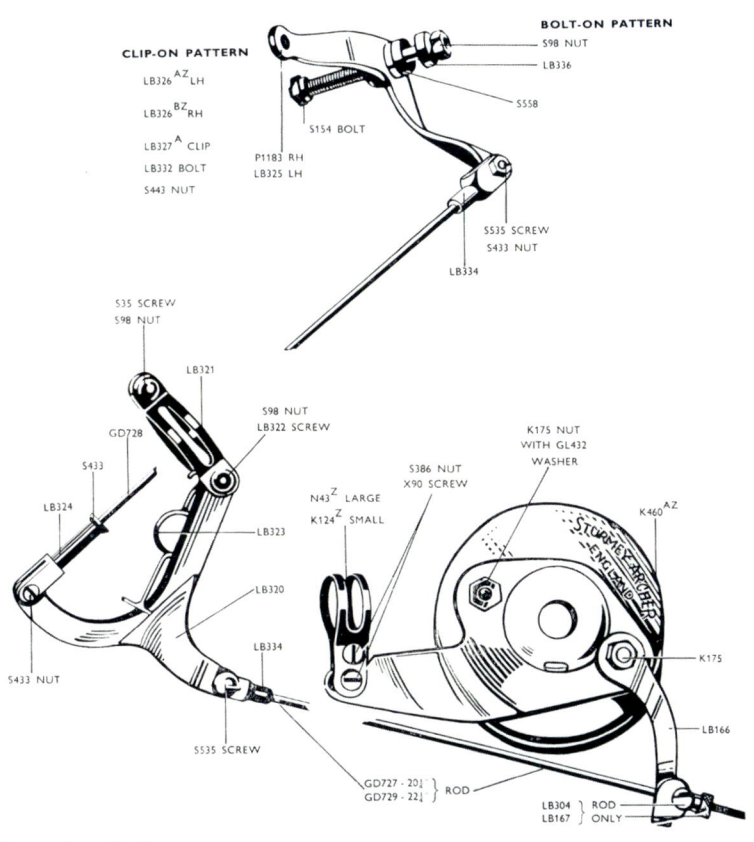

Fig. 12.13. Rod linkage for the BR rear drum brake.

improve efficiency. The new shoes, complete as a unit with the fulcrum plate, could be interchanged with the earlier type but new shoes alone could not be fitted with the old type fulcrum plate.

In spring 1955 Sturmey-Archer managing director Donovan Schnabel Robinson reported that demand for drum brakes was slackening because several Continental firms were making them for mopeds and selling the hubs at cut prices and customised to manufacturers' requirements.

## Jubilee

The original Sturmey-Archer gear was invented in the year of Queen Victoria's death; the company celebrated its Golden Jubilee in the accession year of Queen Elizabeth II.

To celebrate the company's jubilee Sturmey-Archer produced a splendid large format souvenir brochure entitled *50 Years of Leadership*. The introduction stated:

> On the occasion of our Golden Jubilee we are proud to present a brief history of Sturmey-Archer; the story of designers, technicians, riders and the hubs they produced and tested – the story of 50 years of leadership – in both home and overseas markets.

The brochure was beautifully illustrated with hubs, components and personalities past and

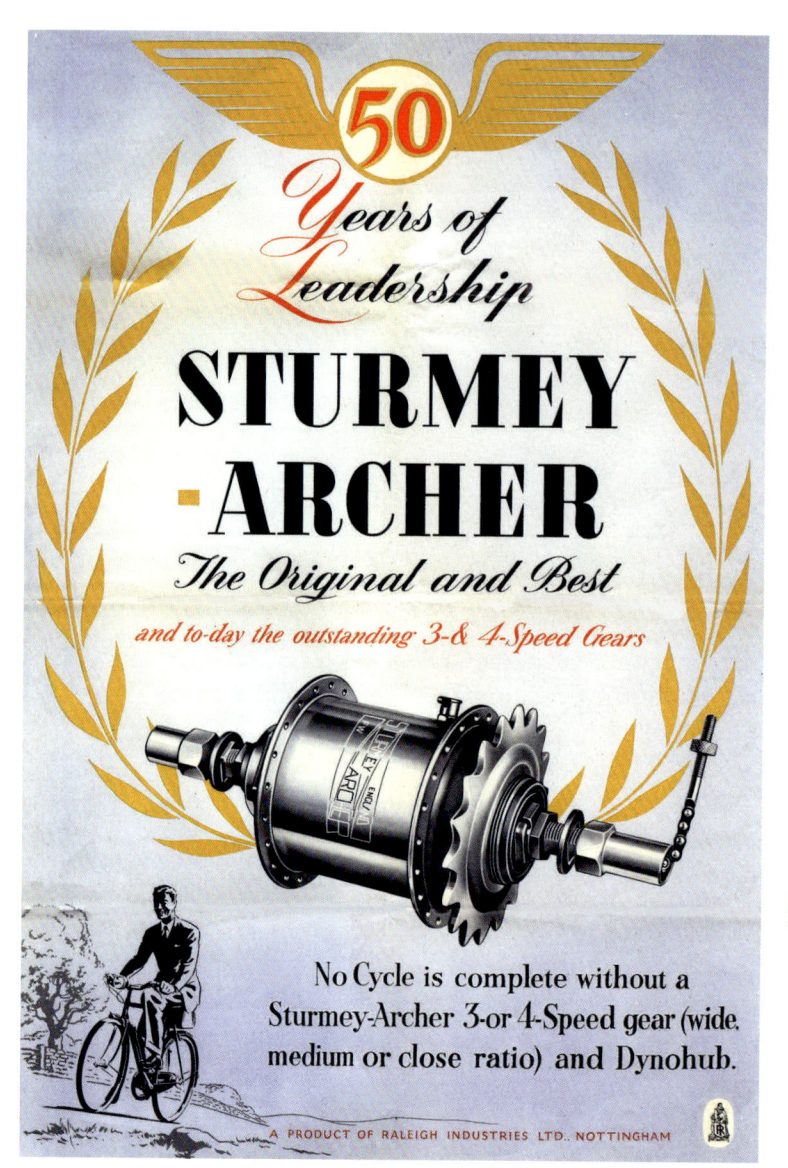

Fig. 12.14. Poster celebrating '50 Years of Leadership'.

present. It even included a photograph of William Reilly although his true contribution was not mentioned; he was merely referred to as a cycling expert 'who had earlier invented a 2-speed hub gear' and who 'reinforced' the Sturmey-Archer team.

*50 Years of Leadership* radiated confidence in the future of hub gears, some of it wishful thinking, as this example shows: 'Whilst many still prefer the 3-speed gear, there is no doubt that the 4-speed, by offering two normal gears, provides advantages which will ensure its pre-eminence in the future.' The brochure proudly proclaimed that '2,000,000 Sturmey-Archer hubs will be produced in 1952' and that half the 1951 production had been exported to over 100 overseas markets.

Europe remained the largest market: Belgium and Switzerland preferred simple 3-speeds whereas Holland and Scandinavia favoured gears combined with drum brakes. The English-speaking countries also constituted a significant market and the brochure noted that 'the Sturmey-Archer ranges are incorporated in American-built bicycles to help meet British competition on something like equal terms'.

### Factory No. 2

The back cover of *50 Years of Leadership* showed the newly extended 40 acre (16.2 hectare) Raleigh factory, described as 'the largest and most modern cycle plant in the world.' It employed 7,000 people and a section within it produced Sturmey-Archer gears. A 10 acre (4 hectare) factory extension, known as No. 2 Factory, was opened in autumn 1952 by the Duke of Edinburgh. It was linked to the older works complex by a bridge crossing Faraday Road, the railway and the River Leen.

### Return of the Tricoaster – the TCW Mk 1

1953 saw the reintroduction of a Tricoaster hub, the first Sturmey-Archer back-pedal brake of any sort since the mid 1930s. William Brown and Sturmey-Archer applied for GB patent 703,992 at the end of 1950. It covered a 3-speed combined with a multi-disc coaster brake. However, this type of brake was not fitted to the production hub which was given the designation TCW (Tri-Coaster Wide-ratio). In summer 1952 William Brown and Sturmey-Archer filed GB patent 723,164 which also dealt with Tricoasters.

The TCW Mk 1 passed internal testing in summer 1952. Testing by 'real' riders then commenced. One such was Cliff Smith, an amateur racing cyclist and Raleigh enthusiast from Leicester. He sent Sturmey-Archer three letters with feedback about the hub at the end of 1952 and beginning of 1953. The TCW Mk 1 went into production soon after this and all early hubs were exported; initial feedback from customers and dealers was excellent. There was, however, some final tweaking: in spring 1953 Sturmey-Archer wrote to Cliff Smith saying 'certain modifications have been made to this hub and we are anxious that the latest internals should now be fitted into the wheel you are testing for us'.

Fig. 12.15. The TCW Mk 1 3-speed coaster.

Fig. 12.16. Cutaway drawing of the TCW Mk 1.

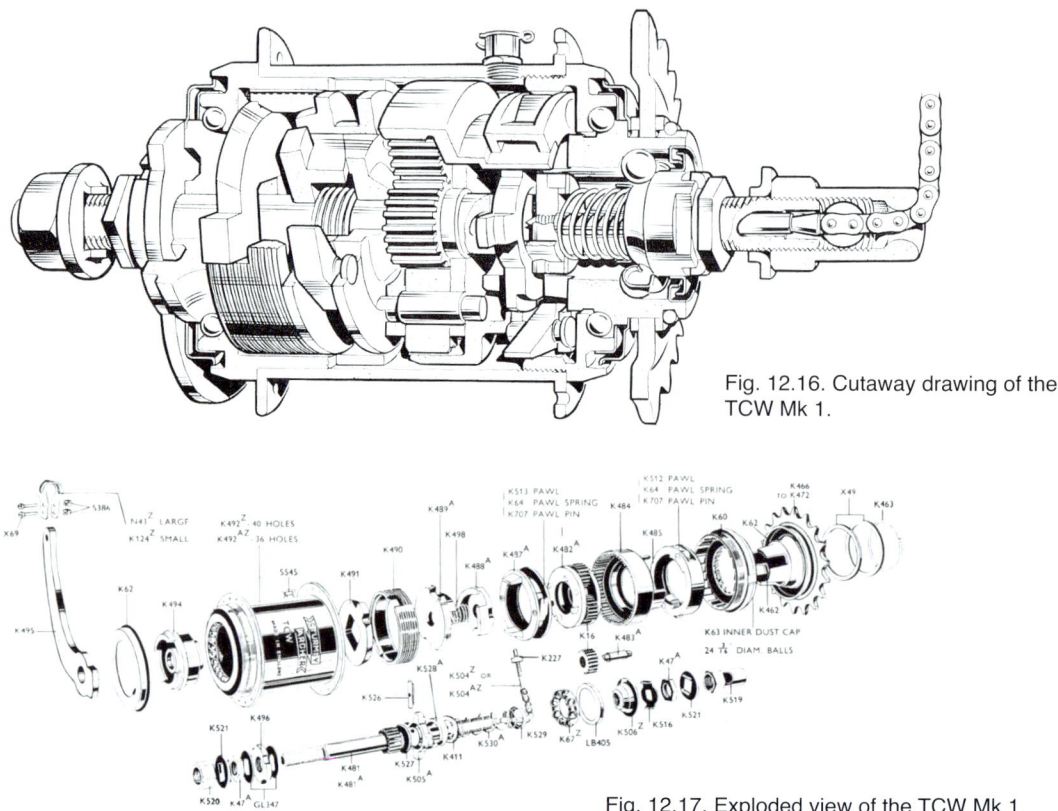

Fig. 12.17. Exploded view of the TCW Mk 1.

## Principles covered by patent 723,164

The patent noted that with certain 3-speed/coaster combinations:

> One problem still remains, namely that ... locking of the wheel by use of the pedals to apply the brake may synchronise with the engagement with the wheel hub of a forward driving pawl of the gear, thereby preventing forward releasing movement, relative to the wheel, of the brake-actuating mechanism of the gear.

This could result in damage to the mechanism.

The new patent covered an improved coupling mechanism between the gear and brake; the solution to the wheel locking problem involved the use of lost motion (slack movement) between certain internal components. The high gear pawls were mounted in a separate pawl ring loosely dogged to the gear ring, which allowed some free rotational movement between the parts before taking up drive. The low gear pawls were similarly mounted relative to the planet cage.

The brake was a split ring type with internal conical surfaces held between two conical plates: one was plate fixed, the other moved along the axle, squeezing the brake ring open so it rubbed against the hub shell. The moving conical plate was driven by an opposing ramp system: one ramp was on the back of the moveable plate, the other was on a member attached to the planet carrier of the gear, the two ramped facings being separated by ball bearings.

Fig. 12.18 TCW hub with prominent self-adhesive label reminding the user to oil the hub frequently.

When the planet carrier rotated backwards (i.e. when back-pedalling) the action of the opposing ramps moved the conical plate to the left and operated the brake. When forward pedalling resumed the conical plate was moved back to the right by a spring.

The production TCW Mk 1 was very similar to the hub described in GB patent 723,164 except that the ramps were not separated by ball bearings. It had a bronze-lined aluminium one-piece brake band. Because the gear section was based on the AW, it still had a 'no-drive/no-brake' spot between top and middle gears, and the rate of braking depended on which gear was selected – in low or middle gear the brake was operated through low gear, whereas in high gear the brake bypassed the gearing.

### TCW Mk 2
In spring 1955 a modified TCW was under test but about four years passed before the TCW Mk 2 went on sale. New features were a bronze-lined split-steel brake band and a modified drag spring system.

### An ultra-wide-ratio 4-speed
Sturmey-Archer and William Brown applied for GB patent 738,338 in spring 1953. This concerned hub gears with primary and secondary gear trains working on the 'cascade' principle. The specification noted that:

> Hitherto, the secondary train has been added for the purpose of obtaining a close-ratio gear by coupling the parts of the two gear trains together so that the sun and planet carrier of the primary train are coupled to suitable members of the secondary train whereby through an alternative coupling the planet carrier of the primary gear train could provide a closer ratio somewhere between the normal reduction ratio of the primary gear train and a direct drive, with the option in some instances of being able to obtain also the said normal reduction ratio of the primary gear train.

The object of the new patent was to use the same kind of gear for a new range of ratios. The gear illustrated was a 4-speed which in the top three speeds worked like a standard wide-

Fig. 12.19. Sturmey-Archer was also active in Belgium. This photo shows VW delivery vans in Brussels, led out by a 'Beetle' with a large model hub gear on its roof.

ratio 3-speed. The lowest gear was obtained by locking the secondary sun to the axle to obtain a compound reduction, the drive output being from the secondary planet cage. The result could be the equivalent of an AW wide-ratio 3-speed with an additional ultra-low gear. With a 20 tooth primary sun and a 60 tooth gear ring the percentage changes could be 43.75% decrease, 25% decrease, direct drive and 33.3% increase; typical gears offered could be 38, 51, 68 and 91". But this was another hub that never got into production.

## Demand for 5-speeds ignored

In touring circles there was interest in a hub that gave a really low gear combined with a reasonably high top – something not achievable even with an FW wide-ratio 4-speed. The subject of 5-speed hubs was raised in the *CTC Gazette* in 1952 when columnist Skipper wrote:

> I believe Sturmey-Archer did invent a 5-speed hub some years ago, but it was never launched on the market – a great pity, as I am sure it would have met with a wonderful response. I do hope we shall not have to wait for some Continental manufacturer to meet our needs.

But Sturmey-Archer still did not launch a 5-speed.

## Demand exceeds supply

By summer 1952 Sturmey-Archer hubs were in very short supply for the export market. At home the company also failed to meet demand. Standard AW 3-speeds were 'severely rationed'. By early 1953 the situation was acute, partly because American cycle manufacturers had decided that 35% of their output would be lightweight machines, most of which would require 3-speed hubs. British cycle manufacturers tried to get as many AWs as possible for the US market where, as the board's June 1953 minutes put it, a Sturmey-Archer 3-speed hub was regarded as an essential fitment. New plant was ordered to enable production to be increased.

### A new managing director – and record production

In autumn 1953 Donovan Robinson, formerly sales director for Dunlop Rubber in South Africa, became managing director of Sturmey-Archer. He spent three months familiarising himself with the whole Sturmey-Archer operation before taking effective day-to-day control at the start of 1954. In the autumn Robinson reported that Sturmey-Archer had sold over 2 million hubs in a single year for the first time ever and production was soon increased to 35,000 a week.

### Sturmey-Archer in the Netherlands

In 1955 Sturmey-Archer terminated their agency agreement in the Netherlands with NV de Groninger Rijwielfabriek A. Fongers. Instead a Dutch Sturmey-Archer company, Sturmey-Archer Gears (Holland) NV, was formed with headquarters in Amsterdam: Mijnheer Westerhoek, formerly of Fongers, was in charge. The burgomeister of Amsterdam officially opened the office early in 1956. A return of at least £45,000 a year (£1 million today) was expected from this operation. In 1957 bicycle sales in the Netherlands fell significantly, reducing the profitability of Sturmey-Archer's Dutch operation. But the Dutch market remained generally profitable for Sturmey-Archer and was to remain of pivotal importance to the future of the company.

### Factory No. 3

Sturmey-Archer's sales increased by 13% in the 1955 financial year. The company could sell more than it could produce of all its products other than front drum brakes. But early in 1956 Donovan Robinson highlighted the adverse effect on Sturmey-Archer of the considerable downturn in bicycle output from Raleigh's British competitors. Meanwhile construction of Raleigh's new works on Triumph Road and Orston Drive had recently commenced. Known as No. 3 Factory, it spread over 20 acres (8.1 hectares) and cost £5 million (£107 million today) to build.

Sturmey-Archer occupied about half the building complex and the aim was to achieve the desired output using normal day shift working. Additional space would be made available in the hardening, auto and plating shops, so that full advantage could be taken of a night shift should higher production be required. No. 3 factory was officially opened in autumn 1957 by Field Marshall Lord Montgomery of Alamein but it was not fully utilised until some time later.

### Production processes

A Raleigh factory tour souvenir booklet from the late 1950s provides an insight into the organisation and operation of the Sturmey-Archer factory at this time.

The machine shop was where pinions, axles, planet cages and other small high precision parts were made. Hydraulically-powered automatic broaching machines cut splines and teeth in gear rings, pinions and drivers. Sturmey-Archer hub cones were made on fully-automatic, centreless grinding machines, at a high output rate, to an accuracy of 3/10,000-inch. Other machinery used included gear cutters and multi-drilling machines.

Seven hundred thousand components per week were produced in this department, using 460 high precision machine tools. Many of the parts were then sent to the hardening shop.

Fig. 12.20. The new factory, completed in 1957.

Fig. 12.21. 'Monty' meets female employees at the opening of the new factory.

The assembly department depended on nimble-fingered operators manually assembling the hubs on a moving belt production line. The hubs were inspected at each stage of assembly. Finally the assembled gear, complete with trigger control and cable, was tested for strength, accuracy and efficiency.

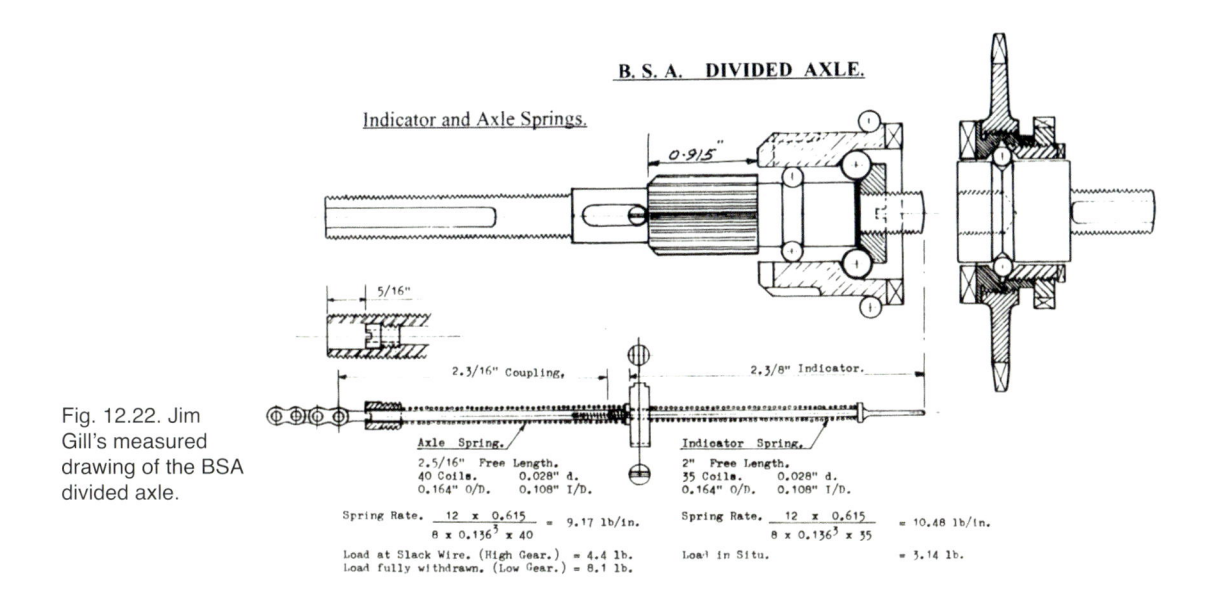

Fig. 12.22. Jim Gill's measured drawing of the BSA divided axle.

## BSA's last hub gear – the Quick Release 3-Speed

Early in 1954 a new type of hub gear came on the British market – the BSA Quick Release 3-Speed. A Sunbeam advertisement in *The Bicycle* proclaimed 'Wheel removed in 30 seconds. No more struggling with gear case or greasy chainwheel.'

During some 50 years of hub gear production, BSA introduced few new designs; this was to be their last. The new BSA Quick Release 3-speed was particularly intended for use with traditional-style Sunbeam roadsters with their famous 'Little Oilbath' gearcase. BSA acquired the Sunbeam brand during World War 2. Single-speed Sunbeams had been available fitted with Sharp's divided axle, enabling the rear wheel to be removed leaving the sprocket in place with chain and gearcase undisturbed. The new Quick Release 3-speed offered the same advantage but was introduced half a century too late for its potential market: gearcases were very unfashionable in the UK by the 1950s.

The Quick Release hub had the toggle chain on the left. To remove the wheel, the toggle chain was uncoupled, the left-hand wheel nut slackened by about six threads and a spacing piece removed from inside the fork end. A suitable spanner was then fitted to the spindle detaching washer which was rotated, unscrewing and moving the axle to the left. This released the wheel, leaving the sprocket and carrier fixed in the frame.

The coupling between the sprocket carrier and the rest of the hub was achieved by a single driving dog, only 2.5 mm deep. When refitting the rear wheel it was easy to screw the axle apparently fully home without the shallow single dog engaging. Later a multiple dog system was substituted which was remarkably similar to that used in the Palladini split-axle hub for derailleur freewheels. It is said that one of the BSA designers saw and examined the Palladini hub in the now defunct shop of David Wilson Cycles in Birmingham and thereafter incorporated its features into the BSA Quick Release 3-Speed.

Apart from the split axle feature and the left-hand changer coupling, the new gear was a standard BSA 3-speed and therefore basically a Sturmey-Archer type X. Some trouble was experienced with axle slip caused by insufficient tightening of the left-hand wheel nut, so a special detaching washer and chain adjuster were fitted to later hubs.

In autumn 1954 Raleigh tried to persuade BSA to stop making hub gears but to no avail.

Raleigh meanwhile reached an understanding with Phillips Cycles to increase delivery of Sturmey-Archer hubs to at least 5,000 a week during 1955. In return Phillips committed to using Sturmey-Archer gears for the next five years. If Phillips subsequently decided to make their own gear, they would give Sturmey-Archer at least two years notice.

Early in 1956 George Wilson told the Raleigh board that, following further negotiations, BSA would probably stop making their own 3-speed and instead buy from Sturmey-Archer. But the following year BSA's bicycle interests became part of the Raleigh group and production of BSA hub gears ceased.

## Hercules and Brampton

Sturmey-Archer continued to suffer problems with unauthorised copies of their products, particularly the AW 3-speed. One of the main offenders was Hercules and it is worth looking back at the relationship between Hercules and Sturmey-Archer over the previous couple of decades.

It seems that, starting with the AW 3-speed about 1937, Raleigh badge-engineered Sturmey-Archer gears for Hercules. But in 1945 Hercules started selling copies of the AW without Sturmey-Archer's approval. Raleigh served a writ on Hercules for transgressing a minor patent by William Brown and Sturmey-Archer concerning selector splines, so Hercules merely changed the spline design slightly and carried on with impunity.

It is probable that most post-war Hercules AW copies were made by Brampton Fittings, who also sold unauthorised copies of the AW 3-speed branded with their own name. In 1956 Tube Investments' British Cycle Corporation, having acquired both Hercules and Brampton, entered formal agreements with Raleigh to stop making hub gears and use only Sturmey-Archer hub gears. Thereafter, Sturmey-Archer resumed badge-engineering hubs for Hercules.

## Scintilla and Trix

The previous chapter described how Sturmey-Archer had done a deal with the Swiss firm Scintilla to buy all their stock of Sturmey-Archer copies, and how Raleigh then formed the Trix SA company in Switzerland, initially to sell these copies. But in summer 1950 Raleigh director Eric Baker reported that Hercules were trying to break Sturmey-Archer's price maintenance agreement regarding hubs in Switzerland. Sturmey-Archer were already losing money due to devaluation of the pound and a price cut would make the situation even worse.

Raleigh office manager Henry Duvall obtained Bank of England authority to buy up to 235,000 Swiss francs (£19,600 today) on behalf of Raleigh to offset the losses due to devaluation. This prevented Trix showing heavy losses and having to be wound up. It also enabled the loss to be transferred to Raleigh, who then obtained tax relief on it. The overdraft in Raleigh's name with Union Bank of Switzerland was cleared by summer 1952.

Early in 1951 Raleigh managing director George Wilson forecast that all the X hubs (AW copies) bought from Scintilla would be sold by the end of the summer, as would all but 1,000 of the Scintilla-made ABC and BFC brake hubs. The remaining 1,000 would be held in store to meet 'isolated future orders'. From thereon genuine Sturmey-Archer internals would be supplied for use with X shells and trigger controls.

George Wilson and Eric Baker visited France, Italy and Switzerland in spring 1951. Their Swiss trip coincided with Hercules reducing their hub gear prices. 'The measures necessary to counter this move were taken,' the board minutes record, and Wilson was confident that opposition in Switzerland from Hercules would be largely eliminated. Hercules meanwhile

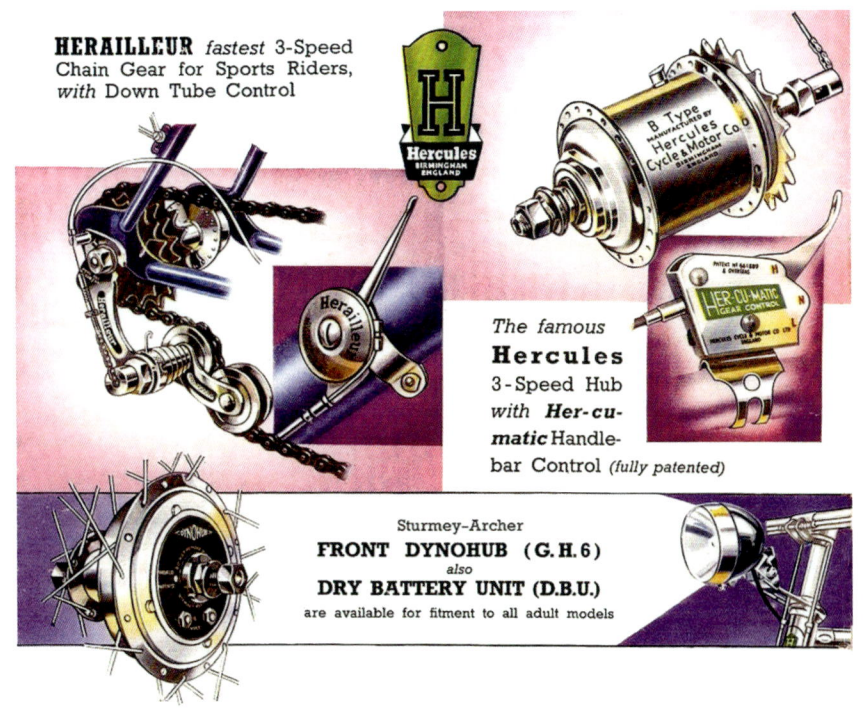

Fig. 12.23. Options from Hercules in 1953 included their own indexed 3-speed derailleur, a copy of the Sturmey-Archer AW 3-speed and genuine Sturmey-Archer Dynohubs.

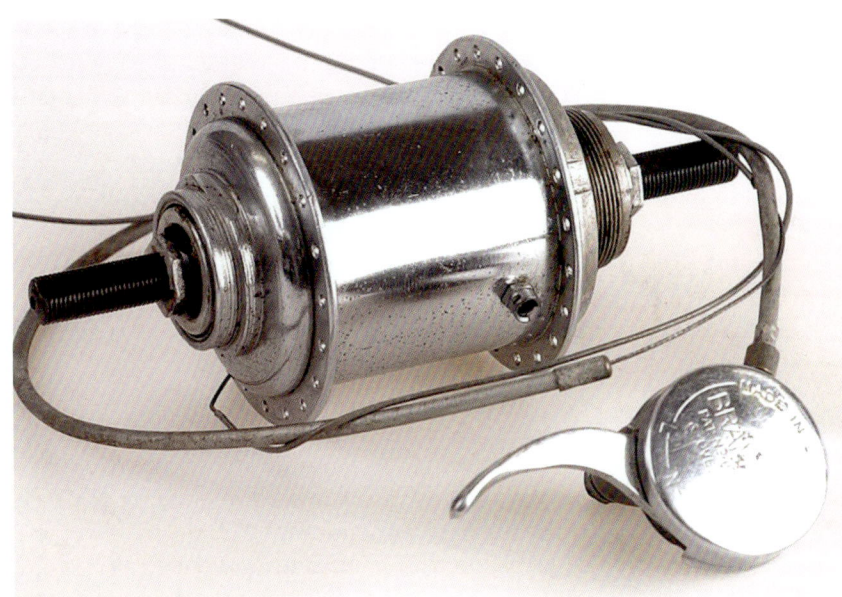

Fig. 12.24. An early Brampton AW clone.

libelled Sturmey-Archer in an advertisement in the Swiss technical press. Following a complaint from Raleigh, Hercules agreed to make 'an ample apology'.

Early in 1952 George Wilson reported that he had agreed to buy the tools and equipment formerly used by Scintilla to make hub gears and brakes. The price was 87,500 Swiss francs (£7,300 today). Discussions were held with Scintilla about them making hub shells, triggers and spare parts for Sturmey-Archer.

By spring 1953 Trix had enough hub shells to last for 18 months and shell production therefore ceased. In the summer it was decided that no further purchases would be made from Scintilla: the X-branded hub shells and triggers would be made in Nottingham.

### Puch, J.C. Higgins, Schwinn and Fichtel & Sachs
By spring 1955 Steyr-Daimler-Puch in Austria were making copies of the AW 3-speed at a rate of 10,000 a month. The Graz-based firm produced nearly two million AW Styria-branded copies between 1954 and 1972. In 2019 Chris Morris compared the internals of a Styria AW copy with a Scintilla AW clone. He concluded that the Styria was a copy of the Scintilla, rather than a direct AW clone, apart from the clutch which was closer to the superior Sturmey-Archer original.

Other AW copies made by Steyr-Daimler-Puch were sold in the USA marked as J.C. Higgins, the sporting goods brand of Sears, Roebuck and Company, and as 'Schwinn approved Steyr' for the Schwinn bicycle company.

Competition was also hotting up in West Germany. Fichtel & Sachs introduced a Tricoaster-style hub of their own design but it was heavier and more expensive than the Sturmey-Archer product. It was thought that Fichtel & Sachs were designing another Tricoaster and also a wide-ratio 3-speed.

Sturmey-Archer managing director Donovan Robinson visited the two main competitors during 1955. He went to Steyr-Daimler-Puch and proposed that they stop making hub gears in exchange for assurance of supply from the Sturmey-Archer range. One of Puch's managing directors visited Sturmey-Archer that autumn. Robinson also visited Fichtel & Sachs and saw them making a wide-ratio 3-speed apparently designed so that a coaster brake could be added. A 'very favourable understanding' was established with Fichtel & Sachs and three of their managing directors visited Nottingham.

### Wide-ratio 6-speed
In spring 1954 Sturmey-Archer and William Brown applied for another patent that broke new ground. GB 767,523 covered an arrangement

> which gives more ratios than are normally available and at the same time gives a greater overall range of gear and a choice of spacing between adjacent gear ratios.

This gear used primary and secondary epicyclic trains arranged to drive in series (cascade). The primary epicyclic train functioned as a simple epicyclic 2-speed which gave direct drive or a reduced drive; its output was fed into the secondary train which acted like a simple 3-speed. By this means six speeds were available.

Two versions were described in the patent. The percentage variations were: 46% decrease, 31% decrease, 22% decrease, direct drive, 13% increase and 45% increase – giving typical gears of 37, 47, 53, 68, 77 and 99"; or 46% decrease, 31% decrease, 22% decrease, 11% decrease, direct drive and 28% increase – giving typical gears of 37, 47, 53, 61, 68 and 87". This was another ingenious William Brown design that never got into production.

### Plastic lubricator
During the mid 1950s Sturmey-Archer and William Brown filed several patents for unexciting but useful detail refinements to hub gears. GB patent 739,997, applied for in 1954, covered

Fig. 12.25. An unauthorised Styria brand AW clone made by Puch in 1954.

**STYRIA 3-Speed hub**
Made in Austria 1954 - 1972

Fig. 12.26. An AW clone made for Sears' sporting goods brand J.C. Higgins by Steyr-Daimler-Puch.

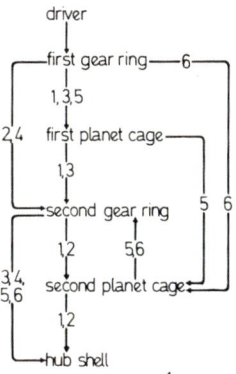

Fig. 12.27. Flowchart for the 6-speed patent.

```
               driver
           first gear ring ——6——
              1,3,5               |
         2,4  first planet cage   |
              1,3                 |
           second gear ring     5 6
              1,2    5,6          |
         3,4  second planet cage——
         5,6
              1,2
           hub shell
```

1 = compound reduction
2 = simple reduction
3 = simple reduction
4 = direct
5 = compound reduced increase
6 = simple increase

PRINCIPLE OF STURMEY-ARCHER SIX-SPEED
(1954 PATENT)
Clutches not shown.

201

Fig. 12.28. The plastic lubricator.

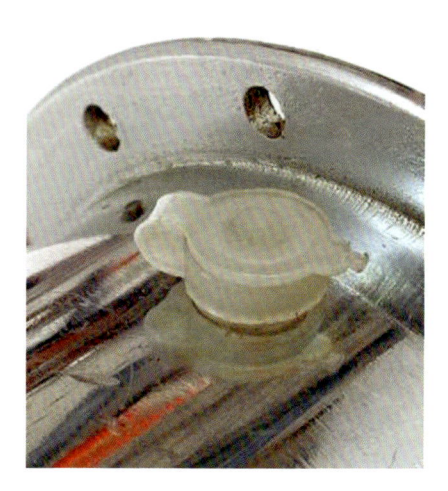

Fig. 12.29. A standard mid 1950s Sturmey-Archer single-speed freewheel.

the plastic lubricator found on Sturmey-Archer hub gears from the mid 1950s until the 1980s, with its 'strap-like connection between the body part and the closure.' The specification pointed out that other types suffered from disadvantages such as the time taken to assemble and susceptibility to loss or damage.

The plastic lubricator was successfully trialled in 1955 on FG hubs, after which it replaced the hinged-lid metal lubricator that tended to leak oil. The plastic lubricator was discontinued in the 1980s when Sturmey-Archer adopted a grease-based 'lubricated for life' policy.

## Improved axle key
In 1955 Brown and the company filed GB patent 789,462 covering a new type of axle key for the gear change mechanism within hub gears. To increase the strength of the axle key it was usually necessary to reduce the axle strength, by making the slot in the hollow axle wider to accommodate a thicker key. One solution would be to make a pin with a bulbous centre but this would be difficult to assemble. Brown's solution was a two-part axle key made from flat strip. This offered the advantage of the bulbous-centre pin while also being easy to assemble and cheap to make. But it could not be threaded and would require some means, such as an indicator rod, to anchor the gear change linkage to it; the solution to one problem created another, so the two-part axle key was not put into production.

## Self-adjusting freewheel
GB patent 796,670, applied for in 1955, was for improved freewheel sprockets. Brown's design used crescent-shaped unsprung pawls seated in the inner ring of the freewheel; these engaged with ratchet teeth cut in the inside of the outer ring (the sprocket itself). The inner ball race was fixed and the outer race was 'axially movable on the inner ring and resiliently loaded towards the … rigid inner ball race part'. The resilient loading was achieved by three tiny coil springs, making the free-wheel self-adjusting for easy assembly and to take up wear as it occurred. There must be some doubt as to how well this arrangement would have worked in practice; it was another patented idea that did not go into production.

Fig. 12.30. A pair of Dry Battery Units, one a chrome-plated rarity. Filter Switch Units could be fitted into the caps of the DBUs, which (despite the label) have been removed in this photograph.

## Dry Battery Unit and Filter Switch Unit

By 1950 the DAU (Dry Accumulator Unit ) had been quietly replaced by the DBU (Dry Battery Unit). This was almost the same as the DAU but used ordinary disposable dry batteries. In its basic form the DBU required the rider manually to switch between Dynohub power and battery power. However, Sturmey-Archer produced a useful accessory that did the job automatically: the Filter Switch Unit (FSU), invented by engineer Leslie Arthur Holliday of 50 Milton Road, London W7.

Raleigh filed a patent for the FSU in 1949 (GB 662,678). It was a small rectifier circuit that fitted into the top of the DBU. The production version switched to battery power at speeds below 9 mph (15 km/h); above that speed the Dynohub took over. A bleed resistance in the FSU allowed a small reverse current to flow through the disposable cells, giving them a longer life than usual, perhaps by depolarising the cells. A new diode-based FSU circuit appeared about 1955. From 1965 until production ceased in 1983, more than 759,000 FSUs were made.

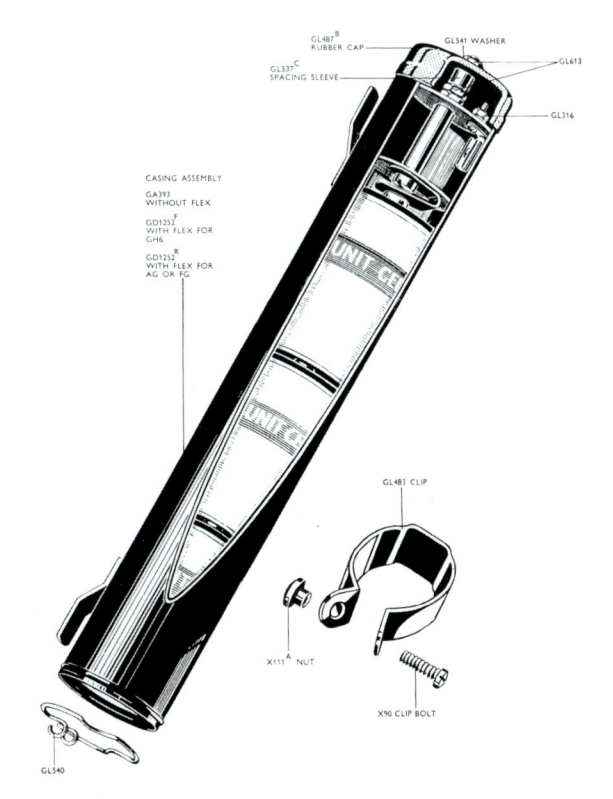

Fig. 12.31. Cutaway drawing of the Dry Battery Unit.

## New lamps

During the mid 1950s new headlamps were introduced. These were of more streamlined appearance but still necessitated use of a screwdriver to remove the rim and lamp front. The roadster lamp was available in black or silver, the smaller sports lamp only in silver. Both had

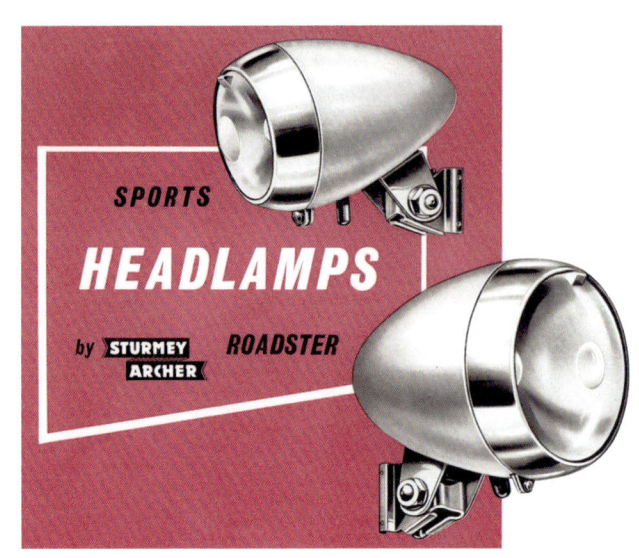

Fig. 12.32. Mid 1950s Sturmey-Archer Sports and Roadster headlamps.

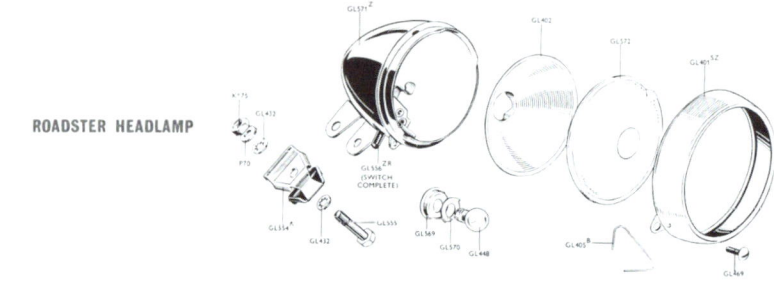

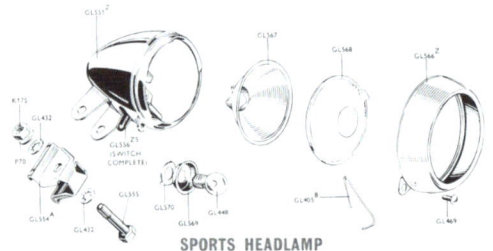

Fig. 12.33. Cutaway drawings of the Roadster and Sports headlamps.

chrome rims and a three-position switch on the underside, the third switch position being for the DBU.

After the war, despite opposition from cycle manufacturers and the Cyclists' Touring Club, rear lights became compulsory for bicycles ridden at night. In the 1950s, as lighting regulations became more stringent, rear lights had to be redesigned. An all-plastic streamlined rear lamp was introduced 'unique in its simplicity and appearance and designed to comply with the new lighting regulations'.

GB patent 762,422, filed by William Brown and Sturmey-Archer in 1954, covered an improved headlamp. The object was 'to provide a simple lamp construction in which the rim may be secured to the body or removed therefrom without the use of tools, and in which no means, external of the lamp, are necessary for securing the rim in position'.

The proposed lamp body incorporated a forwardly projecting flange of reduced diameter and a removable beaded rim adapted to fit onto the flange with a locating lip and a catch to

Fig. 12.34. The mid 1950s plastic rear lamp.

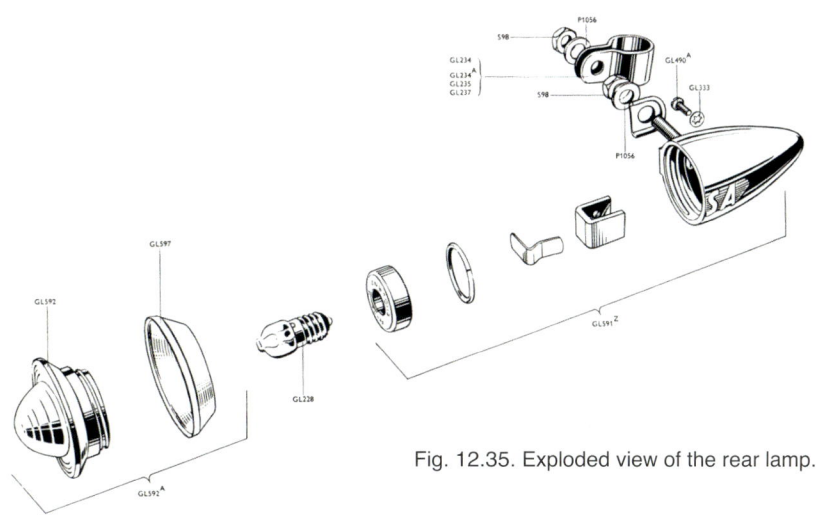

Fig. 12.35. Exploded view of the rear lamp.

engage behind the flange. The rim was rotated to lock it to the lamp body but this design did not get into production. Nor did the 'new form of friction driven Dynohub' mentioned by George Wilson early in 1952, about which nothing more is known.

The robust combined rear lamp and reflector covered by GB patent 829,552 was a clever design that Raleigh used for many years. The patent embodied a William Brown invention but under the Raleigh name, rather than Sturmey-Archer. It was applied for in autumn 1955 and covered a combined rear lamp and reflector for mounting on the rear mudguard in a rubber fairing. The objective was to produce an improved construction for easier assembly 'wherein the resilience of the material of the mounting serves to ensure pressure of the base contact of the bulb onto its associated terminal'. The unit was fixed to the metal mudguard with a single screw that also provided the return circuit path for the bulb.

Fig. 12.36. Leaflet for the SW 3-speed (DDRN 4-13-33-7).

## An improved Dynohub
Sir Harold Bowden passed the chairmanship of Raleigh to George Wilson in 1955 and became life president of the group. He continued to maintain an active interest in Sturmey-Archer's products and complained of the poor light output of the Dynohub, requesting that the highest priority be given to researching improvements. But no magnetic material was found that gave a significantly better output. A more time-consuming re-working of the Dynohub would be necessary to boost its light output significantly.

A patent for an improved Dynohub (GB 824,721) was therefore filed by William Brown and Sturmey-Archer in spring 1957. The object was: 'a new and improved arrangement of parts which will provide a high utilisation of the permanent magnet material and economy in the use of copper'. It consisted of a multi-polar permanent magnet rotor (or stator) having a plurality of poles of alternate polarity which in number is an even multiple of three, and a wound soft iron stator (or rotor) having the same number of poles characterised in that the soft iron stator (or rotor) is divided into magnetically separated 3-pole units.

A prototype, with the internal mechanism speeded up by a gearing system, showed promise but development was abandoned until the 1960s. George Wilson suggested bringing back George Rawlings, inventor of the original Dynohub, but this did not happen.

## SW 3-speed

In 1956 Sturmey-Archer ceased production of the AW 3-speed. It was replaced by the SW (S-series Wide-ratio) which the company described as:

> Revolutionary! Fewer working parts than any other wide-ratio 3-speed hub and 4 oz lighter than its predecessor. Smaller and neater in every way with an increase of 38.4% and a decrease of 27.7% from normal. An outstanding contribution to the well-being of the everyday cyclist.

Unfortunately the SW was a dismal commercial failure and ultimately led to William Brown leaving the company after some 20 years as head of the design and development department.

The SW gear was indeed smaller, lighter, neater and had fewer working parts than the AW. It also gave slightly wider ratios – an increase over direct drive of 38.4% and a decrease of 27.7%. Like the Micrometer-type freewheel used in the first Sturmey-Archer 3-speed, the SW had crescent-shaped un-sprung pawls for lightness, simplicity and compactness.

Production of the SW began in autumn 1954. The first 3,000 SW hubs were fitted to Raleigh bicycles and sold only on the home market. About half broke, due to failure of the planet cage fixing plate, so introduction of the SW was halted. In spring 1955 1,000 modified SW hubs were fitted to Raleigh bicycles sold on the home market. There were only a few minor faults, although some users complained of the difficulty shifting from high gear to middle gear. Subsequently, via depots and dealers, 200 cyclists who used AW hubs were supplied with wheels containing the SW hub, free of charge. Just over 45% had no adverse comments but nearly 19% thought the ratios too wide and 24% disliked the gear change.

More than a year after SW production started, Donovan Robinson reported to the Raleigh board on progress and William Brown said he had gone as far as he could to ease the gear change. The board therefore approved the changeover from AW to SW production commencing on 1 April 1956 – which ominously was April Fools' Day.

So confident were Sturmey-Archer of the success of the SW that a hub-brake version and a Dynohub combination were prototyped, documented and advertised. The Sturmey-Archer master catalogue and 1957 price list shows the standard SW at £2 4s. 6d. (£50 today), the SB hub-brake version at £3 2s. (£60 today) and the SG Dynohub version at £4 10s. 4d. (£100 today), sold loose with all fittings. There was even a badge-engineered version of the SW made for Hercules. But in light of the problems with the SW, the SB and SG hubs were never released.

The launch of the new 3-speed was supported by prominent advertising in *Cycling* and *Motor Cycle Trader*. This made the point that the SW was 'the smallest, lightest wide-ratio hub gear yet made'. At the same time Reg Harris featured in adverts aimed at teenage boys. In one the famous racer said: 'Whatever kind of cycling you do, for complete efficiency and

Fig. 12.37. The SW wide-ratio 3-speed hub.

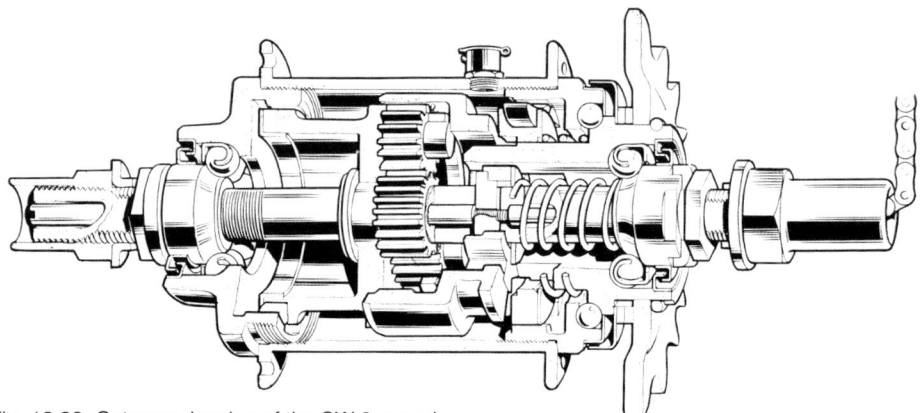

Fig. 12.38. Cutaway drawing of the SW 3-speed.

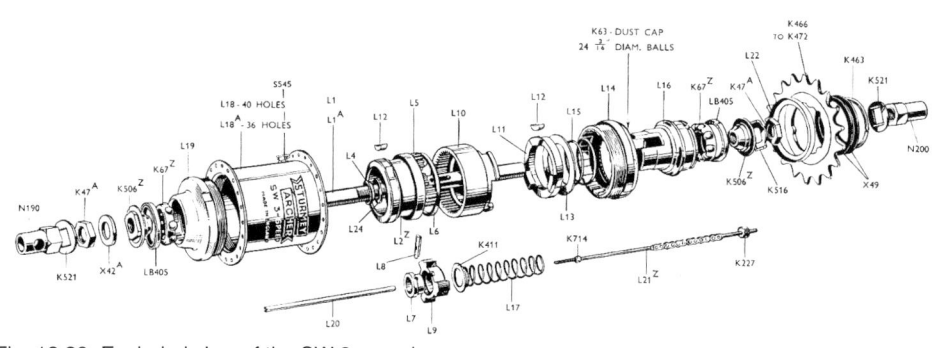

Fig. 12.39. Exploded view of the SW 3-speed.

the fullest enjoyment, you must have a Sturmey-Archer gear.' In another advert he pointed out that 'every moving part of a Sturmey-Archer gear gets eight dimensional tests varying from one hundredth to one thousandth of an inch!' Harris also provided the endorsement in SW advertising aimed at adults: 'It's smaller, lighter and really efficient.'

But the SW proved disastrously unreliable. Not all hubs failed but the failure rate was unacceptably high. In 1958 the AW returned to the range and the SW disappeared like a bad dream.

Fig. 12.40. The SB 3-speed drum brake.

Fig. 12.41. Cutaway drawing of the SB 3-speed drum brake.

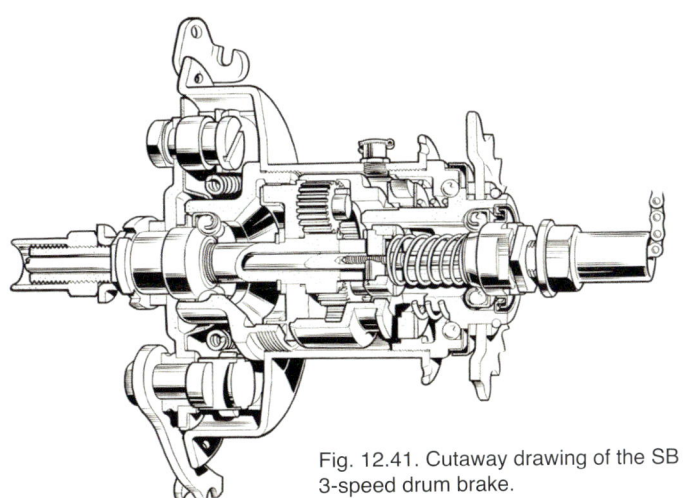

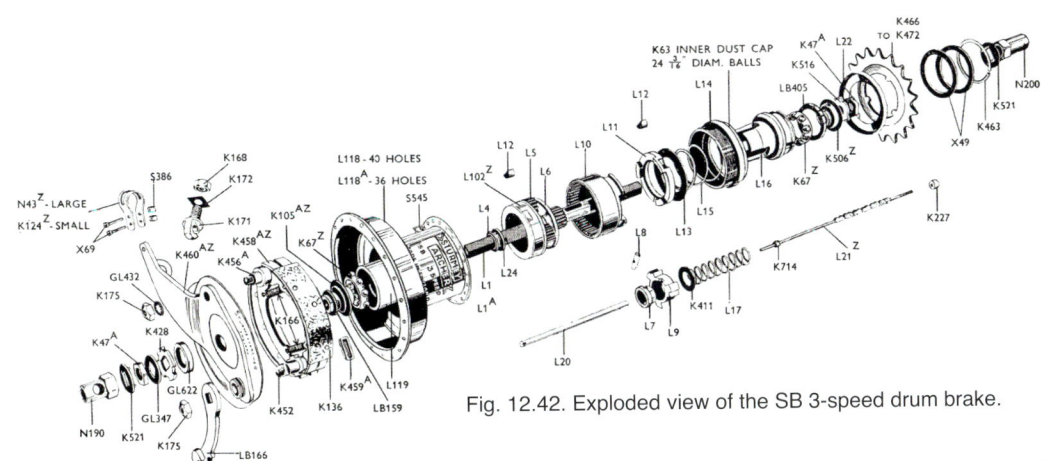

Fig. 12.42. Exploded view of the SB 3-speed drum brake.

209

The Hub of the Universe

Fig. 12.43. The SG 3-speed Dynohub.

Fig. 12.44. Cutaway drawing of the SG 3-speed Dynohub.

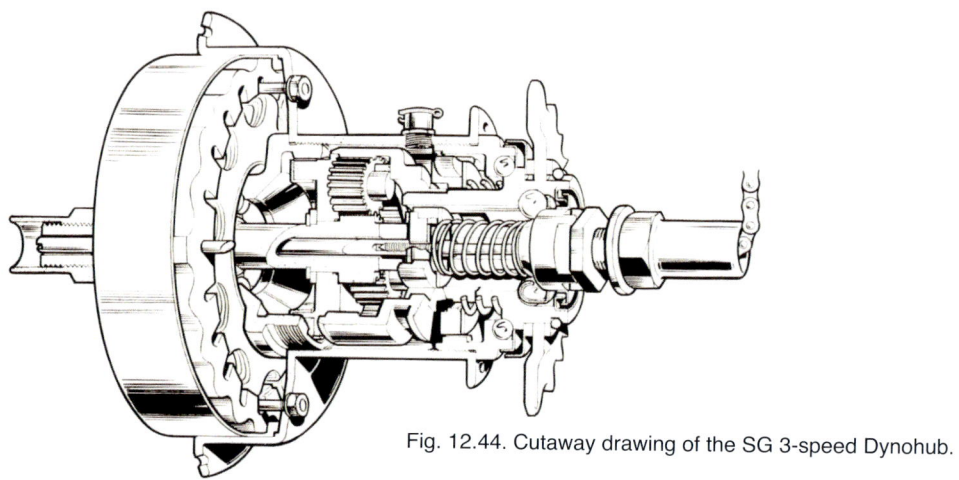

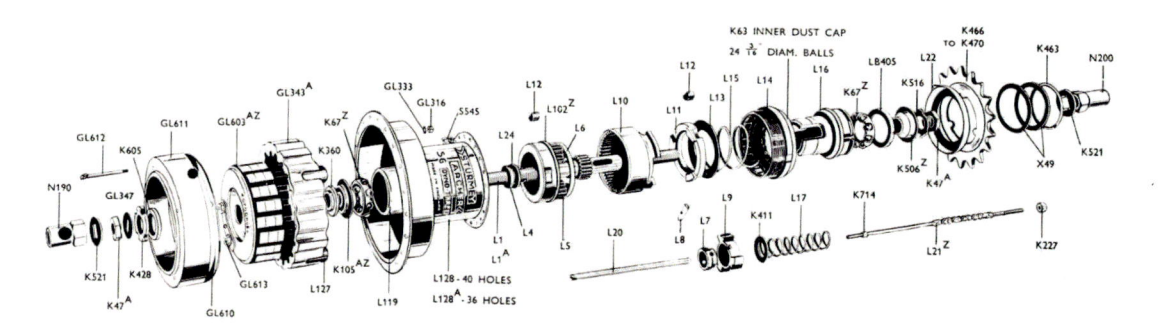

Fig. 12.45. Exploded view of the SG 3-speed Dynohub.

## Why did the SW fail?
In 1989 Martyn Dowell wrote to hub gear expert Denis Watkins suggesting that the problem arose because the pawl ring was under an eccentric thrust from its spring and in high gear the clutch did not support the gear ring. The three dogs between the gear ring and the pawl ring were thus no longer locked together as a unit and tended to 'walk apart'. Dowell suggested that a hub should be cut open and driven against a friction load so that the inner parts could be observed.

In 1995 engineer and Sturmey-Archer enthusiast Jim Gill sectioned an SW hub and built a test rig as Dowell had suggested. Gill produced a report on the SW's shortcomings and how they might be resolved. He noted that slipping occurred in direct and high gears but not in low gear. After extensive testing he concluded that invariably one or two pawls failed to seat fully against the ratchet teeth. The gear ring and pawl ring were thus no longer concentric, so that with each turn of the hub the dogs which locked these two items together moved very slightly in relation to each other and eventually 'walked' apart, causing a slip. Gill concluded that the SW would have worked fine if Sturmey-Archer had slightly increased the depth of the well for the pawls, fitted each pawl with a spring and modified the profile of the ratchet teeth in the ball cups.

The most comprehensive analysis of the SW hub, including how and why it failed and how to repair a damaged SW, was written by Brian Hayes. He and Gill agreed that merely spring-loading the pawls provides an excellent solution to the slipping problems in normal and high gear. It is tragic that nobody at Sturmey-Archer seems to have realised how such a cheap and simple modification could have saved so much investment and reputational damage.

Terry Radford, who worked at Sturmey-Archer from 1956 to 1986, recalled the company exporting 30,000 SWs a week, mainly to the USA. Overtime was plentiful until 'the bubble burst' and the fault, known in-house as 'knocking', became evident. Thousands of hubs were returned for remedial work, costing Sturmey-Archer a huge amount in overtime and import charges.

## The SW patent
The key patent for the SW was GB 749,248, which Brown and the company filed in autumn 1952 and spring 1953. This pointed out that with epicyclic hub gears: 'The size and weight of such hubs is governed in the main by strength considerations and not by the diameter of the gear train as such. The input member must be of a size adequate to carry the input torque and this in turn governs the size of the surrounding member which carries the output coupling pawls normal to such hubs.' One aim of the patent was to provide other forms of improved ratchet output coupling mechanism that provided adequate strength in less space, enabling a lighter hub. Another aim was a simpler method of making the ratchet inoperative to change gear.

The patent showed two solutions, both using a slidable coupling ring, separate from the planet cage, gear ring and driver. One of these coupling rings incorporated crescent-shaped unsprung pawls, like those used in the self-adjusting free-wheel referred to above: this was the solution adopted for the SW. Use of the new coupling ring meant that the gear ring assembly no longer incorporated the high gear pawls.

The coupling ring of the production SW used a pawl retaining washer and a thrust spring. The SW's low gear pawls were interchangeable with those in the coupling ring and both sets could be reversed to spread wear.

For high gear the control cable was slack and the sliding clutch as far left as it would go. This caused it to lock the driver to the planet cage (via the pinion stud ends); the thrust spring forced the coupling ring to its far left position, locking it to the gear ring. Drive passed from the driver via the sliding clutch to the planet cage, through the epicyclic gears and out of the gear ring via the coupling ring and its pawls to the hub shell. The low gear pawls were overrun.

For middle gear the sliding clutch was pulled to its mid position, disengaging from the planet cage and engaging instead with dogs on the inside of the gear ring; the coupling ring remained locked to the gear ring. Drive passed from the driver via the sliding clutch to the gear ring, then via the coupling ring and its pawls to the hub shell, bypassing the epicyclic gears to give direct drive. The low gear pawls were again overrun.

For low gear the sliding clutch was pulled as far right as it would go. It remained engaged with the gear ring dogs but pulled the coupling ring out of engagement with the gear ring. Drive passed from the driver via the sliding clutch to the gear ring, through the epicyclic gears and out of the planet cage via the low gear pawls to the hub shell.

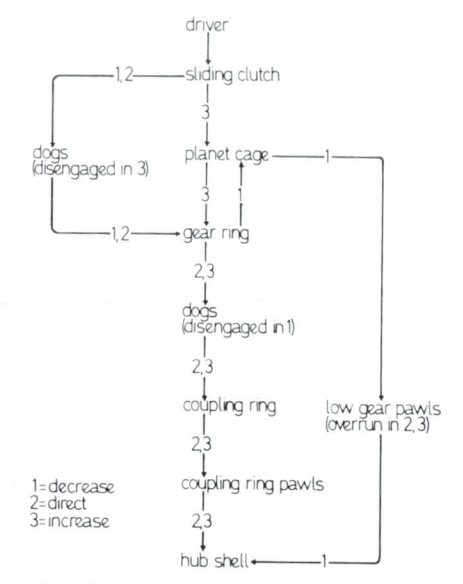

TYPE SW WIDE-RATIO THREE-SPEED
More compact than the AW because the separate coupling ring allowed a smaller gear ring. Unsprung pawls meant it was virtually silent.

Fig. 12.46. Flowchart for the SW 3-speed.

Like the AW gear, the SW had a 'no-drive' position between high and middle gears. Because of the unsprung crescent-shaped pawls the gear was virtually silent in operation. But such pawls do not engage as positively as sprung pivoted pawls and there was sometimes a slight and disconcerting delay in taking up drive.

Apart from the differences described above, the SW was broadly similar to the AW, except that the shell and most internal parts were smaller. Early SWs had an indicator rod in the left side of the axle; those made after mid 1958 had a combined toggle chain and indicator on the right. The ratios were slightly wider than those of the AW, typical gears being 50, 68 and 95" or 46, 64 and 88".

Two special tools were introduced for use with the SW: a 'C' spanner (type DD12418) and a hollow punch (DD12403). The punch was used to fit the planet cage fixing plate to the wheel axle. Later SWs did away with this plate by substituting a deep collar and locking nut – a much more practical solution that did not necessitate a special tool.

## William Brown's departure
The SW debacle cost William Brown his job at Sturmey-Archer. He left and pursued a successful career with Joseph Lucas, manufacturers of cycle and automobile accessories. William Brown was an ingenious engineer whose refinements of epicyclic bicycle gearing

exceeded anything previously seen. For several decades the majority of Sturmey-Archer products were based on Brown's designs.

## Never had it so good

In 1955 Raleigh started offering derailleur gears on sports models for the first time. It was an acknowledgement that trying to produce special hub gears for racing cyclists was no longer an economic proposition. In the eyes of most club cyclists, the victory of the derailleur over the hub gear was complete. By 1963 all hubs designed for the sporting rider would be deleted from the Sturmey-Archer range.

There remained the hope of winning over the younger generation. In 1959 Sturmey Archer ran a series of adverts on the theme 'What's missing?' These were placed in the worthy but dull *Children's Newspaper* and in the *Meccano Magazine*, a more interesting read for technically-minded youngsters. One advert featured a Vulcan bomber with the engine air intake missing; others showed a crane without a hook and an electric locomotive with no headlamp. The message was that, just as these machines were incomplete, so was your bicycle without a Sturmey-Archer gear.

This was certainly a widely accepted view among British boys at this time. Single-speed was almost beyond contempt, whereas derailleurs were weird and clunky. A 3-speed Sturmey-Archer was the norm and a 4-speed was positively exotic.

But among the wider British public cycling was at a low ebb. It had a 'cloth cap' austerity image out of step with the spirit of the time. At a political rally in 1957 prime minister Harold Macmillan famously stated that 'most of our people have never had it so good.' He added:

> Go around the country, go to the industrial towns, go to the farms and you will see a state of prosperity such as we have never had in my lifetime – nor indeed in the history of this country.

Prosperity meant aspiring to own your own car, though fewer than half of British families had access to one. Cycling was increasingly seen as something done only by those too young or too poor to own a car. Moreover, cycling was perceived as sweaty and the coming of commercial TV, with its deodorant and anti-perspirant adverts, made people increasingly aware of 'body odour'. This was an affliction considered so terrible that its name was abbreviated to 'BO': it was whispered behind your back but never to your face, even by your best friend – or so the adverts told us. You might not yet be able to afford that car but better the bus than BO. This did not bode well for cycling in general or Sturmey-Archer in particular.

## Back to internal combustion

In reaction to this situation Raleigh re-entered the market for powered two-wheelers with a simple moped. It was launched late in 1958 and its Sturmey-Archer engine was reviewed in *Cycling* the following spring. The motor had a cylinder capacity of 49.9 cc and an output of 1.3 brake horsepower. *Cycling* described it as sturdy, simple and 'one of the most rational ever designed for a machine which is, in essence, primarily for the rider to whom utility is everything'.

The moped also had Sturmey-Archer drum brakes: a standard BF front hub and a slightly modified version of the BR rear brake, known as the BRM (the M presumably standing for Moped). Originally there was no clutch but this became an optional extra in 1959 and could

Fig. 12.47. The 1958 Sturmey-Archer moped engine.

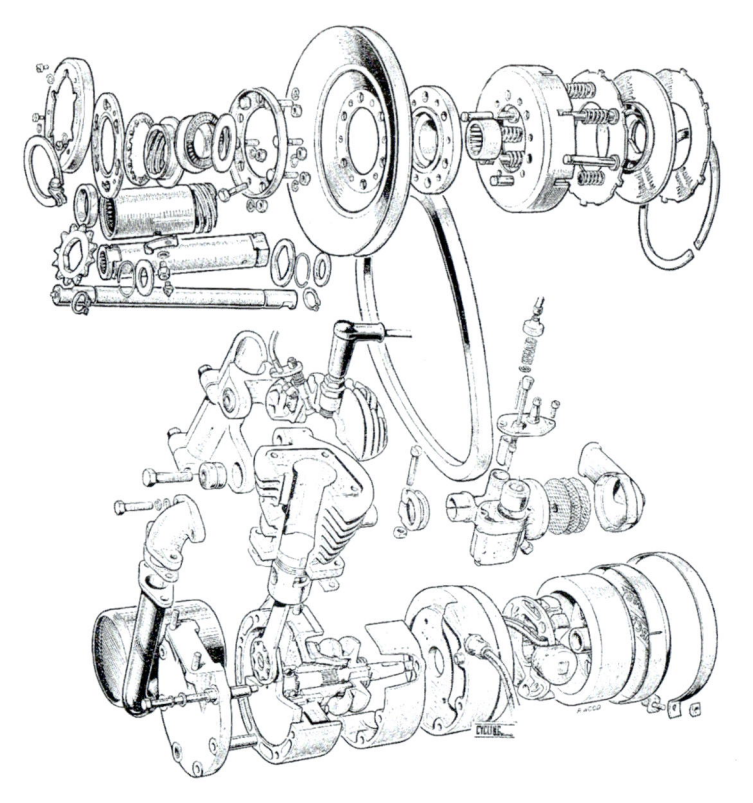

Fig. 12.48. Exploded view of the moped engine, published in *Cycling*'s review, April 1959.

be retrofitted.

The Raleigh Moped was an instant success: in the first 10 months it outsold total UK moped sales for the previous year by 50%. Raleigh meanwhile signed agreements to make Bianchi motor scooters and Motobécane Mobylette mopeds under licence.

# Chapter 13
# Small wheels and big triggers

## Sturmey-Archer in the 1960s

### British cycling's lowest ebb

In the late 1950s and early 1960s British cycling was at its lowest ebb. The annual distance cycled fell by 50% in a decade and sales of bicycles dropped to less than a million per year. As a result the two biggest British bicycle manufacturing groups, Raleigh Industries and the British Cycle Corporation (BCC), merged in 1960. BCC's owner was Tube Investments (TI), a holding company for a wide range of engineering companies making not only bicycles but domestic appliances and products for the construction industry. Among the major brands owned by TI were Creda, Russell Hobbs, Reynolds Tube and British Aluminium. TI bought the Raleigh group but, contrary to expectations, drew the management of the merged enterprise almost entirely from Raleigh personnel and based the company in Raleigh's Nottingham headquarters. Raleigh and Sturmey-Archer both had the prefix TI added to their company names.

At the time of the merger Sturmey-Archer was in good financial shape. Although Raleigh were now fitting derailleur gears on racing bikes, Sturmey-Archer hubs remained the UK industry standard. On the Continent sales by the Dutch and German subsidiaries were increasing and the Dutch company was making a significant contribution to Raleigh group profits. Belgium was also a significant market.

Recognising that the clubman and racer markets had been lost to derailleurs, in 1963 Sturmey-Archer deleted from their range all the remaining close-ratio and medium-ratio hubs: the AM, FM, FC, ASC and AC. Meanwhile, new markets for hub gears were developing for small-wheelers and hi-rise bikes.

### Expansion scheme

A £1 million expansion scheme was sanctioned in 1960 for the installation of equipment for powder metallurgy (sintering), cold extrusion and plastic injection moulding. These were modern technologies not used hitherto by Sturmey-Archer. (See Chapter 16 for more on sintering and cold forming.)

### Tricoaster improvements

In 1961 the TCW Mk 3 Tricoaster was introduced. This used a helical (worm) drive actuator instead of the opposing ramp (end cam) system used in earlier TCWs. But the TCW Mk 3 still suffered from the main disadvantages of its predecessors; it still had a 'no-drive/no-brake' position between high and middle gears; and the braking rate still varied according to the gear in use. The company was obviously aware of these shortcomings and sought to overcome them with GB patent 953,095 which Raleigh and Gordon Herbert Preece filed in 1962.

### S3C Tricoaster patent

Gordon Preece had become design manager at Sturmey-Archer when William Brown was a

Fig. 13.1. Factory assembly area in 1960.

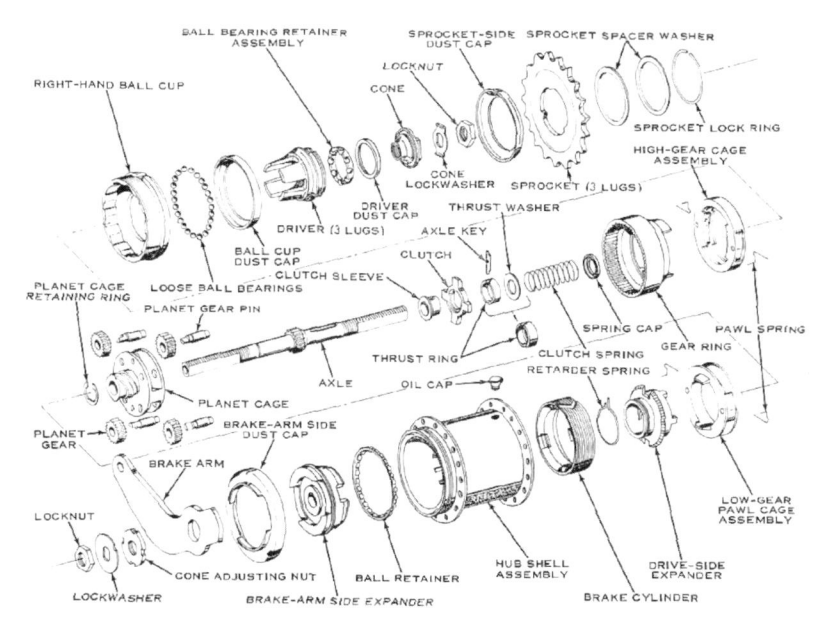

Fig. 13.2. Exploded view of the TCW Mk 3.

director and works manager. His new design, the subject of GB 953,095, formed the basis of the S3C Tricoaster. This used 'a brake actuating mechanism adapted to apply a reverse motion to the annulus thereby to effect brake engagement'. This was done by means of a set of pawls mounted on the driver. When the rider back-pedalled the driver turned backwards and the pawls engaged with ratchet teeth on the gear ring. This drove the gear ring backwards and therefore the planet cage also rotated in reverse. This caused a brake cone to move along the worm and operate the coaster brake. By this means the brake would work whatever gear was selected or even if the gear was in the 'no-drive' condition (between high and middle gears). Furthermore the braking was always via low gear for maximum power and control.

Fig. 13.3. The S3C Tricoaster, designed in 1962 but not launched until 1970.

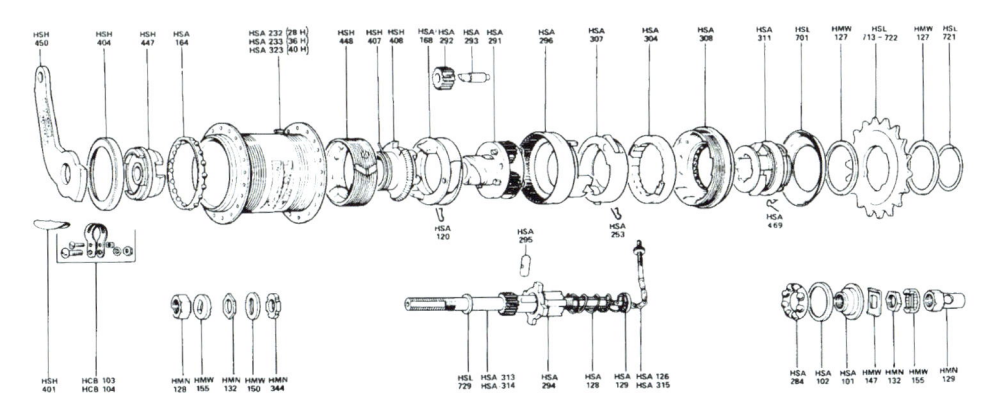

Fig. 13.4. Exploded view of the S3C Tricoaster.

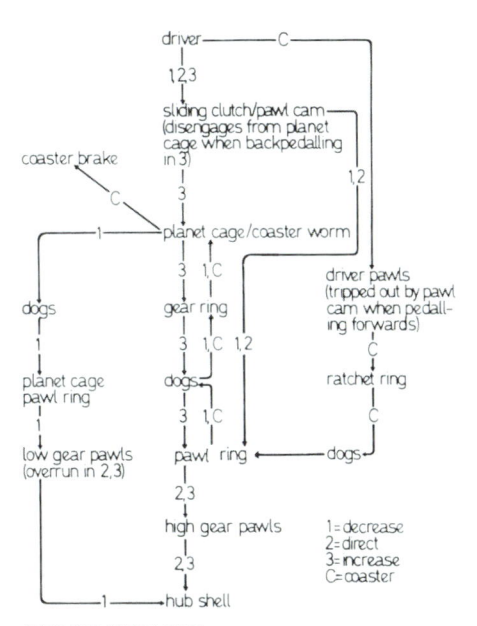

Fig. 13.5. Flowchart for the S3C hub.

TYPE S3C TRICOASTER
This gear uses a single epicyclic train yet the coaster is always operated via low gear.

217

Fig. 13.6. Cyclo Benelux derailleur converters were sold by Raleigh Industries of America.

For forward motion in high gear the brake pawls were tripped out – otherwise the gear would be damaged by the hub shell trying to overrun the pawls and locking against them. At the same time the selector sleeve (clutch) was rendered 'incapable of driving in reverse by reason of co-operating inclined faces' on its dogs and those of the planet cage – otherwise braking in high gear would drive the planet cage direct rather than via the gear ring.

The left end of the S3C's clutch was similar to the four-armed clutch of the AW but ramped dogs on the planet cage ensured that the clutch disengaged when coaster braking in high gear. The clutch extended to the right in the form of a ribbed sleeve; this encircled the axle but rested inside the driver, connecting the clutch to the driver while allowing a slight amount of lost motion between the two parts. This allowed the ribbed sleeve of the clutch to act as a pawl tripping cam: when the driver rotated forwards, the sleeve tripped the tails of the brake pawls; when the driver rotated backwards the sleeve allowed the pawl tails to drop and let the pawls actuate the coaster brake.

This ingenious design was a great improvement on the TCW series but it was not put into production until the following decade.

## Hybrid gearing

The 1962 Raleigh Lenton, as sold in the USA, featured a hybrid gearing system – a Sturmey-Archer AW hub with a Cyclo Benelux 2-speed derailleur converter. Raleigh Industries of America also sold 2-speed and 3-speed Cyclo Benelux converters separately.

The Cyclo Gear Co. Ltd of Aston, Birmingham started selling derailleur converters for hub gears in the 1930s and continued to do so post World War 2. Twin and triple sprocket conversion kits were available to convert 3-speed hubs into 6-speed or 9-speed hybrid gears, or to convert 4-speed hubs into 8-speed or 12-speed hybrids. The derailleur mechanism could be controlled by a top tube lever or a twist-grip.

At this time Cyclo sprocket assemblies were only made for ⅛-inch chains which were standard for use with hub gears. In the mid 1980s Cyclo started offering alternative sprocket assemblies for use with 3/32-inch derailleur chain before abandoning manufacture of

Fig. 13.7. A 1961 UK press advertisement by Cyclo for their derailleur converters. The image is of Fausto Coppi, though it is unlikely that he used such a Sturmey-Archer/Cyclo combination.

converters altogether.

Instead of using Cyclo's twin sprocket assembly, it was possible to use two dished Sturmey-Archer sprockets back-to-back, without sprocket spacer washers on a splined driver. This only worked with fairly large sprockets that were not too different in size. Alternatively a pair of screw-on fixed-wheel sprockets could be used with an old-style threaded driver. Again, some experimentation with the relationship between the sprocket sizes might be necessary.

### Drum brake improvements

Raleigh and Albert Bennett applied for GB patent 976,234 in 1962. This aimed to improve the water resistance of drum brakes. Around the circumference of the fixed end plate was a channel that aligned with a multiplicity of small radial holes in the brake drum. The intention was that water should accumulate in the channel and be thrown out via the rotating holes.

### Toggle chain protection

In 1963 Raleigh and Gordon Preece filed GB patent 993,332. This covered the familiar plastic toggle chain protector and wheel axle end cap. It was not the first Sturmey-Archer toggle chain protector: during the 1920s there was a plated metal cap similar in concept to Preece's plastic device. There was also a metal guard which fitted to the axle and chain stay; this was available during the 1950s but may not have been produced by Sturmey-Archer.

### Pressed-In left-hand ball cups

All hubs using the standard AW-type shell were fitted with a pressed-in left-hand ball cup from 1962 onwards. The ball cup had previously been screwed in and had incorporated flats to facilitate removal in a vice. A further comparatively rare design used a screwed left-hand ball cup without external flats but with internal dogs for a special removal tool.

### Topliss 3-speed

A more interesting development was covered by GB patent 1,004,766, filed by Raleigh in 1963 and

219

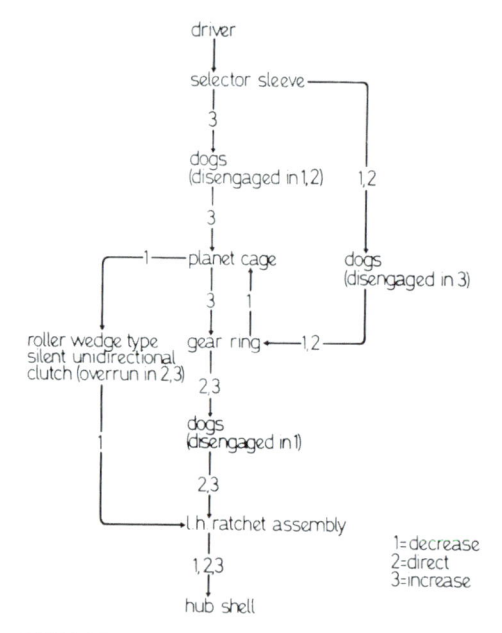

**TOPLISS THREE-SPEED (1963 PATENT)**
Silent except when freewheeling

Fig. 13.8. Flowchart for the Topliss 3-speed.

invented by John Geoffrey Topliss – a simplified slimline 3-speed hub gear making extensive use of pressed components and silent in all gears,

The inner end of this gear's selector sleeve had dogs that abutted the planet pins in high gear. To the left of the gear ring was a ratchet assembly comprising spring-loaded pawls held between a pawl ring plate and a pawl drive plate. The planet cage and the pawl drive plate were connected by an extra unidirectional clutch consisting of a roller-type freewheel device with a drag spring for positive action. The pawl drive plate had dogs to mate with others on the left end of the gear ring assembly.

In high gear the driver turned the selector sleeve which drove the planet cage. This rotated the gear ring at a faster rate. The output was fed from the gear ring via the left hand ratchet assembly to the shell, the extra unidirectional clutch being overrun.

For normal gear the selector sleeve was pulled to the right, disengaging its dogs from the planet pins and engaging with the radial dogs on the gear ring. The driver turned the selector sleeve which therefore drove the gear ring. This delivered the output direct to the left hand ratchet assembly and thence to the shell. The extra unidirectional clutch was again overrun.

For low gear the selector sleeve moved to the extreme right, pulling the gear ring with it and disengaging it from the left-hand ratchet assembly. The driver turned the selector sleeve which drove the gear ring. This rotated the planet cage at a slower rate and its output was fed through the extra unidirectional clutch to the left-hand ratchet assembly and thence to the shell.

This novel gear was not put into production, perhaps because the spectre of the abortive SW still haunted the boardroom.

## The Moulton bicycle

Late in 1962 something happened that arrested the decline in UK cycle sales and gave an unexpected boost to Sturmey-Archer. Alex Moulton launched his small-wheeled bicycle at the Earls Court Cycle and Motor Cycle Show.

Moulton, a keen cyclist and member of the Cyclists' Touring Club (CTC), had been researching and developing his design for an improved bicycle for five years. The final version used 16" wheels with tyres inflated harder than usual. The small wheels gave good acceleration and plenty of space over for wide frame-fixed carriers. Moulton overcame the hard ride of his bicycle's small wheels by incorporating a rubber suspension system. (Moulton was a leading automotive suspension designer, responsible for the rubber suspension used in the original BMC Mini and for the interconnected Hydrolastic and Hydragas systems used in many subsequent BMC, British Leyland and Rover cars.) The Moulton bicycle had an open unisex frame with spannerless adjustment for a wide range of rider heights. Some versions were separable for easy storage or for carrying in the boot of a small car, although he never made a folding bicycle as such.

The bike was an instant success and for a while production exceeded 1,000 units a week. It was the product of extensive research and had not been produced in response to market demand; it was therefore a 'technology push' rather than a 'market pull' product. It nonetheless became fashionable and created the UK market for subsequent small wheelers, such as the Dawes Kingpin, the Raleigh RSW16 and the hugely successful Raleigh Twenty series.

Cycle sales in the UK had been declining rapidly, from 0.9 million a year in 1961 to 0.6 million in 1963. The Moulton went on sale in spring 1963 and bicycle sales started to rise, reaching 0.75 million a year by the time Raleigh bought Moulton out in 1967. Sales then briefly dropped back to the 1963 level but by 1969 were again rising fast, reaching 1.5 million per annum by 1980. Interest in cycling had been rekindled to some extent and the Moulton had helped dispel the 'cloth cap' image that associated cycling with under-privilege: in the 'swinging sixties' celebrities such as Cliff Richard, Lord Snowdon and the Chancellor of the Exchequer were all seen riding the new bike.

Alex Moulton went into bicycle manufacture only after Raleigh had rejected his design as unmarketable. Raleigh still profited from the new bike, as most versions were fitted with Sturmey-Archer gears and some had Dynohubs. The most widely used gear on Moultons during the mid 1960s was the FW wide-ratio 4-speed. The hub gears fitted to the first Moultons had 36 spoke holes and were fitted with 14 tooth sprockets, standard products from the Sturmey-Archer range. But Moulton demand was soon sufficient for Sturmey-Archer to introduce 28 hole hub shells and a 13 tooth sprocket: these became available by early 1964. Until this time most cycles with hub gears used a cable which was open for most of its route to the hub and ran over a pulley wheel. The Moulton used instead a fully-sheathed cable; from about 1965 a special 50 thousandths of an inch (1.27 mm) inner cable was used to resist stretching. Without such a cable, stretch could lead to gear slip. Cable stretch was probably the origin of the rumour that Raleigh had tried to sabotage Moulton by supplying defective FW hubs.

## The Cardiff-London record

The launch of the Moulton was closely followed by another significant event for Sturmey-Archer: the Road Records Association's Cardiff to London record was broken by John Woodburn riding a Moulton equipped with a Sturmey-Archer FC gear. This was the last major British record broken using a hub gear, apart from Cliff Smith's Edinburgh to London success in 1965. The hub gear was used because of the difficulty in getting a high enough gear with a derailleur and such a small wheel size. Nonetheless, the Moulton works had to

Fig. 13.9. John Woodburn broke the Cardiff-London record on a Moulton fitted with a Sturmey-Archer FC close-ratio 4-speed hub.

make their own 11 tooth sprocket. (Alex Moulton later patented and produced a 9 tooth sprocket for use with derailleurs.)

During training for the record attempt, Woodburn used the AC close-ratio 3-speed. With a 68 tooth chainwheel this gave 94, 101 and 107" gears. But finally the FC close-ratio 4-speed was selected which, with a 64 tooth chainwheel, gave a range from 70" to 104".

On his first attempt Woodburn experienced a number of problems, including an injury to his right knee, and he abandoned the ride after 83 miles. But all went well on 9 December 1962 and the 162 miles were covered at approximately 24 mph (38.6 km/h): 18½ minutes were knocked off the previous record, which had stood for five years. Although Cardiff–London was not a frequently contested route, this new record was a great achievement as it defied conventional wisdom in a number of ways: the record was attempted in the middle of winter; the bike had tiny wheels, suspension and no top tube; Woodburn was riding at about six times his then optimal distance; and he used a hub gear.

It was unfortunate that Sturmey-Archer could not capitalise on the success because about this time they deleted the FC hub from their range.

Fig 13.10. The SC single-speed coaster brake.

## SC coaster

Unusually for British bicycles, some Moultons had single-speed coaster brakes. They were used first on the early Moulton Stowaway, the 'take apart' car boot model. The lack of cables from the handlebars to the rear hub meant that the main beam of the frame could incorporate a break joint. Moulton used the B500 Perry Coaster (and possibly the B100 on very early Stowaways). This seems to have galvanised Sturmey-Archer into reintroducing a single-speed coaster: in 1963 they launched the SC, their first since the 1930s.

Something of a mystery surrounds the SC's origins. *Sutherland's Handbook for Bicycle Mechanics* shows almost complete interchangeability of parts between the SC, Perry B100 and Fichtel & Sachs Torpedo coasters and it seems that the SC was referred to as 'the Perry design' by Sturmey-Archer staff. The quick launch of this hub so soon after Moulton started using Perry Coasters suggests that the SC was a licence-built or badge-engineered Perry B100 based on a Fichtel & Sachs Torpedo coaster.

The SC had a solid forged shell and the brake actuator was the opposed ramp (end cam) type. It had a bronze brake band on a split steel liner, like the TCW Mk 2 and Mk 3.

## S2 2-speed

By 1965 Moulton Stowaways were fitted with the Fichtel & Sachs Duomatic. This hub, also used on the Moulton Automatic and Mini Automatic, combined a coaster brake with a 2-speed semi-automatic gear, giving direct drive and a 36% increase. Gear change was by slight back-pedalling.

Sturmey-Archer's response to Moulton's use of the Duomatic was the S2 hub, the subject of GB patent 1,090,410. This was filed by Raleigh in spring 1965, the inventor being Leonard Haydn Fox. The aim was 'a simple yet efficient change speed gear hub in which gear change from one gear to another is effected automatically upon the application of a reverse motion to the chain sprocket'.

Unlike the Fichtel & Sachs Duomatic, the S2 2-speed used direct drive for high gear. The driver drove the selector sleeve, which drove the gear ring via pawls. These were tripped in and out of engagement with the shell by cam faces on the selector sleeve which acted as pawl seatings and followed each other round the sleeve's circumference in the order shallow, deep, shallow, deep. In high gear the tails of the gear ring pawls sat in the deep seatings and hence

Fig. 13.11. The S2 back-pedal shifting 2-speed hub.

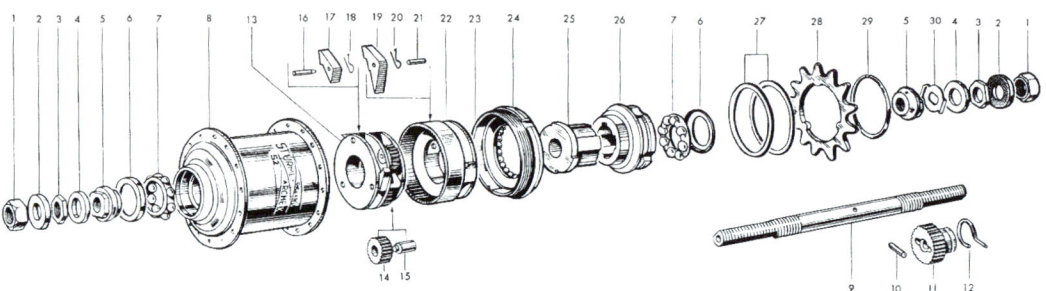

Fig. 13.12. Exploded view of the S2 hub.

engaged with the shell to give direct drive. The planet cage pawls were overrun.

Back-pedalling slightly brought the pawl tails into the shallow seatings, tripping the pawls out of engagement with the shell. Drive then passed from the selector sleeve via the pawls to the gear ring, through the epicyclic train, and out of the planet cage via the low gear pawls to the shell. This gave low gear.

The patent showed two versions of the gear: one with a stepped shell, the other with a constant diameter. It was the second version that went into production in 1966 as the S2, using a standard AW-type shell and giving direct drive and a 28.6% reduction. The S2 was described by Sturmey-Archer as 'admirably suited for small wheel and folding bicycles' yet compared with the Duomatic it was deficient in two respects.

Firstly, it did not incorporate a cable-less braking system and so it was useless for separable bicycles such as the Moulton Stowaway or the 'Take-a-part' version of the Dawes Kingpin. An S2 combined with a coaster brake was mooted by Sturmey-Archer and tentatively designated S2C but never manufactured.

Secondly, unlike the Duomatic, the S2 geared down which effectively limited the top gear on a mass produced 16" wheel bike to no more than 64" (52 tooth being the largest ⅛" chainwheel then commonly available). The Duomatic could offer such a bike a top gear as high as 87". It appears that no bike on the British market was factory-fitted with the S2 hub and most of the 12,500 S2 hubs made went to Scandinavia.

The S2 patent was amended in accordance with a 1970 decision of the Principal Examiner of Patents to make it much more specific to the S2 design. This suggests that another company, probably Fichtel & Sachs, challenged the original wording.

## S3B 3-speed and drum brake

In mid 1965 Raleigh launched their answer to the Moulton: the RSW16, short for Raleigh Small Wheels 16 inch. Like the Moulton it had 16" wheels, an open frame and a large rear carrier. But unlike the Moulton it had no suspension: instead it relied on low pressure balloon tyres and was intended only for short range travel. It was robust, well equipped and cheaper than the comparable Moulton Deluxe. But it was nearly 10 lb (4.54 kg) heavier than the original Deluxe and one wit unkindly described riding the RSW as 'like waltzing in gum boots'. Nonetheless, it rolled better on gravel and soft ground than the Moulton.

The RSW16 Mk 1 had an unusual rear calliper brake that performed poorly. When the Mk 2 was launched two years later, it incorporated the Sturmey-Archer S3B, a new cable-operated drum brake combined with a 3-speed. Like the AB hub, the S3B used a narrow planet cage version of the AW gear but the drum brake had now been made small enough to

Fig. 13.13. The S3B 3-speed drum brake for small-wheeled bicycles.

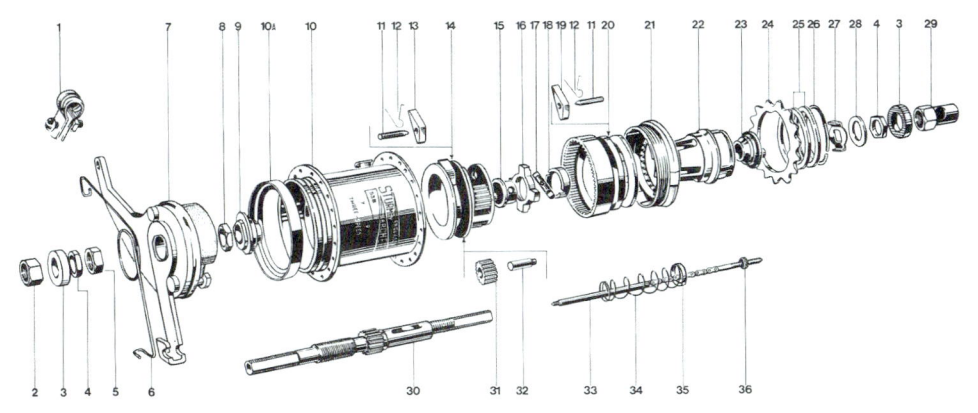

Fig. 13.14. Exploded view of the S3B hub.

225

go in a standard AW shell fitted with a special left-hand ball cup.

Use of the AB hub on the RSW16 would have left only about 4" (100 mm) between the wheel rim and the brake drum. The more compact S3B offered a better appearance, easier wheel building and better water resistance; the bottom of the brake drum was further from the ground, and the junction between the drum and the brake plate was protected by a plastic water shield.

The S3B had an external torsion spring between the brake actuating arm and the fixed plate holding the brake assembly. It was not considered feasible to reline the tiny brake shoes; instead a complete replacement assembly was supplied, consisting of the fixed plate, brake assembly and actuating arm.

The S3B was specifically for use on small-wheeled bicycles, most being fitted to RSW16 Mk 2s. It was an option on late RSW16 Mk 1s, adding £1 1s. 5d. (£17 today) to the price. From 1970 to 1974 it was used on Moulton Mk 3s and RSW16 Mk 3s, although late RSW Mk 3s had AB hubs.

Small-wheels do not need such big brake drums as larger wheels, at least in theory. But in practice, especially because of oil leaking from the gear section into the brake drum, the S3B's braking performance tended to be poor. An additional oil seal was added in a bid to stop oil getting into the brake drum.

## De Gaulle's noes

In 1963 French President Charles de Gaulle vetoed Britain's application to join the European Economic Community. In February the following year Sturmey-Archer produced a report to establish the cost of manufacture in the European Economic Community (EEC): this concluded that the best location for a factory would be the Netherlands.

The report's costings were based on sales in an average year to EEC countries totalling 190,000 AW hubs, 18,000 AB/C hubs and 6,000 TCWs. The biggest market by far was the Netherlands, with 138,000 hubs a year. Belgium was second with 41,000 and Italy third, with 20,000. Germany accounted for 8,000 and France 7,000.

Sturmey-Archer did not proceed with the project but exports were of immense importance to the company. In 1964 a million AW 3-speeds were made and 80% of Sturmey-Archer production was exported.

## S5 5-speed

The 1966 London Cycle and Motor Cycle Show saw the launch of the Sturmey–Archer S5 5-speed hub, forty-five years after Henry Sturmey's 5-speed patent and twenty-eight years after the company's own first 5-speed patent. The S5 was billed as 'The World's first fully enclosed 5-speed gear.'

The S5 was basically a modified FW 4-speed. It had a conventional toggle chain in the right-hand end of the axle. This was connected by the normal cable system to a 3-speed lever on the right. At the left end of the axle was a bell-crank, which was connected by cable to a 2-speed lever on the left. The bell-crank operated a push rod which moved in the hollow axle to control the engagement of the two suns.

The lever on the right acted like a conventional 3-speed selector: with the left lever in the slack cable position, the right lever selected high, normal and low gears. But in effect the S5 contained two 3-speeds: one wide-ratio, the other ultra-wide-ratio, both using direct drive as a common middle gear. When the left lever was pulled back, the ultra-wide-ratio 3-speed

Fig. 13.15. Sturmey-Archer's offices at 387 Nassaukade, Amsterdam.

Fig. 13.16. A 1965 poster for the Dutch market.

227

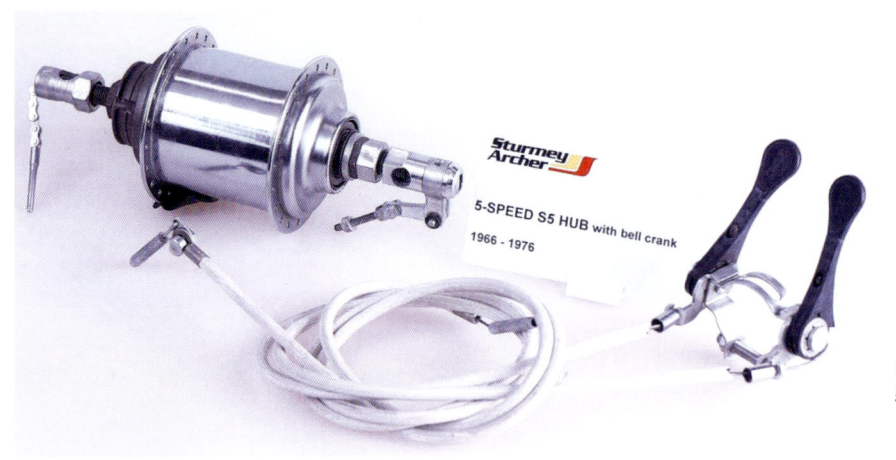

# The Hub of the Universe

Fig. 13.17. The S5 5-speed hub.

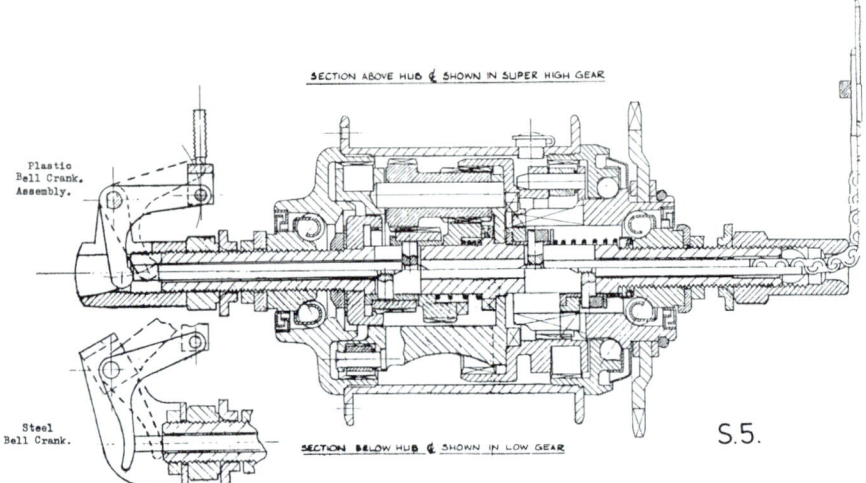

Fig. 13.18. Jim Gill's sectional drawing of the S5, including plastic and steel versions of the bellcrank.

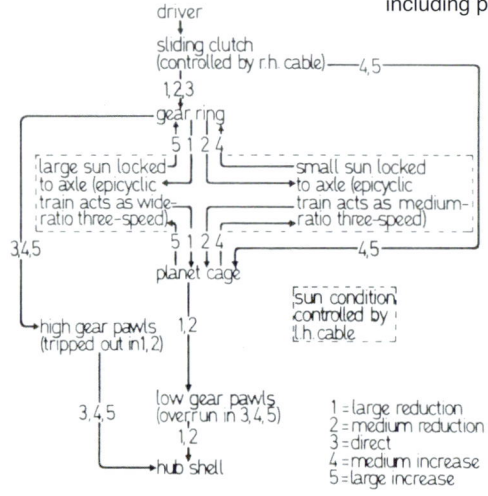

Fig. 13.19. Flowchart for the S5 series of 5-speed hubs.

1 = large reduction
2 = medium reduction
3 = direct
4 = medium increase
5 = large increase

## S5 SERIES FIVE-SPEEDS
Compound planet pinions and two suns give the effect of a double epicyclic system.

Fig. 13.20. Outer pages of a promotional leaflet for the S5 hub (DDRN 4-14-27-5).

Fig. 13.21. Inner pages of the promotional leaflet for the S5 hub, including a cutaway drawing (DDRN 4-14-27-5).

came into effect and the high and low gears became 'super high' and 'super low'. The changing sequence was therefore: super low – left lever back, right lever back; low – left lever forward, right lever back; normal – left lever back or forward, right lever central; high – left lever forward, right lever forward; super high – left lever back, right lever forward.

By leaving the left lever back, the S5 could be run as an ultra-wide-ratio 3-speed; by leaving the lever forward, the hub operated as a medium-wide-ratio 3-speed. In the former condition it was possible to make a precise, positive change from one end of the gear range to the other with just two clicks of the right-hand lever.

The S5 gave the same percentage shifts as the FW (33.3% decrease, 21.1% decrease, direct drive and 26.6% increase ) plus an extra high gear with 50% increase. Typical ratios thus provided were 42, 50, 63, 80 and 95" or 37, 43, 55, 70 and 83".

The S5 was available with the option of dual levers for top or down tube mounting. In 1969 a Twinshift console was introduced 'for the young rider who wants the extra feel of Grand Prix performance' (see below). The S5 could also be used with a pair of standard AW 3-speed triggers.

Having at long last launched a 5-speed hub, Sturmey-Archer made no great effort to sell it in the UK. The major market was the USA, as a component for hi-rise bikes for pre-teens during the 1960s. There was no comparable hi-rise boom in the UK until the launch of the Raleigh Chopper, so the S5 was almost unknown to British cyclists at the time. The FW remained in production alongside the S5 until about 1970.

## Geared front Dynohub

At the end of 1967 Raleigh and Tony Hillyer, who had become Sturmey-Archer's product design manager, applied for GB patent 1,244,726. This covered an interesting development that nearly got into mass production: a geared dynamo for the front hub. This was about a decade after earlier Sturmey-Archer experiments with this idea.

The new device was housed in a cylindrical shell similar in size to the AW's. It featured an armature of 'novel, simplified construction' and incorporated internal gearing to speed up the rotation of the field poles. These rotated in the opposite direction from the wheel 'to give a high rate of flux cutting by the armature coils and to give a high e.m.f. [electromotive force] output and consequentially a higher intensity of light'.

The hub shell incorporated an internally toothed gear ring that engaged with the first of a series of seven gear wheels (three simple pinions and two compound pinions) arranged to form a gear train. These gear wheels were held between two stationary plates fixed on the wheel axle. The output of the gear train drove the field coils. The gear train could be declutched from the field coils for minimum drag: this was done by a push rod activated by a lever riveted to the axle end. There was an overrun device to prevent overloading the gearing: this allowed the field poles to continue spinning if the wheel was suddenly locked by the brake. According to Tony Hillyer, the problem that stopped the geared hub dynamo going in to production was 'gear lash jump' at walking pace due to magnetic effects.

There were relatively few other significant developments in Sturmey-Archer lighting products during this decade. Perhaps the most significant was the introduction of a plastic bodied headlamp with rectangular plastic 'glass'. In the late 1960s Raleigh perfected a process for chromium plating plastic components such as this headlight. The technique was something of a 'black art', easily disrupted by a small change to any of a number of variables.

Fig. 13.22. A 1962 press advertisement for Sturmey-Archer's new twist-grip. By happy coincidence, the twist was a popular dance at the time.

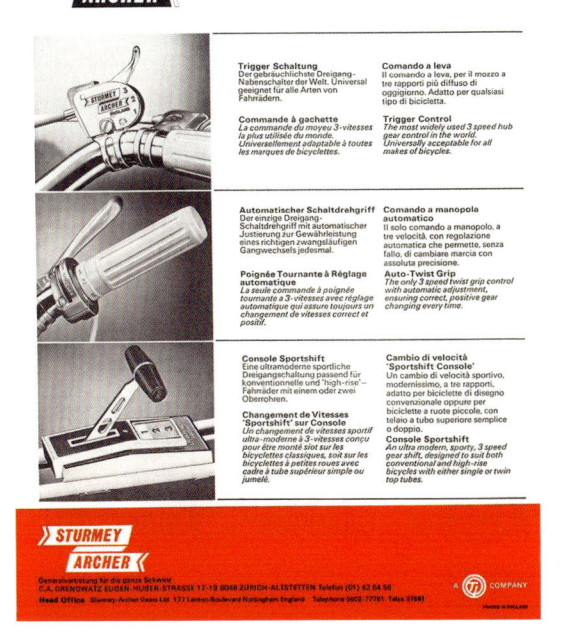

Fig. 13.23. Part of a gear control promotional leaflet in German, French, Italian and English for the Swiss market (DDRN 4-14-27-10).

## Triggers and twist-grips

During the 1960s Sturmey-Archer put a lot of effort into developing various cable control systems for their hub gears. Meanwhile the 3-speed and 4-speed triggers remained virtually unchanged except in minor details: all were now labelled for fixing above the handlebars rather than below. (See Appendix G for a detailed survey of trigger variations.)

Raleigh and Leonard Haydn Fox filed GB patent 951,131 in 1962. This covered an automatic cable adjustment system to take up wear and stretch. The invention was primarily intended for use with twist-grip controls. It involved a cable drum connected to the hand grip and a resilient ring held by friction between the drum and its housing. The unit was designed so that, as the cable stretched, the extra movement of the twist grip to engage bottom gear would slip the assembly round on the resilient ring, automatically resetting it.

Also in 1962 Sturmey-Archer filed the final part of GB patent 1,004,357, the inventors being Raymond John Reed and Gordon Preece. This dealt with the general construction of twist-grip controls and aimed 'to provide an improved twist-grip control which is positive in action, which is reliable, is wear resistant and which is inexpensive in production'.

Sturmey-Archer's twist-grip controls were first marketed in 1961 and the well-known version with automatic adjustment was introduced in 1964. Twist-grips were not a new idea; some gear makers had marketed them before the World War I. In more recent times BSA had produced a twist-grip for their 3-speed hub.

## Sportshifts and Twinshifts

During the 1960s Sturmey-Archer produced a number of exotic changers for young riders. This move was influenced by the American hi-rise market where 'fun' bikes with high-rise handlebars captured a large share of the market.

In 1966 a large triangular-bodied Sportshift was introduced for the AW 3-speed. This device clamped to the top tube. A twin-lever version was made for the S5, the left-hand lever being smaller than the right. The Sportshift was based on GB patent 1,134,807 which Raleigh and Tony Hillyer first applied for in autumn 1966 and amended early in 1967. This noted that often 'when the gear is locked and an attempt is made to alter the gear selection, the cable breaks and must be renewed'. The new invention aimed to eliminate this problem.

The specification drawing showed a large console-type gear lever of the sort seen on juvenile hi-rise bicycles, but the text pointed out that the principle could equally apply to 'a pivoted lever or rotatable sleeve'. The lever was mounted on a pivoted indicator plate that was connected to the changer cable. The connection between the lever and indicator plate was through a looped leaf spring. Under overload 'the spring yields and the lever pivots without pivoting the plate'. This device had the same effect as the changer linkage hold-off spring inside some earlier hubs. The decoupled lever had the advantage that it could be retrofitted to hubs lacking the hold-off feature.

It was probably about this time that Sturmey-Archer introduced a toggle chain/indicator incorporating a 17mm long coil spring. This was the simplest way of retro-fitting a spring hold-off but was soon discontinued.

Another hi-rise lever was shown in GB patent 1,261,210. Raleigh, Hillyer and Kazimierz Tadeusz Dziadosz filed this in summer 1968. It was essentially the construction used in the console versions of the Sportshift introduced during 1968 and 1969 and used on the Chopper and other hi-rise bikes. (The Chopper was introduced by Raleigh in the USA in 1968, test-marketed in Britain the following year and formally launched on the home market in spring 1970.) Choppers sold in the UK were mostly fitted with the AW 3-speed and a single-lever Sportshift. GB patent 1,261,210 included a twin-lever version for use with the S5, some

Fig. 13.24. A 1968 3 x 2 Twinshift for use on 5-speed hi-rise bikes.

Fig. 13.25. A 1969 Twinshift specifically for the Raleigh Chopper.

exported Choppers having the 5-speed hub. The twin-lever versions of the Sportshift console were known as Twinshifts.

Sturmey-Archer also made thinner washers for the drivers of hub gears fitted to Choppers. This was to allow space for the spoke protector typically fitted to these bikes.

## Cost-saving ideas

In the late 1960s Raleigh ran a number of cost-saving initiatives, some of which derived from brainstorming sessions. One was the use of cheaper grease in Sturmey-Archer hubs. The first replacement grease worked well enough in temperate climates but washed out in Far Eastern monsoon conditions. Quality engineer Dave Drinkwater's bike was therefore fitted up with a bottle that dripped water onto the hub as he rode around the factory. Through this practical experimentation with various lubricants a cheaper grease was found that worked well under monsoon conditions.

Another cost-saving idea from this period was to use cheaper coaster brake bands than the normal phosphor-bronze type. Drinkwater's bike was therefore equipped with brake bands made of various different metals to try to find an acceptable cheap solution; none was discovered.

## A turning point

The 1960s saw a turning point for the British cycle industry. Cycle sales in the UK have never dropped as low as they were before the small-wheeler boom initiated by the Moulton. New home markets were created for adult small-wheelers and, boosted by American influence, for juvenile hi-rise bikes. Both categories created considerable demand for Sturmey-Archer gears, and the company rose to the challenge. Gone was the almost obsessive devotion to ever closer ratios for sporting cyclists. As the sixties ended, Sturmey-Archer was more interested in making the 3-speed trigger look like a hot rod gear stick.

## Chapter 14

# The secret seven

### Sturmey-Archer in the 1970s

The first four years of the 1970s were a period of intense inventiveness for Sturmey-Archer. During this time the company proved that it still possessed ingenuity and flair. Sadly, some of its most interesting potential products never saw the light of day.

### SC1 coaster

Sturmey-Archer's first patent application of the decade was GB 1,378,850 filed in December 1970 in the name of Raleigh Industries, the inventor being Tony Hillyer. It dealt with a new single-speed coaster brake, launched eight years later as the SC1. (See later in this chapter for more information.)

The new coaster had a brake actuator that ran along a worm thread (helical drive) on the driver. Back-pedalling caused the brake actuator to move left along the worm thread: a conical left end-face on the actuator forced the brake band open, thus applying the brake. Pedalling forward made the brake actuator move to the right along the worm: teeth on its right end-face meshed with similar teeth on a member dogged to the hub shell, thereby giving positive forward drive. If the rider ceased pedalling, a drag spring caused the actuator to move slightly to the left, thus disengaging drive. By this means freewheeling was provided without the need for a conventional roller or pawl and ratchet mechanism.

This coaster, put into production in 1978 as the SC1, was similar to the original 1922 Sturmey-Archer type CC. The patent also showed a version, not manufactured, that incorporated the same positive forward drive feature but which used 'interdigitated' brake pads and discs instead of the expansible sleeve-like brake shoe.

### S3C Tricoaster

In 1970 Sturmey-Archer launched the S3C 3-speed coaster. This was based on their 1962 GB patent 953,095 and met the standards of the United States Consumer Product Safety Commission (CPSC). For the first time since 1922 Sturmey-Archer's 3-speed coaster had constant-rate braking without a 'no-brake' position between the gears. (See the previous chapter for more on the S3C hub.) There was still a 'no-drive' position between middle and high gears but the new 3-speed coaster was certainly an improvement on the TCW series.

Although known as a Tricoaster within Sturmey-Archer, that name was not generally used in the marketing of the S3C. This may have been to distance the new design from the TCW Tricoaster series.

Later, Sturmey-Archer made a badge-engineered version of the S3C 3-speed coaster for Sachs, in a shell marked Torpedo. There was a matching Sturmey-Archer trigger, with the plastic faceplate bearing the names Sachs and Torpedo. The story behind this collaboration involved Brian Powdrill. He had been sent to West Germany in 1967 to set up a Sturmey-Archer office in Opladen (between Köln and Düsseldorf); this did not work out, so he was transferred to Sturmey-Archer's office in Amsterdam. In late 1979 Powdrill took Mike Smith, then the head

Fig. 14.1. Lamps were restyled for the 1970s, with a more angular look for most of the headlamps.

of Sturmey-Archer, to West Germany to visit Powdrill's contacts at Sachs in Schweinfurt. This resulted in an order from Sachs for 100,000 badge-engineered S3C 3-speed coasters.

Peter Wittering, director of factories, argued that the order could not be produced because of insufficient works capacity. Smith overrode Wittering and serious quality control issues ensued, including poor braking resulting from a bad fit between the Sturmey-Archer internal mechanism and the Sachs shell.

## Hillyer NIG 3-speed

A month after the filing of this new coaster patent, Raleigh Industries and Tony Hillyer applied for GB patent 1,346,068. This covered a new 3-speed hub gear with a 'no intermediate gear' (NIG) feature and that required less accurate adjustment than the AW.

The new gear incorporated a sliding coupling/selector sleeve that could drive the gear ring via a pawl and ratchet mechanism and the planet cage via dogs. To ensure that in high gear there was no damaging effect when back-pedalling or wheeling backwards, the dogs on the coupling/selector sleeve disengaged automatically from those on the planet cage; the method specified was that used in the S3C patent (GB 953,095) – the dogs had 'cooperating inclined faces'.

In all gears the driver turned the coupling/selector sleeve assembly. The gear incorporated the following pawl and ratchet mechanisms:

A – high gear pawls on the gear ring, engaging with the hub shell,
B – low gear pawls on the planet cage, engaging with the hub shell,
C – pawls on the gear ring, engaging with the coupling/selector sleeve.

In high gear the coupling/selector sleeve was dogged to the planet cage. Drive passed through the epicyclic train and output from the gear ring was fed to the hub shell via high gear pawls A. Low gear pawls B were overrun and pawls C connecting the coupling/selector sleeve to

```
                    driver
                      |
          1,2————selector sleeve
                      |
                      3
                      ↓
                    dogs
                   (disengaged in 1,2)
gear ring pawls       |
(tripped out in 3)    3
    |                 ↓
    |              planet cage————1————┐
    |              3 ↑ ↑ 1             |
    |              ↓   |               |
    └—1,2————→gear ring              |
                  2,3         low gear pawls
                   ↓          (overrun in 2,3)
1=decrease     high gear pawls
2=direct       (tripped out in 1)
3=increase         |
                  2,3
                   ↓
               hub shell←————1————┘
```

HILLYER NON-SLIP THREE-SPEED (1971 PATENT)
The gear ring pawls eliminated the need for a 'no drive' position between gears 2 and 3

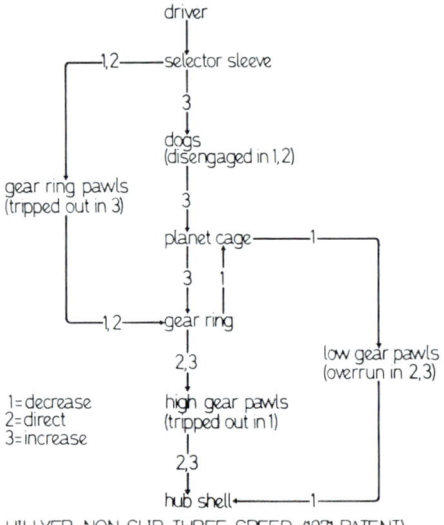

Fig. 14.2. Flowchart for the Hillyer NIG 3-speed.

the gear ring were tripped out, despite being overrun; this protected the gear from damage if the cycle was wheeled backwards.

In middle gear the coupling/selector sleeve moved to its central position, disengaging from the planet cage. Drive went via the coupling/selector sleeve through pawls C to the gear ring and then via high gear pawls A to the hub shell. The epicyclic mechanism was bypassed and low gear pawls B were overrun.

In low gear the coupling/selector sleeve moved to the extreme right and tripped the tails of high gear pawls A. Drive went via the coupling/selector sleeve and pawls C to the gear ring then through the epicyclic train, output from the planet cage being fed via low gear pawls B to the hub shell.

This was another 3-speed that was not put into production.

## A new Chopper console
The only other significant feature of 1971, as far as Sturmey-Archer was concerned, was the launch of the Chopper console type control 72R for the AW 3-speed.

## Cater kick-shift 3-speed
Raleigh filed GB patent 1,452,739 in 1972. It covered a 3-speed with back-pedalling gear change ('kick-shift') designed by Alan James Cater. The design was applicable to hubs with and without coaster brakes. It could be constructed in two versions: one giving the gear change sequence low/normal/high/low; the other giving low/normal/high/normal/low.

Gear change was effected by two devices: cam wheel A on a selector sleeve on the wheel axle; and pawl cam ring B which rotated with the driver but could be moved to the right against spring pressure by a cam track on the right-hand end of the selector sleeve.

There were three sets of pawl and ratchet mechanisms: pawls C feeding forward drive from the selector sleeve to a pawl sleeve and, under certain conditions, to the planet cage; pawls D feeding forward drive from the pawl sleeve to the gear ring; and low gear pawls E on

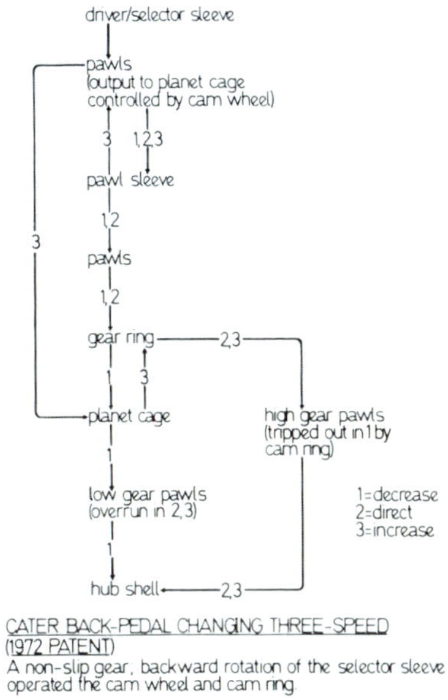

Fig. 14.3. Flowchart for the low/normal/high/low version of the Cater kick-shift 3-speed.

CATER BACK-PEDAL CHANGING THREE-SPEED (1972 PATENT)
A non-slip gear, backward rotation of the selector sleeve operated the cam wheel and cam ring

the planet cage connecting it to the hub shell. There was also a 'resilient clutch' between the selector sleeve and the pawl sleeve to allow about 60 degrees of relative motion between the two assemblies.

With the 'low/normal/high/low' version of this hub, the changes and drive sequences were as follows:

- For low gear, cam wheel A presented shallow cam faces to pawls C, and cam ring B under spring pressure kept the high gear pawls D tripped out. Drive went via the selector sleeve, through pawls C to the pawl sleeve, and from the pawl sleeve via pawls D to the gear ring, then through the epicyclic gears and out via the planet cage and low gear pawls E to the hub shell.

- On back-pedalling, rotation of the selector sleeve caused the cam wheel A to rotate, presenting further shallow cam faces to pawls C; rotation of the selector sleeve forced cam ring B to move to the right against its spring, allowing high gear pawls D to engage with the hub shell. On pedalling forward again, drive passed via the driver and selector sleeve, through pawls C to the pawl sleeve, then via pawls D to the gear ring and from there via high gear pawls D to the hub shell. The epicyclic gears were bypassed and low gear pawls E overrun, giving direct drive.

- On back-pedalling again, rotation of the selector sleeve caused cam wheel A to rotate further, presenting deep cam faces to pawls C; but because of the design of the cam track on the end of the selector sleeve, cam ring B remained on the left, pressed against its spring; so high gear pawls D remained engaged with the hub shell. On resuming forward pedalling, drive passed via the driver and selector sleeve, through pawls C to the pawl sleeve, and (because the deep cam faces of A allowed the pawls C to project further) from the pawl sleeve via the same pawls C to the planet cage; it then passed through the epicyclic train and out via the gear ring and high gear pawls D to the hub shell. Low gear pawls E were overrun and the result was high gear.

- On back-pedalling again, rotation of the selector sleeve caused cam wheel A to present shallow

237

cam faces to pawls C; at the same time the selector sleeve's rotation caused the cam track on its end to allow cam ring B to move left under spring pressure, thereby tripping out high gear pawls D. This returned the hub to low gear.

This was a remarkable hub gear but another that never went into production. The company seems at this time to have had mixed feelings about back-pedal gear changing: in the same year that it applied for this patent it deleted the S2 hub.

Another 1972 deletion was the TCW Mk 3, which had been superseded two years earlier by the S3C 3-speed coaster.

## Munn NIG 3-speed

In spring 1973 Raleigh applied for GB patent 1,399,434. This covered yet another potential replacement for the AW, this time designed by David Curtis Munn. The familiar aims of the inventor were simple construction and reliable operation. An intriguing comment within the patent text pointed out that the control mechanism could be operated 'either manually or by some external automatic control mechanism'. Perhaps the company was responding to Fichtel & Sachs' Torpedo Automatic – a 2-speed coaster with integral, centrifugally operated, fully automatic gear change.

David Munn's 3-speed incorporated four pawl and ratchet systems as follows:

A – connecting the gear ring to the hub shell,
B – connecting the planet cage to the hub shell,
C – connecting the driver to the gear ring,
D – connecting the driver to the planet cage.

In high gear, drive was fed from the driver via pawls D to the planet cage, through the epicyclic gears and out from the gear ring via pawls A to the hub shell; pawls C and B were overrun. For middle gear, two pawl tripping sleeves around the wheel axle were moved to the right against a spring by a control rod, tripping the tails of pawls D. Drive therefore went from the driver via pawls C to the gear ring and from there via pawls A to the hub shell. The epicyclic train was bypassed, giving direct drive. Pawls B were overrun.

For low gear, the control rod moved further right. The two tripping sleeves separated, each being linked to the control rod by a differently rated spring. One of the sleeves continued to hold pawls D out of engagement while the other tripped out pawls A. Drive therefore went from the driver via pawls C to the gear ring, through the epicyclic train and out through the planet cage via pawls B to the hub shell.

This was the third post-SW attempt to redesign the standard cable-operated wide-ratio 3-speed. Like the 1971 Hillyer design, it was a NIG gear eliminating the AWs undesirable problem of 'no-drive' between high and middle gears. It was not put into production.

## A single cable 5-speed

A few days after filing the new 3-speed patent, Raleigh applied for GB patent 1,399,442. This was a design by Tony Hillyer for a 5-speed hub with single cable control. The patent pointed out that the principles 'may be used in the production of multi-speed epicyclic hubs having more than five speeds'.

The example described in the patent offered decreases of 35% and 9%, direct drive, and increases of 36.5% and 50%. Typical gears thus offered were in the order of 42, 58, 64, 87 and

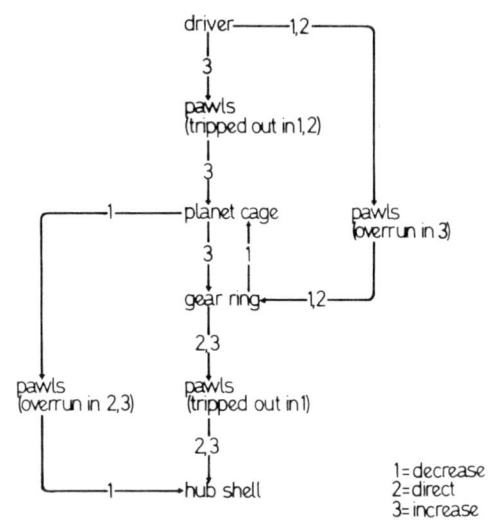

```
       driver────1,2─┐
          │3         │
          ▼          │
       pawls         │
    (tripped out in 1,2)
          │3         │
   ┌──1───▼──────    │
   │   planet cage   pawls
   │      │3    │1   (overrun in 3)
   │      ▼    ▼     │
   │   gear ring◄──1,2
   │      │2,3
 pawls    ▼     pawls
(overrun in 2,3) (tripped out in 1)
   │      │2,3   │
   └──1──►hub shell
```

Fig. 14.4. Flowchart for the Munn NIG 3-speed.

1 = decrease
2 = direct
3 = increase

MUNN NON-SLIP THREE-SPEED (1973 PATENT)
No interlocking clutches but four pawl and ratchet systems tripped in and out by a selector sleeve.

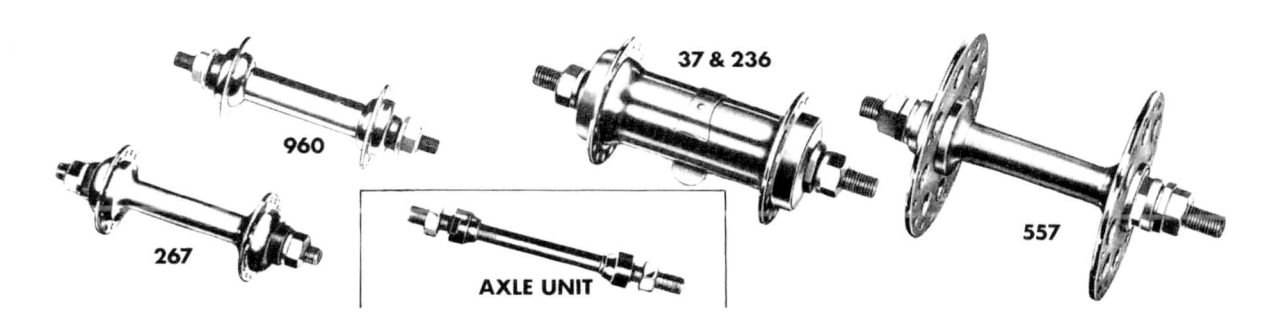

Fig. 14.5. Apart from gear hubs, brake hubs and Dynohubs, Sturmey-Archer produced numerous plain front and rear hubs, such as these front hubs from a 1975 catalogue.

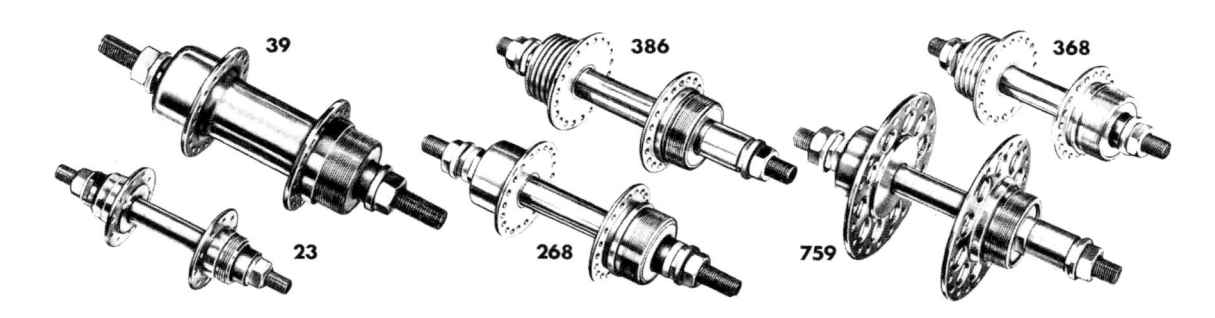

Fig. 14.6. From the same catalogue, these are Sturmey-Archer's standard rear hubs of the mid 1970s.

96". The gear was a twin epicyclic hub with two fixed suns and a common planet cage. One gear ring was fixed, the other slidable. In common with a number of other Sturmey-Archer hub designs of this period, the new 5-speed incorporated a coupling sleeve.

The main version described in the patent specification used the following pawl and ratchet systems:

A – ultra-high gear pawls between the slidable gear ring and the hub shell,
B – high/low gear pawls between the fixed gear ring and the hub shell,
C – pawls between the coupling sleeve and the slidable gear ring,
D – ultra-low gear pawls between the planet cage and the hub shell.

For ultra-high gear the sleeve was held at its furthest left position by the spring-loaded slidable gear ring. Drive went through the sleeve which was dogged to the planet cage, through the epicyclic gear train, out via the slidable gear ring and ultra-high gear pawls A to the hub shell, the three other pawl and ratchet systems being overrun.

For high gear the sleeve was moved slightly to the right, tripping out the ultra-high gear pawls A. Drive went through the sleeve to the planet cage and through the epicyclic system and out via the fixed gear ring and high/low gear pawls B to the hub shell, pawl and ratchet systems C and D being overrun.

For middle gear the sleeve moved further right, disengaging the dogs linking it to the planet cage and allowing the ultra-high gear pawls A to re-engage. The drive went via the coupling sleeve and pawl and ratchet system C to the slidable ring and via the ultra-high gear pawls A to the hub shell. Thus the epicyclic gearing was bypassed to give direct drive, pawl and ratchet systems B and D being overrun.

For low gear the sleeve was pulled further right, moving the slidable gear ring and once more tripping out the ultra-high gear pawls A. Drive went from the sleeve via pawl and ratchet system C to the slidable gear ring then through the epicyclic system and out via the fixed gear ring and high/low gear pawls B to the hub shell, pawl and ratchet system D being overrun. In this gear the two epicyclic trains worked in series.

For ultra-low gear the sleeve was moved to its furthest right position, tripping out the high/low gear pawls B. Ultra-high gear pawls A remained tripped out and drive went from the sleeve via pawl and ratchet system C to the slidable gear ring then through the epicyclic system and out via the planet cage and the

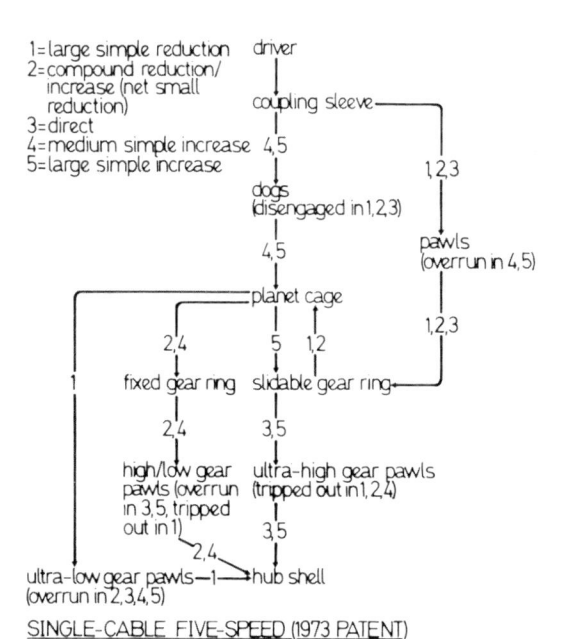

1 = large simple reduction
2 = compound reduction/increase (net small reduction)
3 = direct
4 = medium simple increase
5 = large simple increase

SINGLE-CABLE FIVE-SPEED (1973 PATENT)
Twin epicyclic system using two fixed suns, two gear rings and a common planet cage

Fig. 14.7. Flowchart for the single-cable 5-speed.

ultra-low gear pawls D to the hub shell.

Like Henry Sturmey's 1921 5-speed, the new gear had one great advantage over the S5: single cable control. And it achieved it more simply: Sturmey's hub needed two slidable suns and a slidably mounted epicyclic assembly. But Sturmey-Archer had an ambivalent attitude to 5-speeds at this time: in 1974 they discontinued the S5 without introducing a replacement. This reflected the decline in the American hi-rise market, the main outlet for the S5.

### S2 improvements

Despite having discontinued the back-pedal changing S2 in 1972, the following spring Raleigh applied for a patent covering an improvement to the gear. This patent, GB 1,433,243, was the work of Sidney Simon Standard who became a well-respected Nottinghamshire cycle dealer from 1973 until his retirement in 2000. (He died in 2003 in a tragic accident while leading the junior section of his local CTC on a Sunday cycle ride.)

Gear change of the original S2 was effected simply by two alternate pairs of cam faces (one deep, one shallow) tripping the high gear (direct drive) pawls in and out of engagement. Because the cam was directly connected to the driver, the gear would change four times during one complete backward rotation of the pedals. The problem with this system was the ease of engaging the wrong gear – it all depended on how far back the rider turned the pedals.

Sid Standard's modified gear was designed so that, each time the rider back-pedalled, he could only engage the next gear: if already in high he could only select low and vice versa. The mechanism could also be combined with a coaster brake and it is likely that this patent formed the basis for the mooted S2C 2-speed coaster mentioned in the previous chapter.

The design necessitated a measure of rotational play (lost motion) between certain components. The driver was dogged to a drive ring that was dogged both to the gear ring and to a pawl ring. When the pawl ring's pawls engaged with the hub shell ratchet, the gear gave direct drive (high gear), the planet cage pawls being overrun. If the pawl ring's pawls were tripped out, the drive passed through the epicyclic train and out via the planet cage pawls to the hub shell, giving low gear.

Whether or not the pawl ring's pawls were tripped out was controlled by a cam. But, unlike the S2, this cam did not transmit drive to the pawls. When the rider pedalled forwards the cam rotated with the driver under the action of a special pawl on the drive ring. If pedalling ceased, drag springs maintained the relationship of the cam and pawl ring so the gear could not change. However, if the rider back-pedalled, one of these drag springs prevented the cam from rotating backwards and the special pawl on the drive ring was overrun. The relative motion between the cam and the drive ring let a catch pawl on the drive ring engage with teeth on the cam. This catch pawl rotated the cam by the required amount to effect a change of gear when forward pedalling was resumed.

Sid Standard's improved S2 was not put into production and Sturmey-Archer did not market a kick-shift gear during the remainder of the twentieth century.

### Improved derailleur block

Despite their derailleur patents of 1949–50 Sturmey-Archer had never got deeply involved with this type of gear. But in 1973 Raleigh patented an improved derailleur block invented by John Michael Allen. GB patent 1,482,075 covered a splined block that carried a number of lugged sprockets. They were retained on the block by a threaded outer sprocket which could be a single or double. The sprockets could easily be changed without the need to remove

Fig. 14.8. The abortive Sturmey-Archer multiple freewheel system.

the whole freewheel cluster and without the necessity of a special tool.

In 1977 Sturmey-Archer announced a range of multiple freewheels (14-28, 14-32 and 14-34 teeth) based on the patent. Apart from easy sprocket replacement and interchange, the freewheels featured factory-set caged ball bearings and sealed ball races. Pre-production examples were made and brochures produced but mass production did not proceed.

## S7 NIG 7-speed

In the run-up to Christmas 1973, Raleigh patented the most advanced hub gear invented by Sturmey-Archer up to that time. GB patent 1,494,895 covered a 7-speed hub with single cable control and no intermediate gear (NIG). The name of the inventor was not stated but Tony Hillyer was deeply involved.

The prototype 7-speed, known as the S7, dispensed with the familiar toggle chain. Instead it had a spring-loaded pulley wheel outboard of the drive sprocket. The control cable was anchored to, and wrapped round, the pulley wheel: when the control trigger pulled the cable, the pulley rotated. The pulley was spring-loaded by means of a clock-type spring.

The pulley was linked to a camshaft sleeve around the wheel axle. Each gear change was effected by tripping various pawls in and out of action. Cam followers were used to relay the movement of the camshaft sleeve to the tails of the pawls, so there was no need for a hollow axle. The gear consisted of two epicyclic trains that could be connected in series. It was similar in concept to a hub gear containing a wide-ratio 3-speed driving a medium-ratio 3-speed. This should offer at least nine speeds (3 x 3) but in this case the lowest and highest were omitted. Presumably they were considered not worth the additional complication.

The gear had six pawl and ratchet systems:

A – between the driver and the gear ring of the first epicyclic train,
B – between the driver and the planet cage of the first train,
C – between the gear rings of the first and second trains,
D – between the planet cages of the first and second trains,
E – between the gear ring of the second train and the hub shell,
F – between the planet cage of the second train and the hub shell.

The drive sequences were as follows:

- First Gear (lowest) – via the gear ring of the first train, through the first epicyclic train, out via the first planet cage, then through the second planet cage and finally out to the hub shell. Thus the low gear of the first 3-speed drove the direct drive of the second.

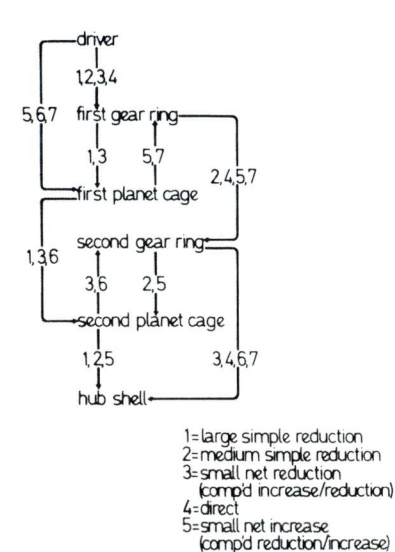

Fig. 14.9. Flowchart for the 7-speed hub.

- Second gear – via the first gear ring to the second gear ring, then through the second epicyclic train and out via the second planet cage to the hub shell. Thus the direct drive of the first 3-speed drove the low gear of the second.
- Third gear – via the first gear ring, through the first epicyclic train, then out via the first planet cage and into the second planet cage, through the second epicyclic train and finally out via the second gear ring to the hub shell. Thus the low gear of the first 3-speed drove the high gear of the second.
- Fourth gear – via the first gear ring to the second gear ring and out to the hub shell. Thus the direct drive of the first 3-speed drove the direct drive of the second.
- Fifth gear – via the first planet cage, through the first epicyclic train, then out via the first gear ring and into the second gear ring, through the second epicyclic train and finally out via the second planet cage to the hub shell. Thus the high gear of the first 3-speed drove the low gear of the second.
- Sixth gear – via the first planet cage to the second planet cage, through the second epicyclic train and out via the second gear ring to the hub shell. Thus the direct drive of the first 3-speed drove the high gear of the second.
- Seventh gear (top) – via the first planet cage, through the first epicyclic train, out via the first gear ring and finally out via the second gear ring to the hub shell. Thus the high gear of the first 3-speed drove the direct drive of the second.

A working prototype of the S7 was made and housed in an AW-type shell. It gave reductions of 35, 25 and 13.3%, direct drive and increases of 15.4, 33.3 and 53.8%. Thus it could offer typical gears of 42, 48, 55, 64, 74, 85, 98 or 36, 41, 48, 55, 63, 73, 85". The S7 marked the zenith of Sturmey-Archer's creative burst of the early 1970s. There was little innovation during the rest of the decade.

243

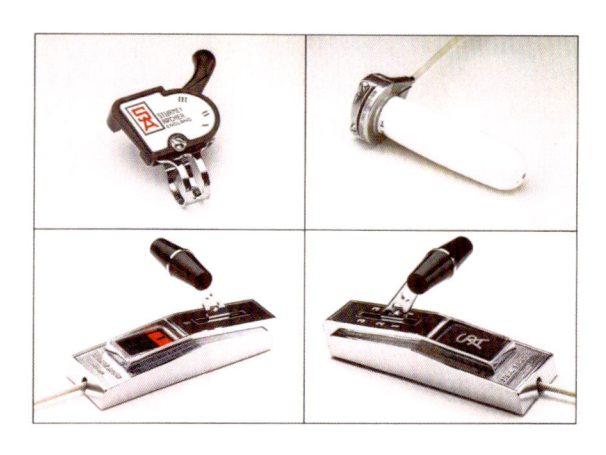

Fig. 14.10. 1978 3-speed controls. Clockwise from top left: the CPSC approved Trigger Control, the Auto Twist Grip, the Standard Sportshift and the De-Luxe Sportshift (with gear number indicator panel).

## A safer trigger and a deletion

The standard AW 3-speed trigger was modified to comply with the United States' Consumer Product Safety Commission (CPSC) safety standards in 1976. This necessitated the bulbous plastic knob that was added to the end of the lever.

In the same year the S3B 3-speed drum brake for small-wheelers was deleted from the product range. The only bikes on which it had been used since 1970 were the Moulton Mk 3 and the RSW Mk 3, sales of which were so disappointing that both had been discontinued.

## 70 mm drum brakes

In 1977 the SBF drum brake was introduced, the S standing for 'small'. This was an internally expanding front drum brake with a 70 mm drum, designed by Sid Standard. The following year saw the launch of the matching rear hub, the SBR, which was suitable for single-speed and derailleur gears. Both had die-cast alloy brake shoes with bonded brake linings and both were also available with equal size flanges to meet the needs of automatic wheel building machines. They were additions to the drum brake range, the 90 mm drum brakes remaining in production. Incidentally, during the 1970s British manufacturing industry widely adopted the Système International d'Unités (SI) metric system and Sturmey-Archer ceased quoting brake drum diameters in inches.

Sturmey-Archer experimented with brake shoes made from glass-reinforced polyester (GRP), Mintex brake linings being moulded into the shoes. Unfortunately the shoes went soft due to heat when braking, so the idea was abandoned.

Fig. 14.11. The SBF front drum brake.

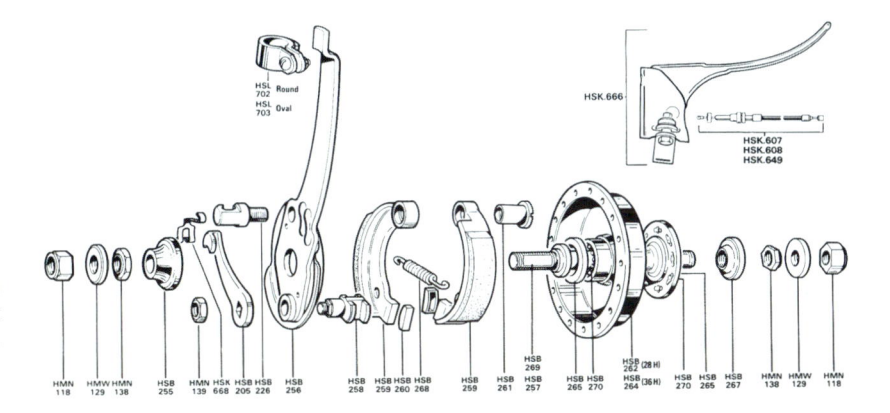

Fig. 14.12. Exploded view of the SBF front drum brake.

Fig. 14.13. The SBR rear drum brake, shown here with derailleur.

Fig. 14.14. Exploded view of the SBR rear drum brake.

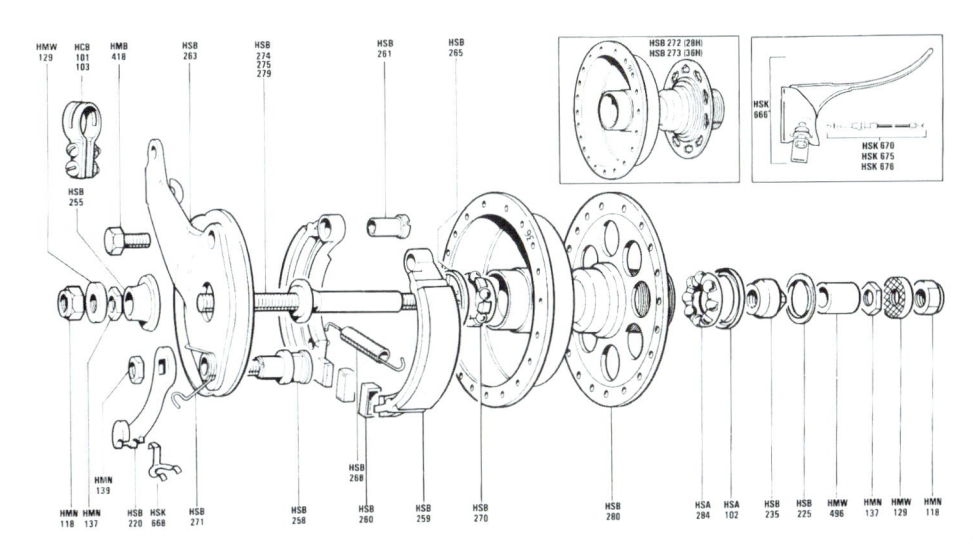

245

## Return of the 5-speed

1977 saw the launch of the S5/1, after several years in which no 5-speed was marketed. The S5/1 was a modification of the original S5; the main difference was in the mechanism for shifting the suns and thereby selecting which was clutched to the wheel axle.

In the original S5, when the left cable was slack, the suns rested in the position for the middle three ratios: the left sun was locked to the axle and the right sun was free. When the left-hand control lever was pulled, the cable tightened and acted on a bell-crank screwed to the left end of the wheel axle. This bell-crank pushed a rod in the left side of the axle, moving the suns to the right against a spring. This movement freed the left sun and locked the right sun to the axle, thereby enabling the ultra-high and ultra-low gears to be engaged.

The S5's bell-crank was not particularly well made and could give trouble in operation. (Steel and plastic versions had been used but neither was as substantial as the bell-crank used on some Shimano 3-speed hubs.) The bell-crank and push-rod system gave the experienced

Fig. 14.15. The S5/1 5-speed.

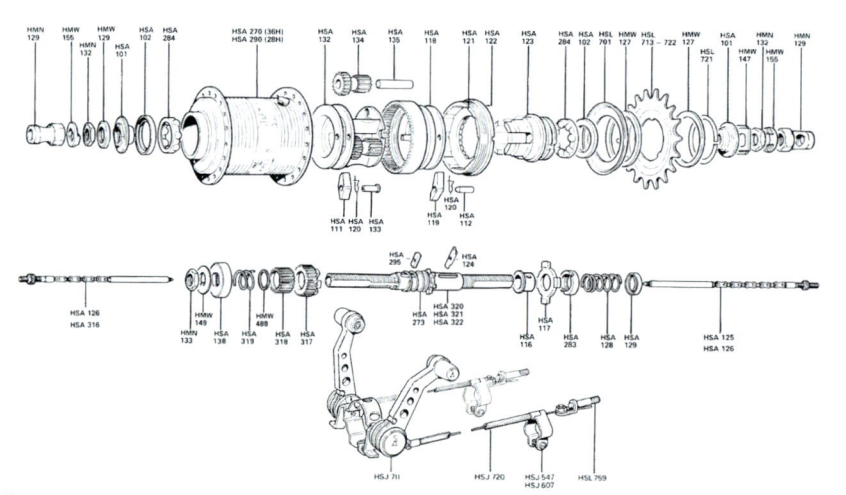

Fig. 14.16. Exploded view of the S5/1 5-speed, showing another twin-lever variant.

cyclist good 'feel' to the selection of the ultra-high and ultra-low gears but responded badly to crash changing by the inexperienced.

The S5/1 eliminated the bell-crank and push-rod system. Instead a toggle chain was fitted to the left end of the axle, like that used on the right. The twin suns now rested on the right when the left cable was slack, ready for selection of ultra-high or ultra-low gear. Pulling the left lever brought them into position for the three middle gears. (With all versions of the S5, direct drive could be selected regardless of the position of the left control lever.)

The pull-chain system incorporated a spring hold-off for the sliding suns to prevent damage during crash changing. This prevented sideways movement of the suns until pedal pressure was slightly eased. This necessitated two springs for the suns where the S5 used only one: an added complication but one that made the hub more useable by inexperienced riders. Use of the standard toggle chain instead of the bell-crank also made production a little cheaper.

The styling of the dual lever unit shown on the exploded view suffered somewhat from the Chopper legacy. Type HSJ 711 was a version for top tube or down tube fitting, whereas HSJ 773 fitted on the handlebar stem.

## Two coasters added, another deleted

The SC1 single-speed coaster was launched in 1978, eight years after it was patented. It had an extruded body with separate flanges and was similar in concept to the original 1922 CC.

Sturmey-Archer also wanted a cheaper and less powerful coaster hub for fitting to juvenile

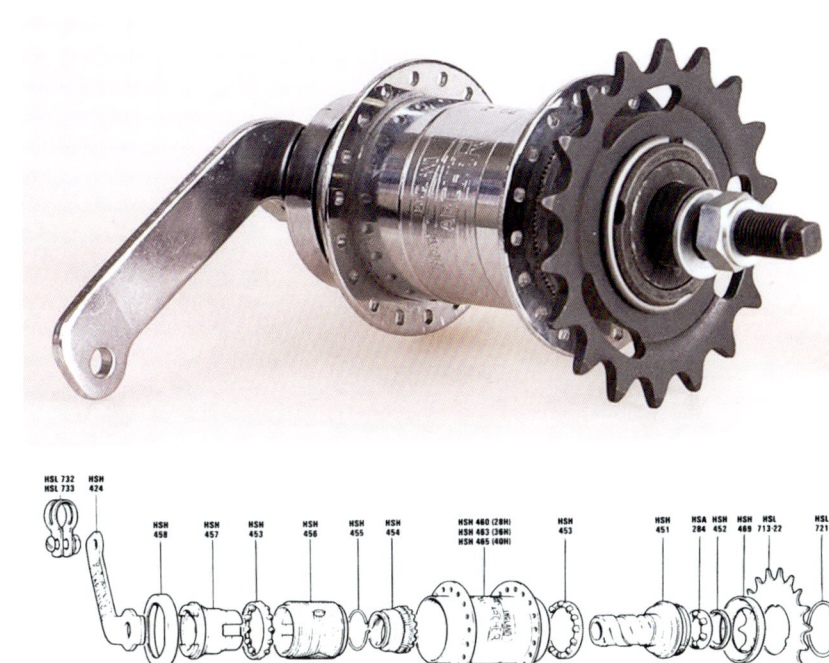

Fig. 14.17. The SC1 coaster brake.

Fig. 14.18. Exploded view of the SC1 coaster.

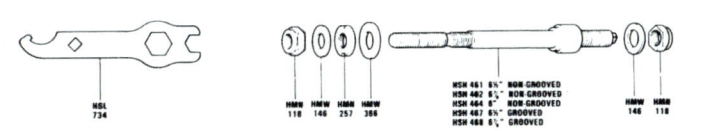

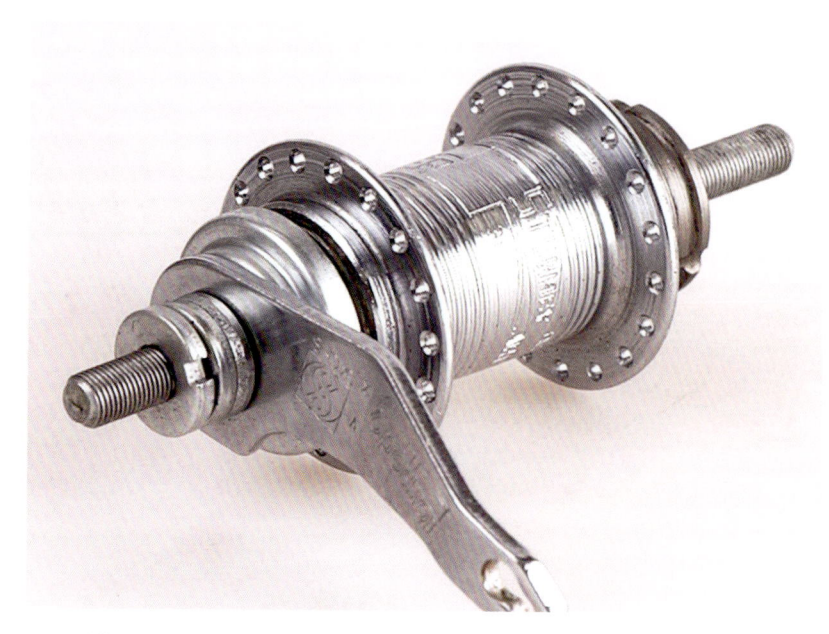

Fig. 14.19. The SCC (Sachs) coaster brake.

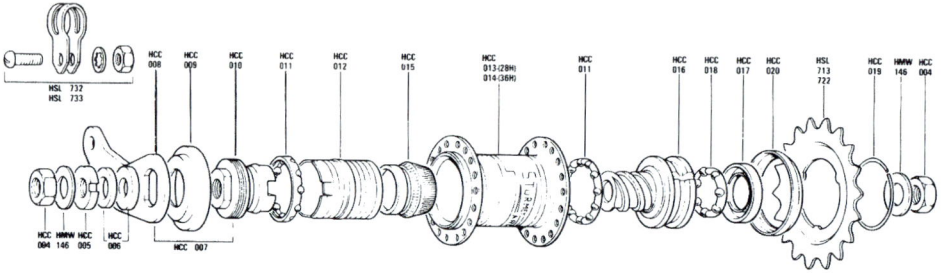

Fig. 14.20. Exploded view of the SCC coaster.

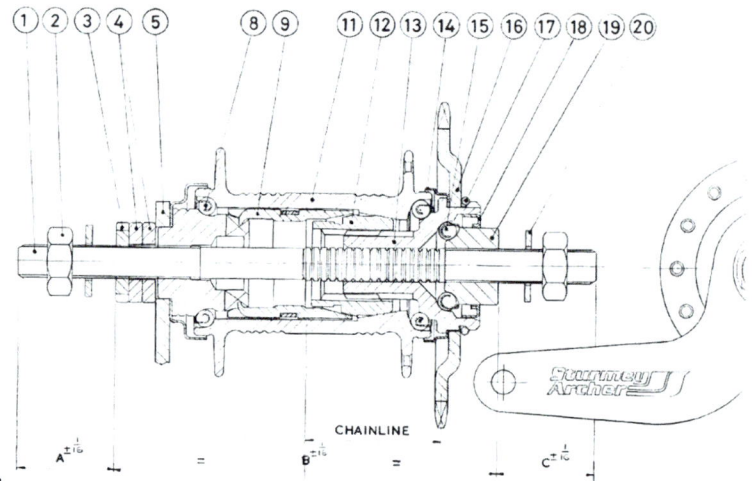

Fig. 14.21. Sectional drawing of the SCC coaster.

Fig. 14.22. The SAB 3-speed 70 mm drum brake.

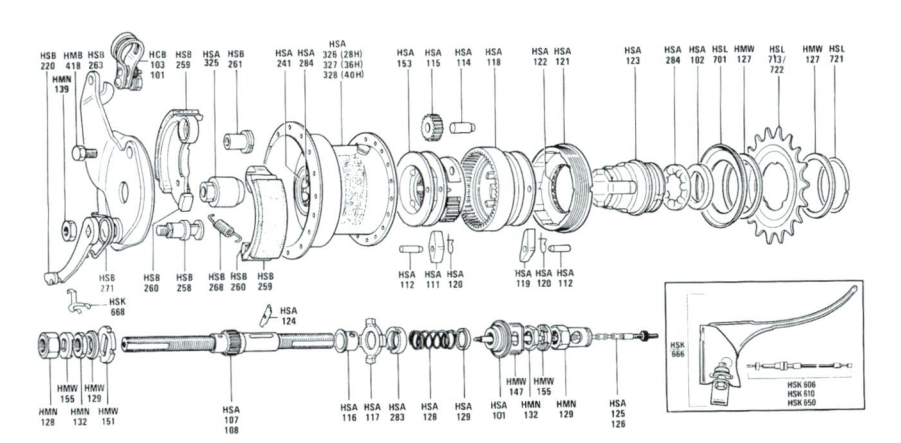

Fig. 14.23. Exploded view of the SAB hub.

cycles made by Raleigh, so in 1978 the SCC coaster brake was introduced. This was the Sachs Jet hub, bought in from West Germany and badge-engineered by fitting a Sturmey-Archer brake arm.

The most significant difference between the two coasters was that the SC1 had positive forward drive via teeth on the right end of the brake actuator, whereas the SCC drove via a serrated friction cone on the brake actuator.

With the launch of these coaster brakes, the Perry-type SC coaster was deleted.

### SAB3 3-Speed drum brake

Another new introduction in 1978 was the SAB3. This was essentially an SBR 70 mm drum brake combined with an AW wide-ratio 3-speed. It was an addition to the range and did not replace the AB 90 mm 3-speed drum brake.

### Improved twist-grip

In 1978 Raleigh filed GB patent 2,024,381, the inventor being Leonard Haydn Fox. It covered an improved twist-grip control that included acetal resin plastics components and was designed for simple economical manufacture. Unlike earlier Sturmey-Archer twist-grips this one provided 'an aural indication of the change of gear' that could 'also be sensed through the hand'.

## Silent freewheel

Leonard Fox was also the inventor of a silent freewheel, the subject of an apparently unsuccessful GB patent application in 1979. It used ball bearings in tapered spaces formed by cutaways in the sprocket. When drive was applied the balls were driven into the tighter ends of the tapered spaces, locking the sprocket to the body of the freewheel and giving drive. But when starting to freewheel, the sprocket was held back relative to rotation of the freewheel body, allowing the balls to move into the wider part of the taper and disconnecting the drive. The concept was an old one, which was probably why the patent application was rejected.

## Contract work

In 1975 an engineering division was formed within Sturmey-Archer to offer a wide range of services to other manufacturers. A 1977 brochure in English, German and French stated:

> A large percentage of motor cars on the roads today use Sturmey-Archer manufactured components – from starting to stopping – in ignition, starter, engine, seating, suspension and brakes. And not only cars – but leisure goods, furniture, hand tools, lawn mowers, domestic appliances, commercial vehicles, earth movers, fighting vehicles, armaments – the list is endless.

The company offered sintering, auto turning, cold forming, general machining and a wide range of finishing and hardening treatments. (See Chapter 16 for more on sintering and cold forming.)

## Phillips and Brooks

Also in 1975 the former Phillips Credenda factory, used for making cycle components, and the J.D. Brooks saddle works, both in Smethwick, were integrated into Sturmey-Archer as part of the restructuring of the Raleigh group. The Credenda factory was very out of date but Sturmey-Archer tried to revive it with manufacture of new components, such as frame lugs and aluminium handlebar stems. These ventures were unsuccessful and in 1982 the Credenda factory was closed, its remaining production being absorbed into the nearby Brooks saddle factory.

There was even a proposal to close the Brooks works, at which point Alan Clarke expressed an interest in buying it. This seems to have made the owners reconsider the situation, as Sturmey-Archer then invested heavily in high quality advertising of Brooks products in Holland and Germany. This resulted in the operation becoming very profitable.

## Metal hardening

In the mid 1970s Sturmey-Archer's metal hardening plant used two techniques. The older one involved dipping the parts in molten cyanide. This gave off carbon monoxide which, in passing over the metal, hardened it by changing the molecular structure of its surface by adding carbon. The treated items were then quenched in cold water or oil, locking the carbon into the surface and completing the case hardening process.

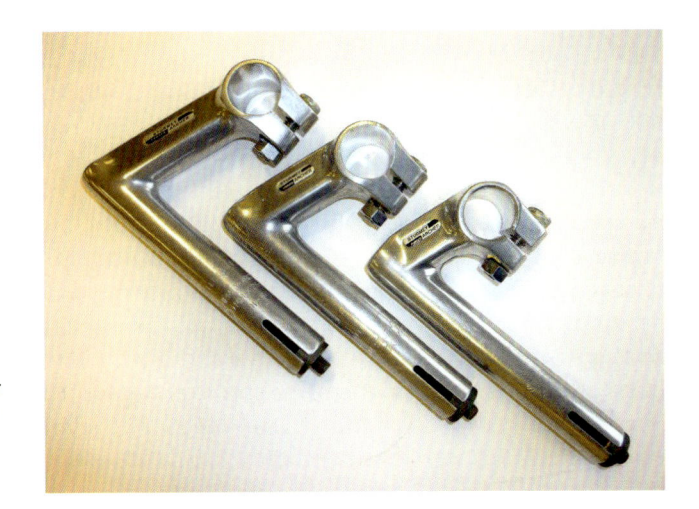

Fig. 14.24. Sturmey-Archer alloy handlebar stems made at the former Phillips works in Smethwick, Birmingham.

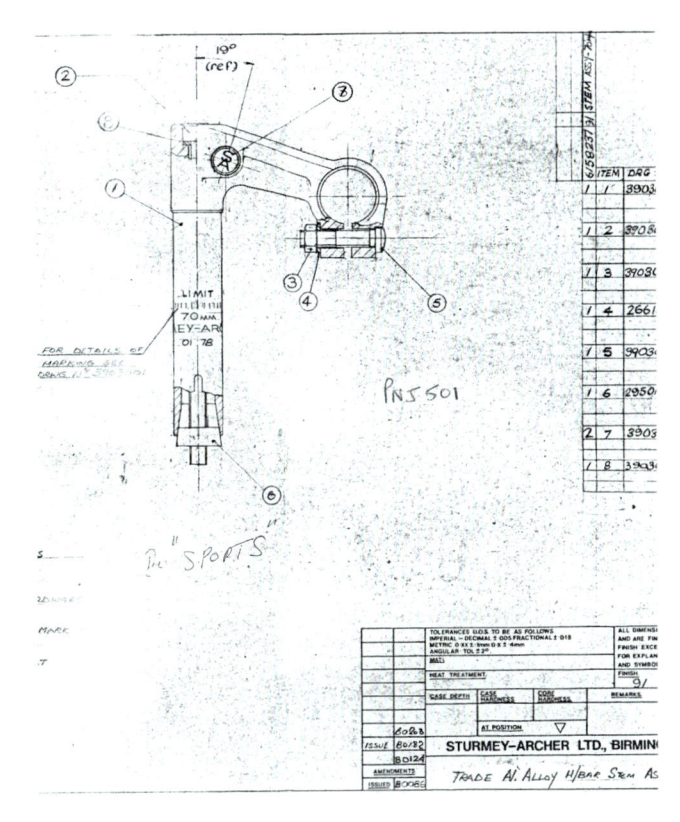

Fig. 14.25. Technical drawing for handlebar stem made at Smethwick

The newer technique involved heating the components in a carburising furnace until all the oxygen had been burned off. Superheated natural gas or propane was then introduced, together with ammonia and propane. In the absence of oxygen, the gases did not ignite but circulated among the metal components. As with the cyanide process, the surface was hardened by carbon transfer and the process was completed by quenching.

## Restructuring continues

Sturmey-Archer produced about 2.5 million hubs a year in the mid 1970s. In 1978 the gears division sold more than half its output to companies other than Raleigh, with 80% of these sales being exported.

In 1976 TI divided Raleigh into four relatively independent entities: Cox car seats, cycles, services and Sturmey-Archer. Substantial capital expenditure commenced at Sturmey-Archer with a view to improving productivity and competitiveness.

Raleigh were already under commercial pressure to use more imported components. The separation from Sturmey-Archer made it easier for the cycle maker to look abroad, especially to Japan. The managing director of Sturmey-Archer complained to the Raleigh board at the suggestion that Japanese imports should be limited only by price and merit, and not by cartel. The board replied that Raleigh 'had to maintain its premier position by producing the best possible bicycles and utilise the components most suitable for building competitive machines, but having said that, there had to be the fullest co-operation between the two companies in maximising utilisation of S-A produced components whenever this was acceptable within the market's demands'. Raleigh meanwhile badge-engineered imported components, either with their own name or with the importers' name, to prevent 'foreign components becoming too familiar in the market place in their own brand names'.

Patrick Bramman, who worked in Raleigh's advertising department from 1972 to 1984, recalled Sturmey-Archer-branded derailleur mechanisms being exhibited. However, these do not seem to have been marketed. The samples were presumably badge-engineered, like the SunTour Cyclone and GT mechanisms badged by Raleigh with their own name. The reverse applied to SunTour's 3-speed hubs, which were secretly made by Sturmey-Archer.

Bramman also remembered the little robot-like figures made from Sturmey-Archer components by the apprentices. These had a long tradition and were displayed by Sturmey-Archer at trade shows and exhibitions. An example is used as a prize in the annual Tin Can Ten race for hub-geared cycles.

There was soon friction between semi-independent Sturmey-Archer and Raleigh about

Fig. 14.26. Bucking the trend to badge-engineer imported components as Raleigh products, Sturmey-Archer secretly made 3-speeds for SunTour of Japan. This example is from 1976.

Fig. 14.27. Robot-like figures made from Sturmey-Archer components by apprentices. This display was photographed in 1975.

product changes, quality and ability to meet demand. Raleigh complained that Sturmey-Archer had fitted die-cast brake shoes without their approval. They also commented on the suitability of the SC coaster initially fitted to the Strika juvenile cycle, as UK parents were totally unfamiliar with coaster brakes and were worried about their children's safety. And Raleigh wanted 1,500 S3C hubs per week at a time when Sturmey-Archer could only supply 700.

In 1978 Raleigh chairman Ian Phillips highlighted the need for much closer liaison between the companies. Matters of concern included rationalisation of axle lengths, changes likely to affect production capacity and version control of design drawings. The separation of Sturmey-Archer and Raleigh at this time did not prove a great success.

## Market situation at the end of the decade

The 1970s was a period during which bicycle sales in the United Kingdom almost trebled: by the end of the decade annual sales were running at about 1.5 million. The annual distance cycled by Britons stabilised during this decade, at about 2,500,000 miles (4,000,000 km); until 1970 it had been falling steadily from the 1955 figure of about 12,500,000 miles (20,000,000 km). However, 2,500,000 miles per year is hardly impressive, as it equates to 9 inches (23 cm) per day per person.

Despite the buoyant market for bicycles Sturmey-Archer still faced a struggle. Not only were there internal battles with Raleigh but derailleur-geared bikes were claiming a larger share of the market and foreign hub gears were making inroads. One consolation was that Shimano and Fichtel & Sachs made only 2-speeds and 3-speeds. In 1978 the US market for Sturmey-Archer products was still considered big enough to justify the opening of a warehouse and sales and service centre in Chicago.

The brainstorming of the early 1970s produced a number of clever designs that failed to get into production, in particular the 7-speed hub. The company seemed reluctant to invest in new products. Nonetheless some worthwhile improvements were made to existing designs, notably the 3-speed coaster and the 5-speed hub. The range of drum brakes was expanded and the product deletions were well reasoned. Few would mourn the passing of the S2 or the S3B. Rather more would have been saddened by the non-appearance of the single-cable 5-speed and 7-speed hubs, had they known about them.

# Chapter 15
# A wavering relationship

### Sturmey-Archer's last years with TI, from 1980 to 1987

## The product range contracts
The 1980s began with continued contraction of the Sturmey-Archer product line. In 1980 the SC1 coaster was dropped from the range after only two years in production. Two years later the SCC coaster was also withdrawn: once again Sturmey-Archer pulled out of the market for single-speed coasters. There was little demand for such hubs in Britain, demand in the USA had decreased as Americans turned to derailleur-geared bikes, and Europe was well served by Fichtel & Sachs.

In historic terms, output was still very high, with 2.2 million hubs made in 1980. By way of comparison, here are annual production figures at five-yearly intervals from 1915:

1915 – 200,000
1920 – N/A
1925 – 130,000
1930 – 200,000
1935 – 750,000
1940 – 60,000
1945 – N/A
1950 – 1.0 million
1955 – 2.4 million
1960 – 2.0 million
1965 – 1.5 million
1970 – 1.9 million
1975 – 2.6 million
1980 – 2.2 million

Moreover, Sturmey-Archer remained a major component supplier to the wider cycle trade, providing not only hubs but lighting equipment and saddles. Sturmey-Archer's 1982 comprehensive component catalogue included the following: hub gears and controls, touring drum brakes, sports drum brakes, 3-speed coaster brake, calliper brakes and levers, cables and fittings, Dynohub lighting, rim dynamo lighting (with bought-in dynamos), Brooks race saddles, Brooks sports and touring saddles, Brooks BMX saddles, BMX crash pads, bags and holdalls, toe clips and straps, single-speed hubs, spokes and nipples, frame fitting components (including seat pillars, head race sets, cotter pins and bottom bracket sets).

## Fixed-wheel conversions
Between the deletion of the ASC fixed-wheel hub in 1963 and prior to the introduction of the S3X many years later, there remained a limited demand for a fixed-wheel hub gear, some of it from people with disabilities for whom such a hub could be particularly useful. In 1981

Fig. 15.1. Despite some fall in demand, Sturmey-Archer still had a high output. Here Alan Clarke (left) receives the millionth hub made in 1980. More than another million would be made before the year's end.

Fig. 15.2. Advertisement in the cycle trade press for Sturmey-Archer components, including Brooks saddles.

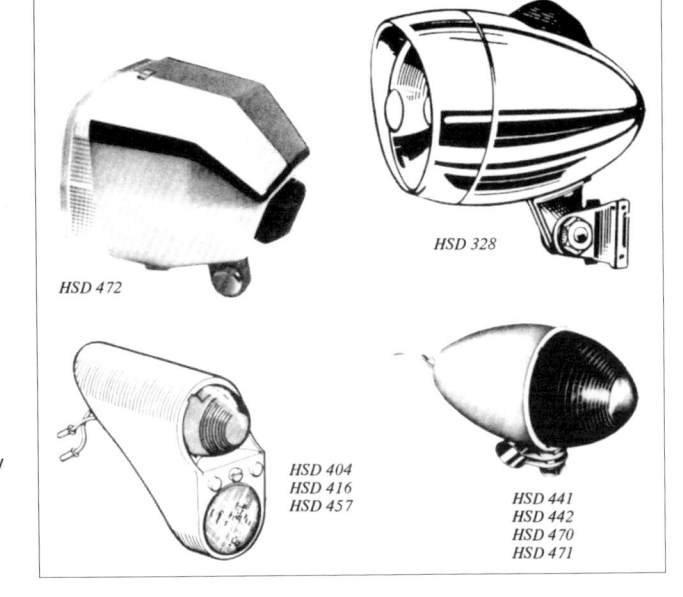

Fig. 15.3. Sturmey-Archer lamps in the 1970s and 1980s included these models. The mudguard-fitting combined rear lamp and reflector (bottom left) was a particularly practical design.

255

The Hub of the Universe

Fig. 15.4. The S5/2 5-speed hub.

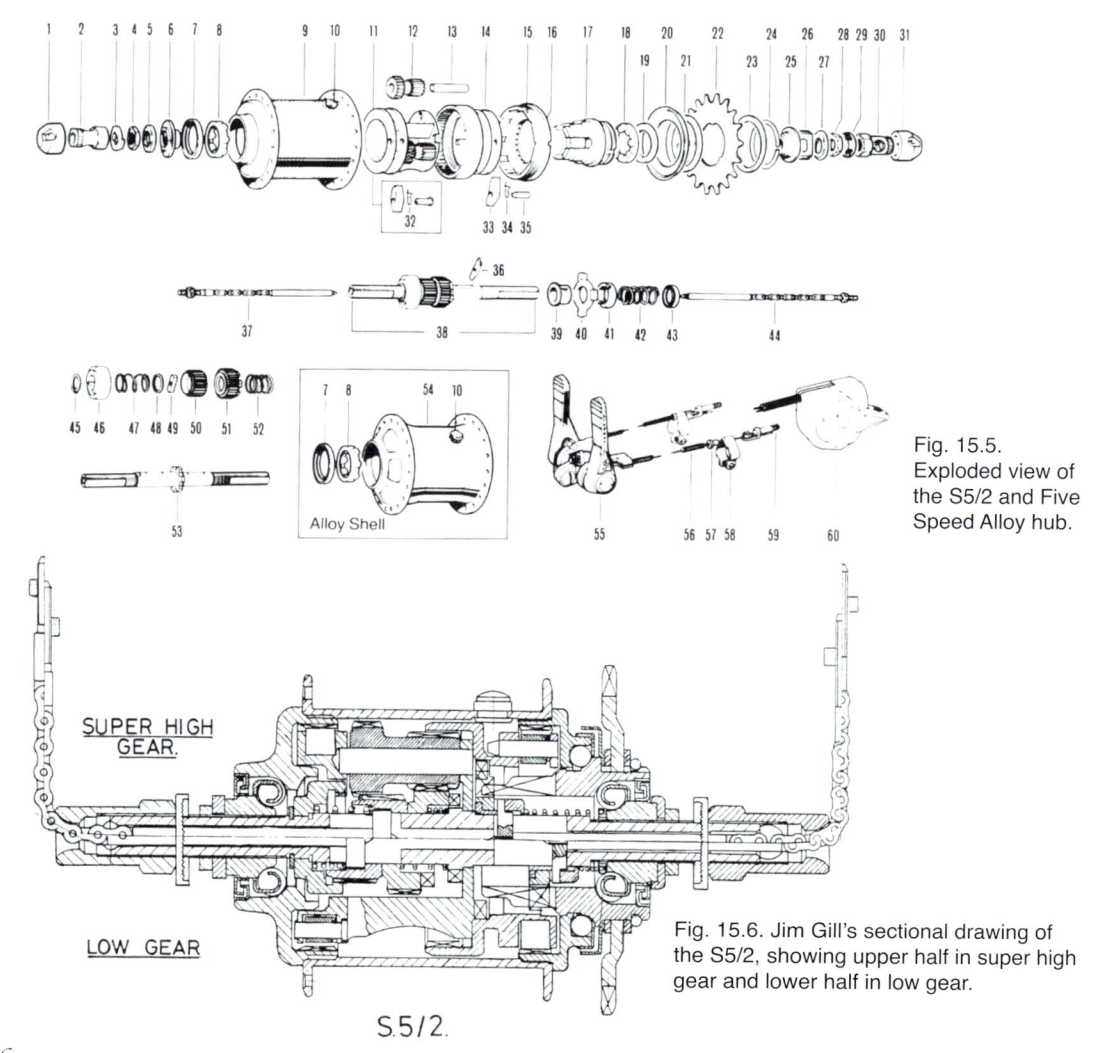

Fig. 15.5. Exploded view of the S5/2 and Five Speed Alloy hub.

Fig. 15.6. Jim Gill's sectional drawing of the S5/2, showing upper half in super high gear and lower half in low gear.

256

Sturmey-Archer therefore issued drawings showing the conversion of an AW 3-speed to 2-speed fixed-wheel mode.

Jim Gill wrote detailed instructions to accompany the Sturmey-Archer drawings. John Fairbrother documented a similar conversion. Both men also wrote instructions for creating a 3-speed fixed hub: Gill's were based on an FM or FW 4-speed, whereas Fairbrother's used a pre-2002 5-speed hub. All these instructions may be accessed at: https://hadland.wordpress.com/2012/07/02/esoteric-info-for-sturmey-freaks/

### S5/2 5-speed
Sturmey-Archer now concentrated on improving their remaining products. In 1981 the 5-speed hub gear was slightly modified and renamed the S5/2. It was essentially the same as the S5/1 except that the wheel axle, sliding suns, dog ring, sun pinion return spring, low gear axle key and low gear spring were no longer available as separate parts. Instead they came as a complete service assembly. Three versions of the axle assembly were offered, the only difference being the axle length: 5⅞" (149 mm), 6⅛" (155 mm) and 6⅜" (162 mm).

### Differences between the S5/1 and S5/2
The adoption of the pre-assembled axle and sun unit resulted from persistent criticism of the left-hand changing mechanism, the usual complaint being that the gears slipped. The mechanism that moved the suns of the S5/1 depended on two springs acting in opposition. With the left cable slack, the stronger spring (sun return) was intended to overcome the weaker one (low gear spring), forcing the suns to the right. This freed the secondary sun and dogged the primary sun to the axle. As the left cable tightened it pulled the sun pinion return spring to the left, taking pressure off the low gear spring which then pushed the suns to the left. This dogged the secondary sun to the dog ring, locking it to the axle and freeing the primary sun.

The S5/2 used the same system but included a stronger sun pinion return spring for a more positive changing action. Whereas the dog ring of the S5/1 relied on a locknut to keep it in place, that of the S5/2 was held by a circlip and therefore less likely to work loose or be tampered with or misassembled.

This new axle assembly was also a gift for anyone wishing to convert an FW 4-speed into the latest 5-speed hub. All that was needed was to remove the axle of the FW (complete with suns, axle keys, etc.) and replace it with an S5/2 axle assembly, a task requiring relatively little skill.

### 5-Speed levers
Sturmey-Archer announced a new alloy stem-fitting twin lever assembly for the S5/2 in 1982. This looked more like a conventional derailleur lever assembly than some of its predecessors but it was remarkably heavy for an alloy product. It has been described as 'styled rather than stylish'.

Three twin lever assemblies were briefly available simultaneously: the new alloy stem fitting levers; chrome-finish frame tube fitting levers; and chrome-finish stem fitting levers that worked back-to-front compared with the other levers.

## New alloy shell
Sturmey-Archer reintroduced an alloy shell in 1983 – a new design rather than a re-launch of the 1940s pattern. It was about 4 oz (113 gm) lighter than the steel shell and was produced only in a 36 hole version. The S5/2 and AW, when encased in the new alloy shell, became known respectively as the Five Speed Alloy and Three Speed Alloy.

## XAG lightweight 3-speed hub dynamo
In 1982 Sturmey-Archer announced the XAG, an alloy-shelled hub combining an AW 3-speed with a new version of the Dynohub. This was exciting news for Dynohub devotees and the new hub was prominently featured in the cycling press. The new dynamo section had a 30 pole ceramic magnet and generated 3 watts at 6 volts. It was claimed to be up to four times as efficient as conventional tyre driven dynamos and exceeded all the new international lighting standards such as ISO DP674 and BS 6102.

But the hopes raised by the XAG were not to be fulfilled. It never got to the shops and Sturmey-Archer later stated: 'The XAG was a one-off test sample to test market reaction to the concept. None went to the trade and the samples were scrapped.' A few survived and there are two examples in Sturmey-Archer's museum.

Fig. 15.7. The prototype XAG high output Dynohub.

## Farewell to the Dynohub
There were to be greater disappointments: early in 1984 it was announced that production of all hub dynamos was to cease. The blame was put on falling demand and the inability of the existing designs to meet new lighting standards. If demand had been higher it might have been worthwhile for Sturmey-Archer to invest in new plant. This would have enabled Dynohubs to be produced using the newer ceramic magnet technology.

Sturmey-Archer had been making dynamos since 1936 and the GH6 had been in production almost unaltered since the end of the World War 2. It was a good product that deserved updating.

## BMX
In the 1980s the popularity of the BMX (Bicycle Motocross) had a marginal effect on Sturmey-Archer. Very few BMX bikes used variable gears but the 1983 AW brochure listed an optional strengthened 6¼" (159 mm) BMX axle alongside the standard 6¼" and 5¾" (146mm) types.

## Columbia AW NIG 3-speed
The original AW 3-speed had many points in its favour, not least robustness and simplicity. But a recurring criticism was that an incorrectly adjusted AW could slip between second and third gear, possibly with harmful results. In 1984 Sturmey-Archer introduced a 'no intermediate gear' (NIG) version of the AW that overcame the problem. It was produced exclusively for US cycle maker Columbia and some 60,000 of the special hubs had been made by February 1987.

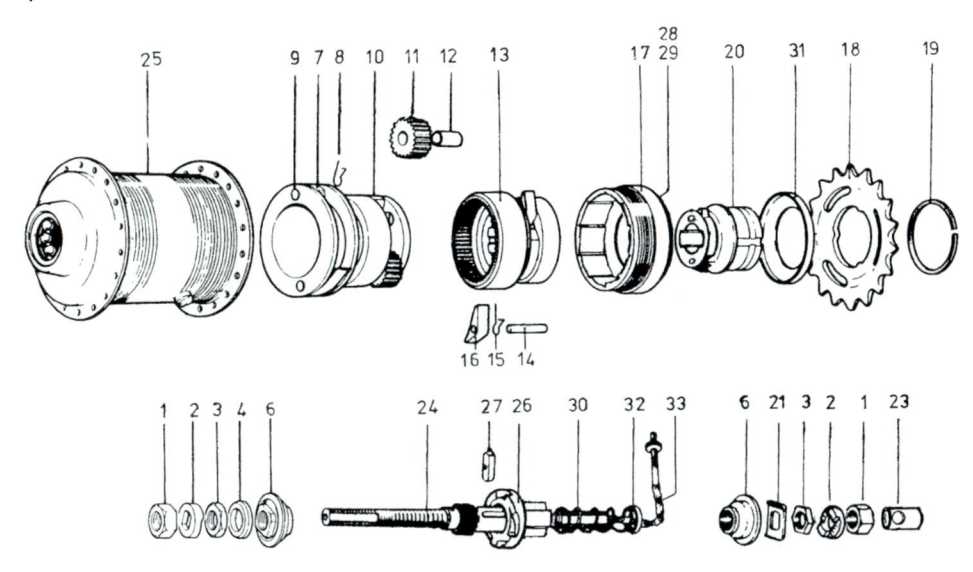

Fig. 15.8. Exploded view by Jim Gill of the Columbia NIG version of the AW.

## AB and BF drum brakes
From 1983 these drum brakes incorporated a new labyrinth seal to keep water out of the brake drums.

## Elite range of drum brakes
In 1984 the Elite range of alloy shell 70 mm drum brakes with sealed bearings was launched. This was an additional upmarket range to compete with products such as the Fichtel & Sachs Galaxie and Orbit drum brakes. It consisted of the VT front drum brake, the ST rear drum brake (which could be used with derailleur gears) and the AT3, which combined an AW 3-speed with the ST's drum brake mechanism. The Elite range included optional black Delrin plastic brake levers for the export market.

The following year the AT5 Elite Alloy 5-speed with 70 mm drum brake was added to the Elite range. It used slightly redesigned S5/2 internals to fit into the same shell as the AT3 Elite Alloy.

## The Hub of the Universe

Fig. 15.9. The peripheral channel of the new labyrinth seal can be seen in the detached end-plate in the foreground.

Fig. 15.10. The Elite VT 70 mm alloy front drum brake. VT is short for 'voortrommel', Dutch for front drum.

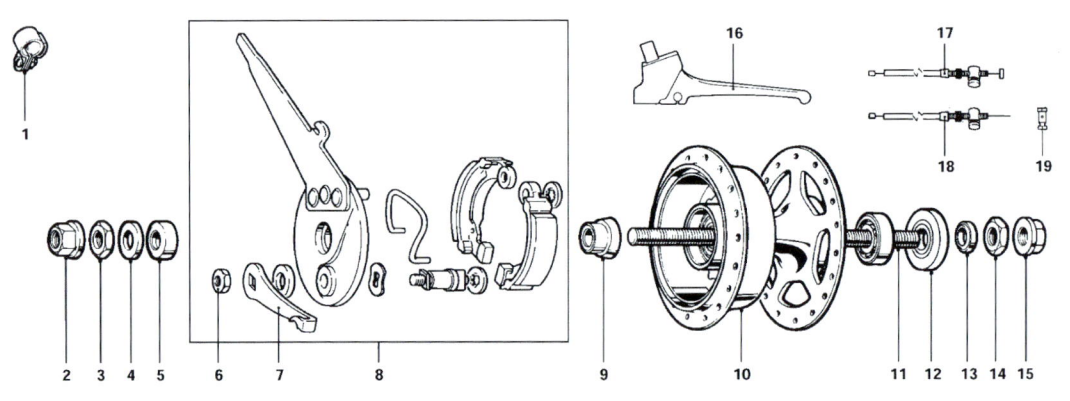

Fig. 15.11. Exploded view of the Elite VT front drum brake.

Fig. 15.12. The Elite ST 70 mm alloy rear drum brake, for single speed or derailleur.

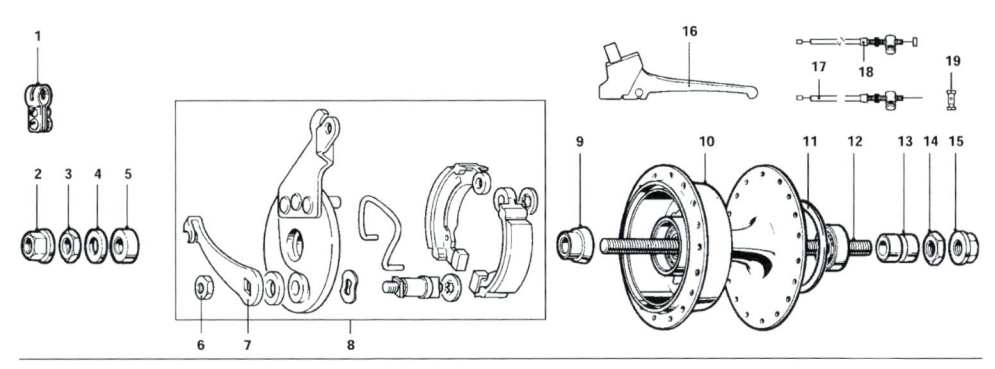

Fig. 15.13. Exploded view of the Elite ST rear drum brake.

Fig. 15.14. The Elite AT3 alloy 3-speed and 70 mm drum brake.

261

The Hub of the Universe

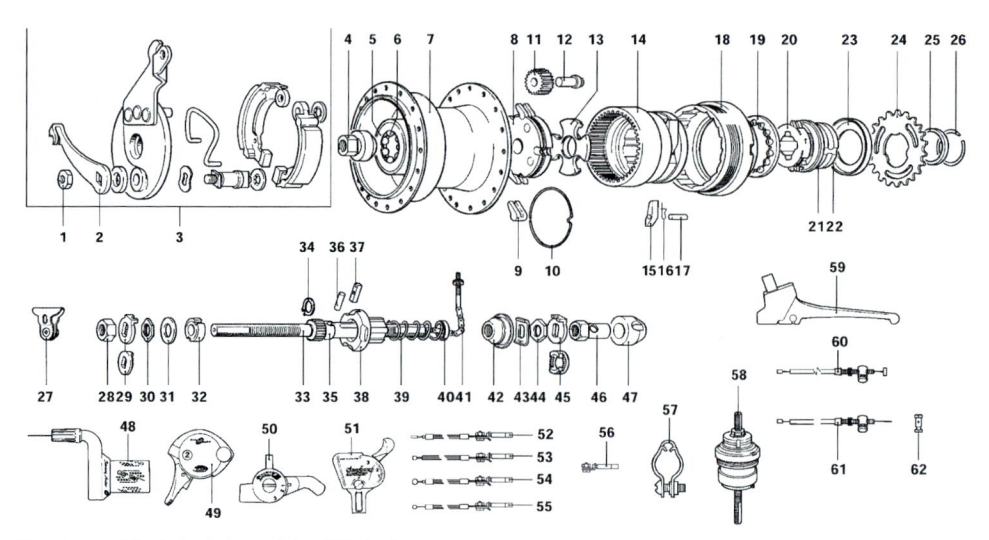

Fig. 15.15. Exploded view of the AT3 hub.

Fig. 15.16. The Elite AT5 alloy 5-speed and 70 mm drum brake.

## Drum brakes for Gazelle

In 1985 a 90 mm diameter, steel-shelled, front drum brake with sealed bearings, was announced – the GBF. The G stood for Gazelle, the famous Dutch bicycle maker which like Raleigh and Sturmey-Archer was owned by TI at this time. The hub was supplied only to Gazelle.

Gazelle previously made their own 3-speed drum brake hub and matching front drum brake hub. After Gazelle was bought by TI, the Dutch company had stopped making their own 3-speed drum brake and instead used the Sturmey-Archer type AB hub. In 1986 production of Gazelle's front hub was transferred to Sturmey-Archer and became the type GBF. Apart from its diablo-shaped hub body, the brake was on the other side of the hub and the Gazelle name was printed on the brake plate, making it exclusive to them. In 2016 Gazelle switched to an alloy-shell version of the GBF, the GLFD.

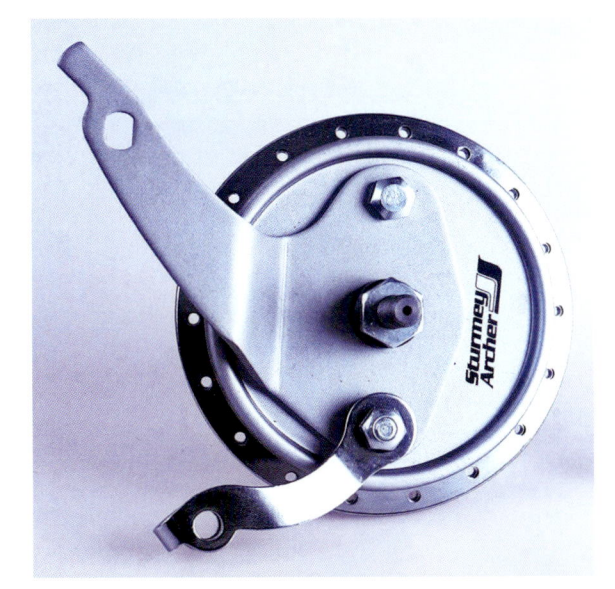

Fig.15.17. The GBF 90 mm steel-shell front drum brake with sealed bearings, made exclusively for Gazelle.

Fig. 15.18. The Steelite SAB 3-speed with 70 mm steel drum brake, in three optional finishes.

## Steelite range of drum brakes
The Steelite range of 70 mm steel shell drum brakes was launched in 1987. These were revamped versions of the SBR rear hub, the SBF front hub and the SAB 3-speed/brake combination. Interestingly, some Steelite hubs were slightly lighter than the corresponding Elite alloy-shelled hubs.

Why were 70 mm drum brakes introduced? In the mid 1980s AB and BF 90 mm drum brake sales were taking off in the Netherlands but there was insufficient factory capacity to make enough 90 mm brake pans. This was because of huge demand from Nigeria for Raleigh bicycles, many of which were equipped with GH6 or AG Dynohubs: the 90 mm Dynohub pan was made on the same machines as the drum brake pans. Introducing 70 mm brakes solved the capacity problem and by chance proved that 70 mm hubs were acceptable in the market, which led to the introduction of the Elite and Steelite ranges.

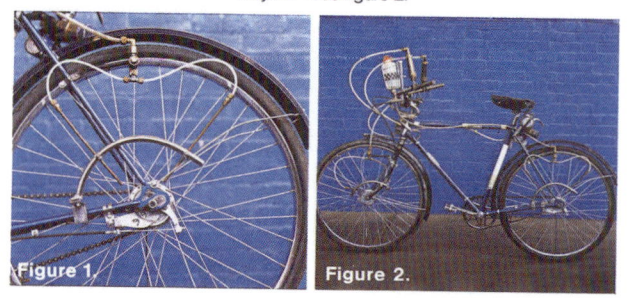

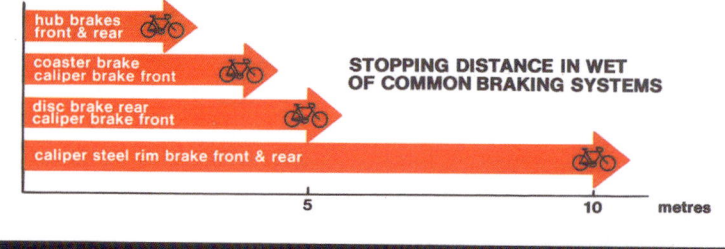

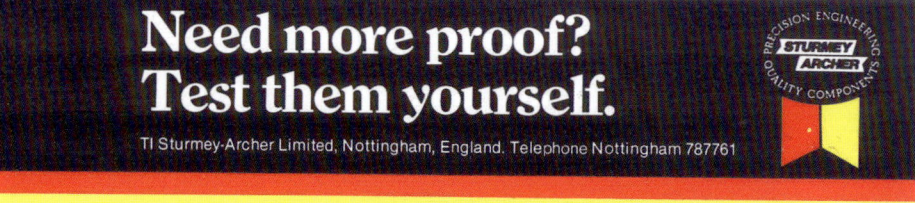

Fig. 15.19. Advertisement for the new 70 mm hub brakes following a convincing live demonstration on BBC TV's Tomorrow's World show.

# Better Bicycle Brakes
## Tested tried and proved

The new Sturmey–Archer lightweight hub brakes are designed and tested to provide better braking. All models are tested for braking performance under strictly controlled conditions.

Tests ensure that *every* brake provides more than 600 lbf in (67.8 Nm) output torque with a cable load of 50 lbf (222.4 N).

**TEST EQUIPMENT**

**MINIMUM PERFORMANCE GRAPH**

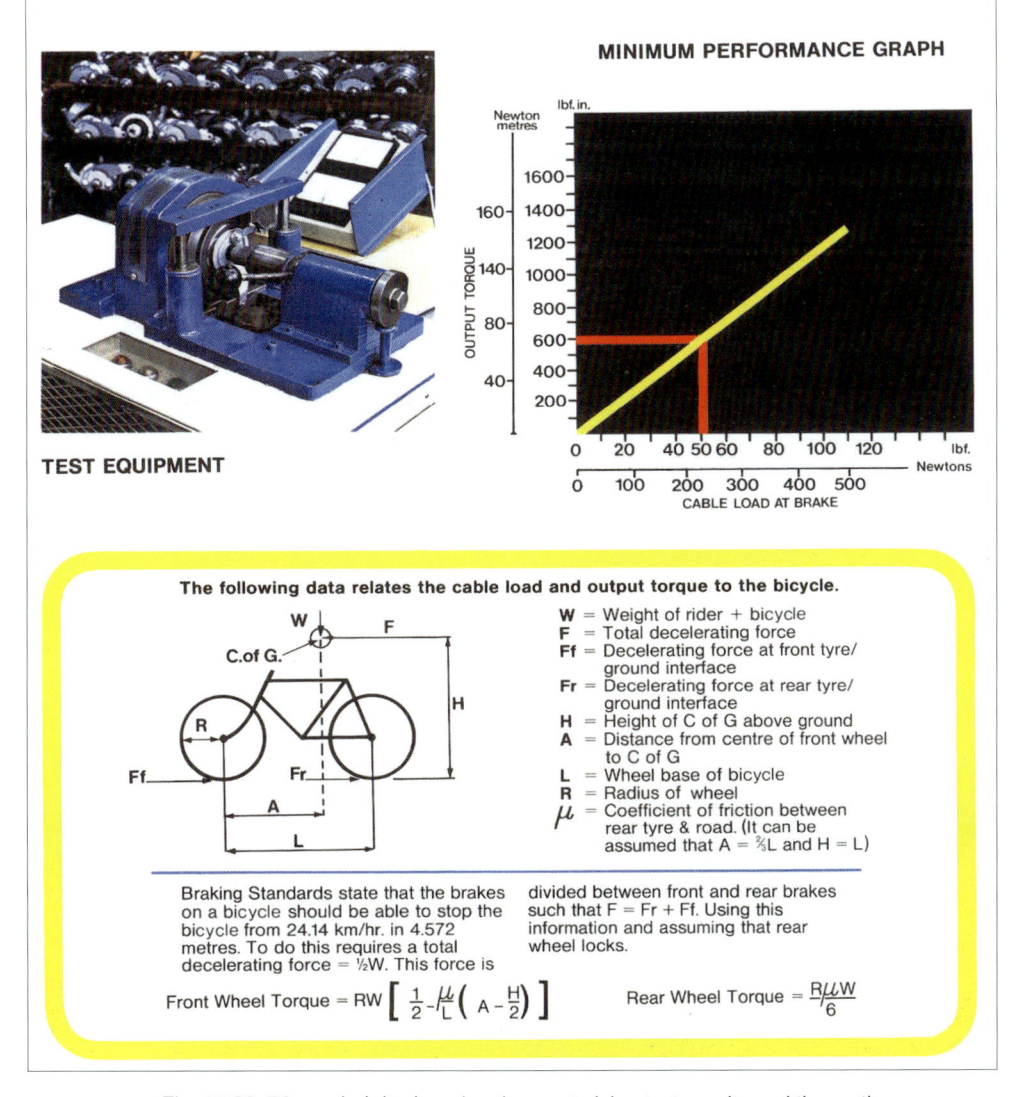

OUTPUT TORQUE (Newton metres / lbf. in.) vs CABLE LOAD AT BRAKE (Newtons / lbf.)

The following data relates the cable load and output torque to the bicycle.

- W = Weight of rider + bicycle
- F = Total decelerating force
- Ff = Decelerating force at front tyre/ground interface
- Fr = Decelerating force at rear tyre/ground interface
- H = Height of C of G above ground
- A = Distance from centre of front wheel to C of G
- L = Wheel base of bicycle
- R = Radius of wheel
- $\mu$ = Coefficient of friction between rear tyre & road. (It can be assumed that A = ⅔L and H = L)

Braking Standards state that the brakes on a bicycle should be able to stop the bicycle from 24.14 km/hr. in 4.572 metres. To do this requires a total decelerating force = ½W. This force is divided between front and rear brakes such that F = Fr + Ff. Using this information and assuming that rear wheel locks.

$$\text{Front Wheel Torque} = RW\left[\frac{1}{2} - \frac{\mu}{L}\left(A - \frac{H}{2}\right)\right]$$

$$\text{Rear Wheel Torque} = \frac{R\mu W}{6}$$

Fig. 15.20. 70 mm hub brake advertisement giving test results and the maths.

## Mountain bikes

In the mid 1980s the British started taking notice of the mountain bike and in 1984 news began circulating of the Sturmey-Archer Trailguard. The *Epicycling* newsletter stated: 'The Trailguard Universal Hub Gear Protector (GSA 361) is a rod skeleton which protects the axle nuts and indicator of your S5 Mountain Bike. It rests on the chain stays, and is mounted under the axle nut. It looks well made and functional'. This product was made for the American market and its manufacture was demand-dependent and intermittent.

There was a certain amount of correspondence in the cycling press about the suitability of Sturmey-Archer gears for mountain bikes used in a true off-road situation. Much of the British cycling press seemed uncertain. Early in 1985 *Bicycle* magazine stated

> Not enough testing has been done but it is generally regarded that a Sturmey-Archer 3 or 5 speed hub is not sufficiently strongly built … There is no doubt about the attraction of an enclosed gear mechanism for such cycles.

Sturmey-Archer shared this uncertainty; there were shades of the tandem-use controversy of the 1920s. Sturmey-Archer stated that the Five Speed Alloy hub 'is, in part, targeted at the mountain bike which has come down "off the hills" and is used in American cities'. An example of such a machine was the Philadelphia-built Sterling Metro 5, a 28½ lb (13 kg) city bike fitted with the Five Speed Alloy hub.

It is interesting to note that Sturmey-Archer hubs were used successfully in off-road bicycles for competitive trials in the Darlington area of north-east England circa 1960.

## Vektar

The Vektar was a BMX-based 'fun' bike for children, launched by Raleigh in 1985. The upmarket version featured an electronic console incorporating a radio and sound generator. The Vektar incorporated a 3-speed Sturmey-Archer hub and the company made a specially modified control system based on a twist-grip with paddles for use with forefinger or thumb.

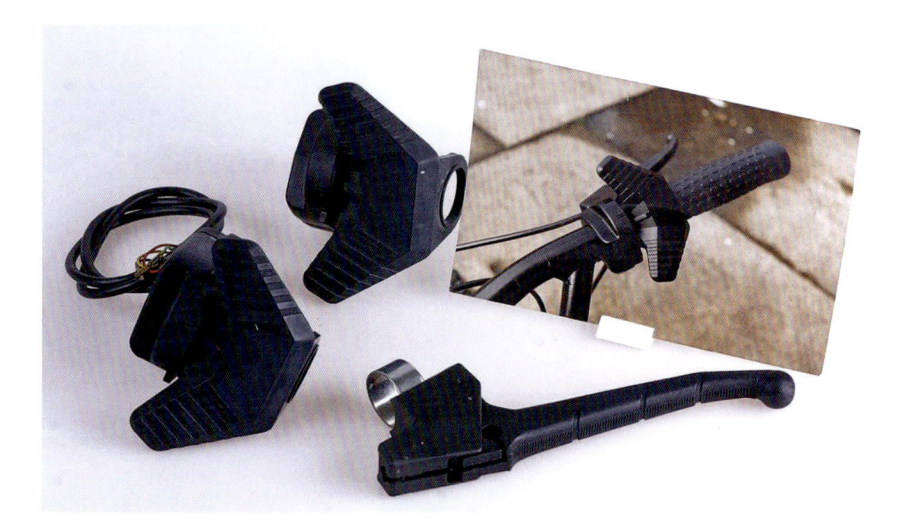

Fig. 15.21. Sturmey-Archer made gear controls and brake levers for the Raleigh Vektar.

Fig. 15.22. Single-lever dual-cable control trigger for the S5/2 5-speed hub.

### New control levers for the S5/2 and AW
There was some rethinking of hub gear controls during the mid 1980s. A BMX twist-grip was included in the 1983 controls catalogue but this was deleted the following year along with the conventional twist-grip.

Early 1985 saw a major step forward for the S5/2: the introduction of a single lever control system intended to overcome the bafflement felt by many cyclists trying to master the twin-lever system.

No modification was required to the gear itself and the new changer could be retro-fitted to the S5/2 and S5/1. However, if fitted to the original S5, an incorrect gear change sequence resulted. Both control cables fed into the one changer which was designed for handlebar mounting. The unit was constructed principally of black plastic. The lever was spring-loaded in two directions and rested in a central position.

To change up one gear the lever was pulled back and allowed to return to its central rest position. To change up another gear the process was repeated. To change down the procedure was similar except that the lever was pushed forwards for each gear change. A recessed indicator disc rotated to give a visual indication of the gear selected.

A parallel development was the introduction of a rectilinear black plastic trigger for the 3-speed, known as the 3-shift. This triggered down to the lower gears but changed up by means of a push button on the changer casing. The number of the gear selected was shown in an aperture in the casing.

### 1985 product range
The 1985 range of hub gears and drum brakes was as follows:

> **5-speed hubs (no brake)**
> S5/2 & Five Speed Alloy. Stem fitting alloy dual lever or plastic single lever.
> **3-speed hubs (no brake)**
> AW & Three Speed Alloy. Steel trigger with plastic faceplate or plastic trigger/push button.

**3-speed coaster**
S3C. Changers as AW.
**3-speed cable-operated brakes**
AB (90 mm drum), SAB (70mm drum), AT3 Elite Alloy (70 mm drum). Changers as AW.
**5-speed cable-operated brake**
AT5 Elite Alloy (70 mm drum). This was new in 1985 and used slightly redesigned S5/2 internals to fit into the same shell as the AT3 Elite Alloy. Changers as S5/2 and Five Speed Alloy.
**Other cable-operated drum brakes**
BF (front 90 mm drum), BR (rear 90 mm drum), SBF (front 70 mm drum, large or small flange), SBR (rear 70 mm drum, large or small flange), VT Elite Alloy (front 70 mm drum), ST Elite Alloy (rear 70 mm drum).

Hubs made exclusively for other companies, such as Columbia and Gazelle, were not catalogued.

Sprockets for hub gears were available in a range from 14 to 22 teeth inclusive (all ⅛"), a 21 tooth sprocket having been introduced into the range about 1983. The 13 tooth sprocket was discontinued in 1984 to the annoyance of owners of early Moulton bicycles.

In 1985 Sturmey-Archer produced a leaflet entitled *Five Speed Hub Gears and Controls*. This referred to the new AT5 Alloy Drum brake offering all the benefits of five speed gearing along with the smooth, controlled, powerful braking performance of the Elite range'. The same leaflet mentioned a retro-fit pack 'enabling cycles fitted with Sturmey-Archer's world famous AW 3-speed hub gear to convert to the five speed system'; this was a complete set of S5/2 internals that replaced the AW mechanism. But this retro-fit pack would not fit AWs made after March 1984. Prior to that date, the left hand ball cup was manufactured in a form suitable for the AW, S5, S5/1, S5/2 and the discontinued FW and AM. Thereafter a simpler internal shape was adopted for the AW ball cup, minimising production costs but precluding the easy conversion of AWs to 5-speeds.

## The wavering relationship with Raleigh and the move to Triumph Road

The relationship between Sturmey-Archer and its parent company Raleigh varied over the years. The 1976 separation of Sturmey-Archer and Raleigh did not prove a great success. In 1982 TI Sturmey-Archer was therefore re-merged with TI Raleigh 'to effect yet further overhead savings and improve management control'. Harold Briercliffe, in his annual review of the UK cycle industry, wrote:

> Since Raleigh bicycles, Raleigh and Sturmey-Archer components all come from the same Nottingham factory the move was a sensible one. Less palatable was news of redundancies for 400 Sturmey-Archer workers.

In the 1983 Raleigh directors' report and annual accounts, heavy losses by Sturmey-Archer were noted. A major reconstruction was planned for 1984 to eliminate unprofitable products and make large savings in manufacture. There was also to be more expenditure on product development for the core gear and hub business. As part of the restructuring, Sturmey-Archer's production and administrative facilities were condensed into the south end of Factory No. 3 on Triumph Road. For more than 50 years the administrative headquarters had been on Lenton Boulevard, some distance from the manufacturing areas.

The restructuring ran to course, reducing losses. Product development proceeded to plan

Fig. 15.23. Inside the Triumph Road factory in 1986.

Fig. 15.24. The company name and the TI logo on the façade of the factory in 1986.

with development of a new 5-speed and the first alloy drum brakes. The organisation was now smaller and better organised. Most of its unprofitable products had been discontinued. Sturmey-Archer no longer had a direct involvement in magnetics, plastics, alloy forging or manufacture of alloy rims, all such items being sub-contracted or bought in.

Unlike its major European rival Sachs-Huret (the recently merged Fichtel & Sachs and Huret), Sturmey-Archer produced no single-speed coasters, no 2-speed coaster, no hybrid gears (derailleur/hub gear combinations) and no derailleur mechanisms. Instead Sturmey-Archer specialised in what it was good at. This included making products for other industries,

269

including numerous components for the automotive and white goods industries, many produced using powder metallurgy.

But in 1985 Sturmey-Archer's financial performance was markedly worse. It was not helped by Raleigh's failure to support Sturmey-Archer in certain respects: on the home market Raleigh had never yet marketed a cycle with a 5-speed hub and they were now pitching derailleur-geared bikes to British women.

TI decided again to separate the gear maker from Raleigh. From 1986 Sturmey-Archer became a self-accounting company within the automotive products division of TI but this situation did not last long. In January 1987 TI Group announced that it had sold all its bicycle interests, including Sturmey-Archer. The buyer was Derby International Corporation SA (DICSA), a specially formed American-managed company backed by leading UK financial institutions and registered in Luxembourg.

# Chapter 16
# The rise and fall of Derby

## Sturmey-Archer's last years in Britain, 1987 to 2000

### Ed Gottesman and the founding of Derby

Derby was a private company the name of which derived not from Nottingham's rival city but from the American term for a bowler hat, in the sense of 'top drawer'. Its founder was A. Edward Gottesman, an American tax lawyer domiciled in London since 1962. It was somewhat ironic that a century after Frank Bowden, a British lawyer with American connections, bought the fledgling Raleigh company, an American lawyer with British connections should head the group purchasing it.

Ed Gottesman was (and at the time of writing still is) senior partner in the law firm of Gottesman Jones & Partners. It was one of the first independent US law firms in the UK. The practice specialises in corporate acquisitions, reorganisations and disposals, US securities law, private equity transactions, US and international taxation, international financing and exclusive distribution, licensing and joint venture agreements. In addition to his legal practice, Edward Gottesman was involved in a wide range of commercial pursuits. His investment holdings included the historic British porcelain and bone china manufacturers Spode and Royal Worcester, and a company formed to acquire Olivetti's personal computer business. Gottesman, like Bowden, was both entrepreneurial and interested in bicycles. He knew the Bowden family and the senior executives of TI long before Derby was formed. He had heard that TI was keen to dispose of Raleigh and appreciated the value of the Raleigh brand, especially in America. He therefore got together with some associates, put in his own money and more from colleagues, obtained the support of financial institutions and formed Derby. An astute tax lawyer, he considered it advantageous to register the company in Luxembourg.

### Alan Finden-Crofts recruited

The banks required a chief executive officer with a proven record of accomplishment, so accountant Alan Finden-Crofts was recruited. He was chief executive of Dunlop Slazenger International from 1985 to 1987 and had been director of Dunlop's consumer group from 1982 to 1984. He was also on the operational board of the British industrial conglomerate BTR from 1982 to 1986. From 1968 to 1982 he was managing director of various subsidiaries of Norcros, the shower and ceramic tile group. He was an investor with Ed Gottesman in the fine bone china and porcelain makers Spode and Royal Worcester, and became chairman and chief executive of Royal Worcester and Spode. The Porcelain and Fine China Company Limited was a subsidiary of Exeter International Corporation SA, controlled by Finden-Crofts and by Gottesman's Centenary Corporation SA.

At his first meeting with Raleigh dealers Alan Finden-Crofts said he had sunk everything he personally owned into Raleigh. He wanted to make it clear that Raleigh was now a small company whose chief executive officer had financial commitment.

When Derby took over Raleigh a whole layer of management was removed at a stroke. For many of the survivors it was a liberating experience: Finden-Crofts told them that all he

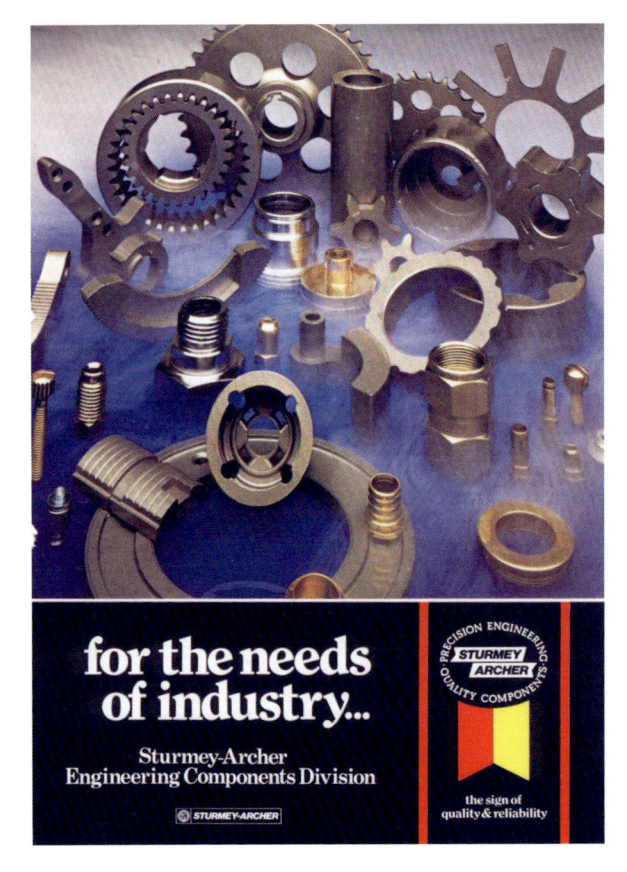

Fig. 16.1. 'For the Needs of Industry' brochure for contract work.

wanted to do was apply a slight touch on the rudder. He was a strategist and did not wish to be involved in the day-to-day activities. He said he believed in choosing the right people then letting them get on with it.

## Early Derby acquisitions

Derby's 1998 annual report neatly summarises the early years: 'The Company was organised in 1986 to acquire the Raleigh, Gazelle and Sturmey-Archer bicycle and bicycle component businesses from TI Group plc. In 1988 the Company acquired the assets of Neue Kalkhoff, the second largest bicycle manufacturer in the former Federal Republic of Germany at the time, and established Derby Germany. Also in 1988 the Company acquired the assets of Raleigh Cycle Company of America from Raleigh's US licensee, Huffy Corporation, and the West Coast Cycle division of Medalist Industries Inc. (owner of the Nishiki brand in the United States). These two businesses were merged to form Raleigh USA. The Company formed the Probike South Africa operating company with the acquisitions of Cycle and Hardware Factors in 1989, J.H. Slotar in 1990 and Cycle Centre Wholesale in 1991. In 1992 the Company acquired Musing, the German bicycle manufacture.'

By 1992 Derby was the largest cycle group in the world, with a sales turnover of $500m. It later acquired Winora, Staiger, Univega, MS Sport and Diamond Back.

## Sturmey-Archer's relationship with Raleigh

Raleigh and Sturmey-Archer became just two of Derby's many brands: the other Derby

Fig. 16.2. Cold formed components leaflet.

Fig. 16.3. Sintered components leaflet.

acquisitions were not Raleigh subsidiaries. In 1994 this was reflected in the name change of the Raleigh holding company from Raleigh Holdings Limited to Derby Holding Limited.

For decades Raleigh had supported Sturmey-Archer by fitting an AW 3-speed hub in the entry-level model of each bicycle range. But by the 1990s there was an image problem with hub gears and a basic derailleur was cheaper and more fashionable. So there was no longer any special favouring by Raleigh of Sturmey-Archer products: a Raleigh bicycle was as likely to be fitted with a Shimano 7-speed hub from the other side of the world than a Sturmey-Archer product from literally the other side of the road.

## Contract work continues

During this time Sturmey-Archer continued carrying out contract work for many firms and industries via the engineering components division. Customers ranged from the automotive industry to computer manufacturers. In 1992 the company published three brochures to promote this part of its business.

One brochure dealt with cold forming in which 'accurately cropped and lubricated billets of material are extruded under controlled striking pressure to form consistently high-quality components'. A multi-million pound investment had recently been made in this technology including 'the siting of three new transfer presses with capacities up to 1000 tonnes'. Complex secondary machining could be carried out in-house and a wide range of specialist finishes and surface treatments was offered.

Sturmey-Archer also specialised in sintering, sometimes referred to as powder metallurgy, which they had been using for some 30 years. Raleigh installed sintering plant in the early 1960s and circulated a technical treatise produced in-house to raise awareness of the technology's possibilities. By 1963 sintered metal components made at Nottingham included tricycle and scooter bearings, washers, lamp bracket bosses and various bushes.

Like cold forming, sintering involved pressing but using a very different process. The brochures explained:

In sintering a fine blend of metal powders is compressed to a virtually solid state [the 'green' compact] in a precision die and then undergoes a carefully timed exposure to varying degrees of heat. This bonds the particles together to produce a pure component, which is accurate to fine tolerances. This process bonds the metal particles together to produce a component free of impurities, accurate to fine tolerances, with precise control maintained over both unit density and porosity.

For this work Sturmey-Archer had more than two dozen presses, with capacities ranging from 15 to 400 tonnes. Where very high precision was needed, as with gear wheels, there would be a second stage of pressing to eliminate any slight dimensional change caused in the heating process. The company used best grade Swedish sponge iron powder with additives such as copper, carbon and zinc stearate. The powder was gravity fed from hoppers into the presses.

Sturmey-Archer did not use sintered metal for heavily stressed components in hub gears such as sun and planet pinions. They sometimes used it in parts such as planet cages (e.g. in the 5-StAr hub to be described shortly) and brake shoes (e.g. in the AWC coaster). The technology was ideal for making items such as car engine cam-belt sprockets and internal parts for domestic appliances such as washing machines.

The company offered a wide variety of finishing operations. Sintered components could be steam treated or resin impregnated and all components could be surface plated in various ways. Secondary machining could be carried out in-house with new Computer Numeric Controlled (CNC) equipment.

Sturmey-Archer stressed that they could assist with all aspects of design and manufacture:

> Years of experience combined with the latest technology means that our designers, production engineers and metallurgists can actually function as an extension of your team, from day one, as part of our total service. As well as being in a position to aid your design process, Sturmey-Archer retains a complete in-house tool making function, which features the latest technology, such as sophisticated spark and wire erosion equipment.

## Re-engineering the range

During the Derby era Sturmey-Archer substantially re-engineered their product range. Apart from the AW 3-speed, all their hub gears eventually incorporated NIG (No Intermediate Gear), the AT3, SAB and AB/C from 1989 onwards. The NIG feature maintained positive drive through the hub regardless of control cable adjustment. The introduction of NIG required precautions to prevent the hub locking up when wheeling backwards or pedalling backwards. Therefore a retracting plate was incorporated. When back-pedalling or wheeling the bicycle backwards, the retracting plate disconnects the pawls in the driver so they no longer connect with the gear ring. The gear ring can therefore rotate unimpeded, preventing lock-up.

Following the example of their competitors Sturmey-Archer lubricated their hubs for service life, omitting the traditional oiling point. Longer axles were fitted to some Sturmey-Archer hubs such as the Sprinter range to be described shortly. This was because most bicycle frames were now produced primarily for use with derailleur gears and could not easily accommodate the shorter rear axles hitherto used in hub gears. By this time Sturmey-Archer's engineering drawings were created using Computer Aided Design (CAD).

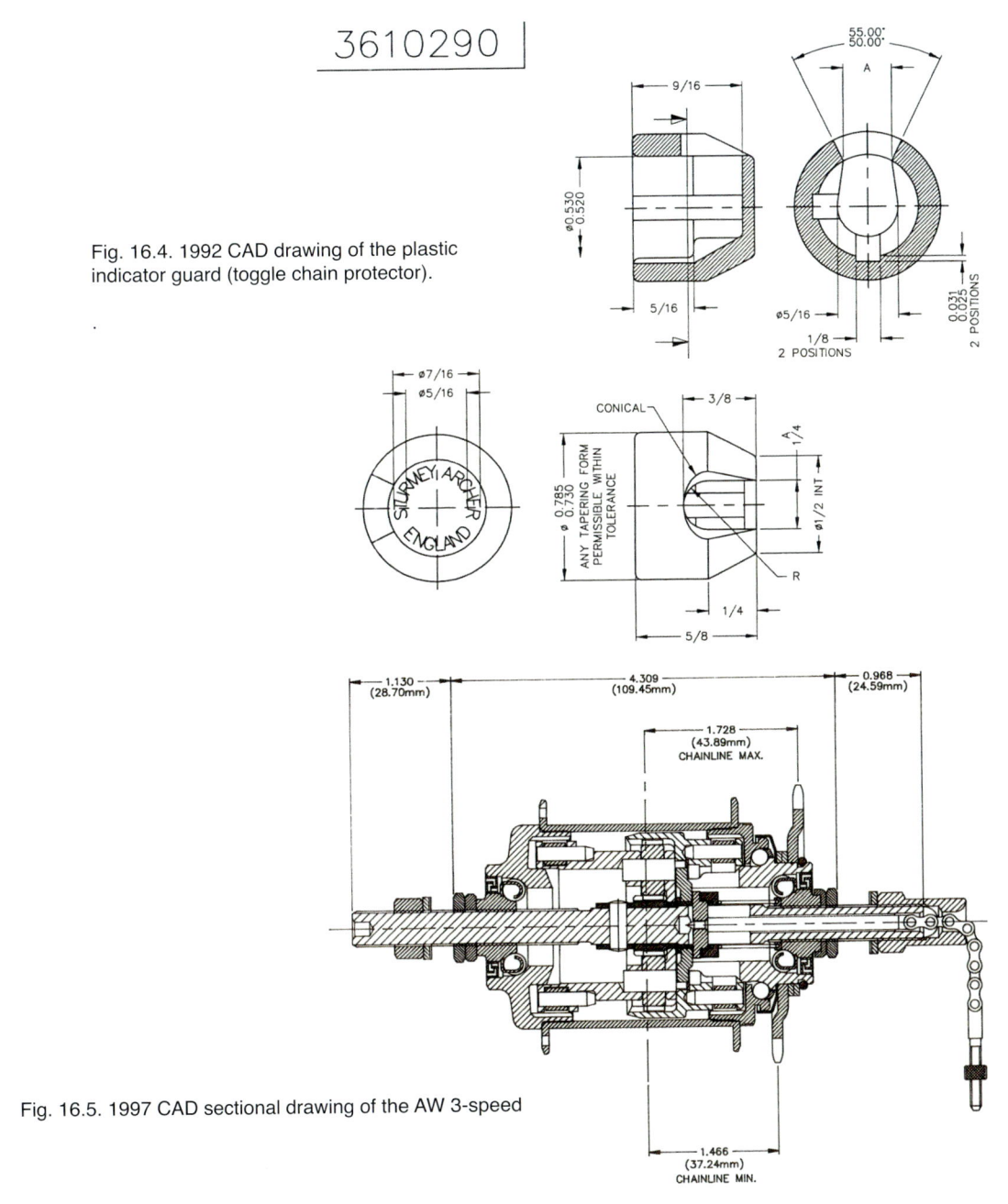

Fig. 16.4. 1992 CAD drawing of the plastic indicator guard (toggle chain protector).

Fig. 16.5. 1997 CAD sectional drawing of the AW 3-speed

## AWC Tricoaster

The AWC 3-speed coaster was launched in 1988; it incorporated NIG from the outset and had a different brake actuator to the S3C. The Mk 2 version was introduced in 1991 and had three brake shoe segments rather than the earlier single split-ring shoe.

Tony Hillyer was responsible for GB patent 2,207,966 which covered the new brake actuator. A pawl and ratchet mechanism was 'arranged such that the back-pedalling torque always follows the same path through the gear irrespective of the gear selection to thereby give uniform braking'.

Fig. 16.6. The AWC Tricoaster.

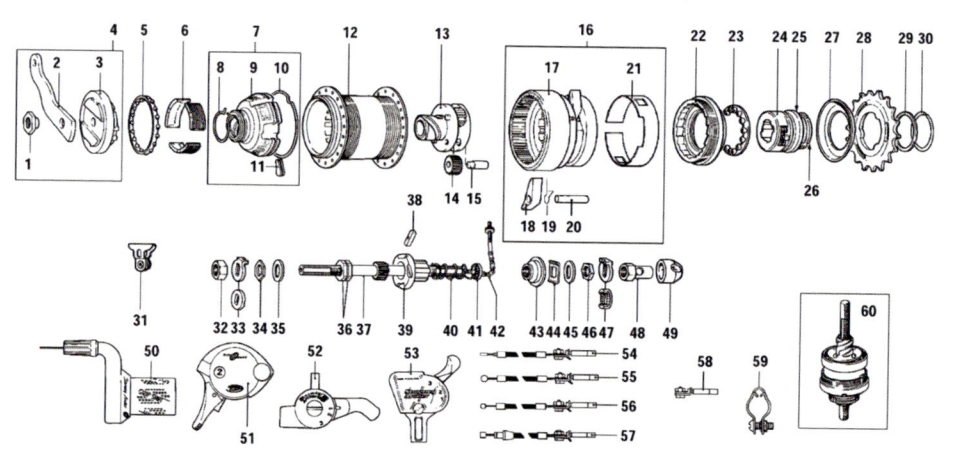

Fig. 16.7. Sectional drawing of the AWC Tricoaster.

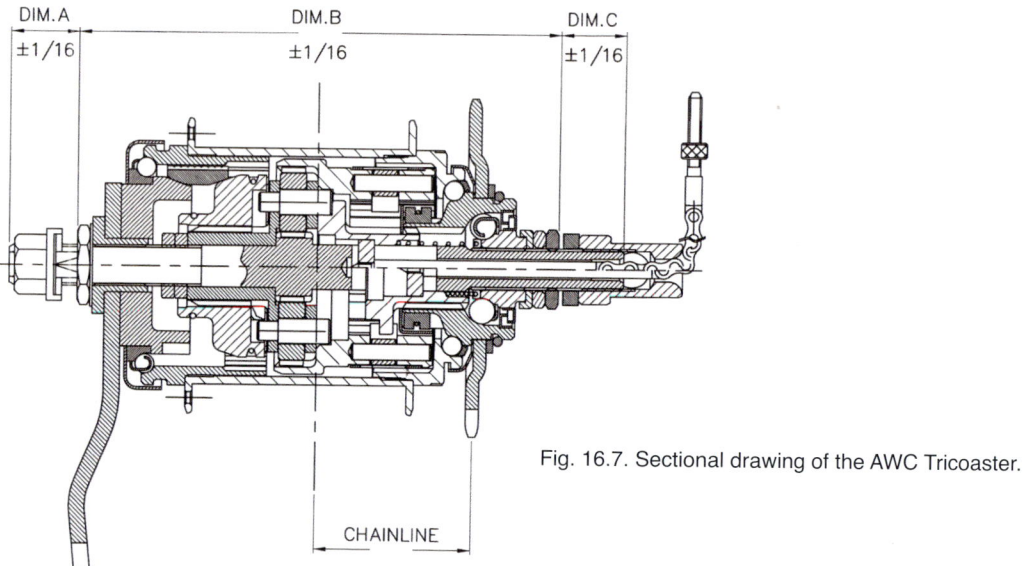

Fig. 16.8. Exploded view of the AWC Tricoaster.

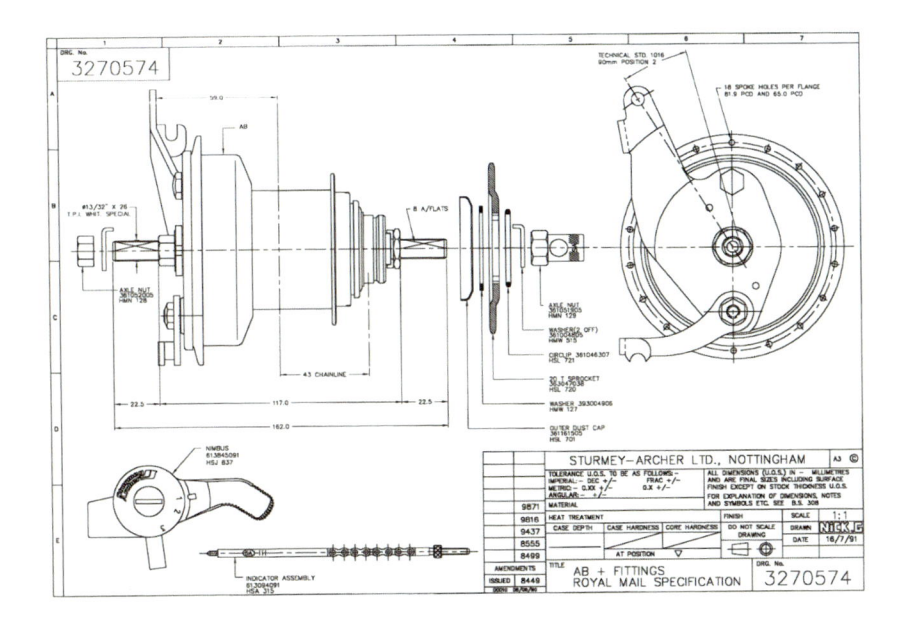

Fig. 16.9. Sectional drawing of the Royal Mail AB hub.

### Royal Mail AB 3-speed drum brake
Sturmey-Archer designed a version of the AB 3-speed drum brake combination specifically for the UK's Royal Mail as this 1991 drawing shows.

### Steelite and Elite 70 mm drum brakes
The Steelite 70mm drum brake range mentioned in the previous chapter was introduced about the time of the Derby takeover. It comprised steel-shelled versions of the Elite drum brakes.

The Steelite hubs replaced the earlier versions of the SBF, SBR and SAB. Minor changes were made to all 70 mm brake mechanisms in 1992. Also, in 1992 and 1993 respectively, the gear mechanisms in the Steelite SAB and AT3 Elite 3-speed 70 mm brake combinations were extensively modified: a new compact planet cage was adopted in place of the long-established design used in the AG, AB and AT3 hubs.

### Modifications to the S5/2 and Elite AT5
In 1988 there was a major modification to the S5/2 5-speed hub. Instead of having the movement of the sun pinions controlled by two springs and a spring washer (which acted as a 'hold-off' when changing gear until pedal pressure was eased), the hubs were now fitted with just one stronger spring. Thus the gear change was made more positive but at the cost of crash changes if foot pressure was not eased when changing gear.

### 5-StAr 5-speed and Elite AT5 5-StAr
The S5/2 5-speed was replaced in spring 1991 by the short-lived 5-StAr (as in **St**urmey-**Ar**cher). This used a different steel shell than the S5/2 and the internals were not interchangeable. The 5-StAr had NIG (No Intermediate Gear) from the outset.

Some early 5-StArs suffered from rough running, a production problem that was quickly remedied. But the hub proved to be relatively weak and axle breakages were unacceptably common. This led Sturmey-Archer to issue a warning that the chainwheel to sprocket size ratio should not be less than 2:1, the company's aim being to limit the torque to which the

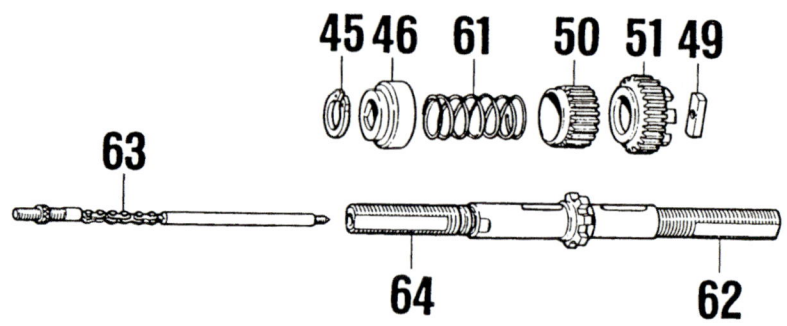

Fig. 16.10. Modified axle and sun assembly for the S5/2 and Elite AT5 hubs.

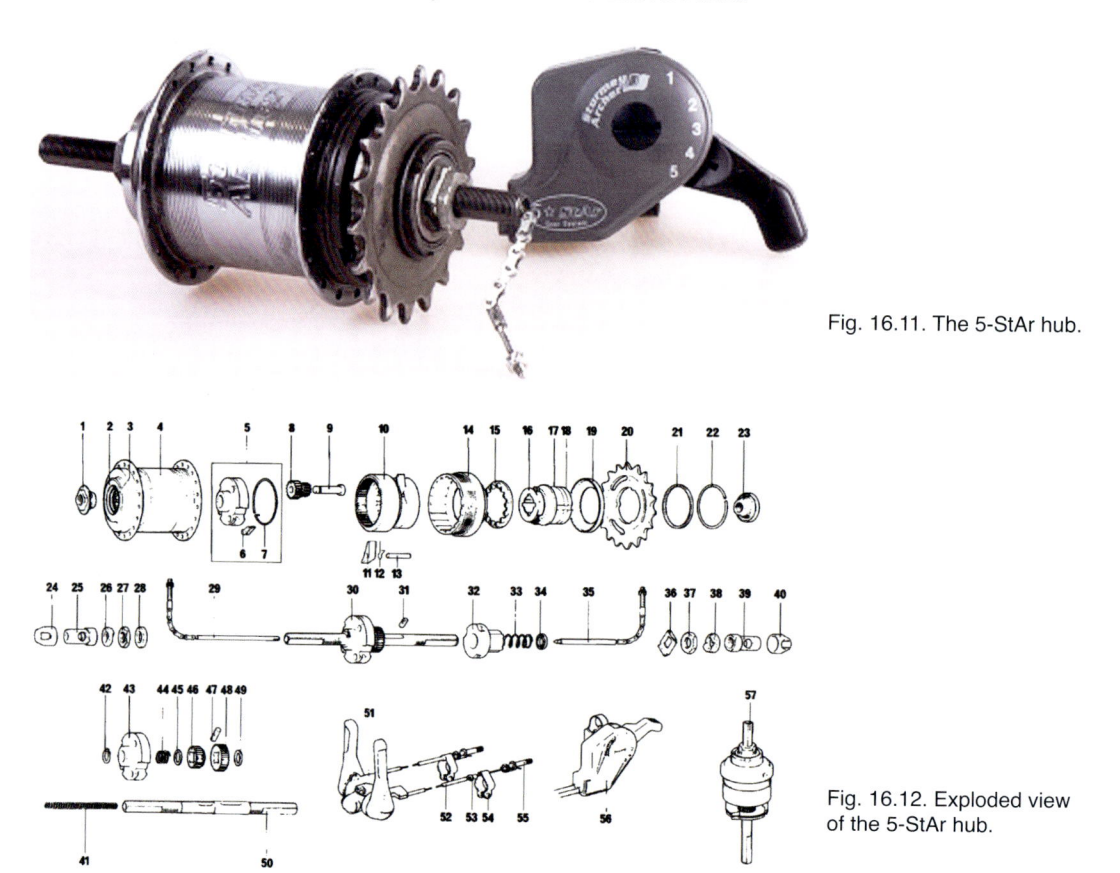

Fig. 16.11. The 5-StAr hub.

Fig. 16.12. Exploded view of the 5-StAr hub.

hub was subjected.

The Elite AT5 5-StAr combined the standard 5-StAr gearing internals with the 70 mm drum brake in an alloy shell.

Production of the 5-StAr was the subject of a 20 minute video commissioned by Sturmey-Archer from the Preview production company of Leicester and released in 1992. The video promoted Sturmey-Archer's quality systems which had recently earned them BS 5750 (ISO 9001) quality assurance certification. Various members of the staff and workforce appeared on screen, including sales director John Macnaughtan and production manager Roger Airey.

Fig. 16.13. The Elite AT5 5-StAr hub.

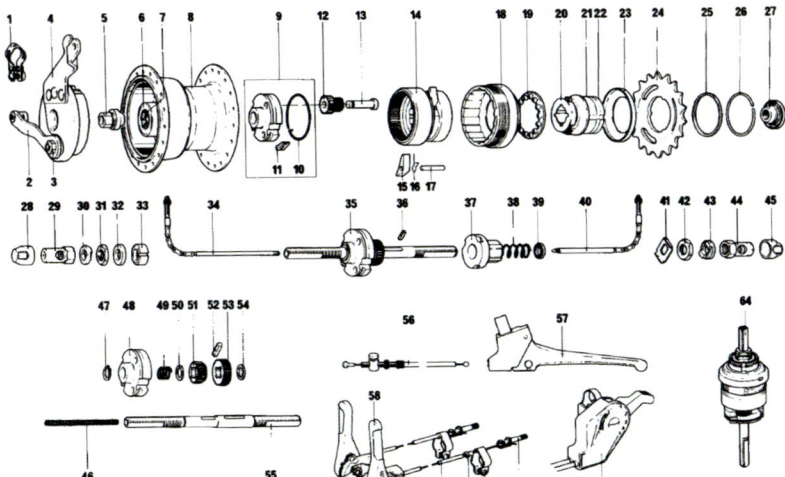

Fig. 16.14. Exploded view of the Elite AT5.

The video was filmed in the Triumph Road factory and offices, providing an interesting record of the latter days of British production.

Sturmey-Archer produced a prototype 7-speed version of the 5-StAr but did not market it.

## Sprinter single-cable 5-speed
In summer 1993 the 5-StAr was replaced by Sturmey-Archer's first single-cable 5-speed, the Sprinter – a mere 72 years after Henry Sturmey patented such a hub. It was available with a steel shell (identical to that used by the 5-StAr apart from the engraving) or in an alloy shell. Like the 5-StAr the Sprinter had the same ratios as the S5 series. The driver, its retracting plate and the planet pinions were interchangeable between the Sprinter 5 and the 5-StAr.

The planet cage was redesigned to give better support to the planet pinions. The clutch spring was the same as in the 5-StAr but the Sprinter had an additional axle spring to control the gear selector key. The key had two steps (one for each sun) and the axle spring allowed these to part if the key slots in the suns were not in line during a gear change. Tony Hillyer, who retired in 1995, was responsible for GB patent 2,249,364 which covered a selector key of this type.

The Hub of the Universe

Fig. 16.15. The Sprinter 5-speed hub in steel shell.

Fig. 16.16. The Sprinter Alloy 5-speed hub in alloy shell.

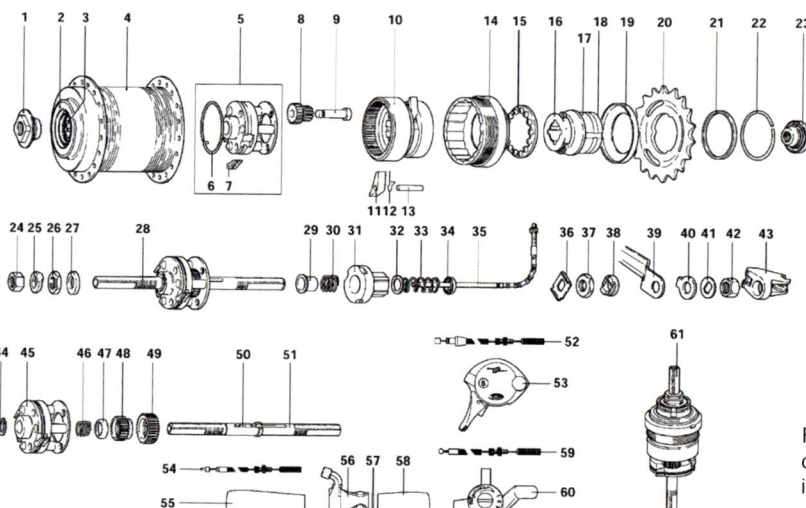

Fig. 16.17. Exploded view of the Sprinter 5-speed, including control options.

280

The Sprinter's arrangements for routing the toggle chain into the hub were novel in that there were four options: the traditional flared wheel nut; a pulley in a housing that slid over the wheel nut; and in either case with or without an axle-fitting cable fulcrum clip. These options were felt necessary because of the high cable tension necessary for single cable selection of five gears (2.5 times the maximum pull required for the 5-StAr). An ordinary flared nut could give stiff operation and a banded-on fulcrum clip could slip along the chainstay. But with a brazed-on cable stop the traditional flared nut could work quite well.

The Sprinter had a new 5-speed trigger, there never having been a Sturmey-Archer single-cable 5-speed trigger previously.

## Elite AT5 Sprinter 5-speed and 70 mm drum brake

In 1993 the Elite AT5 Sprinter 5-speed 70 mm drum brake was introduced. It combined the standard Sprinter hub internals with a 70 mm drum brake in an alloy shell.

Fig. 16.18. Elite AT5 Sprinter.

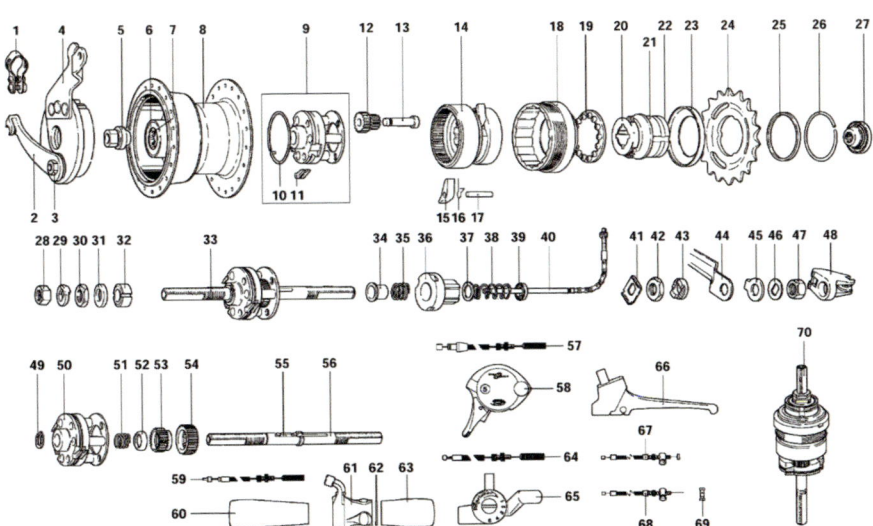

Fig. 16.19. Exploded view of Elite AT5 Sprinter, including control options.

The Hub of the Universe

Fig. 16.20. Sprinter S5C 5-speed coaster hub.

Fig. 16.21. Sectional drawing of Sprinter S5C 5-speed coaster.

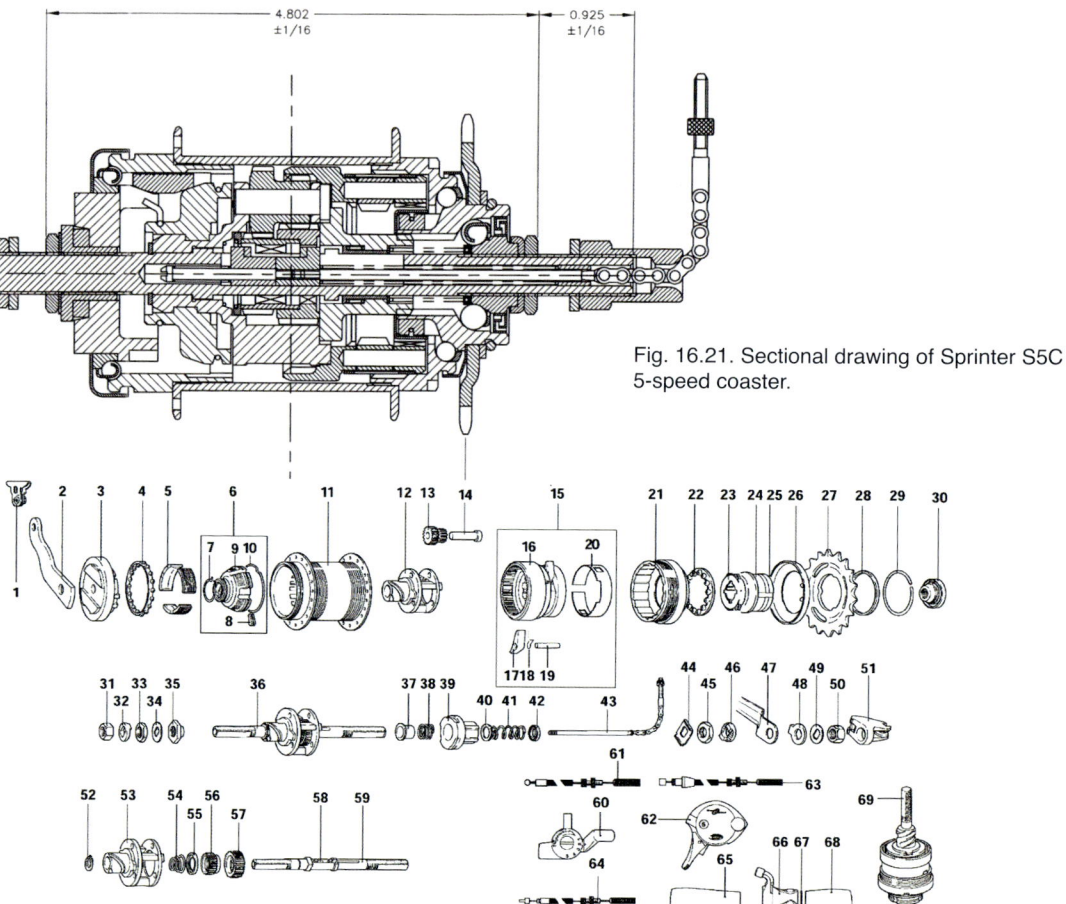

Fig. 16.22. Exploded view of Sprinter S5C 5-speed coaster.

Fig. 16.23. 5-speed controls as at 1993.

## Sprinter S5C 5-speed coaster hub
This derivative of the Sprinter was introduced in autumn 1993.

## BR 90 mm drum brake
The BR steel shell 90 mm rear drum brake for use with a derailleur was re-introduced in 1997 after a break of 13 years.

## Rivals win the 7-speed race
In the late 1980s Sturmey-Archer approached Shimano to explore the possibility of cooperation in the declining hub gear market. Coincidentally, in 1988 Shimano designed a 7-speed hub gear and wanted to produce it close to the largest potential market in Europe. Alan Clarke explains what happened:

Fig. 16.24. The re-introduced BR 90 mm drum brake.

> In January 1989 the Sturmey-Archer CEO, technical, manufacturing and sales directors all visited Japan. They met Keizo Shimano and he proudly showed the high tech factory in Osaka (then building the high end derailleur sets) and the gear hub factory at Shimonoseki. They were also given a prototype of their new 7-speed hub. There was also a formal lunch hosted by Shozo Shimano and, on the way home, a visit to the Singapore factory. Shimano also visited Nottingham but a deal was never done.

Time passed and it was believed by some in the trade that Shimano were working on a 5-speed hub. Then in 1992 they circulated samples of their 7-speed within the German cycle

Fig. 16.25. The Sturmey-Archer factory in 1994.

trade. It was a single-cable compound epicyclic medium ratio hub, similar in many ways to Sturmey-Archer's 1973 prototype S7. Known as the SG-7, the Shimano hub was designed to shift under reasonable pedalling load; it had outstandingly even proportionate spacing between the gears but no direct drive. Cynics said this was to mask the inefficiency of the indirect gears but customer reaction was positive.

Also in 1992 Sturmey-Archer's other major rival, Sachs (formerly known as Fichtel & Sachs, and more recently as Sachs-Huret) moved its European headquarters to the Netherlands. Shimano's announcement of the SG-7 surprised Sachs who immediately revealed details of their own prototype 7-speed to the German cycling press and accelerated their development programme. The result was the Sachs Super 7. Soon both of Sturmey-Archer's rivals had 7-speeds in production, Shimano's becoming generally available in 1993. Shimano set up a 7-speed hub manufacturing operation in the Czech Republic which later destroyed both Sturmey-Archer and SRAM sales.

Launch of the Shimano and Sachs 7-speeds put pressure on Sturmey-Archer to respond. What followed was seven years of woe during which all manner of problems were encountered trying to get the 7-speed Sturmey-Archer range into a saleable and reliable condition. The end result was Sturmey-Archer losing the 7-speed market despite being the first to invent a 7-speed hub gear.

The story is so complex that an internally produced summary of the debacle is 15 pages long. The saga involved poor communication between various parts of Raleigh and Sturmey-Archer, poor liaison with potential customers, lack of promotional samples and sales literature, late deliveries, poorly designed gear shifters, and quality control issues. This led to clients rejecting whole consignments of hubs and ceasing to specify them. Against this background many potential clients turned to Shimano or SRAM for 7-speed hub gears.

Sturmey-Archer's 7-speed was first displayed publicly at the autumn 1994 Anaheim cycle show in California (including in 'exploded' form) but it was virtually ignored by the cycling press. At IFMA, the corresponding European event that autumn, the launch was aborted just prior to the show. At the Brussels show early in 1995 Raleigh displayed 7-speed bicycles, whereas Sturmey-Archer had no 7-speed display or sales literature. A few weeks later Sturmey-Archer officially launched the 7-speed in Europe at the RAI show in the

Fig. 16.26. Twist-grip controls for 3- 5- and 7-speed hubs, as at 1997.

Netherlands. (RAI stands for Rijwiel en Automobiel Industrie, Dutch for 'Bicycle and Automobile Industry'.) The Shimano Nexus-7 hub was 18 guilders (£11 today) cheaper than the Sturmey-Archer 7-speed.

Much of the development of Sturmey-Archer's 7-speed from 1994 onwards took place in the Netherlands and involved the Gazelle bicycle company which, like Raleigh and Sturmey-Archer, was owned by Derby. Gazelle made numerous suggestions for improvements.

By autumn 1996 the 7-speed range had been introduced only in the Netherlands. Eventually it became available in the UK as original equipment on a small number of cycles by Raleigh, Alex Moulton and Pashley.

### 7-speed variants, the Summit range and ball-locking suns

The 7-speed put into production was a triple sun version of the Sprinter, with an overall range of 278%. The first brochure was produced in 1997 and showed three variants:

Sprinter S7 – steel shell,
Sprinter S7C – steel shell with coaster brake,
Sprinter Elite AT7 – alloy shell with 70 mm drum brake.

Sturmey-Archer's alloy shell hub range was renamed Summit in 1999. The sub-set of alloy shell 7-speed hubs was expanded to include a freewheel (i.e. non-brake) version – the Summit S7, and a coaster version – the Summit S7C. The Summit alloy shells had a slightly different parabolic shape from the Elite. Model codes for other Summit hubs followed the pattern X-RD5, where R indicated rear, D a drum brake and 5 the number of gears; X-FD was therefore a front drum brake.

Major problems continued with the 7-speed range. Consequently, when Sturmey-Archer was acquired by Sun Race in 2000, as described shortly, these hubs were not put into production in Taiwan.

Sturmey-Archer worked for some years on an improved mechanism for locking the sun pinions in hubs with multiple suns (such as 5-speeds and 7-speeds). To this end, between 1993 and 1997, Stephen Terence Rickels was responsible for European patents EP0686113,

# The Hub of the Universe

Fig. 16.27. Sprinter S7 7-speed with steel shell.

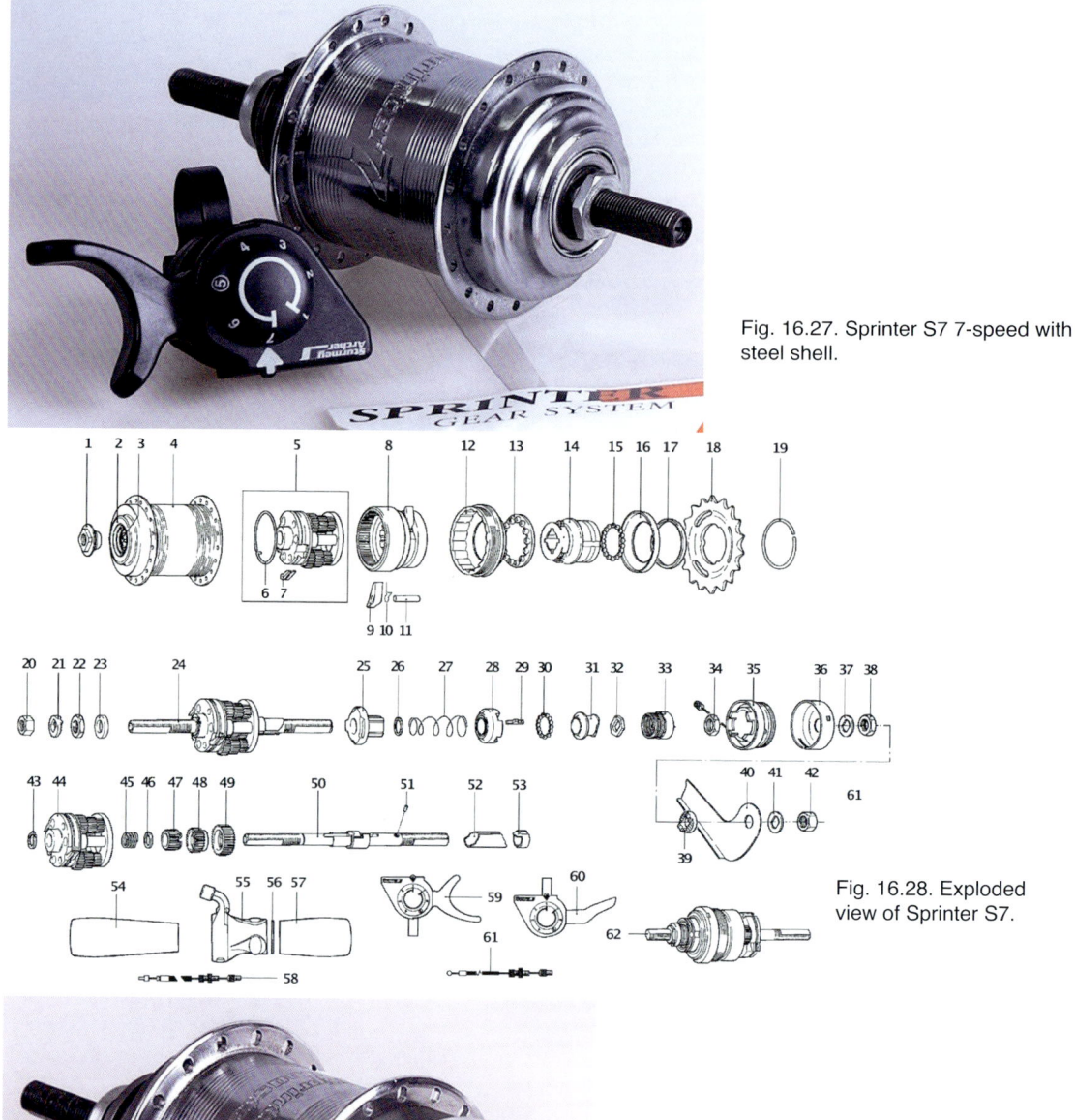

Fig. 16.28. Exploded view of Sprinter S7.

Fig. 16.29. Sprinter S7C 7-speed with steel shell and coaster brake.

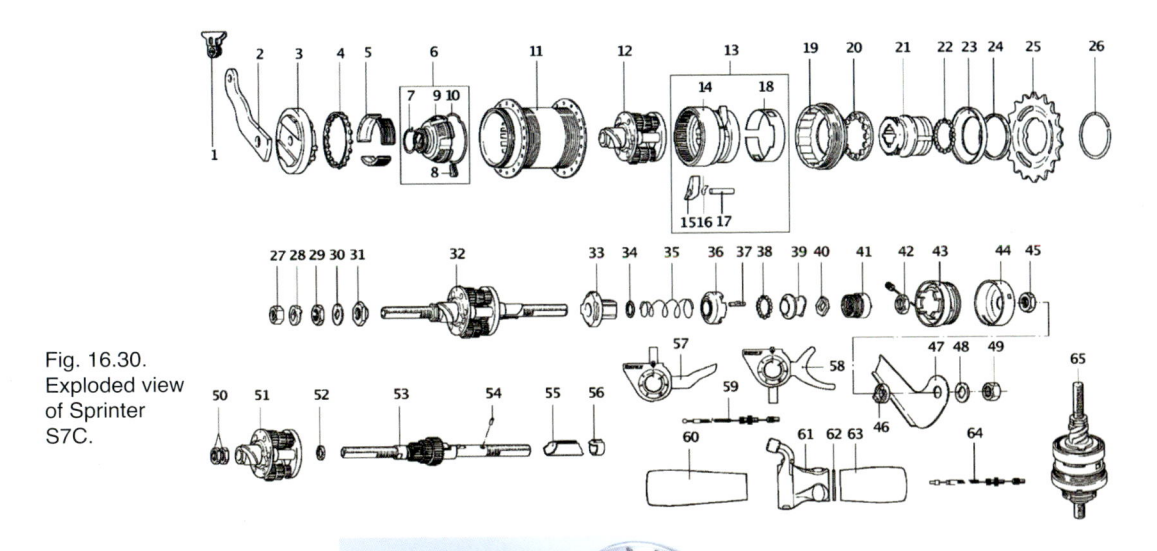

Fig. 16.30. Exploded view of Sprinter S7C.

Fig. 16.31. Sprinter Elite AT7 7-speed with alloy shell and 70 mm drum brake. This illustration clearly shows the axle-fitting fulcrum lever/clip.

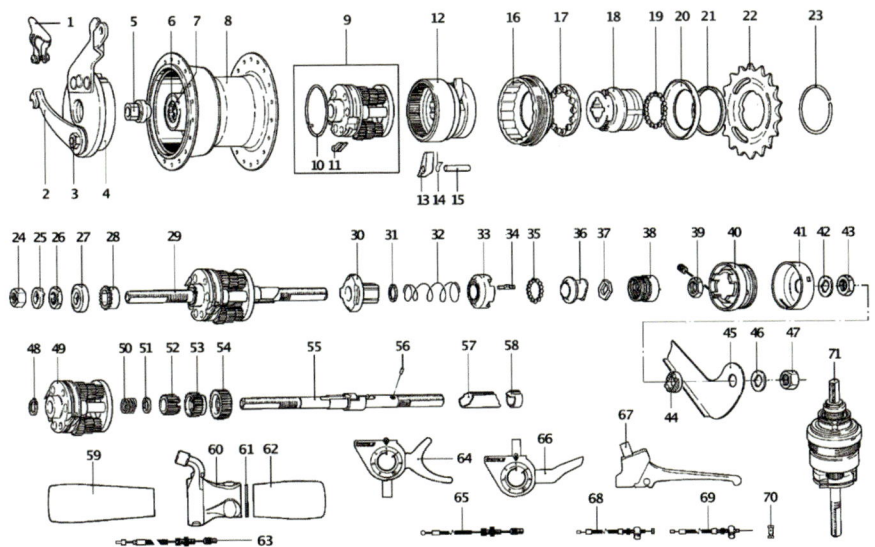

Fig. 16.32. Exploded view Sprinter Elite AT7.

287

Fig. 16.33. The range of hub gear controls available in 1998 for 3-, 5- and 7-speed hubs.

Fig. 16.34. The Sturmey-Archer stand at the 1999 RAI trade show in the Netherlands.

Fig. 16.35. In 1999 Sturmey-Archer pitched the Summit range to Dutch riders of recumbent cycles.

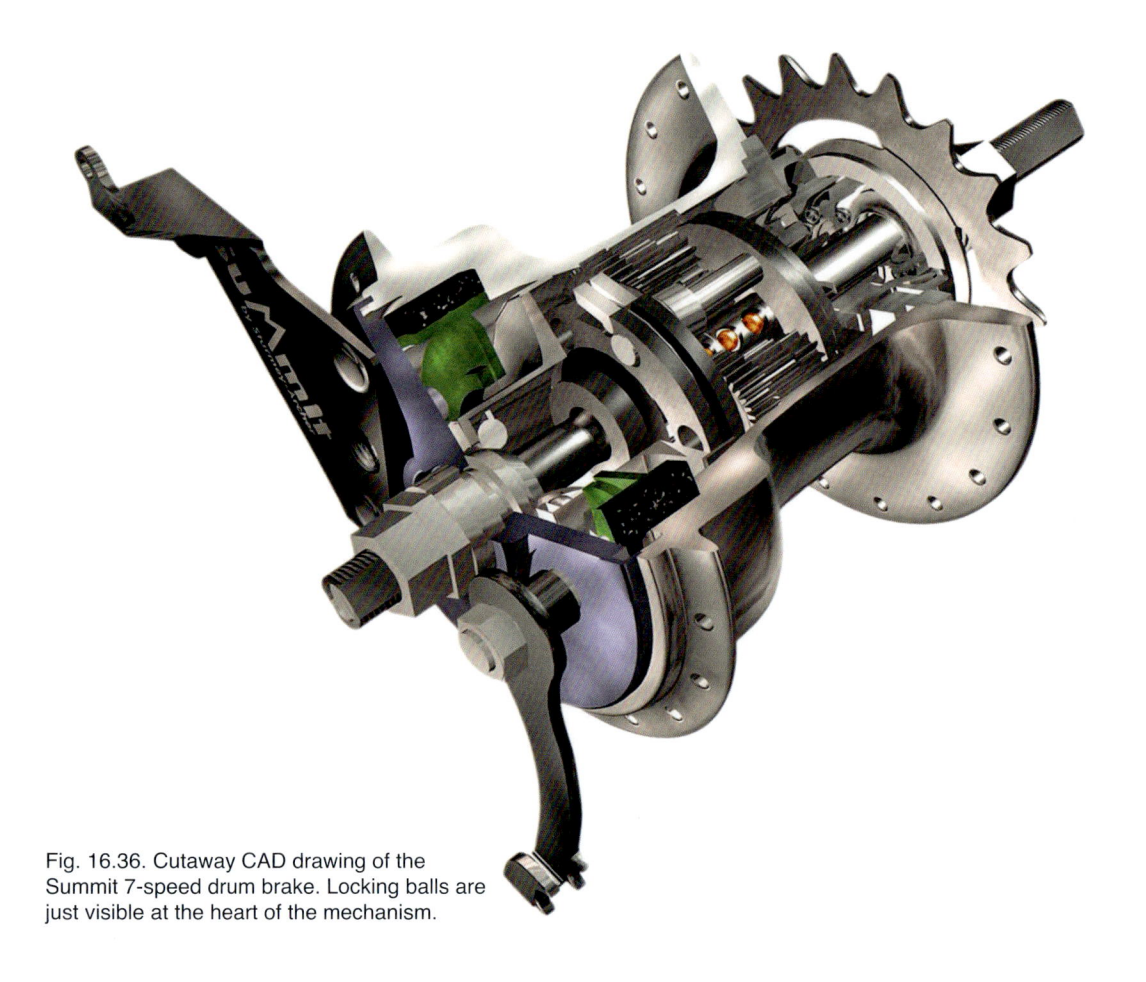

Fig. 16.36. Cutaway CAD drawing of the Summit 7-speed drum brake. Locking balls are just visible at the heart of the mechanism.

EP0762968 and EP0926057. The mechanism as implemented used three ball-bearings per sun to lock it to the axle and was incorporated into existing products.

## Other changes in 1999
In spring 1999 all 3-speed drum brake hubs were fitted with a new planet cage with planet pinions supported at both ends. The 3-speed axle was changed to a one-piece design incorporating the sun pinion into the axle to increase strength.

The Steelite SAB5 was introduced that summer. This was a Sprinter 5-speed combined with a 70 mm steel shell drum brake. Also launched then was the AB5, similar except that it had a 90 mm brake drum.

## Derby Mk 2
Derby's annual turnover in the UK was about £70 million in the mid 1990s. Considerable investment went into rationalising production at Nottingham. This impacted the bottom line and Derby's profit before tax from the UK dived to a mere £130,000 in 1995 but soon recovered to £2.6 million.

In 1997 Alan Finden-Crofts and Ed Gottesman started the process of selling 80% of Derby

TYPE SAB-5 HUB
Steelite 5-speed drum brake hub
1998 - 2000

Fig. 16.37. Two examples of the SAB5 in different finishes.

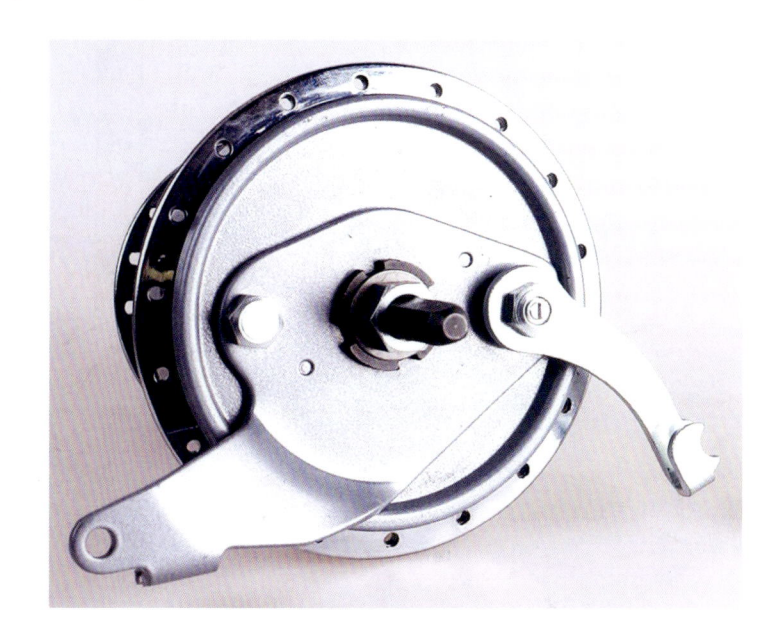

Fig. 16.38. The AB5 5-speed with 90 mm drum brake.

International Corporation SA (DICSA) assets to American investors. After a year during which some $13 million was spent on fees (mostly for investment banking), the majority of the assets of DICSA became American owned and registered. Gottesman and Finden-Crofts got what they considered a very good price.

The new company, Derby Cycle Corporation, was based at Kent in the US state of Washington and registered in Delaware. It was privately owned, 65% of total voting power of the capital stock being held by a subsidiary of Thayer Capital Partners and 13% by a subsidiary of Perseus Capital. DICSA retained 20% of total voting power via a subsidiary, Derby Finance SARL.

Derby manufactured in five countries. It planned to expand through acquisitions in the US and Europe, and by diversifying into accessories and clothing. It held the leading market share in the UK, Ireland, Netherlands and Canada, and was a major player in the USA.

### New management

Gary Matthews became chief executive officer of Derby Cycle Corporation in January 1999. He was appointed a director of Raleigh Industries Limited in August 2000. Alan Finden-Crofts acted as a consultant to Derby for four months after Matthews' arrival to ensure a smooth transition. Finden-Crofts remained an indirect shareholder and a director of Derby Cycle Corporation.

Matthews was a newcomer to the cycle industry, his background being in alcoholic and soft drinks. Eminent Dutch journalist and cycle historian Otto Beaujon wrote: 'Apparently Matthews has never realized that trade margins and profits in the bicycle industry are smaller than in the food industry, and that only a frugal management can run a bicycle holding.' But Matthews showed no signs of frugality. Instead he established sumptuous new headquarters at Stamford, Connecticut, in the Greater New York metropolitan area. Alan Finden-Crofts had run Derby with a staff of 5, whereas Gary Matthews started with 22. Matthews also spent considerable sums on consultancy, whereas Finden-Crofts rarely, if ever, employed consultants.

A characteristic of the Matthews regime was centralisation of control. This was the antithesis of Alan Finden-Crofts' policy of letting the local companies within the Derby group manage themselves. All major decisions now had to be referred back to the USA and sourcing of materials was centralised.

### Sturmey-Archer's markets in the late 1990s

At the time that Derby Cycle Corporation became sole owner of Sturmey-Archer, about 30% of Sturmey's turnover came from its engineering component department, which made sintered and cold forged components for the automotive and domestic appliance manufacturers. These were produced at the Triumph Road factory, opposite Raleigh's main plant and headquarters. Hub gears, drum brakes, spokes and nipples were also made at Triumph Road by the cycle component department. A much smaller factory at Smethwick, controlled by Sturmey-Archer, made Brooks leather saddles.

By the late 1990s about 85% of Sturmey-Archer's bicycle component production was exported, three quarters to countries on the European mainland. The major British specifiers were Brompton and Pashley.

The biggest market was the Netherlands, where there was a separate Derby-controlled sales and distribution company, Sturmey-Archer BV. Sturmey-Archer had about 10% of the European hub gear market, well below the market leader SRAM (who had absorbed Sachs-Huret) and second-placed Shimano.

Sturmey-Archer's turnover dropped steadily from £18 million in 1996 to only £12 million in 1999. Pre-tax profit in 1996 was £2.4 million (13% of turnover), whereas in 1999 a loss was recorded of £300,000. The rise in the value of the pound against the European currencies had pushed Sturmey-Archer into the red.

### How Sturmey-Archer went east

In 1999 the Nottingham-based chief executive officer of Sturmey-Archer retired and Derby brought in a new managing director, Colin Bateman. The 3-speed drum brake hub was re-designed with a solid axle and the whole range given a new look under the Summit brand. Plans were made to buy component parts in Asia but this was arguably too little, too late.

The Derby group had huge borrowings at high rates of interest and the loans were obtained by making promises to the banks about future prospects. If Derby did not show that debt had been reduced by the end of the second quarter of 2000 they could lose control of the company. In early 2000 they decided to sell Sturmey-Archer and offers were requested. Sun Race of Taiwan had been supplying twist-shifter gear controls to Sturmey-Archer for two years and they wanted to add internal hub gears to their derailleur gear range. They visited Nottingham and made an offer to buy based on payment over a period, to enable the seller's claims about company prospects to be verified.

Derby meanwhile sold the land on which the Sturmey-Archer factory was built and used the proceeds to reduce their overdrafts. Sturmey-Archer was loaded with debt and the company pension plan would become more difficult to finance with lower numbers of employees. Because Derby needed to sell before the end of the second quarter the Sun Race offer could not be accepted, even though it was much bigger, and a company called Lenark agreed to buy the debt for a nominal £30 at the end of June 2000. Lenark had similarly purchased the debt of other UK companies. At least one of their managers was a bankrupt, forbidden to be a company director; their managing director was a professional gambler with an address in Las Vegas. Yet Derby said that they had done due diligence before accepting the Lenark offer.

Lenark then took incoming monies from Sturmey-Archer's bank accounts to cover 'administration costs'. Suppliers were not paid. Colin Bateman and Alan Clarke visited Lenark (at their paper envelope company) and came away with a very bad feeling about the future.

The factory had already started to move production facilities to the newly chosen location in Calverton, Nottingham. The existing production facility first produced 10 weeks' stock to cover the transfer period and then the assembly lines were moved. The first payment was due to the owners of the new factory premises but Lenark refused to pay the cost and said the company should find it themselves, despite Bateman and finance director Paul Smith visiting them to explain the situation. Bateman and Smith spent hours explaining the serious nature of the situation to one of the Lenark front men. He eventually appeared to agree that cash should be made available but asked the directors to wait while he went to convince the real Lenark owners. He then went down the rear stairs to the building, got in his car and drove home, where he faxed his resignation to the company. Bateman and Smith were left to return to Nottingham empty-handed.

Amsterdam personnel were meanwhile at the IFMA bike show in Köln. A message was phoned through to say that there was not enough cash in the bank to pay the wages and that staff should shut down the exhibition stand and go home. Administrators were appointed to liquidate the Nottingham operation.

However, Sturmey-Archer Europa was not in liquidation and it was decided that they must fight to continue the company. Alan Clarke first visited all customers at the IFMA show and explained the situation. He asked for their support and largely got it.

After the show there were contacts with personnel in Nottingham who were there trying to save the company. In the weeks that followed potential buyers were approached but just at that time currency exchange rate values changed and turned Sturmey-Archer into a break-even company at best. A potential buyer was not going to pay to take over such a company. In the meantime good former employees found jobs elsewhere and the skills in the factory were lost.

Assembly could not re-start because the assembly lines were at the new premises and the owner refused access. At one stage an employee broke in to salvage some tooling but was caught and the police were involved. The Amsterdam operation bought up large stocks of

## SA Realisations Limited formerly Sturmey-Archer Limited
## (In Liquidation)
## Liquidator's Abstract of Receipts & Payments

| Statement of Affairs | | From 04/10/2004 To 03/10/2005 | From 04/10/2000 To 03/10/2005 |
|---|---|---|---|
| | **FIXED CHARGE ASSETS** | | |
| 280,000.00 | Freehold property | NIL | 300,000.00 |
| | Investment in Subsidiary | NIL | 699,981.00 |
| 1,033,000.00 | Book debts | NIL | 665,496.76 |
| | Shares and investments | NIL | 20.00 |
| | Goodwill | NIL | 1.00 |
| | Records | NIL | 1.00 |
| | | NIL | 1,665,499.76 |
| | **ASSET REALISATIONS** | | |
| 1,700,000.00 | Plant & machinery | NIL | 1,557,106.40 |
| | Fixtures & Fittings | NIL | 297.00 |
| | Motor vehicles | NIL | 2,360.00 |
| 50,000.00 | Stock | NIL | 200,530.34 |
| | Stock - Export sales | NIL | 43,970.80 |
| | Book debts | NIL | NIL |
| | Tax refunds (pre-liq.) | NIL | 100.26 |
| 1,085,000.00 | Cash at bank | NIL | 1,148,699.82 |
| | | NIL | 2,953,064.62 |
| | **OTHER REALISATIONS** | | |
| | Bank interest, gross | NIL | 78,921.51 |
| | Bank/ISA interest, net | 235.62 | 64,793.44 |
| | Other Interest Received | NIL | 52.70 |
| | Sundry refunds | NIL | 1,566.26 |
| | | 235.62 | 145,333.91 |
| | **COST OF REALISATIONS** | | |
| | Cheque/Payable order fee | 4.15 | 892.20 |
| | Secretary of State fee | NIL | 12,500.00 |
| | Lien Settlement | NIL | 93,774.35 |
| | Statement of affairs work | NIL | 15,000.00 |
| | Liquidator's fees | 19,192.50 | 426,455.28 |
| | Liquidator's expenses | NIL | 3,338.62 |
| | Agents'/Valuers' fees | NIL | 76,485.65 |
| | Agents'/Valuers' fees (2) | NIL | 138,136.56 |
| | Legal fees | NIL | 106,002.87 |
| | Notarial Fees | 112.00 | 224.00 |
| | Corporation tax | (1,892.28) | 35,729.68 |
| | Storage costs | 83.14 | 1,668.29 |
| | Statutory advertising | NIL | 492.92 |
| | Other property expenses | NIL | 106,636.73 |
| | Insurance of assets | NIL | 8,692.15 |
| | Wages & salaries | NIL | 144,723.84 |
| | Bank charges | 80.00 | 348.80 |
| | Unclaimed dividends | 188.50 | 6,829.50 |
| | Contamination claim | NIL | 100,000.00 |
| | | (17,768.01) | (1,277,931.44) |
| | **PREFERENTIAL CREDITORS** | | |
| | PAYE income tax etc | NIL | 189,490.54 |

parts from the Nottingham factory so they could still service hubs. (That was difficult because they had to identify loose parts in an unlit factory.) It became clear that production in the UK could not continue. After about ten weeks Alan Clarke decided that it was time to look after Amsterdam personnel.

Sturmey-Archer Amsterdam had paid all its Nottingham invoices and still had about 3 million guilders (approximately £800,000) in the bank, which was moved to another account. If the Amsterdam operation was also to be liquidated, Clarke wanted to arrange a social plan to pay off all dues to employees. The Amsterdam directors had resigned and so the situation was taken to Amsterdam lawyers who opened a court case to claim the company assets. At the same time Nottingham accountants from the liquidator visited Amsterdam because they wanted to use Dutch assets to pay UK debt. They were told that the assets were only there if the company kept operating. If it was liquidated there would be demands to pay off hire contracts for cars and buildings, as well as personnel claims, so there would be nothing left to pay.

As noted previously, Sun Race Taiwan was already supplying twist-shifter gear controls

**SA Realisations Limited formerly Sturmey-Archer Limited**
**(In Liquidation)**
**Liquidator's Abstract of Receipts & Payments**

|  | Statement of Affairs | From 04/10/2004 To 03/10/2005 | From 04/10/2000 To 03/10/2005 |
|---|---|---|---|
| Subrogated EP(C)A claim | | NIL | 100,629.17 |
| Employees' holiday pay | | NIL | 21,502.61 |
| Advances for wages | | NIL | 1,400.00 |
| Trade Union Contributions | | NIL | 2,267.02 |
| | | NIL | (315,289.34) |
| **UNSECURED CREDITORS** | | | |
| Unsecured creditors | | (188.50) | 2,254,060.40 |
| EP(C)A bal. & redundancy | | NIL | 804,374.52 |
| Conts. to pension schemes | | NIL | 85,843.75 |
| | | 188.50 | (3,144,278.67) |
| | 4,148,000.00 | (17,343.89) | 26,398.84 |
| **REPRESENTED BY** | | | |
| VAT receivable | | | 123,521.88 |
| ISA | | | 23,025.75 |
| VAT Receivable | | | 44,220.99 |
| VAT payable | | | (246,383.34) |
| VAT control | | | 82,013.56 |
| | | | 26,398.84 |

Allan Watson Graham
Liquidator

Fig. 16.39 and 16.40. The Abstract of Receipts & Payments from the liquidator's final report.

to Nottingham and Alan Clarke had been introduced to Alan Su at the Las Vegas show a year earlier. Clarke knew that there was interest from Sun Race to buy Sturmey-Archer and his then only option was to help Su do that. So Clarke contacted Su and explained the situation. Su revealed that he had been in The Hague earlier that year because he was looking to establish European distribution for his Sun Race products. Now Sturmey-Archer Amsterdam could be available to him to fill that need. The situation with Amsterdam assets was explained and also how he could buy Nottingham assets using money from the Amsterdam operation. Alan Su said then that, when he had offered to buy the company earlier in the year, his plan had been to move parts production to Asia and leave hub assembly and R & D in Nottingham, but that was no longer an option. Alan Clarke gave him advice about how much he should now offer to buy the parts of the company which he needed. In the meantime Alan Su attended a creditors meeting in Birmingham and it was clear that the company was now doomed in the UK.

Alan Su made his offer but it was rejected by the liquidators. Then they discovered that the court case that had started in Amsterdam was still live and was due to appear before the judge in a few days. Since this would probably mean that Amsterdam assets were no longer available, it made the offer from Sun Race now acceptable. The liquidators also did not want to pay lawyers' costs.

So the offer was accepted and the formalities took place. Technical specifications were airfreighted to Taiwan and work-in-progress and equipment was loaded into 34 containers for despatch by sea. The Nottingham production director and three engineers were approached to work in Taiwan for three months to help set up production there. Factory machinery was auctioned and, while some was purchased by Sun Race, it was later found to be too old and was scrapped. Sun Race had to buy new for many hundreds of thousands of US$.

Employment contracts at Sturmey-Archer Europa (SAE) were continued and Sturmey-Archer Europa was never in liquidation. Personnel pensions had also been safeguarded. But there was still no supply of goods, so Sturmey-Archer Europa concentrated on selling off all their stock of hubs and spare parts. Original Equipment Manufacturer (OEM) customers were forced to buy from competition to keep their assembly lines running.

There had been much discussion in the UK press about this situation, where directors of a firm effectively destroyed their own company. Even MPs were involved, because the law did not recognise that this could happen. It was a situation where the company had been bought for nothing and so Lenark just extracted incoming cost, something they did with several companies in the UK. Despite a lot of talk, no changes to legislation were made and this allowed the 'crime' to be repeated years later with other larger companies and more job losses.

The former sister company Brooks was put up for sale separately and Alan Su asked if he should buy it. Alan Clarke advised against this, largely because he knew that it needed huge investments in new plant. It was auctioned and the highest offer accepted. The highest bidder rang Alan Clarke and said he wanted him to hand over all the sales records, pricelists, etc. but he refused. The new owner said he would pull out of the deal if he could not get the information and he subsequently did so. Consequently the second highest bidder bought Brooks in a contract race. The purchase was led by John Macnaughtan and bought with Adrian Williams in the name of Pashley Holdings Ltd. It was sold by them two years later when it was apparent that Brooks would benefit from both further investment and being marketed by an established saddle maker. John Macnaughtan had known Ricardo Bigolin, founder of Selle Royal, since 1970 making the Italian company the obvious choice to take over this important brand with a firm understanding that manufacture would remain in Smethwick.

Initially Sturmey-Archer Europa (SAE) continued to be Brooks' sales agents but it became clear that SAE's priority had to be with Sun Race sales. Selle Royal were therefore told that SAE would not continue as agents. All stock was therefore returned to Brooks, along with the Brooks museum, including many old catalogues.

## A twist in the tale
In the mid 1990s Sturmey-Archer needed a simple twist-shifter and started buying it in from the Chicago-based SRAM, who made their name selling Shimano-compatible Grip Shifts. The German engineering group Mannesmann AG owned Sachs industries but were making huge profits in telecommunications and wanted to dispose of their less profitable bike interests. A deal was done to transfer those bike assets to SRAM in November 1997. By acquiring the Sachs product range SRAM became a competitor to Sturmey-Archer.

Rather than purchase twist-shifters from a rival hub gear maker, Sturmey-Archer contacted Sun Race and, from 1998, bought twist-shifters from them instead. That first relatively minor involvement led ultimately to Sun Race acquiring Sturmey-Archer.

# Chapter 17
# Sun Race sunrise

### Sturmey-Archer moves to Taiwan, 2000 onwards

### Production starts in Taiwan

In April 2001 Sun Race announced that the Sturmey-Archer production line had been installed in Taiwan under the supervision of three ex-employees of the former Nottingham company. It was anticipated that it would be August 2001 before all hubs from the old Sturmey-Archer range would be freely available. Alan Clarke, general manager of Sun Race Sturmey-Archer Europe BV, said that the external appearance of many hubs would be modernised and that some new gear controls would be introduced. He added that Sturmey-Archer branded chainwheels and cranksets would supplement the range, so that complete drivetrains could be offered.

The first Taiwanese-made hub-gears reached Europe in June 2001. Among the early customers was Derby-owned Raleigh. This was particularly ironic timing, as the old Sturmey-Archer factory had just been demolished. As Carlton Reid wrote on the *Bicycle Business* website: 'Visitors to the Raleigh boardroom now have a different vista to feast their eyes on. No longer will they see the defunct Sturmey-Archer factory: it was blown up yesterday!'

It took another couple of months and about half a million pounds to complete clearing the site. The financial clearing up proceeded in parallel: on 2 July 2001 Sturmey-Archer Limited was renamed SA Realisations Limited, registered at the Guildford offices of liquidators Smith and Williamson.

By the time the factory was demolished Gary Matthews, the Derby chief executive officer who started the Sturmey-Archer disposal rolling, was also history, as far as Derby were concerned.

### What happened to the AW?
Alan Clarke explains:

> When Sun Race took over production, Sturmey-Archer was making two totally different 3-speed hub gears: the original type AW hub and the NIG hub in drum brakes. Alan Su said that he did not plan to continue making both and asked me to choose which one would return to production. I chose the NIG because it was the one used by our biggest customers. I was at that stage grateful if any 3-speed came back into production. I have since regretted that decision. The AW was so simple and its design had been perfected. Customers throughout the world still had spares. Much factory 'work in progress' had been shipped to Taiwan, so some original type AW were made there but in silver painted hub shells because chrome plating was not available. The rest of the parts were sold as spares.

### S80 'Phoenix' 8-speed
The S80 8-speed hub gear (sometimes referred to as the Phoenix, metaphorically rising from the ashes of Sturmey-Archer's recent past) was the first all-new design from Sun Race

Fig. 17.1. RS-RF3 3-speed with rotary cable pulley outboard of the sprocket mount.

Fig. 17.2. Exploded view of the RS-RF3, the NIG successor to the original AW 3-speed.

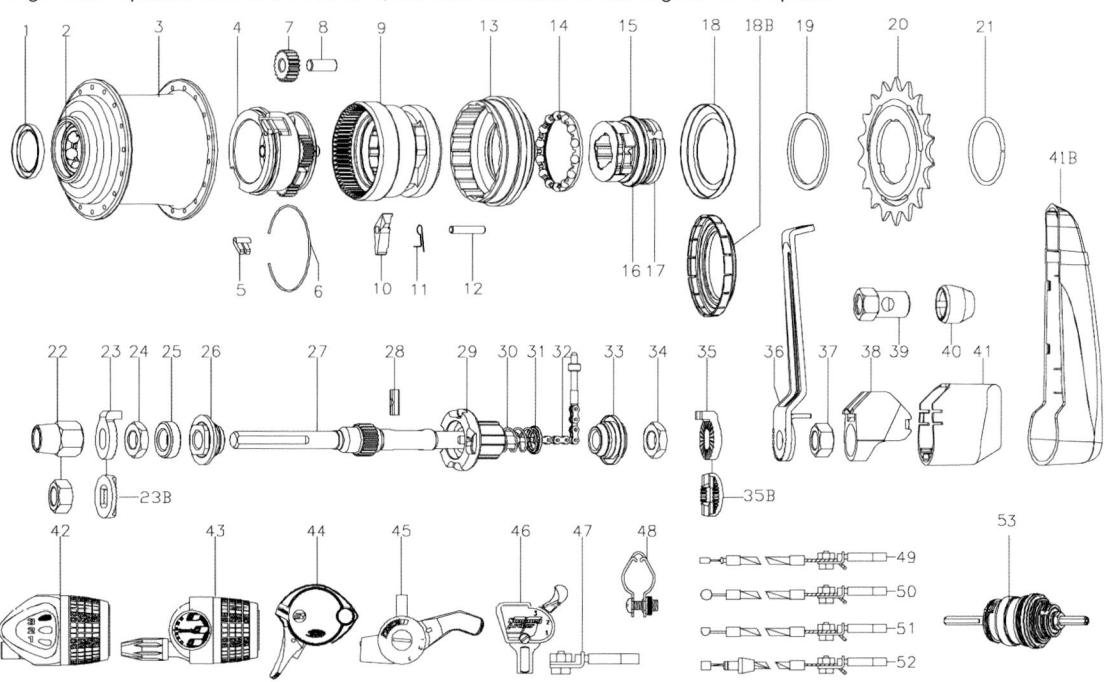

Sturmey-Archer. It made a strong statement that the new owners were prepared to innovate and invest heavily in the future of the company. It also bolstered celebrations of Sturmey-Archer's centenary.

The S80 concept was the work of Stephen Rickels, who went on to become design manager of Brompton folding bicycles. By the time he joined Brompton it had become the biggest cycle manufacturer in the United Kingdom.

Steve Rickels was chief designer at Sturmey-Archer until its acquisition by Sun Race. He

Fig. 17.3. Cutaway drawing of the X-RD8 8-speed hub.

conceived the 8-speed concept not long before this. The world patent number is WO0192094 and priority filing was in May 2000, only a month before Sturmey-Archer was sold to Lenark. The liquidator subsequently sold Sturmey-Archer's name and intellectual property to Sun Race Sturmey-Archer, who developed Rickels' prototype into a production version. They made a number of detailed changes (such as using a smaller diameter wheel axle) without altering the basic concept.

Steve Rickels' design is conceptually elegant. It envisages two or more simple epicyclic modules, each comprising a sun, planets in a planet cage and a gear ring. The only gear selecting mechanism for each module locks or frees the sun. Hence, each module offers direct drive when the sun is free to rotate on the axle or an increased gear when the sun is locked to the axle. Each module can therefore be described as being switched 'on' (gearing up) or 'off' (direct drive).

In the 8-speed application of the concept, three modules are employed, which can drive singly or in series. In the gear's original form, module A provides direct drive and a 1.28 increase. Module B provides direct drive and a 1.644 increase, and module C provides a 1.45 increase.

> Gear 1 has all three modules switched off, therefore providing direct drive.
> Gear 2 has only module A switched on, providing an increase of 1.28 (a rise of 28% from gear 1).
> Gear 3 has only module C switched on, providing an increase of 1.45 (a rise of 13% from gear 2).
> Gear 4 has only module B switched on, providing an increase of 1.644 (a rise of 13% from gear 3).
> Gear 5 has modules A and C switched on, providing an increase of 1.28 x 1.45 = 1.856 (a rise of 13% from gear 4).
> Gear 6 has modules A and B switched on, providing an increase of 1.28 x 1.644 = 2.104 (a rise of 13% from gear 5).

Gear 7 has modules B and C switched on, providing an increase of 1.644 x 1.45 = 2.384 (a rise of 13% from gear 6).
Gear 8 has all three modules switched on, providing an increase of 1.28 x 1.644 x 1.45 = 3.051 (a rise of 28% from gear 7).

Points to note are:

Lowest gear is direct drive and therefore all other gears are gearing up. This necessitates a smaller than usual chainwheel.
Gears 2, 3 and 4 each employ a single epicyclic train. Therefore the four lowest gears should be the most efficient.
Only gear 8 employs all three modules driving in series. This should therefore be the least efficient gear.
The middle six gears are equally spaced medium ratios.
The top and bottom gears are much wider spaced from their nearest neighbours. Gear 1 provides an efficient 'granny' gear, while gear 8 offers a less efficient but nonetheless useful 'following wind' or 'downhill' gear.

## Constructional details of the 8-speed

In each module the planet cage is the driven component. When the module is 'off', an automatic one-way clutch (comprising planet cage pawls acting on a ratchet track on the gear ring) directly links the planet cage to the gear ring, giving direct drive. When the module is 'on', its sun being locked to the axle, the rotation of the planet cage and pinions causes the gear ring to rotate faster than the planet cage and therefore override the one-way clutch, giving an increased gear.

The planet cage of module B is integral with the gear ring of module A. Similarly, the planet cage of module C is integral with the gear ring of module B. Hence the output of each module is automatically fed to the input of the next in a simple and elegant manner. Final output, from the gear ring of module C to the hub shell, is via spring loaded pawls on the gear ring acting on a ratchet track on the hub shell.

Locking and unlocking of the sun pinions (switching the modules 'on' and 'off') is achieved for each sun by a separate 'ratchet pawl gear selector'. This is a spring-loaded metal strip, seated in a groove in the solid hub axle. One end of the selector forms a pawl which, in its up position, engages with a ratchet in the sun, thus locking it to the axle when in the drive condition. The other end sits in a cam plate, rotation of which either:

a) pushes the selector down against spring force, thus retracting its pawl end and freeing the sun pinion, or,
b) allows the selector to rise under spring pressure, engaging its pawl in the sun's ratchet track and locking the sun to the axle.

There are three ratchet pawl gear selectors, one for each module. Each has its own seating groove in the axle and its own cam plate. The three cam plates are mounted side-by-side in a rotatable housing. This is arranged so that progressive rotation selects each gear in descending sequence, from 8 through 1. Rotation is achieved by a spring-loaded cable drum, connected by cable to the hand-operated gear selector. The cable drum functions in a broadly similar manner to the system adopted for Sturmey-Archer's 1973 prototype 7-speed design and subsequently used by them and Shimano in production 7-speed hubs. However, whereas those hubs only needed to accommodate a thin cam sleeve around the axle, the Sturmey-Archer 8-speed's cam plate housing is of much larger diameter. This necessitates a sprocket mounting of larger diameter than usual and prohibits the use of standard three-lugged hub gear sprockets. Instead Sturmey-Archer produce special over-size 23 and 25 tooth sprockets which are complemented by a special range of inexpensive cotterless crank-sets with integral 33, 36 or 38 tooth chainwheels. Standard chainsets can, of course be used but the Sturmey specials offer an easy 'off-the-peg' match aimed at the utility, commuter and roadster markets.

The modular nature of the hub's construction makes it relatively easy for Sturmey-Archer to create a two-module (4-speed) or four-module (16-speed) hub based on the patent. Many components of the 8-speed could be re-used in such hubs.

One wonders what the original members of The Three Speed Gear Syndicate would have made of the 8-speed hub, a century or so earlier.

## Sun Race Sturmey-Archer patents

Sun Race Sturmey-Archer have obtained a number of patents since 2000. The patent numbers quoted below are for the Taiwanese patents, although in some cases there are also corresponding world or territorial patents. The principal bicycle gear patents fall into several groups:

**Gear shifters**
Twist-grip shifter – TW593055, priority date 2003;
Twin trigger – TW201534527, priority date 2014.

**Derailleur multiple sprocket assemblies**
TW201141754, priority date 2010; TW201235256, priority date 2011; TW201504104, priority date 2013.

**Hydraulic drum brake**
TW201420912, priority date 2012. (Sturmey-Archer in Nottingham were working on a hydraulic drum brake in the 1990s.)

**Freewheel mechanism within a hub gear**
TW201303181, priority date 2011.

**Bottom bracket gear with back-pedal shifting**
TW201348060, priority date 2012. Sun Race produced this gear, known as the KS3, specifically for the belt-driven Strida folding bicycle. In 1988 Strida production moved to Nottinghamshire and Sturmey-Archer designed a 2-speed bottom bracket gear with back-pedal shifting but this was not put into production. After Ming Cycle bought the rights to Strida in 2006, they fitted some Stridas with a version of the Schlumpf epicyclic 2-speed chainwheel gear, adapted for belt drive. The Sun Race Sturmey-Archer 3-speed bracket gear was announced in March 2012 and fitted to the Strida EVO model.

**Back-pedal hub gear with coaster brake**
TW201139207, priority date 2010.

Fig. 17.4. Exploded view of the KS3 Strida bottom bracket gear.

**Multi-speed hub gear with back-pedal shifting**
TW201219260, priority date 2010.

**Hub gear speed changing apparatus**
TW201217669, priority date 2010. A very complex patent with many options, including back-pedal, centrifugal and electric shifting.

**Derailleur chain shifter mechanism**
TW201028332, priority date 2009. For use in a fully enclosed chaincase during forward or backward motion. This relates to an idea for Gazelle based on Sturmey-Archer's SD (side drum) hub brake for a bicycle frame with only one backstay and chainstay. It was a derailleur-type gear in a gearcase but about 2013 the project was stopped by Gazelle because they could not obtain a frame of the consistently high strength required to take the stresses. The bike was to have been called the Gazelle Friiik.

**Fixed-wheel hub gear**
TW201028332, priority date 2008, the basis of the S3X fixed-wheel 3-speed (see below).

**Rotary interface on hub gear for cable connection**
TW200514725, priority date 2003, for rotary shifter outboard of hub gear sprocket; TW200514724, priority date 2003, for transmission structure within hub gear to work with rotary shifter (with option of solid wheel axle).

## Sun Race Sturmey-Archer hub range in the mid 2000s
By **2003** Sun Race had three main product ranges:

   S – hub gears and drum brakes,
   M – derailleurs, principally for mountain bikes and utility use,
   R – derailleurs for road racing.

Fig. 17.5. Prototype enclosed derailleur for the Gazelle Friiik.

Fig. 17.6. Dimensioned drawing of the enclosed derailleur mechanism.

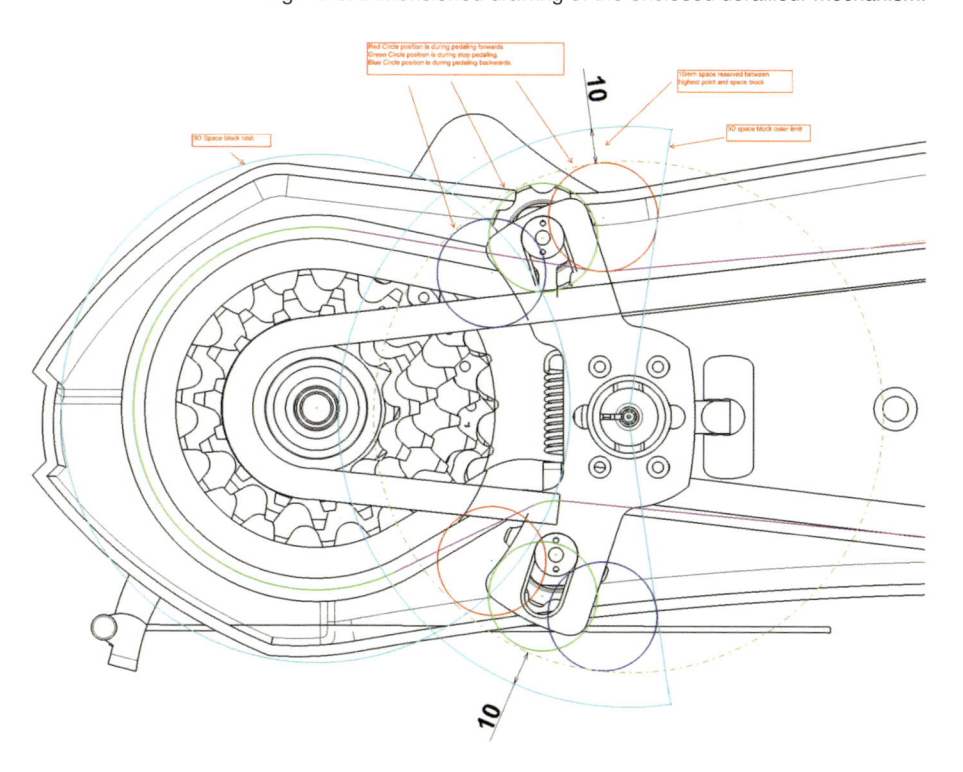

The company also offered single-speed hubs, chainsets, chains and other drivetrain components and accessories.

All hub gears, including those based on Nottingham designs, now had NIG (No Intermediate Gear), thus eliminating slipping of the drive between gears. In the S range of hub gears and drum brakes, there were the following series:

- S80 series of alloy shell 8-speeds with 305% range:
X-RD8 with 70 mm drum brake, X-RR8 with freewheel and compatible with roller brake.

- S50 series of alloy shell 5-speeds with 225% range:
X-RD5 with 70 mm drum brake, X-RC5 with coaster brake, X-RF5 with freewheel.

- S5S series of steel shell 5-speeds with 225% range and ball-locking sun clutches:
AB5 with 90 mm drum brake, S5C with coaster brake, S5 with freewheel.

- S30 series of alloy shell 3-speeds with 177% range:
X-RD3 with 70 mm drum brake, S-RC3 with coaster brake, S-RF3 with freewheel.

- S3S series of steel shell 3-speeds with 177% range:
AB3 with 90 mm drum brake, SAB3 with 70 mm drum brake, AWC with coaster brake, AWB compatible with band/servo brake, AW3 with freewheel.

- Front drum brakes:
X-FD 70 mm drum alloy shell, BF 90 mm drum steel shell, SBF 70 mm drum alloy shell.

- Rear drum brakes (no gears):
X-RD for screw-on single or multiple freewheel 70 mm alloy shell, CBS coaster brake steel shell.

There was a wide range of gear controls. For example, for the 3-speed hubs there was the classic 1970s trigger, the Nimbus thumb shifter, the Orion lever/button shifter, and two new twist-grips. The Orion was a more modern looking version of the 1984 3-shift: unlike its predecessor it was also produced in a 5-speed version. External design and final assembly was done in the Netherlands.

By **2005** Sun Race Sturmey-Archer had added a series of hub dynamos combined with drum brakes – an idea proposed decades previously by Sturmey-Archer but never put into production.

- X-FDD alloy shell hub dynamo and 70 mm drum brake:
choice of 2.4 or 3.0 watt output, with or without sealed cartridge bearings.

Additions had also been made to the range of 8-speeds:

- S80 8-speed additions:
X-RF8(S) with standard length axle and no provision for roller brake, X-RF8(C) with short axle; X-RK8 for disc brake.

Fig. 17.7. Orion shifters for 5-speed and 3-speed hubs.

Fig. 17.8. X-FDD hub dynamo and drum brake.

The C30 range was based on a new 3-speed with a rotary cable pulley outboard of the sprocket, as described in the patents TW200514725 and TW200514724 mentioned above. The variants were as follows:

- C30 alloy shell 3-speed with 177% range:
RS-RF3 with freewheel, RS-RB3 for band brake, RS-RR3 for roller brake, RX-RD3 with 70 mm drum brake.

In **2006** the company launched many additional hubs and related products:

- SX range of hub gears for cruiser bikes, with oversize alloy shell for extra wide tyres:

Fig. 17.9. RX-RD3 3-speed with 70 mm drum brake.

SX-RK3 3-speed for disc brake, SX-RB3 3-speed for band brake.

- CLS range of stick-shift 3-speed levers for cruiser bikes.

- TS range of alloy shell tricycle hub gears:
TS-RF3 3-speed with freewheel, TS-RB3 3-speed for band brake, TS-RC3 3-speed with coaster brake. Strictly speaking not hubs but hub-like countershaft gearboxes. These are supplied with an additional sprocket bolted to the hub shell to drive the trike rear axle.

- QS-RC3 alloy shell quadricycle hub with reverse and coaster brake:
As with the TS range, not strictly speaking a hub but a hub-like countershaft gearbox.

- X-range of alloy drum brakes:
X-SD 70 mm drum brake for single-sided mounting (recumbent or wheelchair) and similar XL-SD 90 mm drum brake both with option of quick-release. The XL-SDD and X-SDD are single-sided drum brakes combined with Dynohubs in 2.4 and 3.0 watt. The X-RDC is a 70 mm rear drum brake with freehub fitting for 7, 8 or 9 speed derailleur cassettes.

- S-range shifter additions:
New twin lever trigger shifters for all 5-speeds and newer 3-speeds. (Separate levers for upshifts and downshifts.)

- C30 rotary selector alloy shell 3-speed range addition:
RS-RC3 with coaster brake.

Fig. 17.10. TS-RC3 tricycle 3-speed with coaster brake.

Fig. 17.11 QS-RC3 quadricycle hub with reverse and coaster brake.

- S30 alloy shell classic 3-speed range additions:
S-RK3 for disc brake, S-RB3 for band brake, XL-RD3 with 90 mm drum brake.

## Brompton specials

- BWR (Brompton Wide Ratio) ultra-wide-ratio 3-speed with 246% range, introduced in 2008 for use with Brompton's own 2-speed derailleur to give 6 speeds.

- BSR (Brompton Standard Ratio) version of the S-RF3 3-speed tailored to Brompton's requirements, introduced in 2009. The Brompton version has 112 mmm over locknut dimension rather than 108 mm, and a different chainline.

Fig. 17.12. BWR Brompton Wide Ratio 3-speed.

Fig. 17.13. BSR Brompton Standard Ratio 3-speed.

Fig. 17.14. XL-SDD Dynohub with 90 mm brake drum for single-side mounting.

Fig. 17.16. X-RD4 4-speed with 70 mm drum brake.

Fig. 17.15. RX-RD5 5-speed with 70 mm drum brake.

## Sun Race Sturmey-Archer hub range in the mid 2010s
If we fast-forward almost a decade, we find further developments have occurred in the product range. Almost of all of these are additions to the products mentioned above:

- X range alloy shell front hub dynamo and drum brake additions, all with sealed cartridge bearings and choice of 2.4 or 3.0 watt output:
XL-FDD with 90 mm drum for conventional fork, XL-SDD with 90 mm drum for single-side mounting, X-SDD with 70 mm drum for single-side mounting.

- HDS range of front hub dynamos without drum brakes:
All with sealed cartridge bearings and choice of 2.4 or 3.0 watt output, HDS10 sub-range without brake provision, HDS20 sub-range for use with disc brake.

- S80(W) new series of alloy shell 8-speed hubs with wider 325% range, replacing S80 series:
X-RD8(W) with 70 mm drum brake, X-RK8(W) for disc brake, X-RF8(W) with freewheel.

- C50 new series of alloy shell 5-speed hubs with wider 243% range and rotary gear selector, replacing S5O series and S5S series:
RXL-RD5 with 90 mm drum brake, RX-RD5 with 70 mm drum brake, RX-RK5 for disc brake, RX-RC5 with coaster brake, RX-RF5 with freewheel.

- S40 new series of alloy shell 4-speed hubs with 210% range and rotary gear selector:

Fig. 17.17. RS-RK3 disc brake compatible version of the rotary selector alloy shell 3-speed.

X-RD4 with 70 mm drum brake, X-RK4 for disc brake, X-RC4 with coaster brake, X-RF4 with freewheel.

- C30 rotary selector alloy shell 3-speed changes:
RS-RK3 for disc brake added, RS-RR3 for roller brake and RS-RC3 coaster both deleted.

- S3S steel shell classic 3-speed range:
AB3 with 90 mm drum brake deleted, AWB for band brake deleted, AWC with coaster brake updated.

- Q-series quadricycle gears:
QS-RC5 5-speed reversible coaster added.

- TS-series tricycle gear additions:
TS-RC5 5-speed coaster brake, TS-RF5 5-speed hub, T-S2C 2-speed coaster brake.

- S3X alloy shell fixed-wheel 3-speed:
With 160% range and choice of shell finishes and optional bar-end, thumb, seat post and braze-on levers. Relates to patent TW201028332 mentioned above.

Fig. 17.18. S3X alloy shell fixed-wheel 3-speed, with sprocket lock-ring.

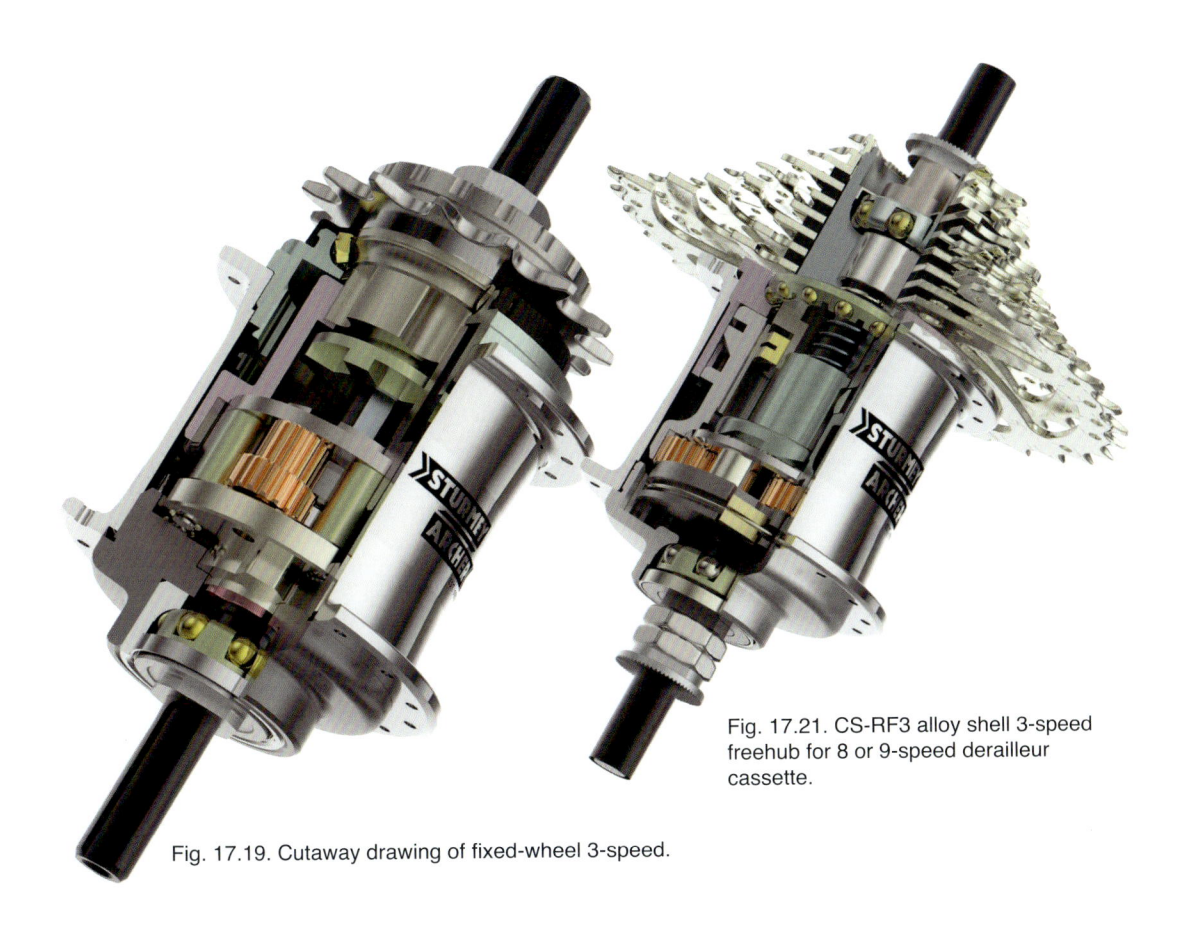

Fig. 17.21. CS-RF3 alloy shell 3-speed freehub for 8 or 9-speed derailleur cassette.

Fig. 17.19. Cutaway drawing of fixed-wheel 3-speed.

Fig. 17.20. Bar-end shifters for the S3X hub.

**SLS3X-B**

311

Fig. 17.22. S1C single-speed coaster.

- F30-series of alloy shell cassette 8 and 9 speed derailleur freehubs with 177% range 3-speed, giving 24 or 27 speeds:
CS-RF3 standard version, CS-RK3 for disc brake, both compatible with standard mountain bike left-hand triple chainwheel shifters.

- S20 series of alloy shell back-pedal shift 2-speeds with 138% range:
S2 standard hub, S2C with coaster brake, S2K for disc brake.

- S1C single-speed coaster brake:
With integral back-pedal brake, available in choice of hub shell colours.

Fig. 17.23. X-SD 70 mm front drum brake for single-sided mounting.

Fig. 17.24. A2D automatic 2-speed with drum brake.

- Front alloy steel drum brake addition:
XL-FD 90 mm drum brake (to replace type BFC steel hub).

- Revised alloy shell drum brake range for single-side mounting:
XL-SD 90 mm front drum brake, in left and right versions.
XL-SD(Q) quick-release 90 mm front drum brake, in left and right versions.
X-SD 70 mm front drum brake, in left and right versions.
X-SD(Q) quick-release 70 mm front drum brake, in left and right versions.

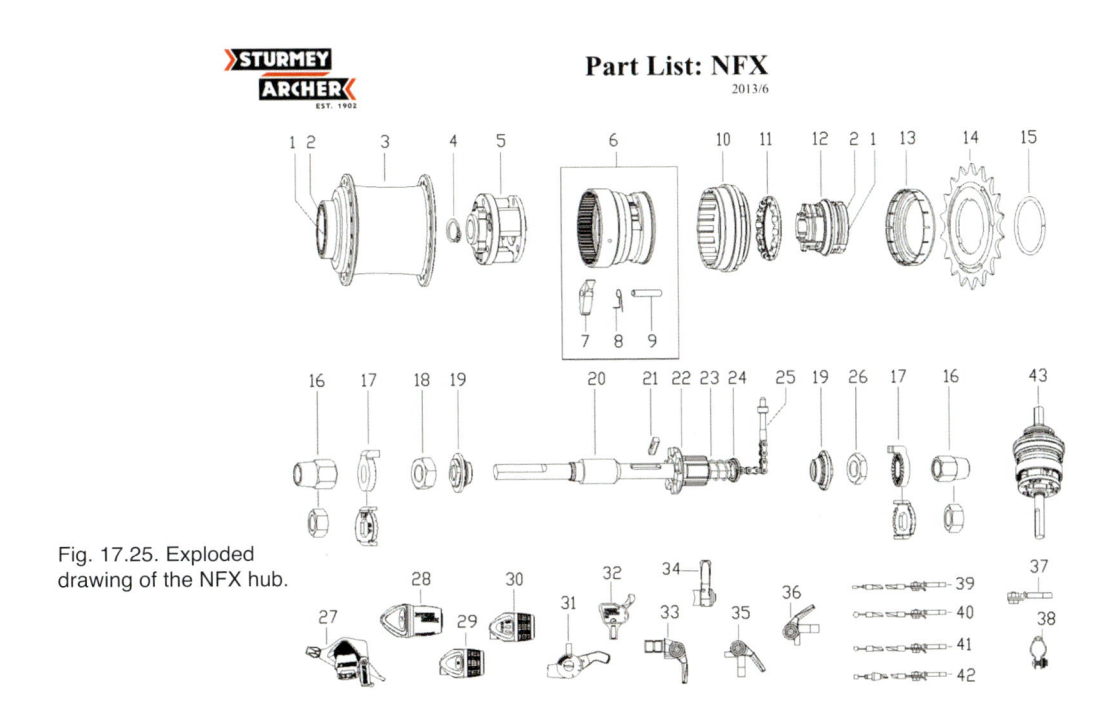

Fig. 17.25. Exploded drawing of the NFX hub.

313

● A2D automatic 2-speed:
A new product added to the range in 2019: a 2-speed with centrifugally-operated automatic gear change and available with drum brake or disc brake attachment. In the past Fichtel & Sachs and their successor SRAM and Shimano have made 2-speeds with centrifugal automatic shifting but no other firm currently does.

● NFX fixed/freewheel/no drive hub:
An unusual product introduced in 2011 for manufacturers of side-by-side tandems for riders with special needs. In these vehicles typically one rider has a disability and the other does not. The hub has three modes:
1. In freewheel mode the disabled rider can choose whether she or he pedals or not.
2. In fixed mode both riders have to pedal.
3. In neutral mode there is no drive for the disabled rider, so he or she can pedal forwards or backwards without effecting the drive.

The above listing was compiled in 2019. For the latest product range, visit www.sturmey-archer.com

# Postscript

## Sturmey-Archer's last years in Britain, 1987 to 2000

Sturmey-Archer is one of the oldest and most famous bicycle component manufacturers. For decades it was the world brand leader in its field and it is still a force to be reckoned with. It is famous for the inventiveness of its designers but has sometimes suffered from misdirected effort, missed opportunities and underinvestment.

Frank Bowden's entrepreneurial skill and risk-taking was key to Sturmey-Archer's foundation and initial success. An important factor was Bowden's understanding of cycling, cyclists and cycle technology, which grew from his own enjoyment of cycling and the health improvements it brought him. But although he had turned Raleigh from a back street bicycle maker into a world class manufacturer, at the time the Sturmey-Archer brand was born his entrepreneurial record was mixed. He had failed to make Raleigh a success in the USA, despite living there for some years and marrying into an American family. He had made loss-making investments in wooden rims and Raleigh's financial situation was still not particularly secure. Furthermore, he was on the rebound from having backed Sharp's continually variable hub gear, which never worked well enough to go into production. But by acquiring the rights to a pair of very similar 3-speed hub gears, he was able to dominate a new market. It was a gamble that paid off handsomely.

The early days of Sturmey-Archer arguably involved too many redesigns of the standard 3-speed. The type X was about as good as a wide-ratio 3-speed can be and could easily be marketed today. Most of the subsequent redesigns were primarily to cut production costs, not to improve the product. An exception was the introduction of ball bearing planet pinions. It was initially a good marketing ploy that gave a small advantage to the user but it led to unexpected hub failures that contributed to the downfall of William Reilly. Another redesign much later led to the exit of William Brown, when unsprung pawls contributed to the failure of the SW hub and resulted in the reintroduction of the trusty AW 3-speed. The AW was a classic design that remained in production relatively unchanged longer than almost any other branded component in the history of the bicycle. It was evidence of the maxim 'the good is the enemy of the best' – simpler and less user-friendly than the type X but reliable, easy to repair and profitable to manufacture.

After the relatively stable complacency of the 1920s, Sturmey-Archer became increasingly inventive in the run-up to World War 2. This was largely in reaction to developments outside the company, such as the marketing of drum brakes for bicycles, the development of hub dynamos and the increasing effectiveness of derailleur gears. But fascinating though the late 1930s product range was, making so many different products was not cost-effective. Soon after the war it became clear that pursuing the racing fraternity was no longer worthwhile and thereafter the product range focused more on utility riders.

Perhaps the company should have stayed better focused on that market throughout the interwar years. If they had manufactured Henry Sturmey's 5-speed hub in the 1920s, could they have weaned the average urban cyclist onto it, so that the 5-speed hub became the norm?

That might have helped maintain the popularity of hub gears in later decades.

Sadly, the accountants in control of Sturmey-Archer developed a longstanding resistance to investment in 'technology push' products, such as 5-speeds and 7-speeds. Decades passed between Sturmey-Archer's inventive designers developing these hubs and product launch. The case of the 7-speed was particularly sad and highlights the malaise the company was suffering from prior to the Sun Race takeover.

In a letter published in *A to B magazine*, June 2010, Alan Clarke wrote:

> When Sturmey-Archer collapsed in 2000, it was in the process of moving to a new factory location, where much less would have been manufactured, so it was already on course to become an R&D plus assembly operation. When we tried to find a buyer to keep Sturmey production the UK, we realised that we could no longer compete by manufacturing here. It hurts me to say it, but product quality is also much better from Taiwan. They have invested in technology which was unavailable in England. SRAM has also recently announced that it will be ceasing hub production in Schweinfurt, Germany. [SRAM subsequently transferred production to Taiwan and, in 2017, ceased making hub gears altogether.] So far as Raleigh is concerned, it lost huge market share, partly because it kept manufacture in Nottingham for too long. Consumers (and bike shops) showed little interest in the 'Made in England' label and bought Trek, Specialised, Giant instead of Raleigh. Anyway, it's all water under the bridge now.

Alan Clarke has maintained the continuity between the old British Sturmey-Archer and today's Taiwanese version. It is impressive to have had a senior manager devote his entire working life to the product range, helping ensure continuity between past and present. Moreover, he has gone out of his way to collect and conserve the history of the enterprise, from the earliest days to the present. In 2004 he organised the purchase of Denis Watkins'

Fig. 17.26. Denis Watkins and his wife Ruby handover Denis's hub collection to Alan Clarke in 2004.

Fig. 17.27. A corner of the Sturmey-Archer museum.

extensive collection of Sturmey-Archer hubs, which now form part of the Sturmey-Archer museum at the company's European headquarters in the Netherlands.

Sun Race are to be applauded for the huge amount of financial and intellectual capital they have invested in keeping Sturmey-Archer alive and profitable. There is no comparison between the modest product range of the 1980s and the much wider range of better-made products coming out of Taiwan today. Sun Race Sturmey-Archer is now the second-biggest hub gear maker in the world and deservedly so.

And what of the future? We can do no better than paraphrase the final paragraphs of this book's 1987 predecessor.

The main contestants in the field of bicycle gearing remain the hub gear and the derailleur. For ease of use the hub gear wins every time. Gears can be selected even with the bike stationary. This makes it pre-eminent for city use. The hub gear enables a stronger wheel to be built with no weakness caused by dishing for the derailleur's sprocket cluster; also spokes are easier to replace and less likely to break. A well-designed and well-made hub gear should prove much more durable than a derailleur. It will also require minimal maintenance.

For non-competitive riders requiring ease of use, reliability and a reasonably wide range of relatively widely-spaced gears (the majority of cyclist?), the hub gear offers the ideal solution. Whether these riders will realise this is another matter – but on this, more than any other factor, depends the future of Sturmey-Archer.

In the meantime we salute the people of Sturmey-Archer, past and present, for building one of the world's greatest cycle component brands.

*Tony Hadland*

# Appendices

*Miscellaneous additional information*

A. Production date list (1902-2018)

B. Glossary

C. Manufacture

D. Efficiency

E. Derailleur converters

F. Dating Sturmey-Archer hubs

G. Triggers, 1938 to 1960

H. Sources

I. Repairs and maintenance

J. Auctioneer's list of Sturmey-Archer plant, 2000

K. Lubrication

L. Sturmey-Archer Heritage website

# A. Production date list (1902-2018)

| DATE | TYPE | DESCRIPTION |
|---|---|---|
| Dec 1902 to 1906 | No Mark | First 3-speed gear hub by Sturmey-Archer |
| Dec 1905 to 1907 | "N" or "C" | First Tricoaster |
| Feb 1906 to 1907 | No Mark | Three Speed-early "X" Type |
| mid 1907 to 1910 | "V" | Three Speed |
| Sept 1907 to 1921 | "N" | Tricoaster brake hub |
| 1909 to 1914 | "X" | Three Speed |
| 1914 to 1918 | "A" | Three Speed |
| 1914 - 1927? | Type S(type F?) | Tricoaster made under licence in US by Sears. |
| 1914 | "FN" | Tricoaster brake hub |
| 1918 to 1938 | "K" | Threespeed |
| 1918 to 1936 | "KB" | Three Speed Hub Brake |
| 1922 | "CC" | Single Speed Coaster |
| 1922 to 1936 | "KC" | Tricoaster brake hub |
| 1929 to 1936 | "SC" or "RD" | Single Speed Coaster Hub |
| 1932 to 1938 | "KS" | Three Speed Close Ratio |
| 1932 to 1942 | "TF" | two-speed fixed or freewheel hub. |
| 1932 to 1942 | "T" | Two Speed Hub (Freewheel) Tandem |
| 1932 to 1942 | "TBF" | 2-Spd Hub Brake (Fixed Wheel) Tandem (Rod operated Brake) |
| 1932 to 1942 | "TB" | 2-Spd Hub Brake (Freewheel) Tandem (Rod operated Brake) |
| 1932 to 1942 | "TBFC" | 2-Spd Hub Brake (Fixed Wheel) Tandem (Cable operated Brake) |
| 1932 to 1942 | "TBC" "TBF" Type | 2-Spd Hub Brake (Freewheel) Tandem (Cable operated Brake) |
| 1932 to 1942 | "TBC" "TB" Type | 2-Spd Hub Brake (Freewheel) Tandem (Cable operated Brake) |
| 1932 to Present | ("LBF") "BF" | Front 90mm Hub Brake (LBF to about 1935) |
| 1932 to 1984 | ("LBR") "BR" | Rear 90mm Hub Brake (LBR to about 1936) |
| 1933 to 1938 | "KSW" | Three Speed (Medium Ratio) |
| 1934 to 1942 | "BFT" | Front Hub Brake for Tandem |
| 1934 to 1942 | "BRT" | Rear Hub Brake for Tandem |
| 1934 to 1939 | "KT" | 3-Spd (Wide Ratio) Brake Hub for Tandem |
| 1936 to 1955 | "AW" | Three Speed (Wide Ratio) reintroduced 1958 |
| 1936 to 1942 | "AT" | 3-Spd Brake Hub for Tandem |
| 1939 to 1959 | "AM" | Three Speed (Medium Ratio) |
| 1936 to 1942 | "AR" | Three Speed (Close Ratio) |
| 1936 to 1942 | "TC" | Two speed close ratio fixed or freewheel. |
| 1936 to 1938 | No Mark | Front Dynohub 12V. |
| 1937 to 1988 | "AB" | Three Speed 90mm Hub Brake |
| 1989 to 2015 | "AB" | NIG three Speed 90mm Hub Brake |
| 1938 | No Mark | Front Dynohub 8V. |
| 1938 to 1941 | "AF" | Four Speed (Close Ratio) |
| 1939 to c. 1960 | "FM" | Four Speed (Medium Ratio) |
| 1945 to 1970 | "FW" | Four Speed (Wide Ratio) |
| 1945 to 1983 | "GH6" | Front Dynohub 6V. |

319

| Dates | Code | Description |
|---|---|---|
| 1946 to 1983 | "AG" | Three Speed Dynohub 6V. |
| 1947 to c.1960 | "FG" | Four Speed Dynohub 6V. |
| 1947 to 1959 | "ASC" | Three Speed Fixed (Close Ratio) |
| 1947 to 1959 | "FC" | Four Speed (Close Ratio) Hub |
| 1948 to c.1960 | "AC" | Three Speed (Close Ratio) Hub |
| 1949 to 1952 | "FB" | Four Speed 90mm Brake Hub |
| 1952 to 1959 | "TCW" Mark I. | Tricoaster brake hub (Wide Ratio) |
| 1954 to c.1960 | "SW" | 3-Spd (Replaced AW for a time) |
| 1958 to 2001 | "AW" | 3-Spd (Wide Ratio)(Re-introduced to replace SW) |
| 1959 to 1961 | "TCW" Mark II. | Tricoaster Hub Brake |
| 1961 to 1972 | "TCW" Mark III. | Tricoaster Hub Brake |
| 1963 to 1978 | "SC" | Single Speed Coaster Hub |
| 1966 to 1972 | "S2" | 2-Spd Hub (Back pedal change) |
| 1966 to 1974 | "S5" | Five Speed Hub (Modified FW) |
| 1967 to 1976 | "S3B" | 3-Spd Brake Hub (55mm for small wheel) |
| 1970 to 1988 | "S3C" | Tricoaster brake hub (Wide Ratio) |
| 1977 to 1981 | "S5/1" | Five Speed Hub (Wide Ratio) |
| 1977 to 1984 | "SBF" | Front 70mm Brake Hub |
| 1978 to 1980 | "SC1" | Single Speed Coaster Hub |
| 1978 to 1984 | "SAB" | 3-Spd 70mm Hub Brake (Wide Ratio) |
| 1978 to 1982 | "SCC" | Single Speed Coaster |
| 1978 to 1984 | "SBR" | Rear 70mm Brake Hub |
| 1981 to 1990 | "S52" | Five Speed Hub (Wide Ratio) |
| 10/1983 | "AB/BF" | Hubs now with Labyrinth seal on brake |
| 1984 to 1999 | Elite "VT" | Front 70mm Alloy Hub Brake (replaced by X-FD) |
| 1984 to 1999 | Elite "ST" | Rear 70mm Alloy Hub Brake (replaced by X-RD) |
| 1984 to 1988 | Elite "AT3" | Rear 70mm 3-Spd Alloy Hub Brake |
| 1985 to 1990 | Elite "AT5" | Rear 70mm 5-Spd Alloy Hub Brake |
| 1986 to 2016 | "GBF" | Front 90mm Hub Brake with Sealed Bearings |
| 1987 to 2017 | Steelite "SBF" | Front 70mm Brake Hub |
|  | "SBR" | Rear 70mm Brake Hub (until 9/2000) |
|  | "SAB" | Three Speed 70mm Hub Brake |
| 1988 to 1991 | AWC Brass brake | Tricoaster Brake Hub with brass brake |
| Jan 1989 to 1992 | Elite "AT3" | NIG 70mm 3-Spd Hub Brake (Wide Ratio) |
| 1991 to Present | "AWC" | Tricoaster Brake Hub with Sintered Steel Brake Shoes |
| 1991 to July 1993 | 5-Star "AT5" | 70mm 5-Spd Alloy drum brake hub |
| 1991 to Aug. 1993 | 5-Star | Five Speed Hub (Wide Ratio) |
| 1993 to 1999 | Elite "AT3" | NIG 70mm 3-Spd Hub Brake (Sintered Planet Cage ) (replaced by X-RD3) |
| July 1993 to 1999 | Sprinter Elite "AT5" | 70mm Five Speed Alloy Drum Brake Hub single cable (replaced by X-RD5) |
| July 1993 to 1999 | Sprinter S5 | Five Speed Hub Single Cable |
| Oct. 1993 to 1999 | Sprinter S5C | Five Speed Coaster Hub brake Single Cable |
| 10/1993 to 7/1999 | Sprinter "S5C" | 5-Spd Coaster Brake Hub Single Cable |
| 7/1997 to 8/1998 | "S7" | 7-Speed Hub |
| 7/1997 to 8/1998 | "S7C" | 7-Speed Coaster Brake Hub |
| 7/1997 to 8/1998 | "AT7" | 7-Speed Drum Brake Hub |

| Date | Code | Description |
|---|---|---|
| 7/1997 to 8/2000 | "BR" | Re-introduction Rear Drum Brake Hub |
| 8/1999 to 9/2000 | "S7" "S7C" "AT7" | Ball-Lock in 7-Speed |
| 3/1999 | Drum Brake Hubs | Solid Axle and New Planet cage in all 3-Speed Drum Brake Hubs. |
| 8/1999 to 9/2000 | "SAB5" | 70mm Steel 5-Speed Drum Brake Hub |
| 8/1999 to 9/2000 | "AB5" | 5-Speed 90mm Drum Brake Hub |
| 9/1999 to 2005 | "S5" "S5C" "X-RD5" | Ball-lock in 5-Speed |
| 9/1999 to 9/2000 | "GBR" | 90mm Rear Drum Brake Hub (sealed bearings) |
| 1999 to Present | "X-FD" | VT with New Shape Shell |
| 1999 to Present | "X-RD" | ST with New Shape Shell |
| 1999 to Present | "X-RD3" | AT3 with New Shape Shell and solid axle |
| 1999 to Present | "X-RD5" | Ball-lock with New Shape Shell |
| 1999 to 9/2000 | "X-RD7" | Ball-lock with New Shape Shell |
| 9/2000 | All Hubs | Final UK production. |
| 2001 | In Taiwan | BR, SBR, S7, S7C, X-RD7, SAB-5 withdrawn |
| 10/2001 | "AW" | NIG in AW 3-Speed |
| 10/2001 | Steelite | Satin Silver Finish |
| 10/2001 | "S-RC3" "SRF3" | Alu Shell AWC/AW |
| 1/2002 | "X-RF5" "X-RC5" | Alu Shell S5/S5C |
| 7/2003 | "SBF" "SAB" | Silver Paint Shell |
|  | "AWC" "AW" | Silver Paint Shell |
|  | "S5" "S5C" | Silver Paint Shell |
| 7/2003 | "AWC" "S5C" "X-RC3"/"X-RC5" | New Brake arm and locknuts 5-speed coaster hubs deleted 2004. |
| 8/2003 | All Hubs | Ground Ball Tracks in Gear Hubs |
| 9/2003 to 2005 | CBS | Single Coaster Brake Hub |
| 9/2004 to 2008 | X-RD8 | 8-speed Drum Brake Hub |
| 9/2004 to 2008 | X-RF8 | 8-speed Freewheel Hub |
| 2005 | RS-RF3 RS-RK3 RS-RD3 | Rotary selector 3-speed with new twistshifter TSS34. |
| 2005 | 5-speed | Ball-locking deleted |
| 2/2005 | CBS 11 | Single Coaster Brake Hub - deleted 2006 |
| 2005 | SX-RK/RB3 | Cruiser hubs for Schwinn Stingray with stickshift |
| 2005 | X-FDD | 3 and 2.4 watt front dynohub drum brake hubs |
| 2005 | HSL 871 | Sprocket dustcap and spacing washer integrated |
| 2006 | TS-RF3 | 3-speed with double sprocket for trike |
| 2006 | TS-RB3 | 3-speed band brake for trike |
| 2006 | TS-RC3 | 3-speed coaster brake for trike |
| 2006 | X-FDH | SD stub axle hubs renamed |
| 2006 | X-RDC | Drum brake hub for 9-speed cassette |
| 2006 | DLS 30/34/50 | Under-bar thumbshifters |
| 2006 | QS-RC3 | 3-speed with reverse gear for quadricycle |
| 2006 | FCS | Single crankset range |
| 2007 | BLS80/81 | Brake levers also with parking button |
| 2008 | X-RF8(W) | First production samples 25 March |

| | | |
|---|---|---|
| 2008 | S5C(W) | First production to MIFA 22 July |
| 2008 | X-FDD | From April with o-ring seals to keep out water |
| 2008 | BWR wide ratio | Samples to Brompton 30 July |
| 2009 | CTS range | Chain tensioners |
| 2009 | FCT20 | Track cranksets in colour |
| 2009 | S3X + bar-end shifter | First hub sets delivered September |
| 2009 | S2 + S2C announced | At Eurobike in September |
| 2009 | BSR for Brompton | August first delivery |
| 2009 | CS-RF3/CS-RK3 | 3 X 9-speed announced at Eurobike |
| 2010 | FCT60 series | Track cranksets |
| 2010 | XL 90mm hubs. | XL-FD, XL-FDD, XL-RD3/5, XL-SD |
| 2010 | SLS thumbshifters | 3-speed, S3X, 5-speed |
| 2011 | Type NFX hub | Neutral, Freewheel, Fixed hub |
| 2011 | S2/S2C | First delivery June |
| 2011 | CS-RF3/CS-RK3 | Samples received October |
| 2014 | SFS30 | Single freewheels 1/8th & 3/32nd |
| 2014 | SFX30 | 13-15t 3-pawl single freewheels |
| 2015 | DYNOHUBS | HDS12 & X-SDD |
| 2015 | S1C | Single coaster brake hub in colours |
| 2015 | C50 | 5-speed drum brake |
| 2015 | C50 | 5-speed freewheel and coaster models |
| 2015 | SBF/SAB | Replaced by alloy shell hubs |
| 2015 | F70 series | Single cranksets with forged alloy cranks |
| 2016 | SLS80-T | Thumbshifter for 8-speed hub |
| 2017 | AB/BF | Replaced by alloy shell hubs |
| 2018 | C40 | 4-speed hub |
| 2018 | A2 | 2-speed automatic hub |
| 2018 | FCSS54/6 | 54 & 56T single cranksets |

# B. Glossary

The meanings given here are simple explanations of terms used in this book.

ALTERNATOR
See GENERATOR below.

ANNULUS
An internally toothed ring in an epicyclic gear, also called a gear ring (plural = annuli).

ARMATURE
The power-producing component of a generator. The armature can be on either the rotating part or the stationary part, and may consist of a permanent magnet or electro-magnet.

AXLE
Generally refers to the wheel axle, sometimes called the wheel spindle. The axles of many hub gears are hollow in order to accommodate the changer linkage.

AXLE KEY
A small cross pin (or similar) that slides in a slot in the hub gear axle. It is the link between the gear change linkage in the hollow axle and the clutching system of the epicyclic gear.

BACK JAW WIDTH
Archaic term for the distance between the rear fork ends. Sometimes called the drop-out width, it should match the hub width or over locknut dimension.

BALL CUP
The circular end plate of a hub shell; it contains one of the ball races for the wheel bearings.

BAND BRAKE
A hub brake in which braking is achieved by tightening a flexible band around a drum or pulley.

BOWDEN CABLE (or WIRE)
A multi-strand control cable running within a flexible sheath, as used for cable brakes and gear control systems.

CAM
A projection (e.g. on a wheel) which, by engaging with another component, converts circular motion into some other form of motion (e.g. reciprocating motion).

CAM FOLLOWER
An intermediate device relaying the motion of a cam to the item to be moved by the cam.

CAMSHAFT
A rotating shaft on which one or more cams is mounted.

CAM SLEEVE
A camshaft encircling the wheel axle.

CHAIN GEAR
Obsolete British term for a derailleur gear.

CHAINLINE
The line followed by the drive chain. When accompanied by a dimension it means the distance from the centre line of the bike to the centre line of the chain (e.g. a chainline of 1¼"). Sometimes hyphenated or two separate words.

CHANGE-SPEED GEARING
Variable speed gearing.

CLUTCH
A means of engaging and disengaging drive.

COASTER
A hub brake operated by back-pedalling. Typically involving an expanding metal brake band rubbing on the inside of the hub shell.

COG
A wheel with teeth around its periphery.

COMMUTATOR
Rotary switch in a generator to convert the electrical output to direct current. Also used in many direct current electric motors.

CONE
The part of a wheel bearing mounted on the axle. The ball bearings run between a fixed race (ball cup) in the hub and a cone (usually adjustable) on the wheel axle.

CONE ACTUATOR
Nothing to do with wheel bearings: this is a conical member in some coaster brakes. When the rider back-pedals, the cone actuator moves sideways thus forcing the brake ring to open and rub against the hub shell.

COUNTERSHAFT
An intermediate shaft between the source of drive and the final destination of the drive (e.g. in a motorcycle at a position between the engine and the driven wheel).

DERAILLEUR
Since the 1920s, the standard four-syllable anglicised form of the three syllable French word 'dérailleur', meaning a chain-shifter gear. Also known in the UK as a chain gear until the mid twentieth century.

DERAILER
More recent American term for a chain-shifter gear, being a literal translation of 'dérailleur' rather than an Anglicisation.

DISC BRAKE
A brake involving callipers that pinch a brake disc fixed to a hub outboard of the spokes. Manually operated by Bowden cable or hydraulic linkage.

DOGS
Interlocking projections as used in some forms of clutch.

DRAG SPRING
A friction device to ensure that an otherwise freely moving component maintains a certain relationship with another component (e.g. if two parts are rotating the drag spring can ensure that one is held back and always follows behind the other). Used particularly in the actuating mechanisms of coaster brakes.

DRIVER
The part of a hub gear or coaster brake on which the chain sprocket is mounted. It feeds drive from the chain to the internal mechanism.

DROP-OUT WIDTH
The distance between the rear fork ends. It should match the hub width or over locknut dimension.

DRUM BRAKE
A brake in which lined brake shoes press against the inside of a drum attached to the wheel. The drum is typically integral with the hub and of larger diameter than the main section of the hub shell. Usually manually operated by a Bowden cable or rod linkage. Also known as an internally expanding brake.

DYNAMO
See GENERATOR below.

END CAM
A cam on the end of a cylinder, designed so that rotation of the cylinder transmits movement, parallel to the axis of the cylinder, to another component.

EPICYCLIC
An adjective describing a system in which a small circle rolls on the circumference of a greater circle. Most hub gears use epicyclic (i.e. planetary motion) gears.

FIELD COILS
Windings of wire around the electro-magnets of a generator.

FIXED-WHEEL
The rear sprocket is fixed rigidly to the wheel; hence it is not possible to stop the pedals turning without stopping the rear wheel. Sometimes two separate words.

## FREEHUB
A freewheel mechanism built into a hub, rather than screwed on, splined to carry a cassette of derailleur sprockets. Freehub is a Shimano-registered trade name but is widely used in a generic sense.

## FREEWHEEL
An automatic mechanism permitting the rider to stop the motion of the pedals at will without stopping the rear wheel from turning. Most freewheels employ a pawl and ratchet mechanism. Sometimes two separate words or hyphenated.

## GEAR TRAIN
A series of interconnected gear wheels. Sometimes hyphenated.

## GEAR RING
An internally toothed gear ring in an epicyclic gear; also known as an annulus.

## GENERATOR
An electrical generator may be an alternator, which produces alternating current, or a dynamo, which produces direct current. However, the term 'dynamo' is commonly used to describe any bicycle generator, although most (including Dynohubs) are actually alternators that do not need the additional complication of a commutator.

## HUB BRAKE
A brake attached to, or integral with, the wheel hub. Hub brakes include drum brakes, band brakes, coaster brakes, roller brakes and disc brakes.

## HUB GEAR
Traditional standard British term for an internally geared hub.

## HUB SHELL
The outer casing of a hub gear or coaster brake.

## HUB WIDTH
The over locknut dimension of a hub, excluding the protruding axle.

## INDICATOR
A device (usually a rod) that indicates when the gear cable is correctly adjusted. Often integral with a toggle chain connecting the gear to the control cable, when it can be described as an indicator coupling.

## INDICATOR COUPLING
A linkage between the axle key and control cable combined with a gear adjustment indicator.

## INTERNALLY EXPANDING BRAKE
See Drum Brake.

## LAYSHAFT
A secondary shaft, usually in a non-epicyclic gearbox, which is neither the input nor output shaft.

## LUG
A projection on a component enabling it to be fixed to another component. For example, most post-WW2 Sturmey-Archer chain sprockets have three semi-circular lugs which engage with three splines on the drive.

## NIG
Abbreviation for 'No Intermediate Gear' or 'No In-between Gear'. It means that, as the control cable moves from one gear position to another, there is no point at which drive is lost or slips. A NIG gear is sometimes referred to as a 'non-slip' gear.

## NON-SLIP
See NIG above.

## OVER LOCKNUT DIMENSION
The hub width, excluding the protruding axle. Abbreviated to OLN.

## OVERRUN
In the context of hub gears, to overrun means to rotate faster than.

## PAWL
A catch (usually spring loaded) which engages with the teeth of a ratchet. In one direction the pawl will lock against the ratchet teeth; in the other it will freely slide over the teeth.

## PINION
A small cog, as in a hub gear.

## PLANET CAGE
A component rotating about the wheel axle and holding a number of planet pinions.

## PLANET PINION
A small cog engaging with a sun pinion and a gear ring.

## RATCHET
The set of teeth with which a pawl engages.

## RATIO
In the context of cycle gearing, the so-called gear ratio is more accurately described as a comparative number. In English-speaking countries, it is usually expressed in terms of the equivalent direct-drive wheel diameter in inches. Thus a 3-speed may give 'ratios' or 'gears' of 48, 64 and 85".

## RETRO-FIT
To fit afterwards, as with a modified component that is retro-fitted to an old machine.

## ROLLER BRAKE
A metal-on-metal hub brake, involving a series of rollers which, when braking, are bunched up to rub on the inside of a brake drum. Typically screwed onto a hub outboard of the spokes.

**SELECTOR SLEEVE**
A clutch actuating device encircling the wheel axle.

**SPINDLE**
A name sometimes used for the wheel axle.

**SPLINES**
Grooves in the wall of a cylinder to enable a component to be fitted to it. Most post-WW2 Sturmey-Archer drivers have splines to engage with lugs on the sprockets.

**SPROCKET**
A cog on the rear wheel on which the drive chain runs.

**STATOR**
The stationary element of an electrical generator or electric motor.

**STUD**
Usually a small axle (e.g. for a planet pinion).

**SUN**
A small pinion meshing with planet pinions that rotate around it in an epicyclic mechanism.

**TOGGLE CHAIN**
The small coupling chain connecting a hub gear control cable to the hub. A widely-used term but never used officially by Sturmey-Archer.

**TOP TUBE**
The so-called cross-bar of a diamond frame bicycle.

**TORQUE**
Rotational force, akin to leverage. Typically expressed in newton metres (N m) or pounds force (lbf).

**TORQUE ARM**
Component anchoring the non-rotating parts of a drum brake or coaster brake to a chainstay or fork blade to prevent undesirable rotation during braking.

**UNIDIRECTIONAL CLUTCH**
A clutch that locks two components together only when moving in one direction (e.g. a freewheel mechanism).

# C. Manufacture

The history of Sturmey-Archer would not be complete without a brief description of how their hub gears were made during much of the twentieth century. The following description is based on a visit by the first author to the Triumph Road, Nottingham works in spring 1985.

The factory produced only a certain number of models from the current range at any one time. These were then passed on to the wholesalers and, by the mid 1980s, the company no longer maintained its own stocks. When the author visited the works, production concentrated on the AW, S5 and AB hubs, these being among the most popular Sturmey-Archer products at the time.

Many of the production techniques employed in 1985 differed little from those used in the early twentieth century. These methods had stood the test of time, as evidenced by the durability and reliability of the product. However, by the 1980s there was some greater automation of production processes.

### Steel hub shells

The main component manufacturing processes could be divided into two classes: pressing and milling/turning. Most of the pressing work involved the manufacture of steel hub shells. Sheet steel in strip form was fed into a machine that stamped out discs of steel sheet about 10" (250 mm) in diameter. Each disc was pressed to the shape of a shallow mug. It was then passed through a series of presses, each time becoming deeper but smaller in diameter. The base of the 'mug' was cut off, leaving an open-ended cylinder; integral flanges were then formed by further pressing.

Hubs with stepped shells, such as those combining a hub brake and gear, were made up of two main sections and separately pressed flanges, which were then joined together.

The 'raw' shells were passed through an automatic machine that trimmed excess metal from the flanges, engraved the scrolled pattern on the shell and cleaned the metal. The shells were then chromium plated.

### Alloy hub shells

In the 1980s some of the most modern machinery at Sturmey-Archer was used for the Elite range of alloy shell hubs. The shells were produced as basic castings by sub-contractors. They were then finished by Sturmey-Archer, using CNC (Computer Numeric Controlled) machinery. This performed all the necessary operations – such as trimming, spoke drilling and polishing – automatically and comparatively cleanly and quietly.

### Small components, axles and gear rings

Many of the small internal components, such as pinion and pawl pins, were manufactured automatically by automatic lathes fed by an arrangement like a Gatling gun. The long rotating 'barrels' contain the raw strips or rods of steel, each of which was fed in turn through the machine.

The more complicated components need an element of human skill and manipulation. One of the more complicated parts was the hollow axle of a 3-speed or 5-speed hub. This was drilled down the centre, slotted (for the axle key or keys) and threaded. The threaded axle ends then had the flats machined to prevent rotation in the stay ends. If the axle was for an

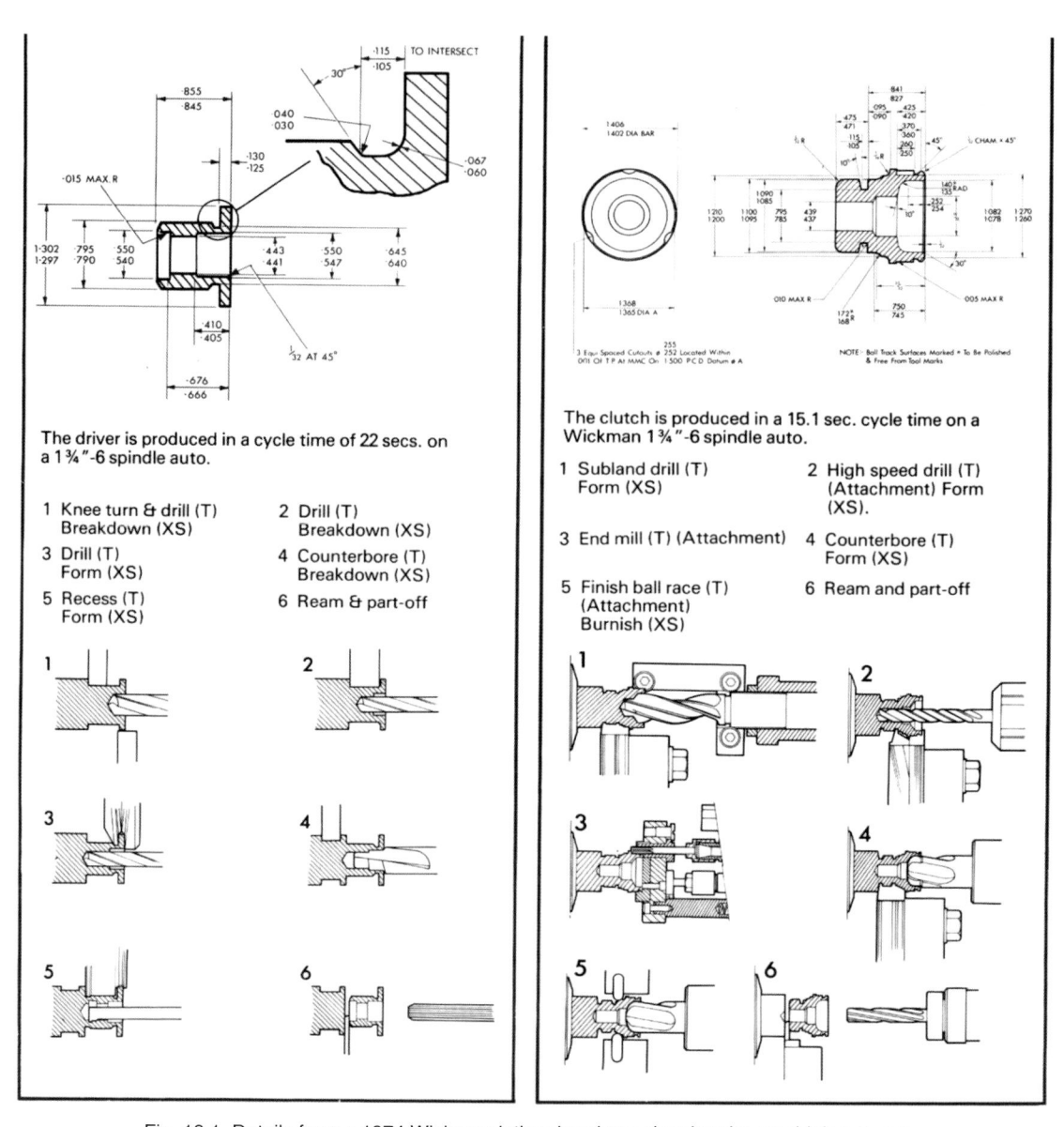

Fig. 18.1. Details from a 1974 Wickman lathes brochure showing the machining stages of a Sturmey-Archer driver and a clutch.

AW 3-speed, a rivet hole was drilled to enable fixing of the sun pinion; if it was for an S5 5-speed, sun clutch dogs were cut from a bulge in the centre of the axle.

Another complicated component was the gear ring. This started as a short length of heavy rod. It was cold forged to form a crude indentation that became the inside of the gear ring. The component was then progressively machined until it assumed its complicated final form, complete with gear teeth and pawl housings.

Internal components subjected to high stresses were case-hardened by heat treatment, which carbonised the exterior of the steel. (At one time case hardening was done by dipping the components in molten cyanide.)

Sprockets were pressed in two stages: first to achieve the basic shape, secondly to chamfer the edges of the teeth. Major sub-assemblies, such as hub brake mechanisms, were assembled at static work stations. Likewise the toggle chain/indicator assemblies; these were manually assembled in jigs and then machine riveted.

Final assembly took place on moving production lines.

## D. Efficiency

Efficiency tests have been carried out on hub gears since the early 1900s. For example, in 1982 Sturmey-Archer tested six new AWs three times each. The results averaged out at 93.8% for low, 96.3% for normal and 92.5% for high gear. Most tests on wide-ratio 3-speeds have given similar results, give or take a percentage point or two.

In 2000 Frank Berto and Dr Chester Kyle carried out a series of rigorous tests in California on a variety of hub gears by Sturmey-Archer, Sachs, Shimano and Rohloff, on a 27-speed Shimano derailleur gear-train, and on 4-speed and 12-speed Browning automatic swinging-gate derailleurs. The frictional losses measured included the bottom bracket, the wheel bearings and an extra chain drive to the dynamometer to measure the power output. Note that some other efficiency tests may give higher results because they do not include all these losses.

The headline findings were:

- 3-speed hubs in direct drive middle gear are typically about 95% efficient, almost as good as a single speed.
- 3-speed hubs in high or low gear typically range from 92% efficiency at 100 watts input to 93% at 200 watts.
- Derailleurs typically range from 92.5% efficiency at 100 watts to 94% at 200 watts.
- Hub gears with more than three speeds tend to be significantly less efficient: 7-speed hubs averaged 85% at 100 watts and 93% at 200 watts.

Other noteworthy points were:

- Hubs that are well run-in tend to be more efficient.
- Light oil rather than 'greased for life' lubrication improves efficiency.
- Sprockets smaller than 15 tooth are less efficient by as much as 2%.
- Precision manufacture improves efficiency, as in the very expensive Rohloff 14-speed hub, which was significantly more efficient than the 7-speed hubs.

For more on this topic, see Frank Berto's paper 'Hub Gear versus Derailleur Efficiency' in *Cycle History 12: Proceedings of the 12th International Cycling History Conference.* Cycle Publishing, San Francisco, 2001.

# E. Derailleur converters

The former technical officer of the Cyclists' Touring Club, Chris Juden, neatly summed up hybrid gearing when he wrote:

> The combination of hub and derailleur gearing known as hybrid gearing certainly appeals to a number of cyclists. Although combining the mechanical losses of the former with those due to out of line running and vulnerability of the latter, it does facilitate a wide range of gears without resorting to front derailleurs or horribly dished wheels.

### Fichtel & Sachs hybrid gears
In the 1980s Sturmey-Archer's German rival, Fichtel & Sachs, sold a version of their 3-speed coaster complete with a pair of sprockets for use with the Sachs-Sport rear derailleur mechanism. About 1990 they introduced a 2-speed hub gear for use with 5, 6 or 7 derailleur sprockets – the Sachs Orbit. They went on to make 3-speed hubs combined with freehubs toa take 7, 8 or 9 sprockets. – the SRAM Dual Drive. But Sturmey-Archer never marketed a hybrid hub until after the move to Taiwan, when they produced hubs similar to the Dual Drive.

### La Gauloise
During the twentieth century various firms and individual engineers produced derailleur converters to allow multiple sprockets to be used with a Sturmey-Archer hub gear. An early example was the Saint-Étienne cycle maker La Gauloise, who in the 1920s offered conversion kits to turn a 3-speed hub into a 6-speed or a 9-speed by adding a 2-speed or 3-speed rear derailleur.

### Cyclo
The Cyclo Gear Company of Birmingham had French origins and produced converters for many years. They took the form of two-sprocket or three-sprocket clusters to fit on the driver of a Sturmey-Archer hub. Until the 1980s, Cyclo converters were produced only for use with ⅛" chains but by the mid 1980s there was also a 3/32" option.

In the 1960s Cyclo made a 2-speed converter with 13 and 15 tooth sprockets for Moulton bicycles. This was an option offered on the Moulton Safari touring machine for use with an FW 4-speed hub to give eight speeds. In the 1980s the smallest Cyclo converter had 16 and 22 teeth. There was also a 19 and 22 tooth unit and another with 16, 19 and 23 teeth.

The units simply clipped onto the driver in place of the original single sprocket and spacing washers. It was best to use a hub gear fitted with a long axle and Cyclo recommended fitting a ⅛" (3 mm) washer to each side of the axle to prevent the chain fouling the seat stay.

Although Raleigh and Sturmey-Archer never sold Cyclo converters in the UK, in the 1960s Raleigh Industries of America did.

### Back-to-back sprockets
A ⅛" chain derailleur converter could also be constructed by using two dished Sturmey-Archer sprockets placed back-to-back (without sprocket spacer washers) on a three-splined driver. To get the necessary chain clearance on the smaller sprocket, both sprockets needed to be fairly large and not too different in size.

Alternatively, a pair of screw-on fixed-wheel sprockets could be mounted back-to-back on one of the old-style threaded drivers. Again, some experimentation could be necessary to get chain clearance.

### Lauterwasser
In the 1970s an ingenious 2-speed lightweight converter was produced in very limited numbers by Jack Lauterwasser, a connoisseur of hybrid gearing. This used 3/32" Maillard Helicomatic derailleur sprockets and could accommodate very different sizes (e.g. 14 and 28 tooth). The whole converter, complete with sprockets, weighed about the same as the largest Sturmey-Archer sprocket.

### Rogers
A number of engineers have produced converters by brazing derailleur blocks onto Sturmey-Archer drivers. In the early 1980s Ernest Rogers of Burbank, California marketed a 5-speed derailleur converter based on a Regina block. A 6¼" (159 mm) or longer axle was required to accommodate the five Regina sprockets. This unit fouled the flange of old style Sturmey-Archer ball rings but Rogers offered to machine the flange off for a modest fee.

### Wodschow
In the 1970s and 1980s Finn Wodschow of Copenhagen supplied a Danish converter that accepted four standard Sun Tour New Winner derailleur sprockets. This converter was used, in conjunction with a 5-speed Sturmey-Archer hub, by two Scandinavian round-the-world cyclists at a time when cycle circumnavigation was relatively unusual.

### Dacon
In the 1980s Dave Connley of Dacon Engineering in Sheffield produced several derailleur converters. The original version accommodated four Sun Tour New Winner sprockets, ranging in size from 15 to 32 teeth. This converter required the Sturmey-Archer hub to have a 6¼" (159 mm) or longer axle, and the rear dropout width (over locknut dimension) needed to be at least 4½" (114 mm).

Dacon's two later converters were replacement drivers. One was designed for use with the standard (short) hub gear axles and a narrow dropout width; it could accommodate three sprockets ranging from 14 to 32 teeth. The other replacement driver was intended primarily for use with small-wheeled bicycles. Like the original Dacon converter, it required a longer axle and wider dropout width but could accommodate four sprockets ranging in size from 12 to 32 teeth. However, if the rider was content with only three sprockets, the unit could be used on a standard axle in narrow dropouts. In this case the smallest sprocket that could be accommodated was 13 tooth.

Dave Connley ingeniously suggested using the 'no gear' position between high and normal gear to enable changing the derailleur gear while the cycle was stationary. He also advocated the use with his converters of an S5/2 hub gear as an ultra-wide-ratio 3-speed, by omitting the left-hand changer, cable and indicator/toggle chain. He referred to an S5/2 thus modified as an S3. This idea anticipated the later ultra-wide-ratio 3-speed made by Sturmey-Archer for Brompton to use with their 2-speed derailleur.

Although Dave Connley no longer sells converters, he was still experimenting with hybrid gearing in 2014.

# F. Dating Sturmey-Archer hubs

Vince Warner of Colwood Wheel Works estimates that pre-1930 serial numbers on Sturmey-Archer hubs can be used to deduce the year of manufacture (plus or minus one year) as follows:

| Year | Serial numbers |
|---|---|
| 1921 | ??–25000 |
| 1922 | 25000–75000 |
| 1923 | 75000–150000 |
| 1924 | 150000–250000 |
| 1925 | 250000–375000 |
| 1926 | 375000–515000 |
| 1927 | 515000–670000 |
| 1928 | 670000–840000 |
| 1929 | 840000–854620 or higher |

It may be that once 999999 was reached the company decided to introduce an alphabetical year code, as hubs made circa 1930-31 are marked with an 'A'. If so they did not stick with it, because from 1932-1939 they used a numerical code: the model designation letters are followed by a single digit indicating the year (e.g. KS4 indicates a KS hub made in 1934).

Hubs made during WW2 do not have dates. Production stopped from 1941 until the end of the war. Hubs and components were stockpiled, with no certainty as to when they would be put on sale. The company probably wanted to avoid marketing products that indicated they had been in storage for some years.

From 1947 to 2000, hubs were stamped with the last two digits of the year followed by the month (e.g. 53 10 indicates October 1953).

However, there are exceptions to the above numbering schemes. Undated hubs from various periods are sometimes found. Also, impossible dates, such as a month 13, have been seen. Explanations may include human error, laziness and mischief making.

Production date codes for Taiwanese production are shown in the table opposite.

| First Code | To Year | 2nd Code | To Month | 3rd Code | to Day |
|---|---|---|---|---|---|
| A | 2001 | A | 1 | A1 | 1 |
| B | 2002 | B | 2 | A2 | 2 |
| C | 2003 | C | 3 | A3 | 3 |
| D | 2004 | D | 4 | A4 | 4 |
| E | 2005 | E | 5 | A5 | 5 |
| F | 2006 | F | 6 | A6 | 6 |
| G | 2007 | G | 7 | A7 | 7 |
| H | 2008 | H | 8 | A8 | 8 |
| I | 2009 | I | 9 | A9 | 9 |
| J | 2010 | J | 10 | B0 | 10 |
| K | 2011 | K | 11 | B1 | 11 |
| L | 2012 | L | 12 | B2 | 12 |
| M | 2013 | | | B3 | 13 |
| N | 2014 | | | B4 | 14 |
| O | 2015 | | | B5 | 15 |
| P | 2016 | | | B6 | 16 |
| Q | 2017 | | | B7 | 17 |
| R | 2018 | | | B8 | 18 |
| S | 2019 | | | B9 | 19 |
| T | 2020 | | | C0 | 20 |
| U | 2021 | | | C1 | 21 |
| V | 2022 | | | C2 | 22 |
| W | 2023 | | | C3 | 23 |
| X | 2024 | | | C4 | 24 |
| Y | 2025 | | | C5 | 25 |
| Z | 2026 | | | C6 | 26 |
| | | | | C7 | 27 |
| | | | | C8 | 28 |
| | | | | C9 | 29 |
| | | | | D0 | 30 |
| | | | | D1 | 31 |

Example
4/9/02     =     BDA9

Fig. 18.2 Production date codes for hubs made in Taiwan.

# G. Triggers, 1938 to 1960

**Sturmey-Archer Trigger Shifters 1938-1960** by Martin Hanczyc
3 November 2004

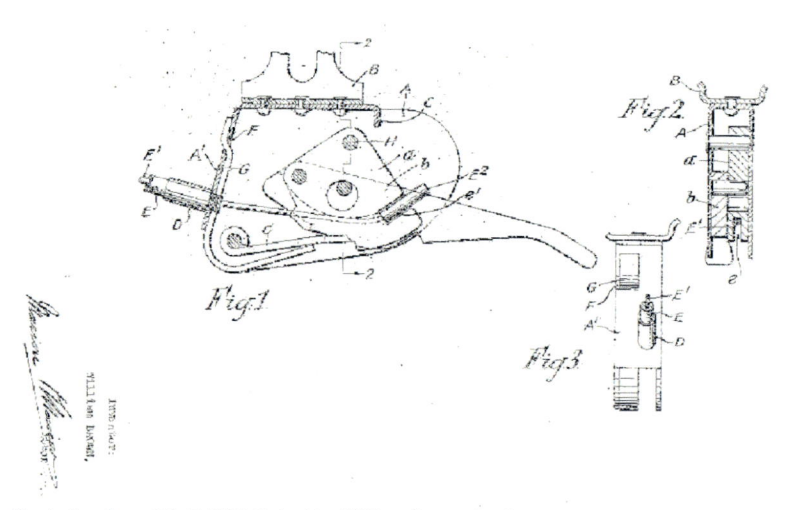

Illustration from CA 491915 Patent by William Brown for Sturmey-Archer Gears Limited 1953

**Purpose:**
My 1950 Maclean Featherweight with a Sturmey-Archer FM hub came with an incorrect trigger. I wanted to install a period-correct trigger and so this investigation began. I present my results as a chronological and descriptive listing of Sturmey-Archer triggers for those who might find this information useful. Even though I rejected any information without documentation and I cite my sources, I do not claim the information is all correct or complete. I welcome any comments, information or contributions. The list covers the period from 1938 to 1960 with an addendum of post-1960 examples.

**Indexed Shifting:**
Sturmey-Archer trigger shifters represent an early embodiment of indexed shifting. Shifting was effected with one finger, and with proper adjustment the correct gear was found instantly, every time. The essential design of these triggers remained constant over many decades. Therefore they can be interchanged for use with many models of Sturmey-Archer hubs (with the exception of the ASC), and also with hubs from different eras. As a consequence newer triggers sometimes can be found on older bikes, as replacements were needed. Here is an attempt to properly designate the years for which a certain style of trigger was produced. Many of these triggers from my workshop are well used and the illustrations may be replaced as I come across cleaner examples. Many thanks to P.C. Kohler for allowing me to use some pretty pictures from the now defunct Roll Britannia archives and to Chris Barbour for proof reading, suggestions and samples.

**Sources:**
Raleigh The All-Steel Bicycle catalogue, 1947.
The Sturmey-Archer service manual, 1948, 1951 and 1956.
Rudge Bicycles catalogue, 1949.
Luxury Cycling by Raleigh catalogue, 1951.
Raleigh The All-Steel Bicycle for Luxury Cycling catalogue, 1951.
Raleigh The All-Steel Bicycle USA catalogue, 1954.
Humber Bicycles catalogue, 1955
Spare Parts List for Sturmey-Archer Gear Hubs, Brake Hubs and Dynohubs, 1956.
The Sturmey Archer Story by Tony Hadland, Pinkerton Press. 1987

A precursor to the trigger shifter is the quadrant shifter (GC1). This typically was used for the Sturmey-Archer K series hubs. It had three positions Low, N (Normal) and High. It was mounted on the top tube.

Model GC3. The first trigger. 1938-48. For three speed Sturmey-Archer hubs, with original patent number 498820 and long handle, The trigger was made for below the handle bar mounting with the print facing away from the rider. The four-speed version (not shown) is GC4.

The Model GC2 - used with three and four-speed Sturmey-Archer hubs from 1948-1953. Although the design on the medallion (face plate) of the triggers changed over time, they all were designated GC2 as they had the same internal parts. This style looks like the 'improved design' described in patent number 649009, however early examples display only the original patent number 498820. Later examples of the GC2 listed below have a window in the medallion. Interestingly, although the print on the medallion indicates below the bar mounting, the gear designation in the window is the opposite – for above the bar viewing. Model GC2A is for ASC hubs only as indicted on the medallion.

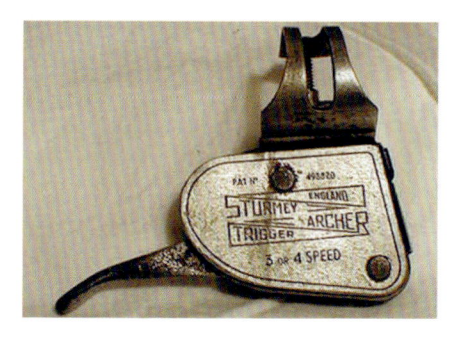

Model GC2.
Introduced 1948-9 for 3 or 4 speed hubs with original patent number 498820.

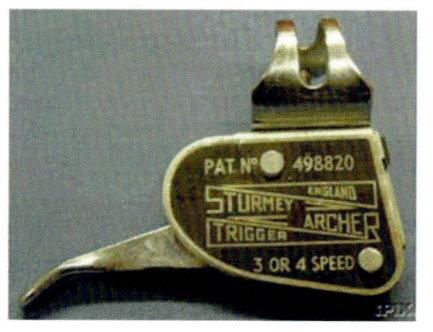

Model GC2.
1948-9. Same as above except with different font and finish on the medallion.

Model GC2.
1950-3 Trigger for 3 or 4 speed, with window showing the gear - B (base), L (low), N (normal), or H (high) - and original patent number 498820. "Pat Nº." switched to "PAT G.B."
**STURMEY ARCHER** in red lettering.

Model GC2.
1950-3. Variant of the above with STURMEY ARCHER in black lettering. Note that the writing on the medallion specifies below the handle bar mounting, but the letter in the gear window (L) is inverted for viewing above the bar.

In 1953, triggers were redesigned for either three speed hubs or four speed hubs (not both as above) and were designated model GC3A or GC4A respectively. These now carry the improved design patent number 649009.

Model GC3A.
1953-56. Designed for a 3-speed with original patent number 498820 and improved design patent number 649009.

Model GC3A.
1953-56. An interesting variant that has the internals for four speeds (note the trigger is shown in base gear), but the medallion specifies three speed meaning low, normal and high. Perhaps this is a transition trigger from GC2 to GC3A or made with stock parts from the GC4A (below). **Courtesy of C. Barbour**

Model GC3A.
1953-56. 3-speed trigger with window as above but with different coloration and font size. Larger font as pictured in the 1954 Raleigh and 1955 Humber catalogues.

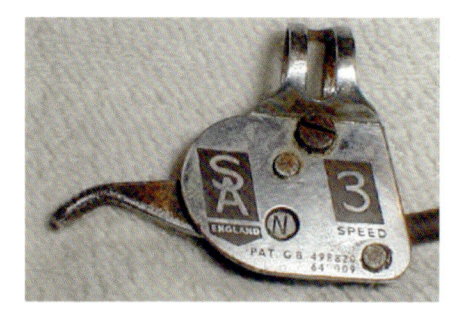

Model GC3A.
1953-56. Yet another variant. This one has the fixing bolt through a smaller body as found on my 1956 Raleigh Sports with SW hub. This trigger displays features of both model GC3A and its successor, model GC3B.

Model GC4A.
1953-56. Designed for a 4-speed with both patent numbers as illustrated in Tony Hadland's book, The Sturmey-Archer Story.

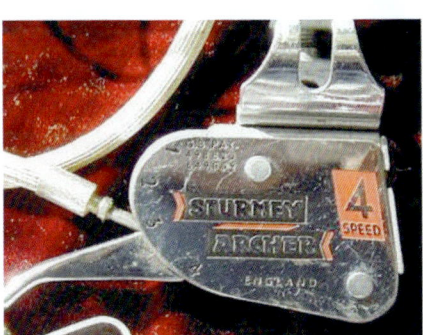

Model GC3B.
1956 - ? was designed for three-speed hubs without a window in the medallion. Note fixing bolt goes through medallion as on later models with plastic cover. Both patent numbers included.

Model GC4B.
1956 - ? Designed for four-speed hubs without a window in the medallion.

1960. Included are a few examples of the evolution of the Sturmey-Archer trigger; the years of manufacture are estimated from the catalogues and some period correct examples of cycles. At some point in the 1960's the below-the-bar orientation of the trigger was inverted for above the bar usage as in all the examples below. In addition the patent numbers were no longer included on the trigger medallion. Later triggers were introduced with plastic parts as some examples below illustrate.

**Sources:**
Raleigh goes places in 1962 catalogue
Raleigh lightweight bicycles 1974 catalogue
Raleigh lightweight bicycles 1976 catalogue

A common three speed trigger for above the bar mounting and fixing screw through body; in use until around 1966.

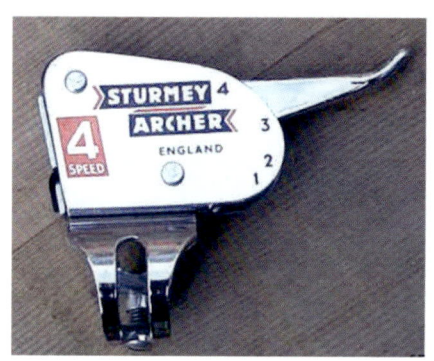

A four-speed trigger for above the bar mounting similar to the trigger above without the fixing screw through body design.

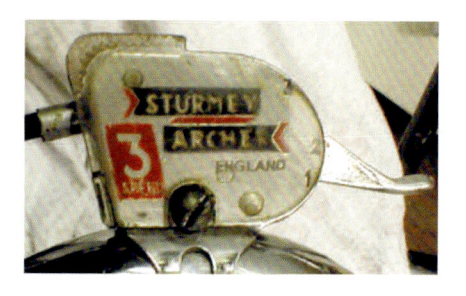

Trigger with plastic cover. The design is similar to the triggers above but the print is located on the plastic cover and not the medallion. Fixing screw through body. Introduced after 1966.

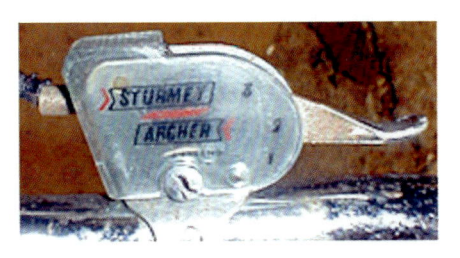

A version with plastic cover but without the large red 3 speed label was in use from approximately 1971 until the mid-1970s.

Another trigger with more plastic parts. Fixing screw through body. Introduced in the early 1970s.

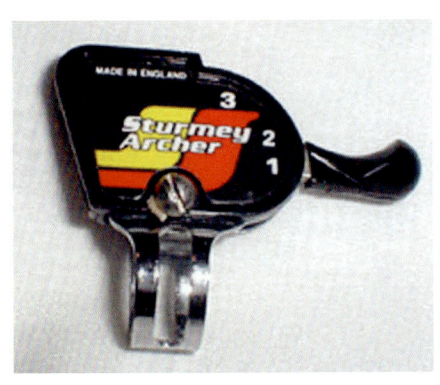

Yet another trigger with more plastic parts. Fixing screw through body. Introduced in 1976.

Postscript: During the 1950s Hercules hubs were produced which were Sturmey-Archer AW clones. Here is an example of a Her-cu-matic gear control made for three-speed Hercules hubs circa 1958. Note that it displays the same Sturmey-Archer patent numbers.

# H. Sources

**The main information sources for this book are:**

- The Raleigh archives (including Sturmey-Archer) held by Nottinghamshire Archives. These are categorised as follows:
    DD/RN/1 Minutes and Annual Reports
    DD/RN/2 Returns, Certificates, etc.
    DD/RN/3 Financial Records
    DD/RN/4 Advertising, Marketing and Promotional Material
    DD/RN/5 Press cuttings
    DD/RN/6 Photographs and Negatives
    DD/RN/7 Cycling History
    DD/RN/8 Publications
    DD/RN/9 Production and Design Records
    DD/RN/10 Legal Records
    DD/RN/11 Administration/Personnel
    DD/RN/12 Social and Staff Events
    DD/RN/13 Buildings and Construction
    DD/RN/14 Films

- A detailed catalogue of these records is accessible online via The National Archives Discovery search engine.

- Patents cited in the text, generally accessed on line via Espacenet. Most patents quoted in the text are British but in many cases there were versions issued in other jurisdictions, especially the USA, major European countries and more recently the Far East.

- The Sturmey-Archer Heritage collection, assembled and curated by Alan Clarke of Sun Race Sturmey-Archer (available online).

- Sturmey-Archer product literature and press cuttings collected and curated by the Veteran-Cycle Club Library (available online).

- Sturmey-Archer product literature and press cuttings collected by the late Denis Watkins.

- Sturmey-Archer product literature and press cuttings collected by Tony Hadland, some of which is now held by the National Cycling Archive at Warwick University.

- *Purchasing Power of British Pounds from 1270 to Present*, MeasuringWorth.

**The main additional sources per chapter are as follows:**

## Chapter 1: The Crypto principle
a. Logos. *Variable Gears*. London, 1908.
b. Variable Speed Gears. *Cycling*, 3 October 1903.

c. F.R. Whitt. 'Some Hub Gear History'. *The Boneshaker*, No. 86, Southern Veteran-Cycle Club, 1977.
  d. *Variable-Speed Gears*. Seabrook Brothers, 1905.
  e. Catalogues and other publicity material produced by the Crypto Cycle Company (1891-97).
  f. Patents cited in the text.

## Chapter 2: William Reilly and the Hub
  a. 'Variable Speed Gears'. *Cycling*, 3 October 1903.
  b. 'Variable Gears Described – The Variable Gears of Today'. *Cycling*, 20 February 1907.
  c. 'Variable Gears Described – A review of all makes of variable gears'. *Cycling*, 19 February 1908.
  d. J.J.H. Sturmey. 'Variable Gearing'. *Proceedings of the Cycle Engineers' Institute*, 1902.
  e. A.B. Demaus. 'Some Engineers' Comments on Cycle Variable Gears'. *The Boneshaker,* No. 103, Southern Veteran-Cycle Club, 1983.
  f. A.B. Demaus. 'An Aviator's Cycle'. *The Boneshaker,* No. 104, Southern Veteran-Cycle Club, 1983.
  g. F.R. Whitt. 'Variable Gears; Some Basic Ergonomics and Mechanics'. *Developing Pedal Power*, The Open University, 1978.
  h. Archibald Sharp. *Bicycles and Tricycles: An Elementary Treatise on their Design and Construction*, London, 1896.
  i. 'Stanley Show'. *The Cyclist and Bicycling and Tricycling Trades Review*, London, 27 November 1901.
  j. Logos. *Variable Gears*. London, 1908.
  k. Patents cited in the text.
  l. Reilly family history research by Mr A.D. Dorsey of Hull, 2001.

## Chapter 3: Archer's involvement
  a. *50 Years of Leadership*. Raleigh, Nottingham, 1952.
  b. F.T. Bidlake. 'Currente Calamo'. *Cyclists' Touring Club Gazette and Record*, December 1902.
  c. A.B. Demaus. 'Some Engineer's Comments on Cycle Variable Gears'. *The Boneshaker*, No. 103, Southern Veteran-Cycle Club, 1983.
  d. The original correspondence on which c. above was based.
  e. H. Walter Staner. 'Variable Speed Gears'. *The Cyclist & Bicycling & Tricycling Trades Review*, 19 June 1901.
  f. H. Walter Staner. 'Combined Free-wheels and Variable Speed Gears'. *The Cyclist & Bicycling & Tricycling Trades Review*, 3 July 1901.
  g. Patents cited in the text.

## Chapter 4: Sturmey's contribution
  a. 'Mr H. Sturmey, Cycle and Motor Industry Pioneer'. *Coventry Herald*, 10 January, 1930.
  b. 'Death of Mr Henry J. Sturmey. A Pioneer of the Cycle and Motor Industries'. *Coventry Standard*, 10 January 1930.
  c. Henry Sturmey. 'Variable Gearing'. *Proceedings of the Cycle Engineers' Institute*, 1902.

## Chapter 5: The 'Sturmey-Archer-Reilly-Mills-Pellant' gear
  a. F.T. Bidlake. 'Currente Calamo'. *Cyclists' Touring Club Gazette and Record*, December 1902.
  b. A.B. Demaus. 'Some Engineers' Comments on Cycle Variable Gears'. *The Boneshaker* No. 103, Southern Veteran-Cycle Club, 1983.
  c. The original correspondence on which b. above was based.

d. *Cycling*, 3 October 1903.
  e. Raleigh company minutes held by Nottinghamshire Archives.
  f. Patents cited in the text.
  g. Census records.

## Chapter 6: Reilly at Nottingham
  a. H. Walter Staner. 'Review of First Sturmey-Archer Three-speed'. *The Cyclist*, 19 November 1902.
  b. Archibald Sharp. 'Notes and Comments on the Shows'. *Cyclists' Touring Club Gazette and Record*, January 1903.
  c. Major article on hub gears. *Cycling*, 3 October 1903.
  d. Midlander. 'The Trade and the Variable Gear Movement'. *Cycling*, 20 February 1907.
  e. 'Variable Gears Described – The Variable Gears of Today'. *Cycling*, 20 February 1907.
  f. F.T. Bidlake. 'Current Comments'. *Cyclists' Touring Club Gazette and Record*, January 1908, July 1909, September 1909, October 1909.
  g. 'Variable Gears Described – A review of all makes of variable gears'. *Cycling*, 19 February 1908.
  h. The Owl. 'How Variable Gears are Made'. *Cycling*, 8 April 1908.
  i. Robin Hood. 'Land's End to John O' Groats Record'. *Cycling*, 5 August 1908.
  j. F.T. Bidlake. 'Tandems, Tricycles, Tyres, Gears and Accessories'. *Cyclists' Touring Club Gazette and Record*, December 1909.
  k. 'Hints on the Selection of a Suitable Variable Gear'. *Cycling*, London, 10 February 1909.
  l. A.B. Demaus. 'Some Engineers' Comments on Cycle Variable Gears'. *The Boneshaker*, No. 103, Southern Veteran-Cycle Club, 1983.
  m. The original correspondence on which l. above was based.
  n. F.R. Whitt. 'Some Hub Gear History'. *The Boneshaker*, No. 86, Southern Veteran-Cycle Club, 1977.
  o. *Variable Gears and all about them.* Cycling Penny Handbook Number 2, c.1903.
  p. P.M. Read. *Sturmey-Archer: the first 90 years – exploded hub gear drawings,* (2nd edition). Milton Keynes, 1994.
  q. Gerry Beardshaw. *Hub Record*. Duplicated list by former Technical Director. Sturmey-Archer, 1984.
  r. 'Logos'. *Variable Gears*. W.A. Standring, London, 1908.
  s. *50 Years of Leadership*. Raleigh, 1952.
  t. I.C. Cohen. Letter about ball bearing planet pinions, *CTC Gazette*, May 1952.
  u. Raleigh and Sturmey-Archer company minutes held by Nottinghamshire Archives.
  v. Patents cited in the text.

## Chapter 7: A motorcycle excursion
  a. Gerry Beardshaw. *Hub Record*. Duplicated list by former Technical Director. Sturmey-Archer, 1984.
  b. A.B. Demaus. 'Some Engineers' Comments on Cycle Variable Gears'. *The Boneshaker*, No. 103, Southern Veteran-Cycle Club, 1983.
  c. The original correspondence on which d. above was based.
  d. Roger Lloyd-Jones & M.J. Lewis. *Raleigh and the British Cycle Industry*, Aldershot, 2000.
  e. Sturmey-Archer advertisements. *Motor Cycling*, 1 December 1914, 15 December 1914, 14 December 1915.
  f. 'Sturmey-Archer Gears; Part 1 – Design, Construction and Action'. *Machinery*, 21 May 1914.
  g. *Sturmey-Archer Three Speed Gears for Cycles and Motor Cycles*. Catalogue, Sturmey-Archer, c. 1913.

h.  Raleigh and Sturmey-Archer company minutes held by Nottinghamshire Archives.
i.  Patents cited in the text.
j.  Census information.

## Chapter 8: Competition and war
a.  Henry Sturmey. 'Variable Gearing'. *Proceedings of the Cycle Engineers' Institute*, 1902.
b.  'Variable Speed Gears'. *Cycling*, 3 October 1903.
c.  F.R. Whitt. 'Variable Gears: Some Basic Ergonomics and Mechanics'. *Developing Pedal Power*. The Open University, 1978.
d.  A.B. Demaus. 'Some Engineers' Comments on Cycle Variable Gears', *The Boneshaker*, No. 103, Southern Veteran-Cycle Club, 1983.
e.  The original correspondence on which d. above was based.
f.  'Variable Gears Described – The Variable Gears of Today'. *Cycling*, 20 February 1907.
g.  'Variable Gears Described – A review of all makes of variable gears'. *Cycling*, 19 February 1908.
h.  'Variable Gears Described – A Review of all Makes of Multi-speed Gears'. *Cycling*, 10 February 1908.
i.  *Hints to Users of the Sturmey-Archer 3-Speed Gear*. The Three Speed Gear Syndicate Limited, c. 1907.
j.  *All about the Sturmey-Archer 3-Speed Gear*. The Three Speed Gear Syndicate, c. 1907.
k.  *Variable Gears and all about them*. Cycling Penny Handbook No. 2, London, c. 1909.
l.  F.T. Bidlake. 'A Four-Speed Hub'. *Cyclists' Touring Club Gazette and Record*, October 1912.
m.  Franz Maria Feldhaus, Dr. Ing.h.c. *Vom Laufrad zur Freilaufnabe*. Fichtel & Sachs AG, Schweinfurt, c.1915?
n.  *Die Fichtel & Sachs Wurde*. Fichtel & Sachs AG, Schweinfurt, c. l941?
o.  'Logos'. *Variable Gears*. W.A. Standring, London, 1908.
p.  Roger Lloyd-Jones & M.J. Lewis. *Raleigh and the British Cycle Industry*. Aldershot, 2000.
q.  Gregory Houston Bowden. *The Raleigh Cycle*. W.H. Allen, London, 1975.
r.  Tony Hadland & Hans-Erhard Lessing. *Bicycle Design: an illustrated history*. MIT Press, Cambridge MA, 2014.
s.  Raleigh and Sturmey-Archer company minutes held by Nottinghamshire Archives.
t.  Patents cited in the text.

## Chapter 9: Conservative consolidation
a.  Gerry Beardshaw. *Hub Record*. List by former Technical Director, Sturmey-Archer, 1984.
b.  'Our Point of View – Future of Variable Gearing'. *Cycling*, 2 May 1924.
c.  Henry Sturmey. 'Variable Gearing: Its Origin, Development and Future'. *Cycling*, 2 May 1924.
d.  'Correspondence'. *CTC Gazette*, May 1924; January 1925; February 1925; June 1925.
e.  Henry Sturmey. 'Improving the Bicycle'. *CTC Gazette*, October 1926.
f.  Micrometer. 'Servicing the Sturmey-Archer Three-Speed Cycle Hub'. *The Motor Cycle and Cycle Trader*, 1 November 1929.
g.  *Sturmey-Archer 3-Speed Gears –Types K, KS & KSW*. Booklet, Sturmey-Archer, April 1935.
h.  A.B. Demaus. 'Some Engineers' Comments on Cycle Variable Gears'. *The Boneshaker*, No. 103, Southern Veteran-Cycle Club, 1983.
i.  The original correspondence on which h. above was based.
j.  *General Cycle Catalogue No. 374*. Brown Brothers Limited, 1934.
k.  P.M. Read. *Sturmey-Archer: the first 90 years – exploded hub gear drawings*, (2nd edition). Milton Keynes, 1994.
l.  Jim Gill. Unpublished detailed hub gear analysis, 2001 and earlier.

m. *Souvenir of the Raleigh Works*, Raleigh, 1922.
   n. Roger Lloyd-Jones & M.J. Lewis. *Raleigh and the British Cycle Industry*. Aldershot, 2000.
   o. Raleigh and Sturmey-Archer company minutes held by Nottinghamshire Archives.
   p. Patents cited in the text.

## Chapter 10: The Hub of the Universe
   a. *Three-Speed Gears*. Booklet. Sturmey-Archer, 1935.
   b. *Hub Gears and Hub Brakes*. Booklet. Sturmey-Archer, Nottingham, 1937.
   c. *Hubs for the Tandem Rider*. Booklet. Sturmey-Archer, c.1934.
   d. *Two-Speed Hubs*. Booklet. Sturmey-Archer, 1938.
   e. *New Range of 3-Speed Hubs*. Booklet. Sturmey-Archer c.1937.
   f. *Types AB, BF and BR*. Booklet. Sturmey-Archer, c.1937.
   g. *4-Speed Hub Gears – Speed with Ease*. Leaflet. Sturmey-Archer, c.1939.
   h. *4-Speed Hub Gears*. Booklet. Sturmey-Archer, c.1939.
   i. Nimrod. 'Sturmey-Archer New 4-Speed Medium-Ratio Hub Gear'. *Cycling*, 8 November 1939.
   j. *Service Manual for Sturmey-Archer Variable Hub Gears, Brake Hubs and Dynohubs*. Sturmey-Archer, c.1948.
   k. 'Sturmey-Archer Introduce New Hub: Close-ratio, Two-Speed Fixed Gear'. *The Cyclist*, 22 July 1936.
   l. 'We Call on the Trade: S.A. Top-Tube Control'. *Cycling*, 7 February 1940.
   m. Gerry Beardshaw. *Hub Record*. List by former Technical Director, Sturmey-Archer, 1984.
   n. Frank Berto, *The Dancing Chain* (3rd edition). Cycle Publishing, San Francisco, 2009.
   o. P.M. Read. *Sturmey-Archer: the first 90 years – exploded hub gear drawings*, (2nd edition). Milton Keynes, 1994.
   p. Jim Gill. Unpublished detailed hub gear analysis, 2001 and earlier.
   q. Raleigh and Sturmey-Archer company minutes held by Nottinghamshire Archives.
   r. Patents cited in the text.

## Chapter 11: War and peace
   a. *FW Wide Ratio 4-Speed Hub Gear*. Booklet. Sturmey-Archer, Nottingham, c.1946.
   b. 'The Servicing and Maintenance of the Raleigh Dynohub'. *Motor Cycle and Cycle Trader*, 22 August 1941.
   c. *Maintenance Instructions and Spare Parts List for the Patent 6 Volt Dynohub, Dynothree and Dyno-Luxe*'. Booklet. Raleigh, May 1946.
   d. *Sturmey-Archer – The Original and Unrivalled 3 & 4-Speed Gears*. Fold-out leaflet. Raleigh, c.1947.
   e. *Sturmey-Archer – The Original Manufacturers of Wide, Medium and Close-Ratio Gears and Hub Brakes*. Fold-out leaflet. Raleigh, c.1948.
   f. Mark Hunt. 'The 32H GH6 Dynohub'. *SA Technical Library, Bulletin No. 14*, Bakersfield, California, January 1984.
   g. *Service Manual for Sturmey-Archer Variable Hub Gears, Brake Hubs and Dynohubs*. Sturmey-Archer, c.1950.
   h. *Spare Parts List for Sturmey-Archer Gear Hubs, Brake Hubs and Dynohubs*. Sturmey-Archer, c.1951 and 1952.
   i. *Master Catalogue*. Sturmey-Archer, August 1956.
   j. Nimrod. 'A Bicycle 5-Speed Gear'. *Cycling*, 1 May 1940.
   k. Cotter Pin. 'New Sturmey-Archer Four'. *The Bicycle*, 7 February 1945.
   l. Gerry Beardshaw. *Hub Record*. List by former Technical Director, Sturmey-Archer, 1984.

- m. Frank Berto, *The Dancing Chain* (3rd edition). Cycle Publishing, San Francisco, 2009.
- n. P.M. Read. *Sturmey-Archer: the first 90 years – exploded hub gear drawings,* (2nd edition). Milton Keynes, 1994.
- o. Jim Gill. Unpublished detailed hub gear analysis, 2001 and earlier.
- p. Raleigh and Sturmey-Archer company minutes held by Nottinghamshire Archives.
- q. Patents cited in the text.

## Chapter 12: From jubilation to rationalisation

- a. *50 Years of Leadership*. Raleigh, Nottingham, 1952.
- b. *Master Catalogue*. Sturmey-Archer, 1956.
- c. *Spare Parts List for Sturmey-Archer Gear Hubs, Brake Hubs and Dynohubs*. Sturmey-Archer, c.1951 and 1952.
- d. *Service Manual for Sturmey-Archer Variable Hub Gears, Brake Hubs and Dynohubs*. Sturmey-Archer, c.1950.
- e. *Sturmey-Archer – The Original and Unrivalled 3 & 4-Speed Gears*. Leaflet. Raleigh, c.1947.
- f. *Sturmey-Archer – The Original Manufacturers of Wide, Medium and Close-Ratio Gears and Hub Brakes*. Fold-out leaflet. Raleigh, c.1948.
- g. *Brampton 3-Speed Hub*. Brochure, Brampton Fittings, c.1956.
- h. Sunbeam advertisement. *The Bicycle*, 20 January 1954.
- i. *BSA Service Sheet No. B1*. BSA, Birmingham, 1954.
- j. *BSA Service Sheet No. B4*. BSA, Birmingham, 1955.
- k. J.E. Harrisson. 'New Sturmey-Archer Ultra Close Fixed Gear under Test'. Letter in *The Bicycle*, 2 May 1951.
- l. Peter Bryan. 'First Public View of New Sturmey-Archer Gear'. *The Bicycle*, 9 May 1951.
- m. *Building Fine Bicycles*. Factory tour souvenir booklet. Raleigh, c. 1958.
- n. David Lowe. 'People and times I will never forget'. *Bygones* No. 50, Nottingham Evening Post, 20 Mar 2010.
- o. Norman Brooke. Letter about Reilly. *Classic Motor Cycle*, June 1987.
- p. Ted Tyndall. Email correspondence with Tony Hadland about AW clones, October 2014 and earlier.
- q. Cliff Smith. Letters to Sturmey-Archer about the TCW hub, 1952-53.
- r. Ted Tyndall. 'The BSA Quick Release Three Speed Hub'. *The Boneshaker*, No. 200, Veteran-Cycle Club, 2016.
- s. Brian Hayes. *Sturmey-Archer SW Three Speed Bicycle Hubs*. 2007. Retrieved 6 November 2018 from www.sheldonbrown.com
- t. Gerry Beardshaw. *Hub Record*. List by former Technical Director, Sturmey-Archer, 1984.
- u. Gerry Beardshaw. *Sturmey-Archer Milestones*. List by former Technical Director, Sturmey-Archer, 1984.
- v. 'Trial of Plastic Lubricator'. *Sturmey-Archer News*, No. 27. Sturmey-Archer, 1955.
- w. Frank Berto. *The Dancing Chain* (3rd edition). Cycle Publishing, San Francisco, 2009.
- x. P.M. Read. *Sturmey-Archer: the first 90 years – exploded hub gear drawings,* (2nd edition). Milton Keynes, 1994.
- y. Jim Gill. Unpublished detailed hub gear analysis, 2001 and earlier.
- z. Raleigh and Sturmey-Archer company minutes held by Nottinghamshire Archives.
- aa. Patents cited in the text.

## Chapter 13: Small wheels and big triggers
   a. Gerry Beardshaw. *Hub Record*. List by former Technical Director, Sturmey-Archer, 1984.
   b. Tony Hadland. *The Moulton Bicycle* (2nd edition). Erdington, 1982.
   c. *5 Speed Wide Ratio Gear*. Parts list and service instructions. Sturmey-Archer, c.1966.
   d. *Automatic 2 Speed Gear*. Parts list and service instructions. Sturmey-Archer, c.1967.
   e. *S3B Spare Parts List and Service Instructions*. Sturmey-Archer, c. 1967.
   f. Howard Sutherland et al. *Sutherland's Handbook for Bicycle Mechanics* (3rd edition). Berkeley, California, 1980.
   g. Robin Roy. *Design Process and Products 2: Bicycles – Invention and Innovation*. Open University, 1983.
   h. Raleigh USA catalogue, 1962.
   i. *Nothing but the best!* Catalogue, Raleigh, c.1966.
   j. Jean Ramsdale. Correspondence with the author about her father, Cliff Smith, April 2010.
   k. Dave Drinkwater. Interview with the author, March 2010.
   l. P.M. Read. *Sturmey-Archer: the first 90 years – exploded hub gear drawings,* (2nd edition). Milton Keynes, 1994.
   m. Jim Gill. Unpublished detailed hub gear analysis, 2001 and earlier.
   n. Raleigh and Sturmey-Archer company minutes held by Nottinghamshire Archives.
   o. Patents cited in the text.

## Chapter 14: The secret seven
   a. Gerry Beardshaw. *Hub Record*. List by former Technical Director, Sturmey-Archer, 1984.
   b. Gerry Beardshaw. *Sturmey-Archer Milestones*. List by former Technical Director, Sturmey-Archer, 1984.
   c. Howard Sutherland et al. *Sutherland's Handbook for Bicycle Mechanics* (3rd edition). Berkeley, California, 1980.
   d. Robin Roy. *Design Process and Products 2: Bicycles – Invention and Innovation*. Open University, 1983.
   e. Dave Drinkwater. Interview with the author, March 2010.f. Patrick Bramman. Email to the author, May 2010.
   f. Gary Hesketh. Interview and correspondence with the author, April 2010.
   g. Peter Read. Email to the author regarding SunTour derailleurs, June 2010.
   h. P.M. Read. *Sturmey-Archer: the first 90 years – exploded hub gear drawings,* (2nd edition). Milton Keynes, 1994.
   i. Raleigh and Sturmey-Archer company minutes held by Nottinghamshire Archives.
   j. Patents cited in the text.
   k. Miscellaneous Sturmey-Archer product literature and service documentation.

## Chapter 15: A wavering relationship
   a. Gerry Beardshaw. *Hub Record*. List by former Technical Director, Sturmey-Archer, 1984.
   b. Gerry Beardshaw. *Sturmey-Archer Milestones*. List by former Technical Director, Sturmey-Archer, 1984.
   c. *S5 104 EN* and *S5 105 EN)*. Leaflets, Sturmey-Archer, c.1982-83.
   d. *Technical Information and Parts List – S5/2 and Five Speed Alloy*. Fold-out leaflets, Sturmey-Archer, May 1983.
   e. Henry Law. 'One for the Roadsters', *Bicycle*, September 1984.
   f. *Parts List – Hub Controls and Fittings*. Leaflet, Sturmey-Archer, July 1983.
   g. Hugh Blakeby. 'Sturmey-Archer: Dynohub and S5/2 hub gear'. *Cycling World*, October 1982.

h. *Technical Information and Parts List – Three Speed Hub Gears – AW and Three Speed Alloy*. Leaflet, Sturmey-Archer, May 1983.
  i. *S5 Five Speed Wide Ratio Hub Gear – Revised Gear Adjustment Instructions.* Leaflet, Sturmey-Archer, c.1983.
  j. 'Workshop – Products: Sturmey-Archer … click'. *Bicycle Times,* April 1985.
  k. Mark Hunt. *Epicycling,* Issue No. 3, Bakersfield, California, 1984.
  l. 'Toolbox – S/A ATB OK?' *Bicycle,* January 1985.
  m. *Sturmey-Archer Cycle Components.* Catalogue, Sturmey-Archer, c. 1984.
  n. *Technical Information and Parts List – Elite Alloy Hub Brakes – VT, ST, AT3.* Leaflet, Sturmey-Archer, 1984.
  o. *Parts List – Hub Brakes (90 mm) – AB, BF, BR.* Leaflet, Sturmey-Archer, 1983.
  p. *Parts List – Three Speed Coaster Brake – S3C.* Leaflet, Sturmey-Archer, 1983.
  q. *Parts List – Hub Brakes (70 mm) – SAB, BR, SBF.* Leaflet, Sturmey-Archer, 1983.
  r. *Parts List – Lighting Equipment and Accessories.* Leaflet, Sturmey-Archer, 1983.
  s. *Five Speed Hub Gears and Controls.* Leaflet, Sturmey-Archer, 1985.
  t. Harold Brierdiffe. 'Rallying Cries', *International Cycling Guide 1983,* London, 1983.
  u. Peter Read. Email to the author regarding SunTour derailleurs, June 2010.
  v. P.M. Read. *Sturmey-Archer: the first 90 years – exploded hub gear drawings,* (2nd edition). Milton Keynes, 1994.
  w. Raleigh and Sturmey-Archer company minutes held by Nottinghamshire Archives.
  x. Patents cited in the text.

## Chapter 16: The rise and fall of Derby
  a. Patents cited in the text.
  b. Derby company reports.
  c. Liquidators' report for meeting of creditors.
  d. Correspondence between the author and Sun Race Sturmey-Archer.
  e. Michael Radford. Article in *News & Views*, Veteran-Cycle Club, June/July 2001.
  f. Otto Beaujon. 'Recent Raleigh History', *The Boneshaker*, No. 159, Veteran-Cycle Club, 2002.
  g. Alan Clarke. 'Industrial Base.' Letter in *A to B* magazine, No. 78, 2010.
  h. Alan Clarke. *7-Speed Hub.* Internal memorandum on development and marketing, Sturmey-Archer (Europa), c. 1999.
  i. Sturmey-Archer brochures and maintenance instructions.
  j. P.M. Read. *Sturmey-Archer: the first 90 years – exploded hub gear drawings,* (2nd edition). Milton Keynes, 1994.
  k. *Bicycle Business* website.
  l. *This is Nottingham* website.
  m. A.W. Graham, Liquidator's final report, KPMG, 2005.

## Chapter 17: Sun Race sunrise
  a. Patents cited in the text.
  b. Sun Race Sturmey-Archer catalogues.
  c. Alan Clarke. 'Industrial Base', letter in *A to B* magazine, No.78, June 2010.

## Appendix E: Derailleur converters
  a. La Gauloise advertisement. *Le Cycliste.* March-April 1924.

b. *Fitting Instructions for 2 and 3 Sprocket Sturmey-Archer Hub Conversion Units.* Cyclo Gear Company Limited, Birmingham, undated.
c. *The Rogers Five Sprocket Conversion for Sturmey-Archer.* Leaflet. Ernest Rogers, Burbank, California, undated.
d. Chris Juden. 'Bits and Pieces – Dacon "hybrid" gear converter'. *Cycletouring*, February/March 1985.
e. *Replacement Drivers.* Leaflet. Dave Connley, Sheffield, undated.
f. *Dacon Sturmey-Archer Conversion.* Leaflet. Dave Connley, Sheffield, undated.
g. Chris Juden. *Chart of sprocket configurations for Dacon converters.* Cyclists' Touring Club, Godalming, undated.
h. Mark Hunt. 'Building a Hybrid Hub Gear'. *Sturmey-Archer Technical Library Bulletin No. 11*, Bakersfield, California, 1984.
i. Mark Hunt. 'Our Sturmey-Archer Hybrid Gearing'. *Sturmey-Archer Technical Library Bulletin No. 10*, 1984.
j. David Sore. Email correspondence with the author, February 2016.
k. David Connley. Email correspondence with the author, January 2015.

# I. Repairs and maintenance

Instructions for a wide range of Sturmey-Archer hubs from 1902 to 2001 can be found on Tony Hadland's website at: https://hadland.wordpress.com/2012/07/02/how-to-repair-old-sturmey-archer-hubs/ The files are in Adobe Acrobat format, making them zoomable and easily printable. The full list is as follows:

**1902 3-speed**

**BSA 3-speeds**
Includes Jim Gill's material on the rare split-axle versions

**K series 3-speeds (K, KS and KSW)**
An 18-page PDF file that includes Jim Gill's analysis of the type K, design changes during its production run, cutaway drawings, Jim's simplified instructions for dismantling and re-assembly, and S-A's parts lists for 1925 and 1935.

**K series 3-speeds with drum or coaster brakes (KB, KC and KT)**
A 13-page PDF file including Jim Gill's description and analysis of the type KB 3-speed and drum brake, and S-A's 1937 maintenance instructions and parts list.

**Type KB 1937**
A 5-page PDF including Jim Gill's description and cutaway drawing of the type KC 3-speed and coaster (back-pedal) brake, plus S-A's 1925 parts list, Jim's dimensioned drawing of the hub shell and his handwritten notes on (and sketches of) the type KC.

**Type KC**
A single page PDF showing S-A's exploded drawing of the type KT 3-speed and drum brake for tandems. Also included are details of the special brake lever fittings.

Type KT

### S-A 1930s drum brakes without gears (BF, BR, BRT and BFT)
A 2-page PDF showing cutaway drawings of the 1932-36 versions of the type BF and BR brake hubs.

### Type BF and BR 1932-36
A 9-page PDF including S-A's 1937 maintenance instructions and parts list for the BF and BR hubs.

### Type BF and BR 1937
A 4-page PDF with cutaway drawings of early and later versions of the BRT and BFT tandem drum brakes.

Type BRT and BFT 1936-41

### General information from the 1956 Master catalogue
Fitting and adjustment
Use and maintenance
Fault finding
General dismantling
Individual dismantling
Inspection
General re-assembling

**SW wide-ratio 3-speed**

**SB wide-ratio 3-speed/hub brake**

**SG wide-ratio 3-speed/Dynohub**

**AW wide-ratio 3-speed (see below for later AWs)**

**AB wide-ratio 3-speed/hub brake**

**AG wide-ratio 3-speed/Dynohub**

**TCW wide-ratio 3-speed/coaster**

**AM medium-ratio 3-speed**

**AC ultra-close-ratio 3-speed**

**ASC fixed-wheel 3-speed**

**FW wide-ratio 4-speed**

**FG wide-ratio 4-speed/Dynohub**

FM medium-ratio 4-speed

FC close-ratio 4-speed

BF & BR hub brakes

GH6 Dynohub

Dry Battery Unit and Dynohub wiring

Other Dynohub and Filter Switch Unit wiring information
FSU circuit diagram and notes
Wiring diagrams

S3B 3-speed with small-diameter hub brake

S3C 3-speed coaster

S5 5-speed

S5/1 5-speed

S5/2 and Five Speed Alloy 5-speeds

S52 1988 modifications

5 StAr and 5 StAr Elite 5-speeds

Columbia NIG 3-speed
Jim Gill's documentation

AB/C & BF/C 90mm hub brake

AW 3-speed

AWC 3-speed coaster

AT3, VT and ST Elite hub brakes

Sprinter 5-speed hub and Sprinter 5 Elite hub brake

Sprinter 5-speed coaster

Sprinter 7-speed hub and Sprinter 7 Elite hub brake

Sprinter 7-speed coaster

Steelite SBF, SBR and SAB hub brakes

**Triggers and Twistgrips, 1950s and 1960s**
SA 1951 trigger instructions
SA 1956 trigger instructions
Twistgrip parts c. 1966
Auto Twistgrip service instructions c. 1969

**Other useful websites:**
Sturmey-Archer Heritage – http://www.sturmey-archerheritage.com/
Sheldon Brown – https://sheldonbrown.com/Sturmey-archer.html
Veteran-Cycle Club Online Library – http://veterancycleclublibrary.org.uk/library/
Colwood Wheelworks – https://colwoodwheelworks.co.uk/

# J. Auctioneer's List of Sturmey-Archer Plant, 2000
*Excludes machinery set aside for export to Taiwan for use by Sun Race*

**Presses – Cold Forging & Deep Drawing**
Liebergeld 1 x 'L1000' and 2 x 'L630' tonne Mechanical Cold Forging Presses (1986).
Craig & Donald 3 x 500 and 6 x 425 ton Mechanical Cold Forging Press.
AIDA 'C2-25' 10-Station 250 ton Transfer Mechanical Deep Drawing Press.
AIDA 'C1-20' 200 ton Transfer Mechanical Deep Drawing Press.
Taylor & Challen '1573' 130 ton.
Geared Deep Drawing Press.

**Other Presses**
HME 'G-100' 100 ton 'C' Press.
HME 'Rigispeed' 70 ton Open Front Press.
Tranemo Double Action Hydraulic Press 200 tonne.
Wilkins & Mitchell 'C30' 150 ton Mechanical 'H' Frame Press.
14 x Taylor & Challen Presses, 12 x Bliss, 15 x HME, 3 x Turner Bros., 5 x Wells 5 ton, Hare Presses
14 x '5BS', 2 x '5IT', 4 x 'Airmiser' Pneumatic, Cincinnati 'Milacron G-30', CVA 25 ton Dieing Press, Lectra & Raskin Presses, 2 x BHP and Humphris Coil Feeders.

**Powder Metallurgy Presses**
Atlas 'MPA15' 15 tonne Powder Compacting Press (1997).
Dorst 'TPA 100' 100 tonne (Rebuilt 1998).
Lauffer 'HPM 200L' 200 tonne Hydraulic Powder Compacting Press.
Bussmann 'HPM 200' 200 ton.
2 x Bussmann 'Simetag' 200 tonne.
Bussmann 'Simetag' 400 tonne.
Dorst 350 ton.
Mannesmann 'Simetag' 15 ton.
7 x Manesty 35 ton.
Mannesmann 'Simetag' 45 tonne.

2 x Dorst 'TPA 60' 60 tonne.
5 x Rotary Cone Powder Mixing M/c's.

## Wire and Spark Eroders
Agie 'Agiecut Sprint 70' CNC Wire Eroder ('93).
Agie 'Agiecut DEM 315 220H' CNC Wire Eroder ('84).
Agie 'Agietron EMS-2' CNC Spark Eroder ('85).
Agie 'Agietron FMS 15' Spark Eroder.

## Multi Spindle Bar Auto Lathes
Wickmans 3 x 1 3/4" – 6 Spindle, 5 x 1" – 6 Spindle, 12 x ?" – 6 Spindle, 1 x 1 3/4" – 5 Spindle.
New Britain Gridleys 18 x 1" – 6 Spindle, 2 x 2 1/4" – 6 Spindle also BSA 1" – 6 Spindle.

## Multi Spindle Chucking Auto Lathes
Wickman 24 x 6" – 5 Spindle, 13 x 6?" – 6 Spindle, 12 x Kummer 'K20' 2 Spindle.

## Single Spindle Auto Lathes
Bechler 'AR10' and 'BR-20' Swiss Type Sliding Heads with Multibar Powered Bar Feeders.
Petermann '10HS' Swiss Type Sliding Head.
12 x CVA 'No. 8' Single Spindle Bar Auto with 12 Station Magazine Bar Loader and 4 x with Vibro Barrel Magazine Feed.

## CNC Machines
Takisawa 'TC-2' CNC Slant Bed Lathes, 4 x Mk. II ('91), 2 x Mk. I ('97).
Sameco 'Monosam 45' Hydraulic Bar Feed.
Kitamura 'MyCenter 1' CNC Vert. M/c Centre ('83).
Ti Herbert-Churchill 'HC3/15' CNC Slant Bed Lathe ('86).

## Grinding Machines
Jones & Shipman 1 x '1305 EIU' Universal Cylindrical ('81), 4 x '1400' Horiz. Surface, 4 x '1300' Universal Cylindrical with Int. Grinding Spindle, 1 x '310' Tool & Cutter Grinder.
4 x '540' Horiz. Surface.
Thompson Horiz. Surface.
Matrix 'GU 065' Universal Cylindrical.
Catmur '2C' Jig Grinder.
2 x BSA Centreless Grinders.
Brierley 'ZB 32' Drill Point Grinder, some with Magnetic Chucks.
Cincinnati 'No. 2' Tool & Cutter Grinder.
Pratt & Whitney Tool & Cutter Grinder.
Also various Off-Hand Grinders.

## Air Compressors/Boilers
Ingersoll Rand 1 x 'SSR ML 132' Packaged Screw ('98) & 1 x 'TMS 300' Air Dryer ('98).
3 x 'EN4C30' Receiver Mounted, 1 x 'SSR ML4' Packaged Screw with TMS Air Dryer, 1 x 'SSR 2000 18L' Packaged Screw with TMS '190' Air Dryer.
Hydrovane 'IP54' Rotary Vane.

Compair Broomwade '6000N' Packaged Screw.
Broomwade 'V200A-F3' Vee Twin Compressor with TMS '190' Air Dryer. 2 x Hoval 'ST 6000' Gas Fired Medium Pressure Hot Water Boiler, 6 Million Btu/Hr. Output ('84).

## Broaching Machines
Lapointe 1 x 'SPD' Vert. Semi-Auto Pull Broacher also 5 x 'FP5' Verticals.
Weatherley Horiz. Broacher.
Weatherley 'XP30X54' 4 Station Vert. Int. Broacher.
Cincinnati '1066' Table Index Vert. Surface Broacher.
Weatherley Cincinnati 'XP30X30' 2 Station Vert. Int. Broacher.

## Sawing Machines
Rohbi 2 x 'RKA62' Auto Vert.
Reciprocating Cut-off Saw ('87/'89).
Kasto 'SSB260VA' Vert.
Cross Cutting Bandsaw ('86).
Do-All 'BWIPG' Vert. Bandsaw.
Clarke 'CHS 8W' Reciprocating Hacksaw.
Birkett 'Cutmaster' Pull Down Cut-off Saw.
Thiel 'Segura 117' Vert. Bandsaw.

## Finishing Machines
1 x Morris-Flex & 1 x Moons Rotary Transfer Polishing M/c's.
3 x Doug Booth Shotblast M/c's.
4 x Acton Vibrota Vibro-Barrel Rumbling M/c's.
10 x Boulton Vibro-Barrelling M/c's.
Also Rhodes, Trowall & Canning Vibratory Barrels.
CM '1000' Shotblast Cabinet.
Vixen 'Jetair' Beadblast Cabinet.
Butterfield 'MCR Airoblast' Conveyorised Beadblast M/c.
Osro High Energy Centrifugal Deburrer.
Acton Vibrota 'VB3' Vibro-Barrel.
Acton Vibrota Vibratory Maize Dryer.

## Treatment Plant
ICI Trichlorethylene Heated Degreasing Tank.
PPC Auto Barrel Transfer Process Plant.
Hockley Semi-Auto Barrel Transfer Process Plant.
Electro Paint Conveyorised Wash Plant.
Hockley 'Barraflow' Wash Plant.
Ohmic Auto Barrel Transfer Process Plant (Rebuilt '90).

## Furnaces/Ovens
2 x Wellman Gas Fired Mesh-Belt Anneal ('85).
2 x Wild Barfield 70Kw.
Electric Temper.

6 x British Furnaces Gas Fired Sealed Quench.
3 x Heat Treatment Services Gas Fired Mesh-Belt Sinter.
3 x Birlec Gas Fired Mesh-Belt Sinter.
EFCO Electric Mesh-Belt Enamel Baking Oven.

**Die Casting Machinery**
EMB 'No. 14' Cold Chamber Die Casting M/c.
2 x EMB 'No. 10'.
3 x Ramsell Naber Electric Crucible Furnace.
2 x Fisher 24 Nipple Die Caster.

**Spoke and Nipple Machines**
7 x Hahn & Kolb 'T3' Vario 9 Station Rotary Transfer.
12 x Aachener Bicycle Spoke Making M/c's.
18 x Amba 10 Station Rotary Transfer.
4 x Amba Aachener Cold Heading M/c's.

**Lathes**
DSG's Straight Bed Centre Lathes.
1 x 13-30 (Rebuilt by DSG in '97).
1 x 1307-30.
Suga Plugboard Auto 4 x 'STS-2', 3 x 'STM-2', 1 x 'STM-3'. 8 x Herbert 'Cri-Dan B' Threading Lathe.
Myford 'Super 7' Lathe.
DSG 'Type 17' 17 x 86 Gap Bed Centre.
Harrison 'M400' Straight Bed Centre.
Herbert 'No. 4' Capstan.

**Gear Machines**
9 x Drummond 'Maxicut 2A' Gear Shaper.
3 x Mikron '132.02' Gear Hobber.

**Drilling/Milling/Tapping Machines**
2 x Adcock-Shipley 'Bridgeport JB' Turret Milling M/c's.
2 x Slack & Parr 18 Spindle Horiz. Drilling M/c's.
7 x Centec 'RE29' Plain Horiz. Milling.
6 x Cincinnati '100' Horiz. Rise & Fall Milling.
2 x Cincinnati '100' Plain Horiz. Milling.
5 x Mollart Twin Spindle Horiz. Deep Hole Drilling M/c's.
3 x Slack & Parr Quick Tap. Elevating Arm Radial Drill.
2 x Thiel 'Duplex 158' Vert.
Milling with Horiz. Milling Spindle & DRO.
Parkson 'M1200' Plain Vert.
Milling. Kearney & Trecker '430' Vert. Milling.

**Miscellaneous Machines**
SIP Societe Genevoise 'Hydroptic-6 HY-6P' Jig Borer.

Sunnen 'MBB-1650A' Precision Honing M/c.
Liebergeld 'STR63' High Speed Bar Cropper ('85).
Hylatechnik Hydraulic Die Splitter.
West 'Mono Arc 222' 8 Kva. Electric Arc Welder.
Edwards 48" Powered Guillotine.
Morgan Rushworth 50" Box & Pan Folder.
Sureweld 'Tigtronic 165' 150 amp Welder.
Heenan & Froude 'S50' and Rockwell '35' Horiz.

**Strip Formers**
US Baird Horiz. Spring Former.
Löser 'KS360' Centreless Linisher ('96).
Flott 'BSM75' Centreless Linisher.
Twin Carousel Enamel Spray Line.
Arc System 801 CD Cap.
Discharge Portable Electric Arc Stud Welder.
Pantograph Engraver. Kitchen & Wade 'E26' 4ft.
Gentry '305' Auto Vert.Lapping M/c.
Ormerod Shaper.

**Inspection & Laboratory Equipment**
Various Inspection and Measurement Equipt. Including Mitutoyo 'BH504' Co-ordinate Measuring M/c., Hommel Int. & Ext. Gear Profile Inspection M/c's.
2 x Baty 'R202' Shadowgraph Projectors with DRO.
Sigma Projector, and Large Qty comparators, Plug & Slip Gauges.
Also Various Laboratory Equipt. including Tensile/Compression Testing M/c's., Microscopes, Hardness Testers, Electronic Balances, Sample Mounting, Houndsfield Tensometers.

# K. Lubrication

**Oil for gear internals**
In the 1950s Sturmey-Archer stopped putting oil in hubs because it usually ran out of the shell while in transit. Bike shops were told to oil the hub before sale and then sell a can of oil with the bike.

The hub internal parts had a black coating which absorbed and retained oil.

In 1989 the oil nipple was removed from the hub and internals were 'greased for life' (or at least to each major service). Weldtite was a long-time supplier of lubricants to Sturmey-Archer but ceased to be in the 2000s because of a high minimum order quantity.

Sturmey-Archer staff were often asked what oil to use in older hubs but Sturmey-Archer oil specifications were never published. Customers were told that Sturmey-Archer was not a specialist in lubricants and many mineral oils were suitable for this use. It was important that the oil was not too thin, or it would run out of the hub, but also not thick enough to stick down the pawls. Something like sewing machine oil (preferred by gear guru Jack Lauterwasser) was usually suitable and good bike shops could offer an appropriate product. Consumers were also always told not to put in too much or it would run out. Little (two teaspoonfuls) and often was better.

In the 1990s the Sturmey-Archer factory used the following lubricants:
    Castrol CLS grease for gear internals.
    Castrol LMX for bearings.
    Spheerol BM2 grease for coaster brake bands and actuators.

In 2019 Sturmey-Archer uses:
    EP 00 (CLS00) semi-fluid grease for gear internals.
    Castrol High Temperature Grease for bearings.
    BNS Grease for coaster brake bands and actuators.

## l. Sturmey-Archer Heritage website

This website, which Alan Clarke personally created and has curated over many years as a labour of love and a separate entity from Sturmey-Archer's commercial website, contains a huge amount of useful, interesting and rare information about the company's older products. Apart from technical information and product specifications, it also contains numerous examples of advertising and other promotional material. Newly discovered material is added whenever it is found and the website is well worth visiting periodically at www.sturmey-archerheritage.com

Figs. 18.5, 18.6, 18.7, 18.8. Four 2019 product posters.

URBAN BLUES
The HBT30 hub has an anodised 6061 aluminium shell, chromoly axle with sealed cartridge bearings and comes drilled for 32 or 36 spokes.
The matching rear hub is for fixed/ freewheel and both are available in five hi-polish colours.
The high quality single freewheel, is available in 1/8" and 3/32" versions and from 16 to 22 teeth.
matching colour single cranksets available
www.sturmey-archer.com
STURMEY
ARCHER
EST. 1902

The grown-up choice...
for grown-up bikes
Most single coaster brake hubs are used in kid's bikes where low cost is more of a priority. But adult city-bikes need better performance, to better withstand the use and abuse of street life. The new Sturmey-Archer S1C single coaster hub has a high precision, low friction, roller operated brake with cromoly M10 axle and aluminium alloy hub shell for increased corrosion resistance.
The anodised hub shell is available in 5 colours to match the FCT60 crankset and HBT30 front hub. So that adult urban bikes can have grown-up looks as well.
STURMEY
ARCHER
EST. 1902
www.sturmey-archer.com

THE Secret OF EASY CYCLING
The new Sturmey-Archer C50 5-speed hub gear features:
• Wide gear ratio of 243%
• Even gear steps of 25%
• Rotary gear selector, with no protrusions outside the frame.
• Heavy duty design.
• Gear change under load.
• Aluminium hub shell.
• Built-in drum or coaster brake options.
• Choice of shifters.
STURMEY
ARCHER
EST. 1902
making cycling easier
making cycling safer
www.sturmey-archer.com
www.sturmey-archerheritage.com

City
Lights
HDS12 2.4w front hub
STURMEY
ARCHER
EST. 1902
making cycling easier
making cycling safer
www.sturmey-archer.com
www.sturmey-archerheritage.com
The current generation of Sturmey-Archer hub dynamos will add power to your sales. The 6v range includes front hub models combined with 70 and 90mm diameter drum brakes and now there is also a single side model for recumbents.
The new type HDS12 2.4w version is for bikes where only the headlamp needs to be powered.
Sealed cartridge bearings are standard and all models are CE and EN compliant.
X-SDD single sided for recumbents

Rototiller 76
Rover safety bicycle 13
Royal Enfield 91
Royal Mail AB 3-speed drum brake 277
Royce Ltd 20, 25, 27
RS-RB3 3-speed for band brake 305
RS-RC3 3-speed coaster 306, 310
RS-RF3 3-speed 298, 305
RS-RK3 3-speed for disc brake 310
RS-RR3 3-speed for roller brake 305, 310
Rudge-Whitworth 91, 167
RX-RC5 5-speed coaster 309
RX-RD3 3-speed drum brake 305, 306
RX-RD5 5-speed drum brake 309
RX-RF5 5-speed 309
RX-RK5 5-speed for disc brake 309
RXL-RD5 5-speed drum brake 309
S Tricoaster 85
S-RB3 3-speed for band brake 307
S-RC3 3-speed coaster 304
S-RF3 3-speed 304
S-RK3 3-speed for disc brake 307
S1C single-speed coaster 312
S2 2-speed 223-225, 241, 253
S2 kick-shift 2-speed 312
S20 range of kick-shift 2-speeds 312
S2C kick-shift 2-speed coaster 312
S2K kick-shift 2-speed for disc brake 312
S30 series 3-speeds 304
S3B 3-speed drum brake 225, 226, 244, 253
S3C Tricoaster 215-218, 234, 235, 238, 253, 268
S3S series 3-speeds 304, 310
S3X 3-speed 254, 302, 310, 311
S40 series of 4-speed hubs 309
S5 5-speed 226, 228-230, 240, 246, 267, 304
S5/1 5-speed 246, 247, 257, 267
S5/2 5-speed 256-258, 259, 267, 277
S50 series of 5-speeds 304
S5C 5-speed coaster 304
S5S series of 5-speeds 304
S7 NIG 7-speed 242, 253, 316
S80 'Phoenix' 8-speed 297-301
S80 series 8-speeds 304
S80(W) range of wider ratio 8-speeds 309
SA Realisations Ltd 297
SAB 3-speed drum brake 249, 263, 268, 274, 277
SAB3 3-speed drum brake 304
Sachs Super 7 7-speed 284
Sachs-Huret 235, 253, 269, 292
Sachs, Ernst 83, 84
SB 3-speed drum brake 207, 209
SBF drum brake 244, 263, 268, 277, 304
SBR drum brake 244, 245, 263, 268, 277
SC single-speed coaster 223, 249, 253
SC1 single-speed coaster 234, 247, 254
SCC single-speed coaster 248, 249, 254
Schlumpf 2-speed chainwheel gear 301
Schönebeck 99
Schütte 157
Schwinn approved Steyr 3-speed 200
Schwinn, Arnold 163

Scintilla AG 163, 164, 179, 198-200
Scott, George 12
Seabrook gear 80, 83
Sears Roebuck & Company 85, 86, 200, 201
Searvogel, Kurt 150
Selle Royal 296
SG 3-speed Dynohub 207, 210
Sharp bracket gear 16
Sharp hub gear 28, 314
Sharp, Archibald 18, 28, 29, 46
Shaw and Sydenham patent, 1882 12, 13
Shimano 253, 273, 283, 284, 292, 300
Shimano SG-7 7-speed 283
Shimano, Keizo 283
Shimano, Shozo 283
Shorland, Frank 14
Simplex gear 80, 81, 83
Simpson patent, 1884 12
Simpson, Alfred 148, 166
Single cable 5-speed (not marketed) 238, 240, 241, 253
Skipper, journalist 194
Smith, Cliff 191, 221
Smith, Mike 234, 235
Smith, Paul 293
Société Industrielle D'Albert 99
Southall, Frank 121
Speedman, journalist 152
Sprinter 5-speed 279-281
Sprinter Elite AT7 7-speed drum brake 287, 290
Sprinter S5C 5-speed coaster 282, 283
Sprinter S7 7-speed 285, 286
Sprinter S7C 7-speed coaster 285
Sprockets, 12-lugged 125
Sprockets, 3-lugged 185
SRAM 292, 296, 316
ST Elite drum brake 259-261, 268
Standard, Sid 241, 244
Staner, H. Walter 25-27, 33
Stanley gear 80, 83
Starley, James 12, 13
Starley, James Kemp 13
Steelite AB5 5-speed drum brake 290
Steelite range of drum brakes 263, 277
Steelite SAB5 5-speed drum brake 290
Sterling Metro 5 bicycle 266
Steyr-Daimler-Puch See Puch
Stick-shifts for hi-rise and cruiser bikes 232, 233, 306
Stoffel, Louis 11
Strida bicycle 301
Studdy, George 107
Sturmey-Archer BV, Netherlands 292
Sturmey-Archer Europa, Netherlands 293, 296
Sturmey-Archer Gears (Holland) NV 195
Sturmey-Archer Heritage website 360
Sturmey, Henry 21, 26, 29-34, 35, 37, 38, 40, 44, 49, 79, 102-106, 226, 315
Sturmey, Henry, prototype 3-speed 33, 37, 45
Sturmey, Henry, prototype 5-speed 41, 102-104, 279, 315
Styria See Puch
Su, Alan 294-296, 297
Summit range of alloy-shelled hubs 285, 292

Summit S7 7-speed  285
Summit S7C 7-speed coaster  285, 286
Summit X-FD drum brake  285
Summit X-RD5 5-speed drum brake  285
Sun Race  285, 292-296, 297, 317
Sun Race Sturmey-Archer Europe BV  297
Sunbeam gears  80, 81, 83, 102
SunTour 3-speed  252
SW 3-speed  206-208, 211, 212, 315
Swiss copies of S-A hubs  163
SX range of hub gears for cruiser bikes  305
SX-RB3 3-speed for band brake  306
SX-RK3 3-speed for disc brake  306
T 2-speed  122
T series 2-speeds  122-125
T-S2C 2-speed coaster for tricycle  310
Tandems, hub gears for  105, 118, 119
Taylor, G.F.  82
TB 2-speed drum brake  125
TBC 2-speed drum brake  125
TBF 2-speed fixed wheel drum brake  125, 126
TBFC 2-speed fixed wheel drum brake  125
TC 2-speed  125-127, 130
TCW Mk 1 Tricoaster  191-193
TCW Mk 2 Tricoaster  193, 223
TCW Mk 3 Tricoaster  215, 216, 223, 238
TF 2-speed  122
Three Speed Alloy  258, 267
Three Speed Gear Syndicate  39, 40, 44, 49, 53, 57, 58, 68, 82
TI  *See* Tube Investments
Tin Can Ten race  252
Toggle chain and flared nut, origination  21
Toggle chain protectors  219, 275
Topliss 3-speed (not marketed)  219, 220
Topliss, John  220
Trade mark registration  105
Trailguard gear protector  266
Triggers  147, 148, 176, 184, 231, 244, 267, 281, 283, 288, 301, 304, 305, 306, 336-343
Triumph gear  80, 83
Triumph motorcycles  71, 73, 74
Trivelox derailleur  121, 125, 179
Trix SA  179, 198, 200
TS range of tricycle gears  306
TS-RB3 tricycle 3-speed for band brake  306
TS-RC3 tricycle 3-speed coaster  306, 307
TS-RC5 5-speed coaster for tricycle  310
TS-RF3 tricycle 3-speed  306
TS-RF5 5-speed for tricycle  310
Tube Investments  215, 270
Twist-grips  231, 249, 266, 267, 285, 294, 296, 301, 304
Twist-shifters  *See* Twist-grips
Uden, E. Boye  157, 159, 161
Ultra-wide-ratio 4-speed (not marketed)  193
Urry, Frank  62
V 3-speed  63, 64, 65, 66, 86
Vaisey, Justice  146
Varlax gear  122
Vibo  163, 164
Victoria coaster  102
Victoria motorcycles  77, 78

Villepigue, Ferdinand  11
Villiers freewheels  109
Villiers gear  80, 83, 121
VT Elite drum brake  259, 260, 268
Walker, A.H  104
Walker, John  39
Wanderer  85
Watkins, Denis  211, 316
Watkins, Ruby  316
Whippet bicycle  16
Whippet gear  16, 32
White, Tom  25, 38
Whitt, Frank  65
Wide-ratio 6-speed (not marketed)  200, 201
Wilkie, William  74
Williams, Adrian  296
Wilson, David  197
Wilson, George  67, 108, 111, 115, 125, 141, 142, 144, 146, 148, 163, 165, 171, 179, 198, 199, 206
Wilson's, patent agents  37
Wittering, Peter  235
Woodburn, John  221, 222
Woodhead and Angois  13
Woodhead, Angois and Ellis  13
Woodhead, Richard  13
Wray, W. Fitzwater  149
Wyatt gear  17
X 3-speed  48, 65, 66, 94, 105, 315
X 3-speed, unnamed early version  49-50, 83
X range of drum brakes  306
X Tricoaster patent  96, 97
X-FD drum brake  304
X-FDD hub dynamo with drum brake  304, 305
X-RC4 4-speed coaster  310
X-RC5 5-speed coaster  304
X-RD drum brake  304
X-RD3 3-speed drum brake  304
X-RD4 4-speed drum brake  309, 310
X-RD5 5-speed drum brake  304
X-RD8 8-speed drum brake  304
X-RD8(W) 8-speed drum brake  309
X-RDC derailleur freehub drum brake  306
X-RF4 4-speed  310
X-RF5 5-speed  304
X-RF8(C) 8-speed  304
X-RF8(S) 8-speed  304
X-RF8(W) 8-speed  309
X-RK4 4-speed for disc brake  310
X-RK8 8-speed  304
X-RK8(W) 8-speed for disc brake  309
X-RR8 8-speed  304
X-SD side-mounting drum brake  306, 312, 313
X-SD(Q) quick-release side-mounting drum brake  313
X-SDD side-mounting hub dynamo drum brake  306, 309
XL-FD drum brake  313
XL-FDD hub dynamo drum brake  309
XL-RD3 3-speed drum brake  307
XL-SD side-mounting drum brake  306, 313
XL-SD(Q) quick-release side-mounted drum brake  313
XL-SDD side-mounting hub dynamo drum brake  306, 308, 309